Asian Law in Disasters

This book is a critical analysis of several of the most disaster-prone regions in Asia. Its unique focus is on the legal issues in the phase of disaster recovery, the most lengthy and difficult stage of disaster response that follows the conclusion of the initial emergency stage of humanitarian aid. In the stage of disaster recovery, the law decides the fate of reconstruction for the individual houses and livelihoods of the disaster-affected people and sets the limit of governmental support for them during the lengthy period of suspension of normal living until full recovery is obtained. Researchers who were participant-observers in the difficult recovery phase after the mega-disasters in Asia analyze the reality of the functions of law which often hinder, rather than foster, efforts to restore disaster victims' lives. The book collects research conducted with an emphasis on empirical approaches to legal sociology, including direct interviews with people affected by the disaster. It offers a holistic approach beyond the traditional sectionalism of legal studies by starting with a historical review and incorporating both spheres of public law and private law, in order to obtain a new perspective that can concurrently achieve disaster risk reductions and human-centered recoveries.

With particular emphasis on the unexplored area of law in the post-disaster recovery phase, this book will attract the attention of students and scholars of disaster studies, legal studies and Asian studies, as well as those who work in the practice of disaster management.

Yuka Kaneko is Professor of Asian comparative law at Kobe University, Japan.

Katsumi Matsuoka is Professor at the Faculty of Humanities and Social Sciences at Iwate University, Japan.

Toshihisa Toyoda is Professor Emeritus at Kobe University, Japan.

Routledge studies in Asian law

Asian Law in Disasters
Toward a human-centered recovery
Edited by Yuka Kaneko, Katsumi Matsuoka and Toshihisa Toyoda

Judicial Review of Elections in Asia
Edited by Po Jen Yap

Asian Law in Disasters

Toward a human-centered recovery

Edited by Yuka Kaneko, Katsumi Matsuoka and Toshihisa Toyoda

Routledge
Taylor & Francis Group
LONDON AND NEW YORK

First published 2016 by Routledge

2 Park Square, Milton Park, Abingdon, Oxfordshire OX14 4RN
711 Third Avenue, New York, NY 10017

Routledge is an imprint of the Taylor & Francis Group, an informa business

First issued in paperback 2017

British Library Cataloguing in Publication Data
A catalogue record for this book is available from the British Library

Library of Congress Cataloging-in-Publication Data
Names: Kaneko, Yuka, 1964– editor. | Matsuoka, Katsumi, editor. | Toyoda, Toshihisa, 1940– editor.
Title: Asian law in disasters : toward a human-centered recovery / Edited by Yuka Kaneko, Katsumi Matsuoka and Toshihisa Toyoda.
Description: New York, NY : Routledge, 2016. | Series: Routledge studies in asian law | Includes bibliographical references and index.
Identifiers: LCCN 2015043503| ISBN 9781138930636 (hardback) | ISBN 9781315680323 (ebook)
Subjects: LCSH: Disaster relief–Law and legislation–Asia.
Classification: LCC KNC630 .A95 2016 | DDC 344.505/348–dc23
LC record available at http://lccn.loc.gov/2015043503

ISBN: 978-1-138-93063-6 (hbk)
ISBN: 978-0-8153-6148-0 (pbk)

Typeset in Times New Roman
by Wearset Ltd, Boldon, Tyne and Wear

Contents

Figures

Tables

Boxes

Contributors

Yuka Kaneko, LL.D., Professor of Asian comparative law, Graduate School of International Cooperation Studies, Kobe University, Japan (Chapter 1).

Li Wei Hai, LL.D., Associate Professor, China University of Political Science and Law, China, specializing in emergency law, military law and maritime law (Chapter 2).

Ali Tolga Ozden, P.D., Assistant Professor, Faculty of Architecture and Design, Çanakkale Onsekiz Mart University, Turkey (Chapter 3).

Burcak Erkan, Ph.D. in statistics, Associate Professor of Statistics, Middle East Technical University, Turkey (Chapter 3).

Taqwaddin Husein, Ph.D., Head of the Aceh Provincial Representative of Ombudsmen of Indonesia; Lecturer of environmental law, communal law, and sociology in law, Faculty of Law, Syiah Kuala University, Indonesia (Chapter 4).

Teuku Alvisyahrin, Ph.D., Lecturer, the Graduate Program in Disaster Science and the Development in Soil Science, Syiah Kuala University, Indonesia (Chapter 4).

Kanongnij Sribuaiam, LL.D., Associate Professor, Law and Development Research Center, Faculty of Law, Chulalongkorn University, Thailand, specializing in environmental law, disaster law, and law and development (Chapter 5).

Ebinezer R. Florano, Ph.D., Associate Professor of the National College of Public Administration and Governance, University of the Philippines, and Director of its Center for Policy and Executive Development, Philippines (Chapter 6).

Joe-Mar S. Perez, Training Specialist, Office of Civil Defense, National Disaster Risk Reduction and Management Council (OCD-NDRRMC), Philippines (Chapter 6).

Abel Táiti Konno Pinheiro, Ph.D., Assistant Professor, Department of Architecture, Faculty of Engineering, Kobe University, Japan, specializing in urban safety and disaster risk management (Chapter 6).

Eichi Yamasaki, Ph.D., Associate Professor, Faculty of Safety Science, Kansai University, Japan, specializing in disaster law (Chapter 7).

Tamiyo Kondo, Ph.D., Associate Professor, Department of Architecture, Faculty of Engineering, Kobe University, Japan, specializing in urban planning and post-disaster housing recovery (Chapter 8).

Michael J.V. White, LL.M., Barrister and Solicitor of the High Court of New Zealand; Senior Legal Advisor, New Zealand Human Rights Commission (Chapter 9).

Wakana Takahashi, Ph.D. in Political Science, Associate Professor, Faculty of International Studies, Utsunomiya University, Japan, specializing in global environmental politics and comparative environmental politics (Chapter 10).

Takayuki Ii, LL.D., Associate Professor of socio-legal studies, Faculty of Law, Senshu University, Japan (Chapter 11).

Yuichi Honjo, Director, Kobe Institute of Urban Research (Chapter 12).

Katsumi Matsuoka, Faculty of Humanities and Social Sciences, LL.D., Professor, Iwate University, Japan (Chapter 13).

Elizabeth Toomey, LL.M., Professor, School of Law, University of Canterbury, New Zealand (Chapter 14).

Akihiko Hokugo, Ph.D., Professor, Director, Research Center for Urban Safety and Security, Graduate School of Engineering, Kobe University, Japan (Chapter 15).

Yung-Fang Chen, Ph.D., Associate Professor, Coventry University, United Kingdom, specializing in training and exercises for emergencies and crisis events, and post-disaster assistance (Chapter 16).

Toshihisa Toyoda, Ph.D. in Economics, Professor Emeritus at Kobe University, Japan, specializing in development economics and economics of disasters; former president of the Japan Society for International Development Studies (Chapter 17).

Introduction

1 Disaster law for the victims – beyond distrust in the law

> We never trust such harmful concepts as law, rights, and the courts, as we know that they are all mechanisms to deprive us of our basis of living.

These were the words we frequently heard during our recent fieldwork in the villages of the Moken, a minority race who have been suffering due to eviction orders made as part of the post-disaster reconstruction following the Indian Ocean Tsunami that hit southern Thailand on December 26, 2004. Similar words were heard among the Qiang villagers, who lost farm lands to rigorous expropriation for a relocation project led by the famous "partner assistance" that followed the Sichuan Earthquake, which occurred on May 12, 2008. However, this is the fate not only of minority races in developing economies. The victims of the tsunami in the Great East Japan Earthquake of March 11, 2011, after five years of implementation of the post-disaster recovery plan, utter similar words of regret: "It was our mistake to believe in the law." They have simply obeyed the law in an expectation that the law will ultimately lead them to a reasonable solution, but the result is disappointing delay, frictions between the government and the affected communities, and population drain as a result of despair.

If such distrust in the law is a common phenomenon between people affected by disaster across borders, we are urged to reconsider the meaning of law in relation to disasters. The *Hyogo Framework for Action* (United Nations A/CONF.206/6 CORR.1), declared at the United Nations-sponsored Second World Conference on Disaster Reduction held in Kobe, Japan in 2005, emphasized in its first priority the role of the law and institutions in the implementation of disaster management. This encouraged the enactment of basic disaster management laws in a number of countries in Asia, as shown in Table I.1 (see UNDP 2009). The scope of these disaster laws, however, did not go beyond defining governmental organizations and functions for emergency response upon the occurrence of disaster; they did not define a holistic system of norms for law in disaster, as recognized in a civil society. Overcoming this limitation was attempted in the *Sendai Framework for Disaster Risk Reduction 2015–2030* (United Nations A/CONF.206/224, CRP.1), adopted at the Third United Nations World

Table I.1 Disaster-related legislation in Asia

	Laws	*Features*
China	• 2007 Law on Emergency Response • 2005/2006 National Plans on Emergency Response • 1997/2009 Law on Disaster Risk Reduction	• Division of roles between central government and local government
Japan	• 1961 Disaster Countermeasures Basic Act • 1947 Disaster Relief Act • 1998 Act on Support for Reconstructing Livelihoods of Disaster Victims • 2013 Act on Recovery from Large-Scale Disasters	• Public support vs. self-reliance • Build Back Better vs. human-centered recovery
Korea	• 2004 Basic Law on DRR and National Security • 1995 Law on Natural Disaster	• Minimization of damages • Protection of life, limbs, properties
Indonesia	• 2007/24 Law on Disaster Management • 2002 Construction Code • 2007 Law on Space Planning	• Right of community • Development and disaster prevention • Preparation for funds
Myanmar	• 2013 Law on Disaster Management	• Inter-ministry coordination • Local governance
Philippines	• 2010/RA10121 Disaster Risk Deduction and Management Act	• Community awareness
Thailand	• 2007 Disaster Prevention and Management Act • 2004 Law on Land Readjustment	• Integration of disaster management • Development and disaster prevention
Vietnam	• 2006 Decree on Disaster Risk Reduction • 2007–2020 National Plan	• Implementation of national plan

Conference on Disaster Reduction held in Sendai, Japan in March, 2015. The Sendai Framework calls for a broader reach of disaster law in the priority area of "governance," which is included as one of the four priority areas (awareness, governance, investment, and preparedness for "Build Back Better"). Disaster law is now expected to establish the procedural basis for public disaster prevention projects (sec. 27a), to provide regulations addressing land use, planning and construction codes for urban safety (sec. 27d), and to encourage community participation and local autonomy (sec. 27f, g).

The Sendai Framework is nevertheless silent on the detailed designs of the thus broadened disaster law. Despite the abundance of emphasis put on the role to be played by the law, there is limited argument on the substance of how to form the law and what exact policies should be attained. We lawyers have to take up this task of elaborating upon the minimum common standards desired of disaster law, based on the hard-learned lessons gained from recent and previous experiences in disaster management.

This volume intends to focus on the legal issues of post-disaster recovery, the most lengthy and difficult stage of disaster response that follows the conclusion of the initial emergency stage of humanitarian aid. In the recovery phase following mega-disasters affecting developing countries in Asia, and the rural areas of developed countries as well, the need for disaster risk reduction (DRR) frequently contradicts with, and is often overridden by, the "development" needs. Although the Sendai Framework calls for the integration of post-disaster reconstruction into the economic and social sustainable development of affected areas (sec. 33 j), the term "development" can invite a centralization of macroeconomic growth. In this development-oriented reconstruction, the law largely decides the fate of reconstruction for the individual houses and livelihoods of the affected people. To analyze the real functions of laws which sometimes hinder, rather than foster, the endeavors of disaster victims to restore their lives, the contributors in this volume have accumulated empirical knowledge as participant-observers in the difficult recovery phase after mega-disasters in Asia.

This volume is, in this sense, an empirical approach to comparative disaster law that is a product of international collaboration between researchers in the field of law and public administration at universities located in the most disaster-prone regions in Asia. Methodologically, the contributors are constantly led by the keen interests in the socio-economic impacts of the law onto the reality of disaster-affected people and communities in reconstructing their self-organized governance (see Ostrom 1990, IRP 2011). The reader will acquire a comparative legal perspective across borders on the different solutions being sought in each jurisdiction to the common problems of disaster management. A comparative approach will lead us beyond the general commonness of the problems to various contexts of individual and collective legal issues in the interface with state involvement, such as land acquisition and compensation for post-disaster public projects, damage claims, public assistance, participation in the governmental decision-making process, as well as dispute resolution mechanisms as the last resort for affected people.

Through a methodological attempt of comparative analysis across borders on the impact of the law on people and society in times of disaster, we will be able to contribute to the emerging field of comparative Asian disaster law.

2 Scope of disaster law

To start an analysis of disaster law, we first need to identify the boundary of "disaster" to be covered by the law. Whether to narrow it to natural disasters or to widen it to cover human-caused damage of extraordinary scale would result in a different understanding on the purpose of disaster law, either as a basis for humanitarian aid or as a system of sharing the burden of social costs. Given the reality that humanitarian aid is often dependent on the state's discretion, the latter seems to be the preferable approach in order to induce an obligation of the state to stably maintain the whole system. For example, Japan's Disaster Countermeasures Basic Act (art. 2, sec. 1) includes both natural and human-caused disasters within its scope for disaster-prevention planning and budgetary arrangements.

Then, what about the reach of human-caused damage: whether it should be narrowed to human accidents or be inclusive of security risks such as disturbances, violence and terrorism? The latter's broader definition is an increasing phenomenon in the context of post-September 11 terrorist attacks. However, the "securitization" of the concept of disaster could change the basic humanitarian nature of disaster law into a tool of politics. In order to avoid being trapped in the intentional utilization of disaster as justification for security politics, the reach of disaster law in this volume will be narrowed to the social sharing of risk linked to natural disasters and human-caused accidents.

3 Public law and private law

Disaster law is an intersection of the public law and the private law spheres. Its fundamental nature lies in the form of public law that provides the basis for the organization and implementation of governmental response at each stage of disaster management. The Disaster Countermeasures Basic Act of Japan, for example, is a bundle of provisions for administrative functions addressing the stages of preparedness, emergency response, reconstruction of damaged infrastructure, and (although not explicitly defined) post-disaster recovery to complete a cyclical disaster management system. The stage of post-disaster recovery is, in particular, a crucial phase in both terms of time and space, in which the general public law regime that applies in standard scenarios clashes with the laws established in an emergency that take various procedural shortcuts in the name of promptness, and in which the measures intended for disaster-affected areas may extend into non-affected areas.

These series of public laws, while suffering from their own internal gaps, also operate in the interface with private law. Particularly in the phase of post-disaster recovery hampered by delay, private property rights of disaster-affected people are often largely overrun by public projects that envisage fundamental changes to the pre-disaster status quo of the civil regime. A bridge between public and private law spheres for both normative and procedural viewpoints is an urgent need.

4 Framework of comparative disaster law: across time and space

Then, how can we compare each domestic system of disaster law as a bundle of public and private laws beyond national borders? Methodological frameworks applied in the field of comparative legal studies may give us hints in an attempt to compare between different "legal systems" that pursue common policy goals. For our purpose of comparative disaster law, as well, we will be able to identify several typical patterns of legal systems from historical and regional perspectives throughout Asia, as a temporary methodological approach to better comprehend this emerging field of law in a cross-section of existing disciplines.

Accordingly, Part I of this volume collects a series of contributions introducing legal phenomena arising from mega-disasters in various areas across Asia. In considering the difference in legal designs in each attempt to respond to disaster risks, we will be able to apply the following typology.

4.1 Discretionary protector state model

When we look back at the history of pre-modern Asian disaster law, we recognize a common tendency of a series of emergency laws that provided support for disaster victims. Before the Meiji-Westernization of disaster-prone Japan, every shogunate government had no other choice but to repeatedly issue *tokuseirei*, a law to cancel all prior debts and prohibit foreclosures for the sake of protecting disaster victims. This spirit of law for disaster relief naturally succeeded in the initial stage of the Meiji-era modernization, until taken over by the influence of Western capitalist laissez-faire in the late nineteenth century. However, it has been revived in the contemporary context under the Disaster Relief Act of 1947 (Kaneko, Chapter 1, sec. 2), while new initiatives have been explored in recent years to construct new modes of support, which are led by mutual aid within civil society rather than at the state's discretion (Yamasaki, Chapter 7). The history of disaster law over thousands of years of Chinese dynasties has also seen a succession of disaster relief traditions, which was continued even by the present socialist system in the form of "winter and spring relief" to support livelihood reconstruction, until the famous "partner (twin) assistance" that was a feature following the Great Wenchuan Earthquake in 2008 (Li, Chapter 2). The development of disaster laws in Turkey has also been a typical one of a "healer state" since the era of the Ottoman Empire, in which a history of struggle to establish emergency legislation upon the occurrence of each mega-disaster has resulted in a patch-work response lacking a systemic order (Ozden & Erkan, Chapter 3), which might represent a typical situation observed throughout Asia. A fundamental weakness of such a protector-state model is the discretionary nature of the state's responsibility, which can always be subject to changes according to the priority of budgetary allocations from time to time, and can easily result in a "small government" when neo-liberalist policies become a trend, which then has to be supplemented by a call for mutual aid within the civic society. An implication is the need for a law to firmly establish the extent of state responsibility, which will also increase the motivation for a state to improve its preparedness before the occurrence of disasters.

4.2 Developmental state model

Upon the Westernization of its legal regime in the late nineteenth century, Japan turned to the pursuit of the capitalist state goal of liberalism. This resulted in the rejection of a bill on extensive disaster relief in the then newly-established National Diet, while self-reliance and mutual aid was expected to supplement the retreat of the state's protectionism. The focus of the disaster law regime was then turned to the construction of disaster-resistant infrastructure and city buildings, making it the government's practice to plan and implement large-scale post-disaster public projects upon the occurrence of every disaster (Kaneko, Chapter 1, sec. 3). This tendency of a "developmental state" to utilize disaster law as a tool of urban infrastructure and industrial development seems to have prevailed in various spheres in contemporary Asia. A recent campaign for "Post-Disaster Needs Assessment" to "Build Back Better," led by the initiatives taken by influential international financial agencies such as the World Bank, has invited large-scale post-disaster investments for infrastructure building and industrial development in many developing countries, while victim support fades out upon the cessation of humanitarian aid, which can only ever cover the emergency stage of disaster relief.

In the post-2004 Indian Ocean Tsunami recovery in Aceh, Indonesia, the national government was mainly concerned with the land administration project called RALAS that was backed by World Bank-led multilateral donor assistance. Meanwhile, matters concerning individual livelihoods were left to the autonomy of traditional communities (*gampong*), which was made possible by a series of provincial ordinances granting special autonomous status to the village communities deeply rooted in customary law (Taqwaddin & Alvisyahrin, Chapter 4). Similarly hit by the fatal Indian Ocean Tsunami, the outcomes of post-disaster recovery in the communities in southern Thailand were more acutely influenced by the governmental strategy to prioritize economic development, as typically shown in the reconstruction plan for the tourist industry, which utilized a series of legal frameworks on environmental management and spatial planning (Kanongnij, Chapter 5). The Law on Land Readjustment Projects was coincidently enacted in the very same month of the tsunami in December 2004 under the auspice of Japanese assistance, and was utilized as one of the legal bases of post-disaster development in Thailand. In the municipalities in Leyte and Samar islands seriously hit by the storm surge during Typhoon Yolanda in November 2013, a rush of applications for large-scale public projects occurred, led by the World Bank and the ADB-oriented concept of post-disaster needs assessment (PDNA). Driven by the vigorous campaign for "Build Back Better," faced with the needs of the affected people at the level of village communities known as *balangay* (Florano, Perez, & Pinheiro, Chapter 6).

4.3 Welfare-oriented model vs. neo-liberalism – classification of support, insurance, compensation

In contrast to the mainstream of the developmental state model, however, we can observe some unique new trends in disaster law formation emerging in Asian society. We may call one such trend the welfare-oriented model, in which civic movements have led attempts to re-establish disaster law as being centered on humanitarian support for individual victims instead of large-scale construction projects. Part II of this volume explores such new trends of welfare-oriented Asian disaster law.

A particular focus is on the "early recovery" period in between the stage of emergency disaster relief and the full recovery stage (see IRP 2008), which has not previously been explicitly indicated in the disaster management cycle. Although the disaster management cycle gives the impression that each stage of disaster response automatically progresses in a linear fashion from one stage to the next, in reality, individual recovery via self-help usually cannot keep pace with the recovery of government facilities reconstructed by public projects. Nevertheless, disaster relief is usually ended upon the transition from the emergency response to the recovery phase, according to the neo-liberal argument that the state's involvement with individual disaster victims should be minimized so as not to cause moral hazards (Posner 2004; Kunreuther 1996).

However, the recent development of disaster law in Japan has resulted in an increase in governmental support, in the form of special legislation on subsidies or discretionary ad hoc measures supplemented by local governments, to bridge the interim period of early recovery. Although the criticisms from neo-liberal voices are heard to highlight the weakness of the theoretical basis for this abundance of state involvement, as well as its piecemeal approach, it should be seen as a struggle in pursuit of a better legal framework for a welfare-oriented approach, to realize the baseline of the "national minimum" to be achieved as the obligation of the welfare state (Yamasaki, Chapter 7).

Then, how can this new trend of the welfare-oriented model acquire meaningful recognition among Asian law-makers against the mainstream of the developmental state model as well as the influence of neo-liberalism? An attempt is made by the contribution of Kondo (Chapter 8), who, after differentiating the legal concepts of "assistance," "damage compensation," and "insurance coverage," compares housing reconstruction support in Japan with the American system in the post-2005 Hurricane Katrina context. Despite the basic liberalist policy of FEMA (Federal Emergency Management Agency) that federal support for housing reconstruction is merely supplementary "assistance" for damage not covered by "insurance," an abundance of subsidies of up to $150,000 per household were offered by the states of Louisiana and Mississippi, upon the rhetoric that they were "compensation" for damage suffered which went beyond that foreseen in public safety planning policies. This unnatural justification for genuine "assistance" reveals a reality that welfare-oriented governmental intervention is inevitable when the "insurance" based system faces public distrust.

In other words, the "assistance" in this situation is more aimed at neo-liberalistic support of the financial sector by the government, instead of a supplement to a liberal system for the sake of disaster victims.

In connection with this, it is worth visiting the outcomes following the 2011 Canterbury Earthquake in New Zealand, a renowned example of a liberal regime rooted more simply in the compulsory disaster insurance system. In contrast to the rhetoric of "compensation" used in the U.S., the limit of insurance payments following the mega-disaster in New Zealand was clearly revealed before the public, causing serious distrust in the system's failure. The contribution by White (Chapter 9) describes in detail the outcomes of failing "insurance" based disaster law due to the limit set by the international re-insurance regime, which even the United Nations supervisory bodies on the Convention on Economic, Social and Cultural Rights have given attention to.

A reference should also be made to the experience of Turkey, which once attempted to introduce an "insurance" based disaster law regime upon the recommendation of the World Bank, but subsequently abandoned it after realizing the large gap between the neo-liberal premise and the country's healer state tradition (see Ozden & Erkan, Chapter 3).

Further, the context of the Fukushima Nuclear Power Plant Accident urges us to dig more into the nature of "compensation" beyond the dualistic choice between "assistance" and "insurance." Given our broad definition of disaster, as aforementioned, to be inclusive of human-caused extraordinary accidents, Fukushima's issues fall within our scope. Takahashi (Chapter 10) emphasizes the need to differentiate the legal concept of "compensation" for damage caused by human errors from the "compensation" paid for loss in the public expropriation of private properties, both of which should be differentiated from "relief," which itself is a risky concept that can be used to justify a compromised level of payment for unsettled compensation. This accusation reminds us of the need to give accurate legal labels to the various concepts in disaster management that are often carelessly misused in a confused way, which is one of the responsibilities of lawyers involved in disaster studies.

Ii (Chapter 11) describes the role of legal servicers as the caretakers of disaster victims' reconstruction of living based on his involvement in the 2011 post-East Japan Earthquake volunteer activities in tandem with the urban attorneys who hastened to establish legal services throughout the disaster-affected areas in the regional part which had been known for lacking judicial access.

4.4 Participatory model – due process for human-oriented recovery

Another trend of contemporary disaster law in Asia which invites special attention is the development of participatory procedures, or due process that guarantees the civic voice is heard in the process of governmental decision-making in the public law sphere. Part III of this volume explores the possibilities of the participatory model. A focus will be on the post-disaster town-recovery planning which links the lessons learned from a disaster to the preparation for disasters in the future, enabling an upwardly spiraling mode of perpetual development of the disaster management cycle.

A hard-learned lesson in the recovery path after the 1995 Hanshin-Awaji Earthquake was a need for a procedural framework to enable "human-centered recovery (*ningen no fukkou*)." Although the government of metropolitan Kobe took formal steps in accordance with the then-existing participatory procedure provided in the Law on Urban Planning, both during the formation of the "recovery plan" as an amendment to the city's master plan as well as the urban planning for individual land use, civic criticism calling for more substantial participation gradually grew. It took a barely-made compromise by the mayor of Kobe to utilize a local ordinance for the encouragement of *machidukuri-kyogikai*, or participatory town-planning councils, for the purpose of starting the decision-making steps over from the beginning as well as the plan-reevaluation steps that followed (Honjo, Chapter 12).

What occurred in the aftermath of the 2011 East Japan Earthquake and Tsunami, was, however, something opposite to Kobe's lesson on "human-centered recovery." An emergency law was introduced to supersede the participatory procedures applicable in normal scenarios, as priority was given to the promptness of the implementation of public projects for post-disaster reconstruction. This was further succeeded by permanent legislation in 2013, which materialized the concept of "Build Back Better" type disaster recovery at the sacrifice of community participation and information access. More often than not, the outcome of such prioritization of speed was to jeopardize the due process of the law which protected the legal regime of private properties and constituted the basis of the lives of the affected populations (Matsuoka, Chapter 13).

Similarly, the post-2011 Canterbury Earthquake recovery drew a red zone in the devastated city center where a "Build Back Better" type urban redevelopment plan was envisaged. Civic criticism rose when it was abruptly made known to the affected people that the city-oriented recovery plan, which was established without a meaningful consultation process despite the community approach emphasized under the Canterbury Earthquake Recovery Act, would involve substantially different rates of compensation on opposite sides of the border of the zone (Toomey, Chapter 14).

A warning has been observed that post-disaster town planning can harm the resurrection of individual livelihoods of disaster-affected people when prejudicial prioritization is given to housing reconstruction. Though the response following the 2001 Gujarat Earthquake in India is often cited as a successful example of safety-focused urban reconstruction resulting from a three-year long consultation between the local government and the citizens, the recovery plan led by professional consultants focused only on housing reconstruction without paying much attention to livelihoods (Hokugo, Chapter 15). The involvement of professional consultants is often led by the interests of the housing and construction industries. It must be the role of law to secure the procedural basis for ensuring the true voices of disaster-affected communities are heard in order to realize overall planning which prioritizes the crucial needs in the recovery.

The experience of Aceh following the 2004 Indian Ocean Tsunami is worth revisiting in terms of a successful participatory approach. The special legislative jurisdiction explicitly provided by the national law allowed the Aceh provincial government to introduce a series of local ordinances to vest each traditional village with autonomous status, which allowed the recovery of the pre-disaster status quo of customary order that was the basis of livelihoods as well as dwellings. (Taqwaddin & Alvisyahrin, Chapter 4).

Chen (Chapter 16), a U.K. based expert in disaster education, visits the experience of Taiwanese recovery from the damage suffered in the 2009 Typhoon, in which unique community-based initiatives have been taken in the education for future generations of both inside and outside of the country. An implication is the blooming international educational networks for the common minimum of disaster management based on the human-centered approach.

5 Avoiding the risk of developmentalization of disaster management

Comparative disaster law in Asia can thus aim at differentiating typical models of legal designs chosen by each country, comparing the fates of each choice from the viewpoint of policy balancing, as well as examining varieties of local endeavors that involve participatory approaches at the community level.

Table I.2 attempts to visualize the aforementioned typical models of Asian disaster law.

Many of the disaster-prone developing countries in Asia are put under the influence of the present world's trend of "developmentalization" of disaster management (lower-right dimension in Table I.2). When the 2005 Hyogo Framework for Action (priority 4) emphasized the need to create links between development planning and disaster risk reduction, we trusted that its sprit was driven purely by the intention to incorporate DRR into the mainstream of national developmental planning. During the ten-year implementation of HFA, however, DRR has turned out to be a new means of economic development, as shown in the recent World Bank campaign for a "Disaster Recovery Framework" and the 2015 Sendai Framework for Disaster Risk Reduction (sec. 30 c, sec. 36 c), encouraging public–private partnership (PPP) between "stakeholders" for disaster-preventive investments (lower-left dimension in Table I.2).

Table I.2 Typological matrix of disaster law models

	Allocation by Market ◄——►	Allocation by State
Rule-Centered ↑	Participatory Model	Welfare-Oriented Model
	Neo-Liberal Model	Protective State Model (Victim-centered) or Developmental State Model (Economy-centered)
↓ Deregulation		

It should be remembered, however, that the definition of the very term of "development" has changed dramatically during these decades. Since the early 1990s when the United Nations' "Human Development Report" started to be publicized, "development" has no longer simply meant economic growth, but has incorporated multiple goals of human society as summarized in the Millennium Development Goals. Now that the United Nations is aiming for new Sustainable Development Goals from 2015–2030, some parts of which are expected to refer to the issues relevant to disaster risk management ("build resilient infrastructure" in sec. 9, "make cities inclusive, safe, resilient and sustainable" in sec. 11, and "take urgent action to combat climate change and its impacts" in sec. 13), now is the moment that DRR should be included in the mainstream of development discourses so as to redefine the "developmentalization" of disaster recovery from the inside of the argument (upper-right dimension in Table I.2).

Otherwise, disaster law will only end up with means that are useful in the neo-liberal context of economic development without paying serious attention to the voices, wisdom, and endeavors at the community level in the pursuit for true safety. Not only developing countries but also rural economies in developed countries which maintain a ceiling of local fiscal allocations without meaningful transfer of tax sources are faced with the same danger of nominal DRR promotion that seeks economic investments at the sacrifice of true safety. If the law can make any change to these situations, it should start with the most fundamental aspects of fairness in terms of both substantive and procedural law, to secure the private rights of disaster-affected people and communities against the exploitation by development projects in the name of DRR (upper-left dimension in Table I.2).

A comparative approach will lead us to various contexts of individual and collective property rights in disaster in each jurisdiction, such as compensation, damage claims, public assistance, participatory procedures in governmental decision-making procedures, as well as the dispute resolution mechanisms as the last resort for affected people, beyond the general commonness of the problems. This volume intends to reach to the heart of the phenomena of Asian disaster law, from the grassroots bottom to the national decision-making top, and the international actors that are becoming increasingly influential in national policy making. Given the lack of international binding law on disaster management, the United Nations has played an important role in establishing objectives and general rules for international cooperation. Also, bilaterally, Japan as one of the world's most disaster-prone economic powers is expected to disseminate both successful and unsuccessful lessons from the struggles for achieving a better framework of policy formation and rule-makings (Toyoda, Chapter-17).

With the contributors to this volume having taken direct roles in disaster management in each risk area in Asia, the descriptions in each chapter present primary facts actually seen, heard, and experienced by the authors, and are dedicated to the needs of further comparative reading from various angles by countries and by subjects. This volume is an initial attempt at comparative Asian disaster law from deep inside the affected areas.

References

IRP (International Recovery Platform) (2011) *Cases and Practices on Role of Community in Recovery*, International Recovery Platform, available at www.recoveryplatform.org/.

IRP (International Recovery Platform)/UNDP (United Nations Development Programme)/ISDR (International Strategy for Disaster Reduction) (2008) *Guidance Note on Early Recovery*, available at www.recoveryplatform.org/.

Kunreuther, H. (1996) "Mitigating Disaster Losses through Insurance," *Journal of Risk and Uncertainty* 12: 171–187.

Ostrom, E. (1990) *Governing the Commons*, Cambridge: Cambridge University Press.

Posner, R. (2004) *Catastrophe, Risk and Response*, Oxford: Oxford University Press.

UNDP (United Nations Development Plan) (2009) *Lessons Learned: Disaster Management Legal Reform*, UNDP.

United Nations/ISDR (International Strategy for Disaster Reduction) (2005) *Hyogo Framework for Action 2005-2015,* A/CONF.206/6 CORR.1, United Nations.

United Nations/ISDR (International Strategy for Disaster Reduction) (2015) *Sendai Framework for Disaster Risk Reduction 2015-2030,* A/CONF.206/224, CRP.1, United Nations.

Part I

Typology of Asian disaster law

Beyond the developmental state model

1 Lessons from the 2011 East Japan Earthquake

Issues of participation and early recovery

Yuka Kaneko

1 Introduction

Disaster law in Japan faces a turning point. As one of the most disaster-prone countries in the world, Japan has accumulated law-making efforts for disaster management since the era of its ancient monarchy. In contrast to the basic discretionary nature of pre-modern laws centering on ad hoc disaster relief, modern disaster law has sought a systematic structure of disaster risk management based on the government's responsibility to maintain the disaster-preventive infrastructure as well as implement emergency responses. In particular, the Great Kanto Earthquake of 1923, in which there were more than 100,000 casualties due to fires that spread after the earthquake, initiated the Japanese modern tradition of the government's frequent use of large-scale urban planning methods for post-disaster reconstruction toward better urban safety. The same utilization of urban planning was pursued by municipal governments in the recovery phase of the 1995 Great Hanshin-Awaji Earthquake, which caused 6,000 casualties, again partly due to earthquake-induced fires despite the development of earthquake-resistant technologies during this period. A difference between these two great urban earthquakes was, however, in the distance between the affected people and the local governments in charge of disaster management: in contrast to the pre-war centralized bureaucracy, contemporary spatial planning is under the responsibility of the municipal governments, which sit closer to the citizens. Numerous voices raised by citizens since the Hanshin-Awaji Earthquake have brought actual changes to the disaster law regime under the 1961 Disaster Countermeasures Basic Act. Debates between legal scholars have also been vigorously made.[1] The ultimate question is, essentially, to what extent the state should be responsible for the individual lives and livelihood of disaster-affected people. Whereas influential scholars have strongly emphasized the state role in the "human recovery (*ningen-no-fukkou*)" approach centered on the disaster victims, the slogan "creative recovery (*souzou-teki-fukkou*)" has been the campaign message from the neo-liberal school, promoting the injection of state budget funds into disaster-preventive investments in preparation for future disasters.

In fact, post-disaster recovery in Japan has been guided largely by the sphere of public law on spatial planning and construction of public infrastructure, causing tension with the private rights of disaster victims at the intersection of two spheres of public law and private law. A critical argument has long been made that modern Japanese law on post-disaster recovery has been nothing more than an instrument of wholesale deprivation of private property for the purpose of constructing modern cities and infrastructure, without fair compensation for the victims (Ikeda 1993, etc.). The "creative recovery" slogan after the 1995 Hanshin-Awaji Earthquake was further expanded into the slogan "revival of Japan" after the 2011 East Japan Earthquake, and reiterated in the Law on Recovery from Large-Scale Disaster enacted in 2013, carrying the potential for enriching private investors that receive special disaster-related subsidies while leaving the very recovery of disaster-affected people behind. Furthermore, the recent vigorous ODA (official development assistance) activities meant to export this Japanese legal framework of spatial planning and construction of public infrastructure in post-disaster recovery to other parts of Asia, together with the restated slogan of "Build Back Better," represent the possibility of similar tragic effects on the disaster victims in these countries.

Before the Japanese model of disaster law is established as an Asian standard, it is necessary to carefully reevaluate its outcomes. With this purpose in mind, first, the historical outlook of Japanese disaster law will be reviewed (section 2) before focusing upon the issues of disaster recovery and the decision-making procedure (section 3). Then, the legal framework for victim support and compensation for loss in the course of recovery will be examined (section 4), and finally, the findings will be summarized (section 5).

2 Disaster law of Japan

2.1 A historical overview: victim aid vs. disaster-preventive investment

Since disaster management and support for disaster victims have always been the fundamental tasks of political rulers throughout the history of disaster-prone Japan, it was natural that the modern law-making activities of the Meiji government after the 1868 Meiji Restoration began with a series of ordinances providing for paternalistic aid for disaster victims. It was ironic, however, that such a humanitarian legal policy inherited from the pre-modern period was changed to a capitalist laissez-faire approach by the 1890s, when Western-style codification was completed and a series of laws was introduced to kick-off the vigorous construction of disaster-preventive infrastructure, followed by ordinances on urban building. As shown later in Table 1.2, a legal regime focused on hard infrastructure-centered disaster management has basically been maintained up to now, while law-making for humanitarian aid to disaster victims has been perpetually hindered by policy debates on the limits of the public role in supporting the individual livelihoods of disaster victims. Perhaps, the modernist pursuit of urban building and industrial development has been so deeply rooted in the legal regime of modern Japan since the Westernization in the late nineteenth century that a challenge has to be made against the very basis of such modernist thought in order to realize "human-centered" disaster management.

Indeed, the capitalist approach has not matched the immense needs in disaster-prone Japan. In 1890, the inaugural Diet rejected a Bill on Relief for the Poor that was intended to ensure national budgetary commitments for disaster relief. Instead the Law on Disaster Relief Funds was enacted in 1899, making it the responsibility of prefectural governments to establish funds to prepare for disaster relief. Such funds, however, were not sufficient to meet the intense need for victim support in mega-disasters. Similarly, market-based private insurance was campaigned for following the government's 1881 withdrawal of a draft bill on a government-sponsored compulsory disaster insurance system, which was influenced by a theory proposed by the German expert Paul Mayet. This resulted in serious social disturbance when the private insurance companies relied upon earthquake immunity clauses to reject fire insurance claims after the 1923 Great Kanto Earthquake, which caused not only 140,000 casualties but also the destruction of 447,000 houses due to fires caused by the earthquake.

After the failure of the war-time special compulsory insurance system introduced in 1944, the need for a more advanced system of governmental aid became eminently apparent after the end of World War II. The 1947 Disaster Relief Act was enacted as a fundamental law to declare the primary responsibility of the government to protect disaster victims and the social order (art. 1). This law, however, was only applied in practice to the stage of emergency response. As for the succeeding stages of post-disaster response, it was only after 1966 that the present system of government-sponsored voluntary insurance on houses was introduced by the Act on Earthquake Insurance, while numerous laws providing various types of governmental subsidies, such as the 1972 Act on Provision of Disaster Condolence Grants and the 1998 Act on Support for Reconstructing Livelihoods of Disaster Victims, have been introduced in response to each mega-disaster, lacking systematic consistency (see 2.3 below).

In contrast to this winding path in the development of laws for disaster victim protection in modern Japan, the legal regime for national land preservation and disaster-preventive town planning has steadily developed a solid structure. Starting with three fundamental laws on water management in the latter Meiji period, the legal regime on urban planning incorporated since 1919 has established the governmental practice of applying the land adjustment law to the reconstruction effort that has followed every mega-disaster, giving rise to the aphorism "a disaster is the mother of land readjustments." The present hierarchical regime of post-disaster reconstruction of hard infrastructure is led by the 1950 Act on General Development of National Land and the 1951 Act on National Government Defrayment for Rehabilitation of Disaster Stricken Public Facilities, while the 1951 Act on Land Expropriation provides the detailed procedure for compulsory land-taking in these public projects, which can proceed despite stakeholders' objections. After the introduction of the Basic Act on Disaster Control Measures in 1961, this trend of making laws for hard infrastructure-oriented disaster prevention has continued, while adding a series of special laws on post-disaster town planning to the regime of the 1968 Urban Planning Act. Those include the 1995 Act on Special Measures concerning Reconstruction of Urban Districts Damaged by Disaster introduced after the Hanshin-Awaji Earthquake, the 2011 Act on Special Zones for East Japan Earthquake Reconstruction, the 2011 Act on Town Planning for Tsunami Disaster Prevention, and the 2013 Act on Recovery from Large-Scale Disasters.

Thus, an imbalance between the struggling legal regime for disaster victim support and the solidly established regime for hard infrastructure rebuilding is apparent in present-day Japanese law. In order to overcome this dualism, legal reform is necessary to bridge the two spheres of public law and private law and incorporate greater representation of disaster victims as indispensable stakeholders in the decision-making process for post-disaster public projects.

2.2 Participation in recovery decision-making

Japan lacks a basic law on post-disaster recovery that guarantees a phase for participatory decision-making in the disaster management cycle. The Urban Planning Act, together with its subsidiary laws which provide for decision-making procedures for each category of town development projects, such as the Land Readjustment Act, has governed post-disaster recovery throughout modern history since the 1923 Great Kanto Earthquake. It should be noted that the procedural characteristics of such laws, particularly their degree of civic participation, have seen changes over time. The original 1919 Urban Planning Law had a simple government-led procedure, which was superseded by the present law in 1968 and progressively strengthened toward increased participatory opportunities via a series of amendments. In addition to the original provisions requiring public disclosure of draft urban plans and a chance for public comment before finalization, a 1980 amendment introduced a clause allowing local ordinances to add further opportunities for civic participation in district-level planning (art. 16, sec. 2). Then, influenced by the post-1995 Hanhin-Awaji Earthquake calls for more substantive civic initiatives,[2] further amendments were added throughout the 2000s, including civic proposals of district-level plans (art. 16, sec. 3), and proposals by civic groups on urban plans in general (art. 21, bis.). Also, following the 1999 amendments to the Local Autonomy Act, an upsurge in local ordinances enhanced opportunities for civic participation and information access, which was further encouraged by the introduction of the 2004 Landscape Act.

However, in parallel with this constant trend toward more civic participation within the sphere of the law on spatial planning, the increasing influence of neoliberalism has brought in a series of laws which have deregulated the decision-making procedure to promote privatization of public projects, such as the 1999 Act on the Promotion of Public Finance Initiative, the 2002 Act on Special Measures concerning Urban Reconstruction, and the 2011 Act on General Special Zones. This neo-liberalism appears to have spearheaded the abrupt revival of a government-centered approach in the wake of the 2011 East Japan Earthquake, apparent in the result of a series of special legislation which introduced the administrative procedure for "special zones" (*tokku*). Namely, the 2011 Act on Special Zones for East Japan Earthquake Reconstruction introduced a special procedure for short-cutting the decision-making process of post-disaster town planning, by instituting comprehensive decision-making by an administrative consultation body (*kyogikai*) made up of the representatives of line ministries and local government as well as private investors, to bundle up and give legal effect to all administrative decisions concerning a project upon a single and unilateral governmental notice (art. 50), while narrowing the participatory opportunities which had accumulated under the laws in normal times (art. 48, sec. 8). It is worthy of note that this government-led procedure for *tokku* was not only applied in the 2011 East Japan Earthquake, but also copied in the 2011 Act on Town Planning for Tsunami Disaster Prevention, a permanent law to encourage nationwide pre-disaster town planning in normal times, and further incorporated into Japan's first ever general law on post-disaster recovery projects, the 2013 Act on Recovery from Large-Scale Disasters (for details, see Kaneko 2013a, b).

The choice between government-centered and civic-centered procedures affects not only the speed, but also the quality of post-disaster recovery. In the reality of the post-2011 East Japan Earthquake recovery, according to the observations made in the author's continued fieldwork, administrative decisions on urban plans that decided the fate of post-disaster town planning in most of the tsunami-affected municipalities were completed through the *tokku* method by the middle of 2012, and followed by administrative decisions on each land-use project such as land readjustments by March 2013, without substantive disclosure of information to land owners, leaseholders, and other members of the tsunami-affected communities, often resulting in the adoption of safety measures which went against the expressed will of the local communities.

2.3 Legal framework on early recovery

"Early recovery" is an emerging concept that bridges the gap between the provision of humanitarian aid in the emergency stage of disaster management and the continuing needs of disaster-affected people and communities in the succeeding stages of post-disaster recovery (IRP 2008, 2011, etc.). While international humanitarian aid is usually concluded upon the closure of the field office of UNOCHA approximately three months after the occurrence of a disaster, and substituted by international development financial agencies such as the World Bank leading large-scale investments for infrastructure reconstruction, it is often taken as granted that the reconstruction of individual livelihoods and communal functions is a matter of self-help. However, in reality, individual recovery is not a simple leap from one stage to another. It usually necessitates continued assistance, at least during the suspension of individual reconstruction activities when land use restrictions are often imposed by the government to enable large-scale public works for infrastructure reconstruction and town planning, such as relocations and land-filling. "Early recovery" should also be considered as a necessary condition for implementing participatory decision-making, by supporting the

Table 1.1 Historical development of disaster law in modern Japan

	Law on emergency response	*Law on victim support*	*National land preservation and disaster preventive town planning*
Early Meiji (middle 19c)		1871 Regulation on Temporary Disaster Relief 1880 Law on Preparation for Disasters	
Late Meiji (late 19c)		1899 Act on Funds for Disaster Relief	1888 Ordinance on the Reform of Tokyo City Areas 1896 Act on Rivers, 1897 Act on Landslides Prevention, 1897 Act on Forestry
Taisho period (1923 Kanto Great Earthquake)		1924 Imperial Order on Subsidies for Supporting Fire Insurance 1924 Act on Emergency Settlement of Issues of Land and House Lease	1919 Act on Urban Planning (former) 1922 Special Act on Urban Planning
Post-WWII	1948 Fire Service Act 1947 Fire and Disaster Management Organization Act 1961 Disaster Preventive Basic Act	1947 Disaster Relief Act 1947 Agricultural Disaster Compensation Act 1947 Act on Emergency Settlement of Issues of Land and House Lease in Disaster Stricken Cities 1962 Act on Special Financial Support to Deal with the Designated Disaster of Extreme Severity 1964 Act on Compensation of Fishery Disaster 1966 Act on Earthquake Insurance 1972 Act on Provision of Disaster Condolence Grants	1950 Act on General Development of National Land 1951 Act on National Defrayment for Rehabilitation of Disaster Stricken Public Facilities 1951 Act on Land Expropriations • Urban Planning: 1954 Land Readjustment Act, 1968 City Planning Act, 1969 Urban Renewal Act, etc. • Disaster-Preventive Infrastructure: 1956 Coast Act, 1957 Act on Prevention of Landslides etc., 1960 Act on Emergency Measures for Preservation of Mountains and Waters, 1964 River Act, 1969 Act on Prevention of Disasters Caused by Steep Slope Failure, 1973 Act on Special Measures for Active Volcanoes, 1978 Act on Special Measures Concerning Countermeasures for Large-Scale Earthquakes, 1980 Act on Disaster-Preventive Collective Relocations

Post-1995 Hanshin-Awaji Earthquake	1995 Amendment to the Disaster Preventive Basic Act (strengthened commands of Prime Minister; Discretion of Self-Defense Force, etc.)	1998 Act on Support for Reconstructing Livelihoods of Disaster Victims	1995 Act on Special Measures Concerning Reconstruction of Urban Districts Damaged by Disaster 1995 Act on Special Measures Concerning Earthquake Disaster Management, 2000 Act on Prevention of Disasters Involving Landslides, 2003 Act on Countermeasures against Flood Damage of Specified Rivers Running Across Cities
Post-2011 East Japan Earthquake	2013 Amendment to the Disaster Preventive Basic Act (horizontal support between local governments, assistance to disabled or elderly people, etc.)	2013 Abolition of the 1947 Act on Emergency Settlement of Issues of Land and House Lease in Disaster Stricken Cities 2013 Act on Special Measures on Land and House Lease in Mega-Disasters	2011 Act on Special Zones for East Japan Earthquake Reconstruction, 2011 Act on Town Planning for Tsunami Disaster Prevention 2013 Act on Recovery from Large-Scale Disasters

temporary living conditions of disaster victims who take part in the town planning without the means to support their livelihood during the transition period until full recovery.

In Japan, local governments in disaster-affected regions usually close the budgetary account for disaster relief during the period approximately three months after the occurrence of a disaster, thus terminating the office for emergency response and replacing it with a new office for post-disaster recovery, in order to receive the national budgetary support meant for reconstruction works. However, a unique aspect of law in disaster-prone Japan is the relatively well-developed measures for "early recovery" support for disaster victims during the stages of transition and even into full recovery (see Table 1.2).

As for the support for dwellings, in addition to the provision of temporary houses during the transition period, varieties of subsidies are provided for supporting the reconstruction of individual houses in the full recovery stage. This includes a subsidy of 2 million yen (US$20,000) for each household that reconstructs a lost house, which is provided under the 1998 Act on Support for Reconstructing Livelihoods of Disaster Victims, as well as a variety of ad hoc measures taken by local governments based on national budgetary arrangements, such as the Recovery Fund established by the national government after the 2011 East Japan Earthquake.

There is also support for the livelihoods of disaster-affected people. In addition to non-monetary support, such as the provision of communal-use facilities for agricultural and fishery households under the 1962 Act on Special Financial Support to Deal with the Designated Disaster of Extreme Severity and the provision of temporary shops and factories as ad hoc support for small and medium-sized enterprises, monetary subsidies have also been available, such as the 1972 Act on Provision of Disaster Condolence Grants that provides a subsidy of up to five million yen (US$50,000) for each household which has lost its income earner, and the 1998 Act on Support for Reconstructing Livelihoods of Disaster Victims that establishes a subsidy of up to one million yen (US$10,000) for each household that has lost its house. In addition to these institutionalized measures, the most influential support in the post-2011 East Japan Earthquake recovery has been the ad hoc measure introduced by the Agency for Small-Medium Enterprises under the Ministry of Economy, Trade and Industry, which has provided subsidies in the scale of hundreds of millions of yen (millions US$) for the rehabilitation of communal-use facilities for use by groups of small-medium enterprises (hereinafter the "SME Group Subsidy").

This seemingly advanced lineup of Japanese measures for "early recovery" is, however, problematic in terms of systematic inconsistency, sectionalism in implementation, and confused budgetary burden sharing.

First, the systematic inconsistency has caused unequal consequences. Particularly, a series of measures introduced after the 1995 Hanshin-Awaji Earthquake for the support of housing reconstruction by urban residents does not always match the needs of disaster victims in a rural-set disaster such as the 2011 East Japan Earthquake. For example, a subsidy of up to one million yen

(US$10,000) under the 1998 Act on Support for Reconstructing Livelihoods of Disaster Victims was only available for those households which lost houses (regardless of income levels and the availability of insurance), while ignoring the most seriously affected categories of victims, such as low-income victims who did not own houses and family-owned businesses which lost their only source of income. Similarly, the additional subsidies up to two million yen (US$20,000) under the same 1998 Act as well as the additional ad hoc subsidies by local governments were only available for those who could afford to reconstruct their houses, while disregarding low-income and elderly households who could not manage to do so, revealing the obviously digressive outcomes. Perhaps an overall reform of measures for "early recovery" is necessary, in order to streamline the measures for this transition period based on the degree that living conditions have been affected, instead of solely based on housing loss, while respecting self-reliance in the stage of full recovery (Kaneko 2012).

Second, the bureaucratic sectionalism between ministries as well as between political parties caused inefficiencies such as the redundancy of similar measures on one hand, and the complete lack of necessary measures on the other. For example, regarding measures for mitigating the "double-burden" of pre-disaster and post-disaster financial debts of disaster-affected individuals and entrepreneurs, the Agency of Finance was quick to introduce a series of special financial measures with extremely generous terms and conditions (e.g. 1 billion yen-scale loan facilities for each enterprise over a 20-year period with an initial five-year grace period, and no requirement of collateral for loans of up to 160 million yen) that were meant for restructuring of financial debts of potential entrepreneurial participants in the rehabilitation. It also introduced a special guideline for private rearrangement that was meant to provide the means for quick liquidation to avoid lengthy bankruptcy procedures. Then, given the hesitance of financial institutions to operate directly in the disaster-affected regions, the Agency of Small-Medium Enterprises introduced a separate financial scheme for the restructuring of old loans to be managed by the newly-established Organization for Industrial Recovery in each affected prefecture. A similar financial scheme by the Organization of Recovery Support for East Japan Enterprises followed, under pressure from the Liberal Democratic Party. All these parallel measures introduced by different agencies were not successful at all, since the aforementioned SME Group Subsidies introduced by the Agency of Small-Medium Enterprises created a dependency within local entrepreneurs and financers on the subsidies instead of the financial schemes.[3] Perhaps, better role-sharing between the market (finance) and the state (subsidies) could have been possible if not for the sectionalism inside the government.

Third, the principle governing the budgetary burden for victim support between the national, prefectural, and municipal governments is confused. As shown in the furthest right-hand column in Table 1.2, some of the support measures involve a certain ratio of municipal burden, but others do not. In the recovery stage of the East Japan Earthquake, municipal governments revealed a

Table 1.2 Outlines of victim support after the post-2011 East Japan Earthquake

Stages		*Area of assistance*	*Legal basis*	*Budgetary burden*
Disaster Relief in Emergency Stage		Basic Needs (Protection of lives, limbs, and properties)	Disaster Relief Act	National Government: 50–90% ⇒ After 2011 Earthquake increased to 99% Prefectural Government: 10–40% ⇒ After 2011 Earthquake reduced to 1% Municipal Government: zero
Early Recovery (interim period)	Legislative measures	Temporary housing	Disaster Relief Act	As above
		Removal of debris	Law on Waste Management	National Government: 50–90% ⇒ After 2011 Earthquake increased to 100% Municipal Government: 10–40% ⇒ After 2011 Earthquake reduced to zero
		Basic tranche of the Subsidy for Reconstructing Livelihoods for households which lost houses	Act on Support for Reconstructing Livelihoods of Disaster Victims	National Government: 50% ⇒ After 2011 Earthquake increased to 80% Provincial Government: 50% ⇒ After 2011 Earthquake reduced to 20% Municipal Government: zero
		Condolence Money (subsidies to households which lost its income earner)	Act on Provision of Disaster Condolence Grants	National Government: 50% ⇒ After 2011 Earthquake increased to 70% Provincial Government: 25% ⇒ After 2011 Earthquake reduced to 17.5% Municipal Government: 25% ⇒ After 2011 Earthquake reduced to 17.5%
		Financial aid to primary industries: • Rehabilitation of common facilities • Rehabilitation of aquacultures	Law on Special Financial Aid for Large-Scale Disasters (Fishery Agency etc.)	• Facilities for common use: National Gov. 1/3. Prefectural Gov. 1/3, Fishermen's Association 1/3 • Facilities for individual use: National Government 9/10

	Ad hoc measures	Support for SMEs: • Temporary shops/factories • Special loans, debt-restructuring schemes, etc. Emergency aid for employment: • Flexible use of unemployment insurance, subsidies to employers • Expanded emergency measures for creation of employment etc.	Ad hoc measures (Agency for Small-Medium Enterprises etc.) Ad hoc measures (Ministry of Health and Labor)	National Government: Full ↓ (Municipal Government can receive rents from users) National Government: Full ↓ (Municipal Government contracts with private companies)
Full Recovery	Legislative measures	Additional tranche of the Subsidy for Reconstructing Livelihoods for housing reconstruction	Act on Support for Reconstructing Livelihoods of Disaster Victims	National Government: 50% ⇒ After 2011 Earthquake increased to 80% Provincial Government: 50% ⇒ After 2011 Earthquake reduced to 20% Municipal Government: zero
	Ad hoc measures	Additional subsides for housing reconstruction by local governments	Ad hoc measures (Recovery Fund)	National Government: Full
		Supporting full recovery of industries: • SME Group Subsidies • SME Special Loans • Measures for restructuring loans etc.	Ad hoc measures (Agency for Small-Medium Enterprises etc.)	• SME Group Subsidies: National Government: 50% Provincial Government: 25% ⇒ funded by the SME Support Organization Municipal Government: zero Individual SME: 25%
	Public Works funded by the National Recovery Budget Allocation	• Disaster-Preventive Collective Relocation • Land Re-adjustment for Land-filling Works • Rental of Public Apartments etc.	Act on Special Zones for East Japan Earthquake Reconstruction	National Government: Full (limited to within Disaster Risk areas designated by the two meter-depth rule resulting from tsunami simulation)

strong tendency to avoid increasing their budgetary burden, by avoiding extensive application of measures involving municipal burdens (e.g. condolence money) while actively utilizing the measures to encourage industry for which the national government had made explicit promises to cover all of the burden (e.g. subsidies under the 1998 Act on Support for Reconstructing Livelihoods of Disaster Victims; SME Group Subsidies).

3 Challenges for the participation process

3.1 Tragedies of government-centered recovery in Japan

The decision-making process for post-disaster town recovery in the affected municipalities in eastern Japan followed a government-centered process which included three steps. First, the Recovery Plan (*Fukkou Keikaku*) was decided by the mayor, which involved a minimal participatory step, such as town meetings. Second, the Recovery Adjustment Plan (*Fukkou Seibi Keikaku*) authorized the governmental council to give comprehensive legal effect to all relevant urban plans in a single decision via the fast-track *tokku* procedure under the 2011 Act on Special Zones for East Japan Earthquake Reconstruction. Finally, each spatial project, such as relocation and land readjustment, was decided based on the relevant legal procedures. The first two steps were quickly completed by way of governmental decisions without substantial disclosure of information to the affected people and communities beyond occasional minimal distribution of the general scheme. This resulted in prolonged delay in the third step of the process for each individual project due to the lack of agreement on the part of the affected people.

The result of the government-centered approach taken by the post-2011 East Japan Earthquake legislation has been tragic. The available choices of safety measures proposed by the government included (i) relocation to higher ground, (ii) land-filling, and (iii) construction of seawalls to let the affected people stay in their original land lots in tsunami-inundated areas. According to the questionnaire surveys conducted by various agencies after the disaster, the majority of tsunami-affected people favored the choice of (i), particularly relocation to nearby higher ground (such as commonly-owned forests which were both safe and provided easy access to the original lands where the basis of their livelihood was located). However, the national government, led by the Ministry of Land and Transportation, issued the Basic Recovery Principle in July 2011, which centered on the choice of (iii). This was followed by a decision of the Central Council for Disaster Prevention in September 2011, which authorized the construction of great seawalls 15 meters in height and with bases greater than 100 meters in sections that cover the entire coastline of the tsunami-inundated areas throughout eastern Japan. This tremendous dependency on hard infrastructure was not only against the will of the majority of local people regarding the choice of safety measures,[4] but also caused enormous harm to their properties and resulted in the fragmentation of communities.

Based on the assumptions derived from computer simulations that the great seawalls could create enough time for the evacuation of many households in the next tsunami, the government-led recovery plans narrowed the scope of households eligible for government-sponsored relocation (via designation of Disaster Risk Areas under the Building Standards Act, art.39, which permanently ban residential use) to only those in the limited areas estimated to be hit by a 2-meter tsunami with a velocity of 2 m/s or more (hereinafter the "2–2 line"). Accordingly, after a year's-long reconstruction ban, without compensation, that was introduced by the local governments after the tsunami to give them time to prepare recovery plans, the majority of households were destined to have to reconstruct in the inundated lands under their own efforts. Certain limited areas where there was a concentration of households operating small commercial and industrial businesses were eligible for government-sponsored land readjustment projects for land-filling instead of relocation projects. This seemed to be the result of a governmental measure to avoid the criticisms of such small industries in case of relocation, since it was the government's cost-saving decision to allow the relocation of houses only.

As a result of such a government-centered decision to demarcate the specifications between different safety measures, the households in tsunami-affected communities were split into several categories, namely (i) those which were within the 2–2 line and eligible for government-sponsored relocation and benefits from the government purchase of their original land and the provision of new land in a safer place, (ii) those which were within the 2–2 eligible line but ineligible to participate in the government-sponsored relocation due to the gap in value between their original land and the new land available for purchase, (iii) those eligible for government-sponsored land-filling of a few meters' depth, (iv) those eligible for government-sponsored land-filling for depths of 15 meters or more, who are destined to wait for several more years until the completion of such technically difficult projects, (v) those which were outside of the 2–2 line and destined to have to build themselves on their original land, and (vi) those which were outside of the 2–2 line and could not afford to reconstruct by themselves (see Table 1.2). Households which found themselves in categories (ii), (iv) and (vi) had no choice but to abandon the reconstruction of their houses and either choose to live in a public rental apartment for low-income persons or move away from their home town.

In order to mitigate social criticism, some municipalities decided to provide additional subsidies for reconstruction of houses based on the "Recovery Fund" backed by the national budget. However, no such measures were available for low-income and elderly households which could not afford reconstruction, and thus only resulted in further unfair treatment across the different categories. The pre-disaster community has been split into a few winners and a majority of losers who are drifting away, no longer capable of sitting down together to deliberate a common future.

Thus, the government-led recovery procedure led by the 2011 Act on Special Zones for East Japan Earthquake Reconstruction, and made permanent by the

Table 1.3 Limited eligibility and support in safety measures in East Japan recovery

Safety-based recovery projects	*Eligibility*	*Public support*	*Additional support*
Relocation (e.g. disaster-preventive collective relocation projects)	27,000 households (out of a total of 310,000 households) ↓ • Unavailable for those who cannot afford reconstruction • Unavailable for those who lost leasehold land due to a construction ban	• Public purchase of original land at subsidized price • Public development of new land sites • Subsidized loans	• Additional subsidies for housing reconstruction
Land-filling (land readjustment projects)	3,500 ha (out of a total of 56,000 ha of inundated land) ↓ • Unavailable for those who cannot afford reconstruction • Unavailable for those who lost leasehold land due to a construction ban	• Public construction for land-filling	• Additional subsidies for housing reconstruction
Self-help (protection by seawalls)		–	• Additional subsidies for housing reconstruction
Public housing	About 20,000 rooms (income-based criteria)	• Subsidized rent	

2013 Law on Recovery from Large-Scale Disasters, has resulted in the exact opposite of "human-centered" recovery.

3.2 The model transplanted in developing countries: the case of Thailand

Backed by the increasing influence of neo-liberalism, the same government-centered and pro-investment procedure in post-disaster recovery is gaining popularity in other jurisdictions, in the name of "public-private partnership." The post-2011 Canterbury Earthquake Recovery in New Zealand was led by the discretionary authority of the Minister for Canterbury Earthquake Recovery, while suspending the application of laws that are relevant in normal times.[5] Developing economies are also the target of the neo-liberal approach as the relevant legal models are brought in by international donors. A comparison of the legal designs chosen by the Asian countries hit by the 2004 Indian Ocean Tsunami offers a picture of the different choices in response to the same neo-liberal trend.

Thailand, for example, did not have a regime of disaster management law when the 2004 Indian Ocean Tsunami hit the southern provinces of Pangna and Phuket, causing more than 8,000 recorded casualties and affecting 407 villages. It was not until 2007 that the first basic law on disaster management, namely the Law on Disaster Prevention and Mitigation, was adopted, integrating the two areas previously covered by the 1979 Law on Civic Defense and the 1999 Law on Fire-Fighters, which did not include much provision on the post-disaster phases to follow the initial emergency stage. Accordingly, the laws in normal times, such as the 1992 Law on Environmental Preservation as well as the 2004 Law on Land-Readjustment, were applied in the post-disaster phases of the 2004 Indian Ocean Tsunami. Representing a typical legal design of administrative laws in developing Asian countries, these Thai laws have a government-centered structure. In the post-2004 tsunami recovery phase, set-back regulations and other construction bans were introduced in the six most seriously affected provinces under a series of ministerial regulations based on the 1992 Law on Environmental Preservation (art. 9, 43~45) bestowing the discretion to the prime minister or the provincial governors nominated by the central government to introduce any adequate orders to respond to emergency situations such as natural and environmental disasters.

Also, land readjustment was implemented involving a few villages in Ta Kua Paa district in Pangna province, a famous tourist destination (DPWTCP 2005, p. 2.22~2.26), based on the 2004 Law on Land Readjustment, adopted as a result of Japanese legal assistance and coincidentally in the same month as the 2004 tsunami, which featured a special fast-track procedure for post-disaster land readjustment projects (art. 45). The 2004 Law on Land Readjustment features a dualistic structure which separates the planning process of a basic plan (*pen me-bot*) and the decision-making process for each land readjustment project. The former, a basic plan, is to be completed exclusively by administrative decision-making between national, local, and municipal governments (art. 6, sec. 2, art. 13, sec. 6), which differs from its Japanese counterpart that guarantees civic participation in the plan-making process. The latter decision-making process for each project involves only the landowners, while other stakeholders' objections are heard at the provincial committee (art. 16, 36, 43, 53, 62–70), again differing from its Japanese counterpart which treats land users as equal to landowners.

This separation may result in at least two effects. First, the substance of a land readjustment project can be decided at the discretion of the government, without involving participation by stakeholders. This reminds us of a similar attempt to bypass participatory procedures applicable in normal scenarios by the aforementioned Japanese *tokku* method under the 2011 Act on Special Zones for East Japan Earthquake Reconstruction. Second, in contrast to the Japanese law which provides for equal rights of participation for both landowners and tenants, the goal of a land readjustment project is simplified as a compromise between the government and the landowners only (art. 36, 53), while introducing a complaint procedure for "relevant parties" that becomes final at the provincial level, cutting out recourse to judicial review (art. 43, 70). Although this legal design may realize quicker disaster recovery, it might severely reduce the chances of participation and information access for a broad range of stakeholders other than the landowners, given the socio-economic reality in Thailand that absentee landownership prevails, and that, due to the slow implementation of the Torrens-style land title registration project under the 1954 Law on Land, the legal status of land users is often as weak as customary occupation (*chap-chorn*).

This combination of government-centered planning and ownership-centered decision-making may represent a typical approach taken by many developing countries (FAO 2006), which are actively introducing spatial planning law as a new means of acquiring land for development purposes that has less of a budgetary burden for compensation than expropriation law would require.

3.3 Local ordinances as the basis for a community approach: post-2004 Aceh

The Indonesian experience, in its recovery process from the extreme devastation that involved more than 200,000 casualties in the 2004 Indian Ocean Tsunami, presents an alternative direction of legal designs for better opportunities of participatory disaster recovery. While it has been debated whether the overall recovery was led by the national government or by local communities,[6] post-tsunami land use planning was definitely led by local communal initiatives. Because the national government's initial proposal for a uniform land-use ban over the entire area within 2 km of the coastline received strong criticism from tsunami-affected people who used to make their living on the coastal lands, the recovery blue print (formalized by the Presidential Decree No. 30 in 2005) entrusted each village community to make the decision of whether to relocate to higher ground or to stay in the coastal lands. Those communities which chose to stay were partly backed by the land mapping project performed under the framework of RALAS (Reconstruction of Aceh Land Administration System) and including the involvement of international donors (MDF: Multi-Donor Fund for

Aceh and North Sumatra) in accordance with guidelines set by the national land ministry (BPN Decision No. 114-II 2005) and the government regulation No. 2 in 2005, which emphasized the recognition of the *status quo* of pre-disaster property regimes based on the Civil Code and/or customary law. Given the lack of land registration certificates due to the population's traditional mistrust of formal ownership regimes since colonial days, land-mapping projects had usually no other choice but to depend on the customary rules in each community, in which the village chief together with the religious leader decided land boundaries and the Sharia court gave authentic recognition (Taqwaddin and Alvisyahrin 2013). Based on the special legislative autonomy given by the 2001 Law on Special Autonomy of Aceh Province, a series of Aceh provincial ordinances (such as Qanun No. 7 in 2000 on customary justice, and Qanun No. 5 in 2003 on the basic autonomous government of *gampong*) recognized an enhanced role of customary communities as the basic unit of autonomous government. According to numerous case studies (Fitzpatrick 2012; IRP 2012, etc.), such a community approach is considered successful in fostering effective planning that reflects each different socio-cultural background in the process of post-disaster recovery.

This community initiative, on the other hand, has been criticized in regard to the disparity caused between villages that have had different degrees of access to donor resources (Telford 2012 etc.), as well as the poor integration between the plans of communities and the upper levels of provincial and municipal governments. Reflecting both sides of such divided views on the roles of community in disaster management, Law No. 24 in 2007 on Disaster Management in Indonesia, together with its implementation regulation No. 21 in 2008, centers on extended control by the national disaster management agency (BNPB) and its local-level subsidiaries (BPBDs) over the level of communities, though repeatedly emphasizing the rights and interests of communities (art. 4, 26, 59, etc.).

Parallel to this centralized approach in the area of disaster law, the area of spatial planning also shows a trend toward re-centralization. Law No. 24 in 2007 on Spatial Management, which superseded the preceding law of 1992, has a unique design feature which, while emphasizing a broad mandate for local ordinances to design the details of civic participatory procedures (art. 20 sec. 6, art. 23 sec. 6, art. 26 sec.7, art. 28 for basic plans, and art. 21, 24, 27, 28 for detailed plans), allows central-ministerial regulations to extend controls over such local ordinances (art. 18, which is further detailed in the 2010 Decree No. 15, art. 28, 33, 37). This is essentially a reversion to central control, away from the drastic experiment of decentralization in Indonesia since 1999. Decentralization first took an ambitious form of devolution (the transfer of the majority of administrative authority to the municipal level) under the 1999 Law on Local Autonomy, but was then amended to a mitigated form of decentralization under the revised law in 2004. The scarcity of concrete participatory procedures under the 2007 Law on Spatial Management has led to a similar lack of concrete provisions for civic participation under local ordinances, as shown in the case of the 2011 Jakarta City Ordinance on Spatial Management, which has been a target of social criticism and even involved a lawsuit in the Supreme Court.

The approach taken in local ordinances in Aceh province in Indonesia would, however, suggest a different direction from government-centered disaster recovery. The limited participatory approach in the national laws was supplemented by a series of provincial ordinances, based on the special legislative jurisdiction explicitly established by the Aceh Qanun No. 3 in 2007. Particularly, the Aceh Qanun No. 5 in 2010 on Disaster Management has added important provisions to its counterpart national law in order to enhance the role of communities, including a stress on information access and advisory roles to be played by the communities in the decision-making on disaster management (art. 11), while emphasizing the responsibilities of all levels of actors to disclose true information (art. 21). A unique institutional framework was also devised by the Aceh Qanun No. 10 in 2008 on Indigenous Institutions to stimulate mutual supervision between community institutions that monitors the increased autonomy under the Aceh Qanun No. 9 in 2008 on the Strengthening of Community Law (Taqwaddin and Alvisyahrin 2013).

Similar endeavors have been undertaken in Japan for the strengthening of local ordinances to enhance participatory procedures (Kaneko 2013a&b for details). The 1981 Kobe City Ordinance on District Plans and Town Planning Councils had, for example, added unique provisions (art. 4–8) to encourage broadly ranging civic participation in town planning beyond the mandate given by the national City Planning Act, which merely allowed local governments to elaborate upon procedures for the involvement of stakeholders in district-level planning (art. 16, sec. 2). Such additional provisions in the Kobe ordinance played an important role in the post-1995 Kobe Earthquake recovery as the basis for the certain extent of civic participation which did take place in the post-disaster urban planning, and which further influenced subsequent endeavors in other municipalities to enact ordinances for participatory disaster recovery. For example, the 2006 Ordinance on the Promotion of Town Planning by way of Civic Participation in Katsushika Ward, Tokyo was a product of an active campaign by the Tokyo Metropolitan Government for "pre-disaster recovery planning involving community cooperation" under the framework provided in the 2000 Tokyo Ordinance on Disaster Response and the 2003 Tokyo Manual on the Disaster Recovery.

Nevertheless, an explicit mandate encoded in the basic national law is necessary in order to secure the legal effect of participatory provisions under local ordinances. Aceh Province is a special case in Indonesia, bestowed with certain autonomy of legislative jurisdiction. The aforementioned endeavors by local ordinances in Japan, in contrast, were easily superseded by the 2011 Act on Special Zones for East Japan Earthquake Reconstruction featuring the government-centered procedure. Given the constitutional restraint in Japan that narrows the reach of local ordinances within the mandates given by national laws (the 1947 Constitution, art. 94), a basic law to establish community-centered procedures as a norm seems a crucial need.

4 Protection of the property basis of early recovery

4.1 Differentiation of support, compensation, and damages

In order to actualize "early recovery" or an effective legal framework that directly addresses substantial reconstruction of disaster-affected people and communities, a streamlining of the legal concepts of "support," "compensation," and "damages" seems necessary. In principle, the government is not responsible for the destruction caused by natural disasters, unless obvious fault is found in the governmental management of disaster-preventive facilities,[7] whereas the governmental "support" offered to disaster victims is not an obligation but a matter of discretionary actions of a welfare state. In contrast, the context of "compensation" emerges as a matter of obligation when the government imposes a restriction or any other special sacrifice of private property for the sake of a public use, based on the fundamental guarantee of the freedom of ownership in modern law.[8] "Damage" is, on the other hand, a claim arising as a result of a fault of the government, which should be differentiated from "loss compensation" for lawful restrictions. This differentiation of these three concepts is meaningful, particularly when the neo-liberal school of institutional economists insists on the minimization of governmental "support" to disaster victims based on the arguments that such support causes a moral hazard and harms self-reliance (Posner 2004, Kunreuther 1996, etc.). Even when "support" is reduced at the discretion of a neo-liberal government which favors allocating more of the national budget toward rebuilding infrastructure and economic stimuli, "compensation" remains a mandatory obligation owed to disaster victims that the government cannot avoid.[9]

In the post-2011 East Japan Earthquake recovery, in the course of large-scale public construction projects for infrastructure such as great seawalls, land-filling, and relocations, numerous issues concerning "compensation" emerged in regard to the restriction to the most fundamental property rights of disaster-affected people, such as land ownership, leaseholds, commercial goodwill, and fishery rights, which have been handed down for generations as indispensable bases of living in the rural economy. While fair compensation (Japanese Constitution, art. 29, sec. 3) is necessary when the *status quo* of the living basis is taken or otherwise restricted by the government in normal times, post-disaster recovery sometimes proceeds without such lawful compensation, in an abuse of the discretionary context of "support." According to findings in the continued fieldwork by the author's group in the tsunami-affected areas in Iwate Prefecture since the occurrence of the 2011 East Japan Earthquake, typical cases of such restrictions include:

i Land-readjustment projects without loss compensation: Since the introduction of Western-style urban planning law in Japan in the 1900s, land readjustment as one category of urban planning has been applied by the government to every post-disaster recovery, resulting in the saying mentioned above that "disaster is the mother of land readjustment." One of the main reasons for the propensity of the government to choose this action is the existence of "reduction" (*genbu*), which enables the public expropriation of a certain share of land ownership without compensation. Usually the rate of *genbu* reaches more than 20 percent of each original lot of land. The justification of this taking land without compensation is based on the interpretation of a constitutional clause on the inherent restriction of property rights for social function or "social welfare" (Const. 29, sec.2). In the post-2011 East Japan Earthquake recovery, land readjustment has been used for 3,500 ha in total, a vast area, and has been employed not only for implementing land-filling projects up to 15 meters in depth, a safety measure which has suspended individual reconstruction activities by disaster-affected people for 6–7 years (the completion is expected in the year 2017 or 2018), but also for constructing 17-meter-wide industrial roads and industrial parks, which is arguably beyond the constitutional condition on the inherent restriction of private rights without compensation. Although the precedent of the Japanese Supreme Court used to differentiate governmental restrictions for public use (with compensation) and police purposes (without compensation),[10] the recent stance of the Supreme Court judgments add more detailed criteria for such differentiation, considering the balance between the purpose of restrictions, the type of restricted properties, and the degree of restrictions.[11]

ii Relocation under the 1980 Law on Disaster-Preventive Collective Relocation: Although disaster-preventive collective relocation was featured as the highlight of safety measures taken in the post-2011 East Japan Earthquake recovery, its implementation has involved numerable problems, resulting in a serious population drain from the target areas. One of the reasons for the disappointment is the price gap between the governmental purchase of original tsunami-inundated land and the governmental sale of land lots in the relocation sites. Sometimes the gap is as much as several times, particularly since the market price of the tsunami-inundated lands located in rural fishery areas is valued very low, while the price of relocation sites is decided by the government on a cost-plus basis, which can soar as the cost of governmental land acquisition increases due to the lack of suitable areas for relocation. Disaster-affected households simply cannot afford to buy at such increased prices, and have no other choice but to move away from their ancestral land, since they can neither afford to relocate, nor rebuild on the original land due to the permanent habitation ban applied to the Disaster Risk Areas (Building Standards Act, art. 39). If the government-sponsored relocation was constituted as "compensation" for such permanent restriction, instead of as mere "support," this price gap should have been borne by the government, rather than being shifted to the disaster-affected people, who have already suffered enough from their losses in the disaster and the succeeding suspension of rebuilding due to governmental projects that have lasted several years.

iii Separation of housing and livelihood: Another problem of disaster-preventive collective relocation has been the separate treatment of houses and livelihoods. While the characteristics of the pre-disaster *status quo* in making a

> living in the rural economy centered on petty industries such as agriculture, fishery, and small-sized shops and factories owned and operated by a single household that lived on the same site, the government regulations and ministerial guidelines for the implementation of relocations were amended after the 2011 East Japan Earthquake so as to permit the relocation of houses only, separating dwellings from the land and facilities residents used for their livelihoods. Accordingly, households in the target areas were compelled to choose either (a) the purchase of new land in a relocation site with their own money, while maintaining their business on the original land, or (b) selling the original land and abandoning the reconstruction of their business in order to use the proceeds of such sales for the relocation of their house in a safer place. Actually, many households could choose neither (a) nor (b), but were forced to abandon both the relocation of their house and the reconstruction of their business because of the aforementioned price gap. This outcome is highly questionable when the relocation is reconsidered in the context of "compensation" for the permanent habitation ban in the Disaster Risk Area. Although the governmental guidelines on compensation for loss in Japan have been based primarily on the concept of "property compensation," while the concept of "protection of livelihoods" is only admitted within the discretion that falls outside of the obligatory compensation,[12] there are certain special laws which explicitly refer to the "measures for livelihood reconstruction" which oblige the prefectural governors to prepare plans to equalize the quality of life before and after the expropriation of land for public projects.[13] Given this trend of law-making for the "protection of livelihoods," whether it may be discretionary support or obligatory compensation, disaster-preventive collective relocation should not end up causing the uncompensated destruction of the *status quo* of integrated dwellings and livelihoods.

A possible counter-argument from the neo-liberal school would be that the losses incurred in the course of relocations can be disregarded since relocation is a discretionary "support" linked to the habitation ban imposed for the safety of local citizens as an inherent restriction due to the social function of private properties (Const. 29, sec. 2), which do not fall under the context of loss compensation (Const. 29, sec. 3). Such an argument, however, lacks any basis if the justification of "safety" is contested. The element of "social welfare" (Const. 29, sec. 2) is questionable when compared to the necessity of such huge but ineffective safety measures as the great seawalls that are unable to protect against the next level-2 class tsunami, or the relocation to inland compact-cities several kilometers away from the highland areas of the seacoast that the affected communities proposed for their relocation. If the justification of "safety" is lacking, the issue remains then as "compensation" (Const. 29, sec. 3). Even when the justification of "safety" is admitted, "compensation" cannot be avoided since, as aforementioned, the Supreme Court precedent requires the balance between the purpose (tsunami prevention), properties (integration of habitation and livelihood), and the degree of restrictions (permanent habitation ban).

4.2 A comparative perspective: safety vs. livelihood

Similar property issues in the course of post-disaster recovery projects are observed in other disaster-prone regions in Asia. In the recent fieldwork conducted by the author's group in village communities on the tenth anniversary of the 2004 tsunami in Aceh, Indonesia,[14] villages have been compelled to make a dualistic choice between government-sponsored relocation for the safety of inhabitance and self-reconstruction on the original land for the sake of livelihood. Those villages which chose self-reconstruction on their original land on the seacoast somehow maintain their livelihood but continue to face the problem of safety, since essentially no safety measures have been provided by the government in such areas. In contrast, those villages which chose to relocate several kilometers away from the seacoast have had to address the problem of making a living, particularly for the villagers who used to be farmers or fishermen and lost their agricultural or fishery means. Although the government purchased their original land within the range of 2 km from the coastline, such purchase is questionable because it was without providing any alternative measures for livelihood reconstruction. A better choice to enable both safety and the continuation of livelihoods could have been available if a proper differentiation is made between the legal concepts of "compensation" and "support," as observed in the recent trend in Indonesia of increasing participatory approaches in the legal areas of spatial planning (2007 Law on Spatial Planning, etc.) and land-taking (2012 Law on Land Expropriations etc.), which introduced a highly sophisticated procedure for participation and objections by stakeholders.

Similar issues regarding livelihood protection are observed in the recovery after the 2008 Sichuan Earthquake in China, which involved more than 90,000 casualties and missing people. The post-Sichuan Earthquake recovery featured speedy reconstruction as a successful result of "partner assistance," or a policy for matching each seriously affected municipality with a supporter from among the richest provinces and special cities in the industrialized eastern part of the country. This policy was provided in the Ordinance on the Post-Wenchuan Earthquake Recovery and Reconstruction, art. 3, and the Notice on the Method of Partner Assistance issued by the State Council in June 2008, obliging the supporters to allocate 1 percent of annual gross product for each year in the set three-year period (Gu 2009). While the speedy reconstruction of houses and infrastructure by the partner assistance program has been highly praised by the international society, there remains a question of whether the recovery of individual livelihoods was sufficiently supported under the policy bias of the partner assistance program, which was overly inclined toward hard infrastructure rebuilding. According to a report by local attorneys specializing in post-disaster dispute settlement,[15] numerous administrative lawsuits have been raised in judicial courts in regard to compensation for expropriation of land in the course of the post-Sichuan recovery. In fact, in the recent fieldwork conducted by the author's group in August 2014 in disaster-affected villages in Beichuan district, Mianyang City, which was the recipient of partner assistance from Shandong province,[16] the issues of taking of farmlands without compensation were obvious. In the large-scale collective relocation of the entire Beichuan district capital's center to a newly constructed city site, as well as in the concentration of agricultural villages in nearby safer lands, disaster-affected farmers were compelled to abandon their original farmlands, receiving neither substitutes nor monetary compensation, while they were assigned an apartment or a house together with the new status of "urban-registered" household that meant certain beneficial treatment in seeking formal employment and entering university. It is further problematic that the expropriation of lands for the construction of relocated cites was also done without substitution or monetary compensation for the farmers.

Uncompensated expropriation of farmland is unconstitutional in the socialist constitution of China, as amended in 2004 (art. 10, sec. 3), which explicitly provides for compensation for the taking of private property rights. This right is further detailed in the 2007 Law on Rights in Rem (art. 42, 121, 132, etc.), which defines the principles of compensation as covering not only the loss of property but also the protection of livelihoods for farmers, including social insurance and other lawful interests. Such principles of compensation are applied not only to ownership but also to the other rights in rem. This includes the "rights on farmland management contract" introduced in the socialist reform since the 1980s, established in the 2002 Law on Farmland Contracts as a transferable (art. 32–3) and inheritable right (art. 31), and given the status as one of the ownership restrictive rights (*iura re aliena*) under the 2007 Law on Rights in Rem. It is more than ironic if a neo-liberal trend of market-oriented post-disaster recovery prevails in socialist China, permitting the uncompensated taking of farmland for the purpose of profitable urban development by the stakeholders in partner assistance.

4.3 Formalization of informal rights: basis of community recovery

The legal basis for "early recovery" should include the situation of disaster victims who do not have formally registered private rights such as ownership. In the socio-economy of rural Japan that largely depends on primary industries such as agriculture and fisheries, a traditional style of communal land use still prevails as the common basis of livelihoods. These traditional lands face extinction without fair compensation when they become a part of the post-disaster town recovery projects decided by the *tokku* method under the 2011 Act on Special Zones for East Japan Earthquake Reconstruction (see Kaneko 2014). Similarly, the exclusive fishery rights of the coastal communities over adjoining sea areas have been an indispensable livelihood basis of the fishery folk in eastern Japan since the pre-modern era, but are now largely endangered by the *tokku* system. The recovery projects often compel the eviction of fishery households from tsunami-inundated areas, or ban the reconstruction of ports and fishery facilities in their original places, or introduce 15-meter-high seawalls which hinder fishery activities, and have tended to result in a great number of cancellations and suspensions of individual membership to the fishery rights without any compensation, as a result of the regular nationwide renewal process for registered fishery rights in 2013. Such rights had been the basis of livelihoods handed down for generations in each fishery community.

Another outcome is increased vulnerability of inhabitances, due to the endangered status of leaseholders as a result of recovery projects. Protection of unregistered tenants in disasters has long been a key area in the modern history of property law in Japan, where the separate ownership of lands and houses is a common phenomenon due to the disaster risk-sharing practice between owner and lessee. Particularly designed to protect against the tragic fate of "earthquake sales," where people who make their living utilizing leased land are easily deprived of their rights by absentee landowners selling target properties for profit-seeking purposes, special laws and case law that secure the renewal and the prevalence of a lease against new owners have accumulated since the early 1900s, despite the provisions under the Civil Code allowing the owner full discretion to cancel lease contracts. Such laws, which have been applied to all modern disasters, including the 1995 Kobe Earthquake, however, were not effective in the post-disaster phase of the 2011 Great East Japan Earthquake, mainly due to the governmental decision to suspend the application of a pro-lessee special law,[17] as well as the prolonged temporary land-use ban set by the local governments covering the entire tsunami-inundated area for the preparation of post-disaster public projects. Any lawful actions by tsunami victims to secure their leaseholds were suspended by the ban and, without the protection of the pro-lessee law, it resulted in the termination of leases upon the unilateral cancellation by the owners who initiated investment activities on these lands (Kaneko 2014). Lacking easy access to judicial lawsuits in the rural society, no one could dare to claim the constitutional right for compensation for the lost leaseholds, or the additional rights for participation in decision-making linked to such leaseholds under the Urban Planning Act.

A similar phenomenon is observed in the fieldwork conducted by the author's group in August 2013 in the areas hit by the 2004 Indian Ocean Tsunami, which caused more than 5,000 casualties in the provinces of Pangna and Phuket, South Thailand.[18] Commercial fishermen who held land titles in the coastal areas since settlement in the 1970s have managed to rebuild their fishery business, although they had to assume the same dualistic choice as the fishermen in Aceh and East Japan between safety (relocation to higher lands separated from the basis of livelihood) and their livelihood (self-reconstruction in the original land without governmental measures for safety). In contrast, the minority Moken people, a traditional subsistence fishing group lacking registered land ownership, have faced tremendous difficulties due to eviction orders by ministerial regulations issued after the 2004 tsunami, based on the discretionary mandates given by the 1992 Law on Enhancement and Conservation of National Environmental Quality. Regardless of the fact that the Moken have lived on the coastal lands for generations, maintaining a simple lifestyle and eco-friendly methods of fishery based on traditional wisdom, their claims over the use of land were simply neglected by the government in the course of the post-tsunami recovery, as a result of the literal application of the formal law which makes much of the "domain public" or state ownership of waste lands (1954 Law on Land, art. 2). They can seldom manage to obtain any land title of individual ownership, because the Torrens-style land title registration system applied in Thailand does not permit collective ownership by a village community, and the recent attempt by the 2007 Constitution (art. 66) to define "collective rights" was suspended by the coup d'état in 2013. It is ironic that the same government which forced the eviction of Moken villages on one hand issued land title certificates to commercial developers on the other, followed by numbers of lawsuits raised by such developers against the Moken villagers who have resisted the governmental eviction orders. The outcome of such lawsuits is, at most, an ultimate compromise in a civil conciliation which leads to a 50-50 division of disputed land between the villagers and the developer, which means an uncompensated loss of half of village land.

A similarly tragic fate of unregistered land-use rights is observed in the recovery phases after the 2013 Typhoon Yolanda, which involved 6,000 casualties due to a tsunami-like serious storm surge reaching more than 8 meters in height. In the fieldwork conducted by the author's group in March 2014, in the most seriously affected areas around Tacloban, the capital city of Leyte province,[19] fishery villages were facing a land-use ban applied to areas within 40 meters from the seashore. Given the fact that the storm surge extended more than one kilometer inland from the seashore, the 40-meter ban that split each village into pieces was understood by many village leaders as nothing short of compulsory eviction for the purpose of commercial development. These fishery villages have no means of asserting lawful rights in the context of property law to contest the eviction order, since most of the villagers lack formally registered ownership. This is the result of the "regalien doctrine" introduced in the Spanish colonial reign, utilized by the American colonial rulers as the basis of state authority to grant private ownership, and repeatedly proclaimed in the successive constitutions (see art. 12, sec. 2 of the present 1987 Constitution). Since it is an established Philippine Supreme Court precedent to deny the acquisition of ownership by prescription, the repeated land re-distribution projects have resulted in nothing more than land redevelopment. Further, as the customary land rights recognized under the 1997 Law on Indigenous People's Rights has been ruled by the Supreme Court as unconstitutional, there seems limited hope that the fishery villagers can successfully contest their eviction in the civil court. However, a village chief suggested in an interview with the author that his village would never surrender to any eviction order as long as the village maintained its integrity as a "*Barangay*" or basic administrative body having the status of judicial person under public law. *Barangay* is formally established as the basic administrative unit in the 1992 Law on Local Autonomy in the Philippines, vested with highly autonomous powers, including the legislative power to enact village ordinances and the budgetary autonomy to introduce new taxes. This independence as a judicial person implies the possibility for villagers to claim for the protection of lawful properties inside their community as a whole, as a strategy to ensure the basis of "early recovery" for the whole community.

5 Summary of lessons

This article has reviewed the legal issues of post-disaster recovery in Japan with a particular focus on the results of special legislations introduced after the 2011 East Japan Earthquake, as well as a certain comparative perspective on similar issues in other disaster-prone areas in Asia. A common tendency in both situations is government-centered decision-making regarding public projects for infrastructure and town reconstruction, prioritized ahead of "early recovery" of the individual livelihoods of disaster-affected people and communities. Special laws introduced in the post-disaster phases often provide the legal justification for such prioritization of infrastructure development, as shown in the cases of the 2011 Basic Act on Reconstruction in Response to the Great East Japan Earthquake in Japan, the 2008 Ordinance on the Post-Wenchuan Earthquake Recovery and Reconstruction in China, the 1992 Law on Enhancement and Conservation of National Environmental Quality in Thailand, etc. This fact suggests to us the need for the formation of a basic law on disaster recovery as a mother law at the top of a hierarchal legal regime, which would guarantee the indispensable rights and interests of disaster-affected people and communities against the infringement by flexible introduction of special laws. Findings from this chapter may suggest certain necessary elements for such a basic law as being the following:

First, trust in civic autonomy should form the theoretical basis of the whole procedure for decision-making. In this sense, the Japanese legal model of urban planning being exported to other countries in Asia is highly problematic, since it has been utilized as an instrument for government-centered development of national land and urban building, deviating from its European origin that has been devoted to the pursuit of social welfare by a "social state" and constantly taken the path toward the furtherance of participation. Then, what should be an alternative model? A hint obtained from the post-Hanshin-Awaji Earthquake in Kobe was the utilization of a contractual approach under the city ordinance on town planning, in which an association established by the local community took part in the decision-making process by the mayor, an approach utilized in advanced attempts in many other local governments, including the local ordinances in several advanced wards in Tokyo. Implications from such attempts may include the need for establishing explicit requirements for a community to obtain independent status as a judicial person, as elaborated in the works by Ostrom (Ostrom 1990 etc.), such as the criteria of boundary or membership, decision-making rules, governance mechanisms involving external stakeholders, as well as the right to information access, and the conditions and frameworks of the binding effect over governmental decision-making. The successful experiences of restored autonomy of *Gampongs* in Aceh and the strong independence of *Barangays* in the Philippines are all encouraging episodes. A pessimistic lesson, however, is learned from the post-2011 East Japan Earthquake recovery where the accumulated attempt of local ordinances was shown to be powerless when national legislation disregarded the results of autonomous decision-making, and the local communities lacked autonomous status due to the recent vigorous campaign for inter-municipal mergers, making it difficult for the voices of the community to be heard at the municipal level. In countries such as Japan and Thailand where local communities have a weak basis for political autonomy, the last resort may be collective lawsuits claiming judicial review, such as Mitwirkungsklage in Germany (a category of lawsuit against the governmental infringement of procedural rights to participate). The outstanding increase in administrative lawsuits in China is worthy of further study.

Second, the collective claim on property rights by the disaster-affected communities should be formalized, so as to meet the needs of contemporary society which is vulnerable to disaster risks. Given the fact that the majority of the world's population has made its long-term living on land without formal "ownership" titles, and that there is a strong need to recognize and protect the pre-disaster *status quo* of such a majority of affected people from those taking advantage of a disaster to make unwarranted changes, we need to have a new regime of law beyond the limitation of the modern regime of formal law that admits only individual claims on individual properties. Although changing property law is not an easy task, the historical experience of Japan, a highly disaster-prone country, is worth remembering, particularly for the successful transformation of the Western-oriented ownership-centered regime of the Civil Code into an actual user-friendly model involving unregistered land use, customary land ownership and fishery rights, by way of accumulating statutory changes and case law in the interface with the struggles for the reconstruction of habitats and livelihoods of disaster-affected people. The same transformation of current laws is possible if lawyers take up their responsibilities.

Third, the legal regime of victim aid should be re-designed so as to support the stability of life for disaster-affected people in the interim period of "early recovery" and with this to enable their active participation in the course of recovery decision-making. On the other hand, the theoretical basis is weak for an overly extended utilization of governmental subsidies in the stage of full recovery, for the purpose of reconstructing houses and livelihoods and stimulating industry. Excessive provision of subsidies for households and industries in the full recovery phase after the 2011 East Japan Earthquake has invited an ugly political socio-economy of greed, not only in the disaster affected-areas but all over the country, which is full of calls for more subsidies. This demand exists despite a deficit in the national budget of nearly 300 percent of the GDP, the largest deficit in history, which is worse than the situation in developing countries highly dependent on the grants of international donors. Perhaps, a proper theoretical reorganization of victim aid for the stage of full recovery is necessary; one that would center on a progressive standard for self-help using a disaster insurance system supplemented by a system of subsidies in the case of mega-disasters beyond the scale of the insurance coverage, with explicit limitations established for state interventions.

Perhaps, as shown in a comparative perspective summarized in Table 1.4, each legal system has its own characteristics, and our model basic law on disaster recovery should be customized to meet them, to supplement the weakness

Table 1.4 Comparison of public law–private law relationship in disaster recovery

		Public law: framework for participation	
		Weak ⟵	⟶ *Strong*
Private law: protection of informal property rights	*Strong* ↑	**Indonesia – Aceh: 2004 Tsunami** • Public law: Autonomy of *Gampong* (Aceh Ordinance 2003/5) • Property: recognition of customary rights (Aceh Ordinance 2008/9, 10)	**East Japan Earthquake 2011** • Public law: village autonomy lost; government-centered special laws • Property rights: formalization of informal rights
	↓ *Weak*	**Philippines: 2013 Typhoon Yolanda** • Public law: Autonomy of *Barangay* (1991 RA7160 on Local Autonomy) • Property rights: illegal occupants ⇔ absolute priority of ownership (1983 Public Land Act)	**Thailand: 2004 Tsunami** • Public law: no village autonomy (⇔ *Tambon*-autonomy since 2003) • Property rights: illegal occupants ⇔ absolute priority of ownership (1934 Civil Code; 1954 Land Law)

and utilize the strong aspects of each system. Japanese law has developed a fairly flexible basis for recognition of informal rights and interests indispensable for the lives of disaster-affected people in the sphere of private law, while lagging behind in the formation of a meaningful basis for participation in the sphere of public law. The formation of a Basic Law on Disaster Recovery in Japan should be expected to concentrate energy on the deliberation of the participatory framework, while guaranteeing the historically accumulated victim-friendly designs of private law against the increasing influence of neo-liberalism.

Notes

1 See Abe (1998), Ikeda (2000), Yasumoto (1995), Ikuta (2010), etc.

2 In the aftermath of the Hanshin-Awaji Earthquake in 1995, a well-known episode was that the Kobe City government, backed by strong support from the Ministry of Construction at that time, rushed to a decision on the urban plans for land readjustment within two months of the emergency land-use restriction from the earthquake (Building Standards Act, art. 84), which was later supported by the enactment of the 1995 Act on Special Measures concerning Reconstruction of Urban Districts Damaged by Disaster, despite harsh criticism. This tension between the government-led special procedure and the civic criticism was finally conciliated through a compromise proposed by the Kobe mayor, who introduced the idea of "two-step urban recovery planning." In this compromise proposal, slight changes through civic initiative were admitted to the already valid governmental decision on urban plans through utilizing "town planning councils" (*machizukuri-kyogikai*) based on the municipal ordinance on "district-level plans" under the City Planning Act (art. 16, sec. 2).

3 While the utilization of financial schemes for suspension is merely approximately 400–500 cases in each of two schemes during three years' operation until the end of 2014, the SME Group Subsidies recorded a total amount of 446 billion yen (US$4.4 billion) distributed to more than 10,000 entrepreneurs in 605 groups by the end of the year 2014.

4 The scale of seawalls was designed to protect against level-1 class tsunamis (or the ones occurring in 100-year intervals, such as the Meiji-Sanriku Tsunami in 1896) but are incapable of counteracting level-2 class tsunamis, such as the one in the East Japan Earthquake in 2011.

5 The 2011 Canterbury Earthquake Recovery Act in New Zealand (art. 16~21), for example, provided discretionary authority to the Minister for Canterbury Earthquake Recovery to direct and approve the recovery plan for the areas affected by the Canterbury Earthquake that occurred in February 2011, while explicitly suspending the application of the 1991 Resource Management Act and other relevant laws that provided for participatory procedures in normal times (art. 24, 71), and narrowing the reach of judicial review (art. 70). Although this 2011 Act emphasizes the functions of the "community forum" to be held by the Minister (art. 6) and consultation with local communities (art. 17, sec. 1), it lacks any provision to guarantee the legally binding effects of such consultations.

6 Prompt actions taken by the Indonesian government impressed the international community as it concluded the Master Plan for 2004–2009 for post-tsunami recovery within three months from the disaster, which was soon legalized in the form of Presidential Regulation No. 30 in 2005, and implemented by the special national agency for post-tsunami reconstruction and recovery (BRR). The Master Plan was later consolidated into the Aceh Recovery Framework (ARF 2008–2011, Provincial Governor Order No. 360 in 2007), together with the plan for peace and integration.

7 Although it has been the increasing stance of the lower courts to admit the liability of the government under the Law on National Tort Claim Compensation (art. 2) in the natural disasters where disaster-preventive facilities such as levees were not designed to cope with large-scale disasters, the Supreme Court (Daito flood case judgment in January 26, 1979, *Minshu* Vol. 38, No. 2, p. 53) set the general standard of a transitional nature, in consideration to the budgetary, technical, and social limitations of risk management.

8 Art. 544 of the French Civil Code as well as the Weimar Constitution (art. 153, sec. 2) are often cited as the origins of the modern principle of compensation. This judicial stance seems to have guided the governmental practice of categorizing the safety standards of disaster-preventive facilities into level-1 and level-2.

9 Similarly, even when a neo-liberal government uses the rhetoric of "support" in order to minimize the payment in the case of human errors, such as the accident at the Fukushima No. 1 nuclear power plant, the governmental obligation for "compensation" as well as "damages" remains.

10 See, e.g., Supreme Court judgment on June 26, 1963 in *Keishu* Vol. 17, No. 5, p. 521.

11 See, e.g., Supreme Court judgment on February 13, 2002 in *Minshu* Vol. 56, No. 2, p. 331.

12 The 1962 cabinet approval of the "implementation of essential standards on compensation for expropriation for public works" declared that the government would not pay compensation for lost livelihoods, provided that "measures for reconstruction of livelihoods" should be considered in case of the total loss of the basis of living. In this regard, the government also issued the "essential standards on the compensation of public facilities" in 1967, which introduced the "measures for restoration of social functions" beyond the previous basis of compensation merely for the value of individual properties based on the market price.

13 For example, City Planning Act, art. 47, Law on National Land Development and Road Construction, art. 9, Law on Special Measures for Water Resource Areas, art. 8, Law on Special Measures on Land Taking for Public Works, art. 47, etc., which make it the obligation of prefectural governors to make a plan for the reconstruction of lives (including such measures as introduction of jobs, assistance to obtain relocation sites, arrangement of living environment, etc.), and to implement such a plan within the limit of law, budgetary allowance, and other circumstances.

14 The interview survey in December 20–26, 2013 through the collaboration of Kobe University (Asian Disaster Law Study Program) and Syiah Kuala University (Tsunami Disaster Risk Management Institute) conducted in the villages of Jackie Chen in Neuheun district, Deyeh Man Plam in Leupueng district, Lambung in Ulee Lheu ward, Desa Dea Gulumpan in Ulee Lheu ward, Cadek in Baitsussakam district, and Lambada Lhok in Baitsussakam district.

15 Information obtained in the Asian Disaster Legal Forum, Institute for Disaster Management and Reconstruction, Sichuan University, August 12, 2014.

16 The interview survey in August 11–16, 2014 through the collaboration of Kobe University (Asian Disaster Law Study Program) and Sichuan University (Institute for Disaster Management and Reconstructions) conducted in the villages of Shaba-chin, Angtsu-pin, and Tsu-shan community in Rencha-pin as well as in the city center of the new Beichuan district-capital.

17 A five-year protection period should have been available, if the 1947 Law on Temporary Measures for the Land and House Leaseholders in Disaster-Stricken Cities was applied to the 2011 Great East Japan Earthquake. The Japanese government decided not to apply it to this disaster, for the first time in a great disaster since World War II.

18 The interview survey in August 16–18, 2013 conducted through the collaboration of Kobe University (Asian Disaster Law Study Program) and Chulalongkorn University (Law and Development Program) in the villages of Ban Nam Khem, Tung Wah, and Tub Ta Wa in Pangna province, and Co si-de in Phuket province.

19 The interview survey in March 20–25, 2014 conducted through the collaboration of Kobe University (Asian Disaster Law Study Program) and University of the Philippines Diliman (National College of Public Administration and Governance) in the villages of Barangay 90 and Barangay 60A in Tacloban city, Barangay San Rogue in Tanauan city, and Balangay Palaypay in Basay city.

References

Abe, Y. (1998) *Law and Policy in Great Disasters*, Tokyo: Nihon-hyoron-sya (in Japanese).

DPWTCP, Department of Public Works and Town & Country Planning, Ministry of Interior of Thailand (2005) *Community & Tourist Destination & Environmental Project for Tsunami*, Bangkok: Ministry of Interior of Thailand.

FAO/Nittharatana, P., Cherdchinda, C. and Siriwan, S. (2006) "Pre- and Post-Tsunami Coastal Planning and Land-use Policies and Issues in Thailand," in *Proceedings of the Workshop on Coastal Area Planning and Management in Asian Tsunami-affected Countries*, Food and Agriculture Organization of the United Nations.

Fitzpatrick, D. (2012) "Between Custom and Law: Protecting the Property Rights of Women after Tsunami in Aceh," in Daly, P., Feener, R.M., and Reid, L.S., eds, *Ground Up: Perspectives Post-Tsunami and Post-Conflict Aceh*, Singapore: Institute of Southeast Asian Studies.

Gu Linsheng (2009 "Damages and Recovery Response on the Wenchan Earthquake," *Toshi-Seisaku*, No. 135 (in Japanese).

Ikeda, T. (1993) "A Note on the Historical Meaning of the Ordinance on the Reform of Tokyo City Areas," in Toshiya, N. *et al.*, eds, *Modernism and Contemporaryism in Law*, Tokyo: Nihon-syoron-sya (in Japanese).

Ikeda, T. (2000) "Axes of Laws on Disaster Response and Disaster Recovery and the Issues of Law on Disaster Recovery," in Kai, M., ed., *Great Disasters and Law*, Kyoto: Kyoto Gakuen University Institute for Business Science (in Japanese).

Ikuta, N. (2010) *Law for Disaster-Preventions and its Frameworks*, Tokyo: Toshindo (in Japanese).

IRP, International Recovery Platform (2008) *Guidance Note on Early Recovery*, Kobe: IRP, available at www.recoveryplatform.org.

IRP, International Recovery Platform (2011) *Cases and Practices on Role of Community in Recovery*, Kobe: IRP.

IRP, International Recovery Platform (2012) *Indian Ocean Tsunami 2004: Recovery in Banda Aceh*, Recovery Status Report No. 5, Kobe: IRP.

Kaneko, Y. (2012) "Livelihood Support for the Early Recovery in the Great East Japan Earthquake and Tsunami – Lessons for Developing Countries," *Journal of International Cooperation Studies*, Kobe University, Vol. 20, No. 2, pp. 79–109.

Kaneko, Y. (2013a) "Law and Community in Disaster Recovery: Lessons from 2011 Great East Japan Earthquake on the Civil Rights," *Journal of International Cooperation Studies*, Kobe University, Vol. 21, No. 1.

Kaneko, Y. (2013b) "Procedural Rules for Participation in Post-Disaster Recovery: Comparative Approach to Japan, Thailand and Indonesia," *Journal of International Cooperation Studies*, Kobe University, Vol. 21, No. 2. (in Japanese).

Kaneko, Y. (2014) "Property Law Issues for the Human-Centered Post-Disaster Recovery: An Approach to Asian Comparative Disaster Law," *Proceedings at the Japan-Netherlands Law Conference on August 2013*, Leiden University.

Kunreuther, H. (1996) "Mitigating Disaster Losses Through Insurance," *Journal of Risk and Uncertainty*, Vol. 12, pp. 171–187.
Ostrom, E. (1990) *Governing the Commons*, Cambridge: Cambridge University Press.
Posner, R. (2004) *Catastrophe, Risk and Response*, Oxford: Oxford University Press.
Taqwaddin, H and Alvisyahrin, T. (2013) "Role of Community and Communal Law of Aceh in the Great Sumatra Earthquake and Tsunami Recovery: A Case Study in Lambada Lhok Village, Aceh Besar District, Aceh, Indonesia," *Journal of International Cooperation Studies*, Kobe University, Vol. 22, No. 2.
Telford, J. (2012) "Disaster Recovery: An International Humanitarian Challenge?" in Daly, P., Feener, R.M., and Reid, L.S., eds, *Ground Up: Perspectives Post-Tsunami and Post-Conflict Aceh*, Singapore: Institute of Southeast Asian Studies.
Yasumoto, N. (1995) "Post-Disaster Recovery Town-Planning and Civic Participation," *Jurist*, No. 1070 (in Japanese).

2 Natural disaster relief in China

Experiences and shortcomings in the 2008 Great Wenchuan Earthquake and thereafter

Li Wei Hai

1 Introduction

In the 5,000-year history of China, natural disasters have occurred with such frequency that the famous Western scholar Walter H. Mallory depicted the country as "the land of famine" (1930, p. 95). According to a report published by the United Nations, of the 54 most serious natural disasters that occurred in the world during the twentieth century, eight occurred in China and resulted in direct economic loss that surpassed US$90 billion. With the twenty-first century challenge of global warming, China is facing a more serious situation than ever before. In 2008 and 2009 alone, China saw the southern blizzard disaster, the Great Wenchuan Earthquake and a northern drought that lasted several months.

This chapter will review the development of disaster law in China, which addresses aid for victims and systems of relief from natural disaster. In ancient times, flood control was a contributing factor to the formation of unity of the Chinese nation. Meanwhile, failures in the provision of famine relief, which usually served as a highly political factor in the historical development of China, have also been an important cause of the demise of some dynasties. Since the founding of modern China, the state's capabilities for emergency relief following natural disaster have greatly improved. Especially in recent years, significant progress has been made by Chinese governments in the establishment of natural disaster emergency rescue systems. China has formed a relatively developed emergency management system whose basic principles consist of unified leadership, responsibility appropriate to the level of government, integration between departments and regions at different levels, and dependency administration. Nevertheless, some legal problems exist in the areas of governmental responsibility and funds management, so corresponding measures will be recommended in this chapter to actively overcome these shortcomings.

2 The legal history of Chinese disaster law and victim aid

2.1 In ancient times

To maintain a stable political regime, consolidate the ruling order and alleviate class antagonism and social inequalities, the ruling authority in each ancient dynasty would take measures to help alleviate the damage and suffering of victims of natural disasters. Therefore, disaster relief was of great function in political stability and of high importance in the history of China's rulers.

Disaster relief was not listed in the scope of standard governmental affairs in the Qin and Han Dynasties, and this situation did not change until the Sui Dynasty and Tang Dynasty, when coordination of disaster relief between the monarchy and administrative system was gradually formulated. During the reformation of the bureaucracy by the Qing Dynasty, the Ministry of Civil Affairs was established to take charge of governmental affairs concerning famine. In addition, disaster relief funds mainly came from the state treasury. For example, the funds used to help victims during the Tang Dynasty accounted for 8.7 percent of the national government's expenditure (Deng, 1997, p. 499).

In ancient times, the government took a leading role in disaster relief, which was at its peak in the early period of the Qing Dynasty. However, coinciding with the growing tendency toward basic social autonomy, the government's role in leading disaster relief gradually declined and non-governmental assistance such as "Yi Zhuang" ("Charitable Community")[1] and other charitable institutions sponsored by squires increased rapidly (Yu, 1997, p. 66).

2.2 The Republic of China period (1912–1949)

After the founding of the Republic of China, the Beiyang Government ("Northern Warlord Government") and National Government bowed to social pressure and took measures regarding disaster relief, but with poor effect. The National Government established relief for commerce and agriculture as well as emergency relief and employment. Afterwards, due to rising military tensions, the National Government delegated all matters concerning disaster relief to the China Huayang Voluntary Disaster Relief Institution, which played an important role in drought relief and long-term disaster prevention. In the field of disease prevention and control, the National Government also organized a specialized institution, issued regulations and carried out regular and ad hoc epidemic prevention work.[2] The National Government also set up a porridge factory and warehouse to help famine victims, as well as programs for water conservation and locust prevention. In addition, the National Government issued disaster relief laws in which both broad and specific provisions were included, such as the Local Asylum Rules (promulgated by the Ministry of Interior, 1928), Social Relief Act (enacted by the National Government, 1943), Implementing Rules of the Social Relief Act (approved by the Chief Executive Yuan, 1944), The Asylum Procedures (published by the Executive Yuan, 1944) and Winter Relief

Measures (promulgated by the Ministry of Interior, 1949). According to records, there were 24 primary disaster social relief laws issued between 1927 and 1949.

2.3 The period following the foundation of New China (1949–1978)

In order to effectively respond to natural disasters, the central government established a unified relief leadership system at the very beginning of the new Republic. Soon, the Central Disaster Relief Commission was set up to systematically lead, organize and coordinate disaster relief. The Government Administration Council (GAC) issued "Instructions for Manufacturing Disaster Relief" on December 19, 1949, and requested that:

> people's governments at various levels must organize manufacturing disaster relief commissions, in which representatives from the departments of interior, finance, health, industry, agriculture, trade and civil organizations must be included. This commission shall be directly led by heads of the people's governments at each level.
>
> (Wang & Tian, 2006, p. 29)

The Central Disaster Relief Commission was set up to take charge of national disaster relief works on February 27, 1950. "The Brief Organizational Rules Regarding the Central Disaster Relief Commission," promulgated by the central government, defined the main tasks of disaster management and made clear that day-to-day disaster relief works were the responsibility of the Ministry of Interior.

The central government developed a disaster relief strategy entitled the Chinese Disaster Relief General Organization Charter in early 1950, which was based on the prevailing national conditions. It defined a policy that identified production as a means to achieve self-supporting relief, saving to help people weather periods of famine, the necessity of mutual relief between victims when facing a disaster and that governmental relief was an important supplementary means to help victims. Later on, this policy was gradually revised to include reliance on the populace, collectivity and production to provide self-supporting relief in order to encourage mutual assistance when disaster occurred. Governmental relief and support was an important supplementary means of assisting victims. This policy played an important role in disaster relief work.

2.4 The period from 1978 to the end of the twentieth century

In 1978, the central government adopted a new management system for natural disasters based on the party and government forming a unified leadership, departments shouldering different responsibilities according to their own missions and responses being determined based on classification of the disaster. Under this system, the Party Central Committee and the State Council were charged with the overall command and coordination of responses and responsibility for important decision-making. Relevant departments at all levels of government held certain responsibilities under the unified leadership of local party committees. More attention was given to the mobility of the People's Liberation Army (including reserve components), Armed Police, public police and militia troops. Meanwhile, a comprehensive and effective coordination mechanism for disaster management was formed in order to ensure the effectiveness of relevant departments.

2.5 *The twenty-first century*

Entering the twenty-first century, China has made great progress in the area of legislation on natural disasters, especially in the following aspects:

2.5.1 *Constitutional law*

Article 45 of the Constitution provides that:

> Citizens of the People's Republic of China have the right to material assistance from the State and society when they are old, ill or disabled. The State develops social insurance, social relief and medical and health services that are required for citizens to enjoy this right.
>
> The State and society ensure the livelihood of disabled members of the armed forces, provide pensions to the families of martyrs and give preferential treatment to the families of military personnel.
>
> The State and society help make arrangements for the work, livelihood and education of the blind, deaf-mutes and other handicapped citizens.

The Fourth Amendment to the Constitution added that, "The State respects and preserves human rights" and "The State establishes a social security system compatible with the level of economic development." Such stipulations have laid a strong and solid constitutional basis for administrative relief following natural disaster.

2.5.2 *Statutory law*

The principles provided in the Constitution can be strengthened only through formulation and implementation of laws and regulations. During the decades since the founding of New China, especially the 30 years after the reform and opening up of the country, China has established a dynamic, multi-level emergency management system against natural disasters. Legislation that has been adopted to respond to the diverse range of possible disasters includes the Flood Control Act (2002), the Meteorology Act (1999), which addresses meteorological disasters, and the Act on Protecting Against and Mitigating Earthquake Disasters (1997). In 2007, the Standing Committee of the National People's Congress enacted the Emergency Response Law, which provided a comprehensive legal basis for national disaster response. However, there is still no separate legislation on administrative relief.

2.5.3 Administrative rules and departmental regulations

Administrative rules and departmental regulations play an important role in the legal system of natural disaster relief. The State Council has issued a large number of administrative rules, departmental regulations and other normative documents, which could be seen as concrete operational standards for responding to natural disaster. These rules and regulations include the Interim Measures for Compensation in Flood Restriction Basins (2000) for responding to floods; Regulations on Meteorological Disaster Prevention (2010) for responding to meteorological disaster; Regulation on Destructive Earthquake Emergency (1995), Regulation on Earthquake Prediction Management (1998), Regulation on Seismic Safety Evaluation (2002), Regulation on Earthquake Monitoring and Management (2004), Regulation on Post-Wenchuan Earthquake Recovery and Reconstruction (2008) and National Earthquake Emergency Plan (2012) to address earthquakes; and Regulation on Forest Fire Prevention (2008) and Regulation on Grassland Fire Prevention (2008) to deal with forest and prairie fires. The National Emergency Plans for Natural Disaster Relief issued by the State Council in 2006 is regarded as the most important current regulation on natural disaster relief.

2.5.4 Local rules and regulations

As the administrative relief required differs between regions, local governments have issued their own local rules and regulations, which is permissible as long as they do not conflict with the Constitution or statutes. Some provinces like Guizhou, Shanxi, Zhejiang, Fujian and Guangdong have developed provincial-level general plans for natural disaster emergency relief. Some prefecture-level cities such as Huizhou, Zunyi, Lingbi, Wuxi, Qingdao, Baotou, Xi'an and Hangzhou have also established natural disaster emergency relief plans that address their respective local situations.

2.6 Recent changes

Since the turn of the millennium, China has seen the foundation of a market-oriented economic system, together with significant advancements in information and technology and great improvements in quality of life levels. Meanwhile, China's natural disaster response system as a whole has experienced a process of fundamental adjustments that accords with these advancements. The requirement for society as a whole to respond to a disaster has changed completely, especially after the SARS incident in 2003, which greatly promoted the transformation of disaster response. These changes can be detailed as follows.

First, the goal of victim aid has changed from a focus on mitigating economic loss under the planned economic system to an emphasis on people, that is, the livelihoods of victims. In the past, the primary response after a disaster was to protect the security of property, especially state-owned property, but now the life, health and livelihood of affected people is the first priority throughout the disaster response process.

Second, disaster relief has begun to transform from being solely focused upon post-disaster relief to multi-dimensional, comprehensive assistance, especially in initial emergency relief. In the past, disaster relief mainly focused on post-disaster recovery, which meant a long time was spent investigating and reviewing the effects of a disaster and confirming the costs before beginning to implement the recovery. But in terms of building up an emergency relief system, the foremost function is to provide victims with immediate assistance and relief within the first 24 hours after a disaster. All levels of government burden much more responsibility under the model of multi-dimensional assistance.

Third, the organization and command of disaster relief has moved away from dependence on the individual experience of administrative staff and towards systemic relief plans and orderly operations.

Fourth, there appears much more openness and transparency in the organization process, which means it is essential that victim aid complies with legal procedures and is open to the public. Statistics regarding a disaster, especially the death toll, should be disclosed to the public as soon as possible.

Fifth, the low standard of victim aid under the traditional system has begun improving towards the higher levels expected by international requirements. In the past, preventing deaths due to starvation or exposure to the cold was the basic requirement for victim aid, but now the new standards guarantee victims have access to nutritious food, clean drinking water, warm clothes, temporary housing and medical treatment, as well as adequate schooling for children (Wang & Tian, 2006, pp. 31–32).

Finally, modern information technology is utilized, aiming to substantially improve the efficiency and effectiveness of disaster relief. The Minister of Civil Affairs recently pledged that advanced natural disaster relief information technology would be operational from 2014 (The Bureau of Disaster Relief, Ministry of Civil Affairs, 2013).

3 The present structure and policy issues of victim aid

3.1 Victim aid during emergency response

3.1.1 Organizational structure and responsibility for victim aid

According to the Constitution, the National Commission for Disaster Reduction of China, an inter-ministerial coordination body under the leadership of the State Council, is responsible for formulating China's disaster reduction and victim aid policies, guidelines and plans, organizing and coordinating major national disaster reduction and victim aid activities, presenting guidance and direction to local disaster reduction and victim aid work, and carrying out international exchange and cooperation in disaster reduction and victim aid. But when a great natural disaster occurs – for example, the SARS crisis in 2003 and the Great

Wenchuan Earthquake in 2008 – the central government will usually activate a new non-standing or temporary command organ on behalf of the State Council, with full authority to command, coordinate and control the whole process of disaster relief and victim aid in accordance with the Emergency Response Law.

Most scholars and officials recognize the 2003 SARS crisis as the crucial turning point in China's modern history of emergency response, and since then, local governments at different levels have begun to emphasize that government should play a prime role in fulfilling the social management and public service functions, responding effectively to every kind of public emergency event and providing aid to victims.

The Chinese central government has established nearly 100 disaster relief corps specializing in different professional fields, such as mine rescue, search and rescue, clearing of ruined buildings and emergency medical relief. In particular, by 2010 the People's Liberation Army had established eight disaster relief corps totaling 50,000 service members. When facing a great disaster, the Central Military Commission can deploy the emergency corps at the request of the State Council to support the central and local governments and execute the most dangerous and critical response and relief tasks.

Governments at all levels have formulated victim aid plans that correspond with levels defined by the scale and effect of different disasters. After a catastrophic disaster, central governmental relief teams, including disaster relief corps, must arrive at the disaster area within 24 hours. This is a very special and strict rule that requires a working group at the national level to be sent to the disaster area in the first instance following the initiation of emergency response. The National Development and Reform Commission will send a working group in response to a Level IV disaster, while the State Council will send a working group at Level III.

3.1.2 Fiscal expenditure and relief goods reserve for disaster relief and victim aid

On average, natural disasters have affected 300 million victims, with 3 million houses collapsed, 8 million people needing emergency relocation and US$35 billion direct economic loss annually over the past 15 years (Information Office of the State Council, 2009) Although the central government's relief expenditure has been the most important financial channel, which on average contributes 80 percent of total relief expenditure, the ratio of central relief expenditure to the direct economic loss amounts to between 2 and 3 percent, which is very low and not conducive of effective disaster relief (Qi, 2008, p. 32).

In 1998, the central government started to build a national-level goods and materials reserve system for disaster relief. National-level reserve depots were successively built in 18 cities, including Beijing, Shenyang, Harbin, Tianjin and Fuzhou. Provincial-level depots have reached 92.7 percent completion and county-level depots have reached 80 percent. It can therefore be said that the national disaster relief materials and goods reserve system has been established (Zhang, 2013).

3.2 Victim aid in early recovery

3.2.1 Winter and spring relief system

The winter and spring relief system for disaster victims, one of China's special social assistance systems, has been established since the founding of New China. This system is intended to ensure that victims in rural areas can get timely governmental relief in winter and spring, when victims go through particular difficulty. The spring drought relief system is usually executed from March through May each year in accordance with the prevailing circumstances. Victims have difficulty feeding themselves in the three months following the Spring Festival, while this situation generally improves in May since they should have new grain available. The winter aid is carried out from December through February, namely the three months before the Spring Festival; this is because the lives of the poor are more difficult before the arrival of spring.

3.2.2 Partner assistance for victim aid

Transfer payments, one of the two basic types of fiscal expenditure, refer to the free transfer of funds between governments at different levels. It has two basic characteristics, subsidies and non-profit transfers, which are aimed at realizing balance in regional finances and equality in public services. Transfer payments usually take one of two forms, either vertical or horizontal. Horizontal transfer payments are funds that are transferred freely among governments at the same level, usually from richer governments to poorer ones, so as to help and support each other, narrow the economic gap and balance the financial disparity among different regions. They feature the transfer of distinct social subsidies, national aid and other funds from richer regions in a direct, transparent and effective manner. In the course of recovery following the Great Wenchuan Earthquake and Lushan Earthquake, other provinces (as well as some political entities within Sichuan Province) supported Sichuan Province's reconstruction on a mass scale, which should be regarded as an archetypical model of horizontal transfer payments, which were performed under the promotion and supervision of the central government and Sichuan provincial government.

3.2.3 Disaster relief donations

China did not have specific laws and policies regulating disaster relief donations until 1998. But in that year, as great floods simultaneously occurred in the areas of the Changjiang River, Nenjiang River and Songhuajiang River, significant donations came from all areas of the country and abroad, which brought with them many complicated legal issues that needed to be addressed. In the process of administering flood donations, non-governmental organizations such as the China Charity Federation and the China Red Cross Society played a very positive role in supporting the donation program, led and organized by the Ministry of Civil Affairs and branches of the ministry at different levels. A total of

RMB 3.515 billion yuan was received, exceeding for the first time the total amount of disaster relief appropriated by governments, which was RMB 1.23 billion yuan. After that, the socialization of donation mechanisms began to form, consisting of government promotion, implementation by non-government organizations, broad participation by society and cooperation between stakeholders (The Bureau of Disaster Relief, Ministry of Civil Affairs, 2005, p. 179).

Since then, China has implemented legislation related to disaster relief donations. The Public Welfare Donation Act issued by the Standing Committee of the National People's Congress in 1999 is usually regarded as the fundamental law for disaster relief donations. This act established the basic principles of disaster relief donations, namely that they be voluntary, non-profit, respectful of the donor's willingness and not contrary to the public good.

The Ministry of Civil Affairs issued Disaster Relief Donation Management Measures in 2008, aimed at comprehensively defining the procedure for organizing the raising and acceptance of donations, regulating donations from abroad, donation management and use. But the Management Measures lacked details on how to accept, manage and use donated materials.

4 Evaluating the laws and policies on victim aid

In the 2008 Great Wenchuan Earthquake, 60,560 people from Sichuan, Gansu, Shaanxi and other provinces (municipalities) were killed and 352,290 injured. The government evacuated 4,381,564 people and 455,019,241 were significantly affected by the earthquake. By June 23, 2008, governments at all levels had put RMB 54.3113 trillion yuan into earthquake relief funds, of which RMB 49.6101 trillion yuan was invested by the central government. This contrasts with the RMB 70 billion yuan that the central government had allocated for recovery and reconstruction funding in the 2008 budget (Sohu News, 2008). Though great achievements were made in the Great Wenchuan Earthquake relief, it must be accepted that many problems were exposed.

1 Lack of comprehensive law:
   To date, China has been unable to avail itself of a comprehensive law addressing disaster relief. Provisions concerning the obligations of citizens, the rights of victims and procedures for initial response, short-term relief and post-disaster reconstruction are not clear, and at times very ambiguous. On the laws of preventing natural disasters, China has the Act on Protecting Against and Mitigating Earthquake Disasters (APMED) issued in 1998 and the Act on Dealing with Emergency Incidents (ADEI) promulgated in 2007. The ADEI defines only general rules on early warning, relief and reconstruction systems and lacks detailed provisions, which has led to disorder and inefficiency of justice. The seismological bureau, meteorological departments, civil administration department and other departments each respond to natural disasters from their own perspective only and lack a sense of integration across the whole situation.

2 Limited preparedness:
Governments at all levels have not attached great importance to disaster prevention. Although the disaster area was in an active seismic zone, the design and quality of local buildings had not reached the standards that the government had stipulated in official documents. Governments also lacked comprehensive knowledge related to large earthquakes and had not compiled and published a suitable earthquake relief manual until the occurrence of this catastrophe. Similarly, local governments had not attached great importance on disaster prevention until now. The public as well have lacked necessary education and ignored available training on disaster prevention and mitigation, including preparatory training and practice that would have allowed the provision of mutual aid, one of the most effective forms of disaster relief. The lack of disaster prevention knowledge has greatly limited the psychological endurance and resilience of the government and public, thus affecting the whole process of disaster prevention and relief.

3 Governance questions:
The lack of disaster relief training for emergency personnel introduced great gaps in the quality of emergency personnel available compared to that which was required. Though the country began to systemically build up relief and rescue teams at the national level after the Great Wenchuan Earthquake, local governments, especially grass-roots governments in villages and communities, have not shown a very strong intention to promptly organize autonomous relief teams or mutual aid teams, thanks to shortages of funds, professional skills training and, above all, guidance from higher levels of government and legal obligations.

4 Funding for disaster relief:
Difficulties existing in disaster relief fund-raising led to seriously inadequate appropriation of funds, despite the great attention focused on the Great Wenchuan Earthquake disaster relief work from both international and domestic sources. Disaster relief allocations in China had been relatively separate and struggled to cope with the massive needs arising from the disaster. Public welfare was not prosperous enough to support social fund-raising activities. Even where sufficient funds have been raised, there are no special agencies to manage the supervision and allocation of these assets. As a result of the backward economy in this area, the advancement of mutual aid between victims was difficult.

Due to the separate budgets of the central and local governments, it is hard to pool relief funds from different sources to make overall arrangements. The prevailing local investment patterns lead to obvious gaps between different regions. The amount of funds that local governments put into natural disaster relief has a direct relationship with the government's tax sources (Qi, 2008, p. 27).

The current operational procedures for the allocation of disaster relief funds make it difficult to meet shortages in distribution. The operational mechanism cannot satisfy the requirements for efficient relief. A practical solution to shortcut the intermediate steps would be for the central government to arrange annual disaster relief reserve funds based on average spending in previous years (for example, three years) and appropriate it into a special account for the Ministry of Civil Affairs. How these funds are used can be decided by the Ministry of Civil Affairs, and audits can be conducted after the completion of the disaster relief.

5 Funds preparedness:
Among the numerous problems in the management of government funding for natural disasters, the section on emergency preparedness in the APMED is worth examining:

> 4.1 Funds preparedness
> The Ministry of Civil Affairs shall coordinate with the National Development and Reform Commission (NDRC) and the Ministry of Finance to arrange the central disaster relief funds budget in accordance with the budget law of the People's Republic of China, and urge local governments to enhance investment in disaster relief funding, based on the principles of hierarchical responsibility for disaster relief work and funding and that the local level is the first consideration in disaster work and funding.
>
> 4.1.1 Both the central government and local governments at various levels shall arrange disaster relief budgets in accordance with the principle of hierarchical responsibility for disaster relief work and funding.
>
> 4.1.2 The central government should arrange sufficient natural disaster relief aid funds which are specifically used to help solve the basic difficulties faced by the residents in serious disaster areas, based on the actual expenditure in the previous year.
>
> 4.1.3 The central and local governments should gradually improve the standards of disaster relief fund subsidies and establish a natural growth mechanism for disaster relief funds based on financial growth, inflation, residents' actual living standards and other such factors.
>
> 4.1.4 The reserve funds arranged by the central and local governments should be used for victims when relief budgets are insufficient.

In terms of actual spending, there has been an upwards trend in recent years; however, the total amount and growth rate are unstable from year to year. According to the 2006 China statistical yearbook, China's relief spending has increased from RMB 2.251 billion yuan in 1991 to RMB 62.97 billion yuan in 2005; however, negative growth was recorded in some years (Chinese States News, 2006). Despite this substantial increase, the national disaster relief funds as a proportion of the direct economic loss caused by natural disasters is relatively low at around 2 to 3 percent.

Generally speaking, the following problems have existed in the management of government relief funds:

First, the relief funds are initially allocated by the central government to provincial governments, then to prefecture-level governments, then finally to county-level governments. This process is too long and inefficient. The actual transfer of funds between two levels generally requires at least two months (Lin, 2008, p. 43).

Second, failure to adhere to the principle that relief funds should be used for their specified purpose means some relief funds have been diverted to other unrelated uses. Through auditing, we find that relief funds in most villages and towns have been used to subsidize social and medical costs, or put toward the costs of local leaders visiting affected areas, which is directly contrary to the essential purpose of the funds.

Third, there has been failure to strictly adhere to the principle of openness and fairness *in the allocation of* funds. Since the entire process is not sufficiently open to the public, relief funds in many cases have been diverted by leaders or worn down by corruption (Liu & Sheng, 2007, p. 57).

6 The shortcomings of current audit and supervision mechanisms:

Hardly any provisions in the relevant laws and regulations deal with the audit and supervision of government relief funds. In reality, many irregular actions exist in the process of subsequent audits and supervision – for example, registers of received materials and funds are not maintained and receipts are not provided to donors.

Emphasis should be placed on the following key points to improve the existing mechanism of audit and supervision of government relief funds.

First, a combination of peer review and review by superiors should be adopted within the main auditing bodies. Article 9 of the Audit Act provides that auditing institutions at various levels should report their work to the government at the corresponding level and the auditing institution at the next higher level, and institutions must adhere to the leadership given by the higher-level audit institution. However, Article 11 provides that the funds required by audit institutions to perform their duties shall be included in the budget and guaranteed by the government at the corresponding level. Therefore, as provided in Article 16, the audit institutions exercise supervision of the corresponding level of government through auditing the implementation of the government's budget, final accounts and the management and use of extra-budgetary funds by departments (including units directly subordinate to them). As a result, there are sufficient reasons to believe that institutions should be more dependent on reviews by superior agencies in order to properly supervise government funds for natural disasters.

Second, the principles of preparation must be abided by strictly. Almost all emergency incidents occur with high randomness and great uncertainty. Such problems should be addressed at the site of the disaster as soon as possible. The audit institutions should engage in the use of relief funds in advance. In practice, complete-cycle tracking of funding should be implemented.

Third, the principles of openness and transparency have to be constantly emphasized throughout the audit process. Article 36 of the Audit Act provides that the audit institutions can report the audit outcomes to the relevant governmental departments or disclose it to the public. The auditing of government relief funds should be openly published to the public, which would increase the government's credibility and introduce supervision by society, including the affected victims.

Lastly, the combination of conventional legal compliance audits and field surveys would be a far more efficient approach to supervision. Article 33 of the Audit Act provides that audit institutions have the right to investigate issues relevant to the audit and obtain evidentiary material from organizations and individuals when conducting an audit; the relevant organizations and individuals shall support and assist the audit institution's work, truthfully report the situation and provide related evidentiary materials to the audit agency.

5 Case study: Partner Assistance Policy in the reconstruction following the Wenchuan Earthquake

Throughout the history of China, political philosophy has generally praised unification, benevolence and harmony as prime values. When facing natural disaster, the government would usually make great efforts to mobilize all possible powers, approaches and resources in order to perform rescue and relief work This sentiment is echoed in an old saying: "If one part of China has difficulties, help will come from eight different directions."

5.1 Background of the Partner Assistance Policy

The People's Republic of China has adopted the Partner Assistance Policy (对口支援; PAP) since it was founded in 1949. According to the *Overall Plan of Restoration and Reconstruction after the Wenchuan Earthquake* (The State Council, August 27, 2008), the preliminary estimation was that the required disaster relief funds would reach nearly RMB 1,000 billion yuan. But after the Sichuan Provincial Government's re-estimation, the funds estimated as essential for basic reconstruction reached RMB 1,700 billion yuan (The Center of the CCTV Media, 2009). By comparison, it should be noted that in the fiscal year of 2007, which saw the fastest economic growth rate in the past 30 years, the GDP of Sichuan Province had just reached RMB 1,050.5 billion yuan and its financial revenue was RMB 139.57 billion yuan, which meant that the expected disaster relief funds would be 1.7 times the amount of Sichuan's GDP and 12 times its financial revenue in 2007 (Sichuan Provincial Bureau of Statistics, 2008).

5.2 Legal basis of the Partner Assistance Policy

The Emergency Response Law of the People's Republic of China also provides that when local governments are weakened and incapable of responding to emergency incidents, they shall request for superior governments to provide assistance. The superior governments should provide necessary technical, financial and material support according to the actual situation in the disaster areas.

In June 2008, the State Council rapidly enacted *the Regulation on the Post-disaster Reconstruction of Wenchuan*. Article 13 provided that local governments at or above the county level should take all necessary measures in accordance with the arrangements of the superior government, including PAP to support the post-disaster reconstruction. Further, Article 3 also provided that the post-disaster reconstruction of Wenchuan should observe an integration of the principles of self-dependence and PAP. Thus, the regulation mentioned above serves as the fundamental and direct legal basis for the PAP (The State Council, 2008).

However, the practical implementation of the PAP not only requires abstract principles, but also concrete rules to regulate the approaches, content and procedures of the PAP in detail. In practice, Chinese governments at different levels have been accustomed to the old approach which was generally adopted for disaster relief during the long period of the planned economy, i.e. political mobilization. One month after the natural catastrophe, on June 13, 2008, the central government convened an important disaster relief conference and called on local governments to offer assistance to the disaster areas, which was taken as a special political assignment by many local leaders (Hu & Wen, 2008).

5.3 Practical operation of the Partner Assistance Policy

As mentioned above, the Chinese government has gradually recognized in law the significance of disaster relief administration since the turn of the century. On June 4, 2008, the above-mentioned *Regulations on Wenchuan Post-disaster Reconstruction* was passed by the 11th Executive Conference of the State Council (Hu & Wen, 2008). In order to further embody the details, the State Council then issued the *Programs on the Partner Assistance of Wen Chuan Post-disaster Reconstruction*, which clarified the support parties, mission, objective, approach and standards of the PAP (The State Council, June 11, 2008).

The central government designated 19 provinces and municipalities which were comparatively more developed as support parties, while 18 seriously afflicted counties were chosen as the corresponding recipient parties.

The disaster relief programs also defined the missions of partner assistance as follows: (1) Provide reconstruction planning, architectural design, expert recommendations and project supervision; (2) Reconstruct residential houses and buildings in rural and urban areas; (3) Reconstruct public infrastructure, such as schools, hospitals, broadcast and television facilities; (4) Reconstruct basic infrastructure, such as roads, highways, water and gas facilities, disposal facilities, etc.; (5) Reconstruct agricultural infrastructure in rural areas; (6) Provide mechanical equipment, basic instruments and construction materials, medical services, technical training, educational opportunities, export of labor services, etc.; (7) Encourage the support parties to make investments in the disaster areas in a way that conforms to the rules of the market economy. The support party can invest in constructing factories, logistics centers and any other operating corporations;

(8) Others (the State Council, June 11, 2008). Among these missions, four of them are focused on the reconstruction or restoration of basic infrastructure. Obviously, this corresponded with the emergency requirements in the disaster areas, where there were tens of thousands of victims to be resettled.

5.4 The standards of the Partner Assistance Policy

The partner assistance program describes the general requirements in 32 Chinese characters, which when translated into English are "to strengthen the leadership, elaborate organization, conform with the plan, implement the policies orderly, unify the policies, finish the job cautiously and improve cohesion" (The State Council, June 11, 2008).

First, the PAP covers many fields of work and involves the cooperation of governments at different levels. As a result, a unified leadership and management system is necessary, which requires both the support and recipient parties to establish special coordinating departments or agencies to be responsible for the cooperation.

Second, governments at different levels should make policies that are strict yet reasonable, which means that the reconstruction should conform to strict standards, and budget arrangements should be scientific and rational without any waste, fraud, embezzlement or corruption.

Third, in order to inspire the sustained enthusiasm of partner assistance, social corporations and other organizations should be called upon to participate in the process of decision-making when policies are made with regard to reconstruction and recovery. These social powers can be mobilized to participate in the disaster relief work. Moreover, donations from society would be of great use to the relief work, but should be subject to strict legal regulation and supervision.

Finally, there are two specific requirements in the support program to ensure the effectiveness and efficiency of the PAP. According to the requirement of the State Council's policy, which would be executed for three consecutive years, in principle the support provinces shall contribute at least 1 percent of their financial revenue from the previous year to support the severely afflicted counties (The State Council, June 11, 2008). The Sichuan provincial official statistics showed that by the end of September 2011, the 18 support provinces had finished 3,662 of the planned 3,668 construction programs and invested a total of RMB 856.846 billion yuan, i.e. 98.96 percent of the total investment plan (The Press Office of Sichuan Government, 2011).

5.5 Transformation of the partner assistance model

The model of the three-year partner assistance program witnessed a transformation from unilateral support to mutual cooperation, which reflects the multiple functions of the PAP, that is, not only for disaster relief but to boost the overall economic development and social advancement of the afflicted regions through the mutual cooperation of the two sides.

5.5.1 Unilateral support in the early stage of the PAP

Upon the central government's instructions, the 18 provincial governments took an active role in the implementation of the PAP, which was initially unilateral in the sense that the support parties offered assistance to the recipient parties without any reward. There were two main models of commanding and organizing the PAP: Jiangsu Province adopted an independent PAP model, where its provincial government established headquarters for disaster relief that were fully authorized to coordinate and supervise the implementation of the reconstruction projects. Projects at the county level were controlled by the provincial government, and projects at the town or village level were controlled by the counties of Jiangsu Province (Ni *et al.*, 2009, p. 57).

Alternatively, the Beijing Municipal Government utilized a comprehensive model in which a general headquarters was established to assume the responsibility for all of the reconstruction projects. The headquarters consisted of seven different divisions corresponding to the government's departments and agencies, six of which were based in Beijing and the remaining one serving as the front-line division based in the disaster area (Ni *et al.*, 2009, p. 57).

During this period, the PAP was mainly operated through these four approaches:

1 Construction aid projects. As many buildings and public infrastructure were seriously damaged by the earthquake, the aid projects in the initial period primarily aimed at the reconstruction of schools, hospitals and other public service facilities. According to the statistics presented by the PAP Office of Sichuan Province, in the first year of the operation of the PAP there were 2,376 projects in total, among which there were 133 house-building projects, 311 public facility projects, 262 rural construction projects, 1,042 public infrastructure projects and 408 other public projects (Partner Assistance Office of Sichuan Province, 2009).

2 Support of education and technology. In regards to the actual implementation of the PAP, education and technological assistance refers to the practice where the support party sends to the disaster areas professionals and other skilled people who specialize in education, hygiene, agriculture, tourism and other fields (Liu, 2012, p. 61).

3 Commercial and industrial support. Sichuan is one of the major agricultural provinces in China. The earthquake had destroyed many important traffic channels, which blocked the transportation of agricultural products out of Sichuan. So the first and foremost measure of commercial and industrial support was to help the disaster areas to market agricultural products throughout the country. In October 2008, Shanghai held an exhibition of agricultural products from Dujiangyan County, at which trade contracts worth RMB 1.51 billion yuan were concluded. (East Daily News, 2009). Second, the support parties helped the disaster areas to develop local tourism as well. Sichuan Province has abundant tourism resources with multiple cultural elements, so support parties began to utilize opportunities to recover Sichuan's tourism (Songpan Government, 2009).

5.5.2 Mutual cooperation in the latter stage of the PAP

After the first year of implementing the PAP, local economic development and social order gradually returned to normal, so the PAP began to transform toward long-term mutual cooperation.

1 Support to establish new local industrial zones. These industrial zones were initiated and planned in the earlier stage of the PAP according to administrative order rather than market mechanisms; nevertheless, in the latter period of mutual cooperation, many more enterprises registered in the support provinces were encouraged to invest in the new industrial zones under the administrative guidance of provincial governments.
2 The approach toward supporting local industries became much more popular in the latter period of the PAP. For example, Shanghai Debin Environmental Protection Technology Co. Ltd. invested in a program for garbage disposal in which a total of RMB 40 million yuan was invested to set up an environmental material company. This company can dispose of one million tons of rubbish annually and provides nearly 100 jobs for local residents (Sichan Daily, 2009).
3 In order to stimulate the internal impetus of the PAP, various commercial entities, social organizations and other non-government organizations in Sichuan Province were inspired and mobilized to take part in the recovery of the disaster-affected areas, such that more than 2,000 cooperation agreements were reached by the end of 2009 (Liu, 2012, p. 82).

5.6 Legal problems of PAP after the Great Wenchuan Earthquake

Though the PAP had played an important role in some special periods, it has some serious problems, especially those seen after the Great Wenchuan Earthquake. By May 30, 2009, of the 2,155 partner assistance projects covering the fields of public service, rural and urban reconstruction, 1,411 projects had been initiated, which accounted for 65.4 percent, and 314 projects had been finished, which was 22.3 percent of those initiated (Partner Assistance Office of Sichuan Province, 2009). Of all the ongoing 21,607 reconstruction projects, 14,319 projects had been finished and 112,660 houses in rural areas had been built, which accounted for 89.2 percent. Of the permanent housing projects in urban areas, 204,200 houses were under construction, which was 65.1 percent, and 515,000 houses had been finished, which accounted for 16.4 percent. Moreover, 2,836 schools were under construction, of which 340 had been finished, which accounted for 11.24 percent (Jiang, 2009).

Through the above data, we can see that the relevant regulations of the PAP had set a three-year term for the partner assistance projects, which guaranteed that the projects were constructed with strict conformance to the stipulated plans. As analyzed above, the main motivation of the PAP is political mobilization, in which the central government plays an important role by initiating the PAP.

From the perspective of the rule of law, the lack of institutional guarantee is the main cause for the above contradictions, which embodies three deficiencies in the operation of PAP:

1 The non-legislated nature of PAP acts as a disaster relief policy but not as a long-term effective mechanism. Without an institutional system, the initiation of a PAP is only associated with some special emergency events and depends on leaders, especially the top leader's willingness, and it is hard to avoid waste and unfairness. It is estimated that the per capita allocation of funds was RMB 21,830 yuan on average, but the per capita allocation in Wen Chuan County was RMB 77,257 yuan, which was 31 times the amount of RMB 2,490 yuan in Jiange County during the three-year term of the PAP (Li, 1998, p. 35). It was absolutely unfair that partner assistance funding was distributed according to the administrative jurisdiction rather than the extent of impact caused by the disaster (Partner Assistance Office of Sichuan Province, 2009).
2 It is very hard to coordinate the implementation of the PAP when there is government discretion and rules based on the mechanisms of the market economy. A flexible and efficient system of PAP should rely on a cooperative mechanism of market and government, which would ensure that the market plays a fundamental role in resource allocation and the government legally executes its power. But in practice, some support parties have blindly assisted the disaster-affected areas by establishing many industrial zones without considering the effect on local enterprises. Those industrial zones did not accord with the local rules of economic development and thus resulted in serious pollution, causing subsequent natural environmental crises.
3 The non-legislated nature of PAP hinders institutional innovation: During the operation of the PAP in Sichuan, though the regional governments exploited many auxiliary policies and complementary measures to perfect this mechanism and provide high operability and good local adaptability, the lack of policy mechanisms for transformation and development makes it difficult to turn such successful examples into legal rules applicable to the whole county in the future.

5.7 Provincial Partner Assistance Policy after the Lushan Earthquake

At 8:02 on April 20, 2013, a terrible earthquake struck Lushan County in Ya'an City, Sichuan Province. According to the *Report on Earthquake of Lushan*, the serious disaster affected more than 30 counties, including Ya'an, Chengdu, Leshan, Ganzi and Deyang, with a combined population of nearly 2.184 million. By May 23, 2013, 196 people had died, two people were missing and 14,785 people were injured. Nearly 4,045 aftershocks continually ravaged the area (People's Government of Ya'an, April 22, 2013).

On July 16, the State Council issued the *Notice on the Overall Planning of Reconstruction and Restoration of Lushan* (People's Government of Sichuan Province, July 15, 2013), consisting of nine articles and strictly providing that the provincial PAP shall play a major role and financial arrangements shall be more reasonable and fair. Then, on July 19, 2013, the General Office of the Sichuan Provincial Party Committee and the General Office of the Sichuan Provincial Government jointly issued *The Work Plan of Reconstruction and Restoration in Lushan* (People's Government of Sichuan Province, July 22, 2013). The total sum of assistance should amount to 5 percent of the provincial government's revenue (People's Government of Sichuan Province, July 22, 2013).

Comparatively speaking, the operation of the PAP in Ya'an in 2013 was more reasonable than that in Wenchuan in 2008. The three distinct features are:

1 The dominant position of the local government in the entire process of the PAP's implementation. The Sichuan Provincial Government was authorized to take charge of the disaster relief work independently, which means that the Sichuan Provincial People's Congress and the Sichuan Provincial Government had absolute power to conduct activities and implement policies.

   After the Lushan Earthquake, the central government soon authorized the Sichuan Provincial Government to establish the incident command system, which comprised three levels of province, city and county. After the initial period of urgent rescue operations, the Committee of Restoration and Reconstruction in Lushan County was established, consisting of the General Office and seven working groups. Under the leadership of this committee, the local governments had enough power to make their own decisions, especially concerning the distribution of relief funds based on actual needs.

   At the same time, the central government played an auxiliary support role in the process of reconstruction rather than completely giving up the role of guidance. According to the *Notice on the Overall Planning of Reconstruction and Restoration of Lushan*, the central government is supposed to instruct the local government to execute the PAP policy and actively act as the coordinator and consultant for disaster relief (People's Government of Sichuan Province, July 15, 2013).

2 The arrangement of reconstruction and restoration was more reasonable and in compliance with the democratic system and market-oriented rules. Ya'an was one of the areas most seriously affected in the Lushan Earthquake. Consequently, while making the reconstruction plans, the local government not only paid attention to the current situation, but also considered the comprehensive development of the region in the future (Xinhua Network, 2014). During the reconstruction of Wenchuan, several sites for new buildings were wrongly chosen and aftershocks ruined many new buildings. In order to avoid secondary disaster, reconstruction sites should be cautiously selected. For instance, the houses at the entrance of Baoxin County, where landslides take place frequently, should not be permitted to reconstruct in the future (Xinhua Network, 2014).

The reasonableness of the reconstruction program can be illustrated by the slogan of the government: to complete the reconstruction within three years, to realize progressive development within five years and to be as affluent as other areas within seven years (People's Government of Ya'an, March 11, 2014). But how is the government to guarantee the rationality of all of the reconstruction programs? All recovery and rebuilding projects are to undergo comprehensive assessment and strict supervision, especially ecological and environmental assessments. In particular, all large-scale projects worth RMB 30 million yuan or more must be invested through openly competitive bidding held at the Sichuan Public Resources Trade Center, in accordance with the rules of the market economy (People's Government of Sichuan Province, 2014).

3 Through the *Framework Agreement of Partner Assistance*, the legal relationship of partner assistance is formally established between the support party and recipient party. Thus the local government laid more emphasis on the use of this legalized mechanism to assist the afflicted areas. (People's Government of Ya'an, August 2013). Additionally, the more flexible mechanism of appointing cadres is another distinct feature in the implementation of the PAP. In the process of reconstruction, a group of officials were appointed by the Sichuan Provincial Government to lead the disaster relief work. The mechanism of cadre exchange would be more mature and beneficial. For instance, some professionals were directly dispatched to the disaster areas, serving as leaders in charge of special reconstruction projects (People's Government of Ya'an, March 20, 2014).

6 Conclusion: suggestions for improving the Partner Assistance Policy

After reviewing the two different implementations of the PAP, although the operation of the PAP in Ya'an was much more successful, there is a long way to go in fostering a more reasonable and legalized mechanism that can guarantee the effectiveness and efficiency of the PAP in the long term.

As discussed above, the PAP transformed into long-term mutual cooperation during its latter stage, which should be legalized and institutionalized in the future. The central government should also recognize the validity of cooperative agreements between different local governments, which are favorable to quantifying the mission of assistance and ensuring sustainable assistance. In the process of making the agreements, each party would have equal status, which should fully embody the spirit of private law in the market mechanism. As to the assistance contract, the political mission assigned by the central government is confirmed as a legal obligation, and it seems that the spirit of private law can be reflected into the field of public law and is expected to be a possible approach for partner assistance.

Therefore, it seems that the mechanism of the PAP could be refined through the two approaches of private law and public law, which goes specifically as follows:

A cooperative agreement or contract serving as a new form of PAP: Under the organization, coordination and guidance of the central government, the local governments should establish mutual-profit partner assistance agreements or administrative contracts after comprehensive consultation and negotiation (Zhu, 2007, p. 23). Consequently, the local governments will be authorized with more autonomy according to their economic development level and other aspects of the situation.

The valuable systemic and personal experience gained from the normal horizontal transfer payment mechanism: On account of the defects in the integration of supporting construction planning in the long term, it is necessary to make laws in the near future that provide the rights and responsibilities of both sides relating to the support of construction. The PAP should also be based on the horizontal transfer payment mechanism, but only one which is legislated, so that it can operate efficiently and support the long-term implementation of the PAP.

The incentive mechanism for administrators should be improved: In China, GDP statistics are an important index to evaluate the achievements of local leaders and civil servants (Zhou, 2006, p. 42). Obviously, the administrators of the support party would feel reluctant to invest a large sum of money into the disaster areas without any return in the operation of the PAP. Only when the PAP is comprehensively integrated with the local economy, environmental protection and ecological improvement, would the administrators have strong motivation and spare no effort to promote the implementation of the policies and programs of partner assistance.

In summary, there are three important principles that deserve to be enshrined by legislating the PAP system, which are as follows: First, the mechanism of mutually beneficial cooperation should be established in the form of agreements and contracts between different governments reached through fair negotiation and reasonable planning. Second, it is acknowledged that there are great regional differences in the process of economic development and legal advancement. Therefore, recovery projects should undergo strict planning and assessment procedures according to the relevant laws and addressing the following aspects: (1) local economic, social and cultural factors; (2) medium- and long-term planning of local urban and rural construction; (3) environmental impact; (4) disaster risk assessment. Third, all governmental behaviors, including partner assistance, should be strictly regulated by law. In conclusion, the traditional mode of response to natural disasters, executing a political mission and mobilization, should be replaced by a legal approach featuring concrete and explicit rules based on the market economy.

Notes

1 Yi Zhuang, first established by Fan Zhongyan, is a product of the agrarian society. It established facilities including schools, public farmland, ancestral halls and other facilities to help the poor and victims of natural disaster. However, with changes to social structures, the scope of Yi Zhuang has gradually narrowed. In modern times, this concept almost exclusively refers to ancestral halls.

2 The National Government established a health and epidemic prevention group in 1931. The Ministry of Health issued regulations on infectious disease prevention and an enforcement regulation in 1924.

References

Bureau of Disaster Relief, Ministry of Civil Affairs (2005), *Great Natural Disasters from 1949 to 2004 in China*, internal publication.

Bureau of Disaster Relief, Ministry of Civil Affairs (December 17, 2013), *Chinese Natural Disaster Relief Information Engineering in the Near Future*, accessed on December 25, 2013, http://news.xinhuanet.com/yzyd/local/20131227/c_118743489.htm.

Chinese States News (June 2006), *Chinese Investment in Disaster Relief from 1991 through 2005*, accessed on August 13, 2013, www.stats.gov.cn/tjsj/ndsj/2006/indexch.htm.

Deng, Yun Te (1997), *Chinese History of Disaster Relief*, Beijing: Commercial Press.

East Daily News (November 2009), "The Second Exhibition of Sichuan Agricultural Products Was Successfully Held in Shanghai," accessed on March 26, 2014, http://e-nw.shac.gov.cn/zfxxgk/zwxw/ncjingji/200911/t20091116_1256333.htm.

Hu, Jin Tao & Wen, Jia Bao (June 13, 2008), *Speech on a Conference about the Domestic and International Background on Present Hold by CPC Central Committee and State Council*, accessed on March 28, 2014, http://news.xinhuanet.com/newscenter/2008-06/13/content_8363888.htm.

Information Office of the State Council (May 11, 2009), *The Disaster Mitigation Operation in China*, accessed on December 29, 2013, http://news.xinhuanet.com/newscenter/2009-05/11/content_11351082_1.htm.

Jiang, Ju Feng, Sichuan Provincial Governor (July 29, 2009), *The Report with Regard to Post-disaster Reconstruction Addressed in the 10th Session of the Standing Committee of 11th Sichuan Provincial People's Congress*, Sichuan Provincial Government.

Li, Sheng Quan (1998), "The Progress, Troubles and Strategies on the Project of Immigration of Three Gorges Dam," *Journal of Chongqing Business School*, Vol. 7, pp. 35–40.

Lin, Jia Hua (January 2008), "Study on Improvement of the Use and Management of Disaster Relief Funds," *Development Research*, Vol. 1, pp. 43–47.

Liu, Shi He & Sheng, Dong Gui (June 2007), "The Many Problems Existing in the Management and Use of Disaster Relief Funds," *Auditing and Finance*, Vol. 7, pp. 57–59.

Liu, Yi (2012), *On the Operation and Legalization of Partner Assistance – An Empirical Study Based on the Post-Disaster Reconstruction of Wenchuan Earthquake*, Doctoral dissertation, Southwestern University of Finance and Economics.

Mallory, W.H. (1930), "Famines in China," *Annals of the American Academy of Political and Social Science*, Vol. 152, pp. 89–98.

Ni, Feng, Zhang, Yue Yu & Yu, Tong Zhou (2009), "The Initial Research on Partner Assistance of Wenchuan Earthquake," *Journal of Economic and Management Research*, Vol. 7, pp. 57–60.

Partner Assistance Office of Sichuan Province (2009), *Work Progress Reports about the 18 Provinces Partner Assistance in the First and Second Quarters of 2009*, Sichuan PA office [2009], no. 29.

People's Government of Sichuan Province (July 15, 2013) *Notice on the Master Plan of Reconstruction and Restoration of Lushan*, accessed on February 25, 2014, www.gov.cn/zwgk/2013-07/15/content_2445989.htm.

People's Government of Sichuan Province (July 22, 2013), *The Work Plan of Reconstruction and Restoration in Lushan*, accessed on February 25, 2014, www.gov.cn/jrzg/2013-07/22/content_2452267.htm.

People's Government of Sichuan Province (January 18, 2014), *The News on Sichuan Provincial Public Resource Exchange Supervision Website*, accessed on March 28, 2014, www.spprec.com/sichuan/infodetail/?infoid=a000b168-f190-4d10-a7a5-eb7aea660b50&categoryNum=042001.

People's Government of Ya'an (April 22, 2013) *The Figures Regarding Lushan Earthquake*, accessed on February 22, 2014, www.Yaan.gov.cn/htm/articsearch_The Statistics of Earthquake_1.html.

People's Government of Ya'an (August 2013), *Series of Relevant Reports on Ya'an Recovery and Reconstruction*, accessed on March 27, 2014, www.Yaan.gov.cn/htm/articview_201308140950180200.html, www.Yaan.gov.cn/htm/articview_20130920131736001.html, www.Yaan.gov.cn/htm/articview_201308141009010215.html, www.Yaan.gov.cn/htm/articview_20131203123810000.html.

People's Government of Ya'an (March 11, 2014) *The Report on Ya'an Recovery and Reconstruction*, accessed on March 27, 2014, www.Yaan.gov.cn/htm/articview_20140311133807359.html.

People's Government of Ya'an (March 20, 2014), *The Report on Professional Cadres Dispatched to the Disaster Area during the Ya'an Operation of Partner Assistance*, accessed on March 29, 2014, www.Ya'an.gov.cn/htm/articview_20140320120023062.html, www.Ya'an.gov.cn/htm/articview_200807030941250141.html.

Qi, Yu (September 2008), "Study on Current Situation, Problems and Countermeasures of Natural Disaster Relief Investment," *The Local Financing Research*, Vol. 1, pp. 25–32.

Sichan Daily (October 12, 2009), *The Cooperation between Shanghai and Dujiangyan is Getting Better*, accessed on March 26, 2014, http://sichuandaily.scol.com.cn/2009/10/12/20091012546424654918.htm.

Sichuan Provincial Bureau of Statistics (February 19, 2008), *The 2007 National Economic and Social Development Statistics Bulletin of Sichuan Province*, accessed on March 17, 2014, www.sc.gov.cn/scszfxxgkml_2/sbgt_53/gzdt/sjtj/200804/t20080425_272183.shtml.

Sohu News (June 24, 2008), *The Basic Statistics on the Great Wenchuan Earthquake and its Recovery and Reconstruction*, accessed on August 25, 2013, http://news.sohu.com/20080624/n257690599.shtml.

Songpan Government (September 18, 2009), "The Summary Materials of Conference on Partner Assistance on September 18, 2009," accessed on March 28, 2014, www.sdpc.gov.cn/gzdt/t20091030_311920.htm.

The Center of the CCTV Media (March 8, 2009), *The New Conference on Wenchuan 5.12 Earthquake Relief and Reconstruction*, accessed on March 26, 2014, www.sc.gov.cn/zwgk/zwdt/ldhd/200903/t20090309_617750.shtml.

The Press Office of Sichuan Government (October 14, 2011), *Report About the Reconstruction and Restoration of 5.12 Wenchuan Earthquake*, accessed on March 18, 2014, www.gov.cn/gzdt/2011-10/14/content_1969461.htm.

The State Council (2008), *The Regulation on Post-disaster Reconstruction of Wenchuan*, accessed on March 28, 2014, www.gov.cn/zwgk/2008-06/09/content_1010710.htm.

The State Council (June 11, 2008), *The Programs on the Partner Assistance of Wenchuan Post-disaster Reconstruction*, accessed on February 21, 2014, www.gov.cn/zwgk/2008-06/18/content_1019966.htm.

The State Council (August 27, 2008), *The Overall Plan of Restoration and Reconstruction after the Wenchuan Earthquake*, accessed on February 20, 2014, www.gov.cn/ldhd/2008-08/27/content_1080841.htm.

Wang, Zhen Yao & Tian, Xiao Hong (July 2006), "The Basic System of China's Natural Disaster Emergency Rescue Management," *The Comparative Economic and Social Systems*, Vol. 5, pp. 26–38.

Xinhua Network (February 14, 2014), *The Lushan Model of Post-disaster Reconstruction*, accessed on March 22, 2014, www.sc.gov.cn/10462/10464/10797/2014/1/14/10290796.shtml.

Yu, Xin Zhong (April 1997), "The Social Relief in Late Qing Dynasty-Research in Yi Zhuang, Soochow," *Nan Kai Academic Journal*, Vol. 3, pp. 62–70.

Zhang, Ximin (May 12, 2013), *An Interview with China Disaster Relief: The Ability to Respond the Disaster Is Improved in China*, accessed on December 29, 2013, http://news.sina.com.cn/c/2013-05-12/112527098504.shtml.

Zhou, Lian (2006), "The Motivation and Cooperation of the Government Officials' Promotion Game," *Economy Review*, Vol. 6, pp. 42–48.

Zhu, Yin Li (2007), "Legal Analysis of the Nature of the Regional Economic Cooperation Agreement," *Journal of Jinan University*, Vol. 2, pp. 23–28.

3 From healer state to protector state

A critical evaluation of painful struggles in legal and administrative undertakings in disaster management of Turkey from 1509 to 2010

Ali Tolga Ozden and Burcak Erkan

1 Introduction

Turkey is subject to various natural hazards, most of which change easily into disasters because of the vulnerable structure of the community and the built environmental conditions. This chapter explores how the legal and administrative struggles that have been developed and implemented in Turkey in order to cope with the detrimental effects of natural and man-made hazards have changed the disaster understanding and perception among the governments and institutions as well as the building professionals. In that sense, the legal and administrative shift in disaster coping efforts is examined through the laws and regulations developed from the foundation of the Turkish Republic (1923) to the year 2010.

The following sections of this chapter critically evaluate the development of legal and administrative approaches of disaster concepts from a historical point of view in the years between 1923 (the foundation of the Turkish Republic) and 2010. It is also beneficial to point briefly to some historical advancements and shifts from the period of the Ottoman Empire (1299–1922), which ruled the country before the foundation of the Turkish Republic. Those struggles conducted in Ottoman Empire times are important in order to understand the shift from the rehabilitative (post-disaster) approach to the mitigation (pre-disaster) approach in Turkish Republic times, in chronological order.

2 Acts of God period: post-disaster coping strategies after hazardous events from 1509 to 1922

2.1 Initial documents reflecting both the disaster impacts and the response activities in Turkey's disaster history: 1509 earthquake

Destructions pertaining from hazardous events experienced all over the world for centuries have changed the perception of and response to disaster phenomena among communities as well as institutions. In order to evaluate the shifting understanding and development of this process in Turkey, the first written documents can be dated to the year 1509 in which a strong earthquake struck İstanbul, the capital of the Ottoman Empire. The 1509 earthquake was one of the foremost hazardous events recorded in the history of Turkey (Bayrak, 1996; Evangelatou-Notara, 2001; Ambraseys and Finkel, 2006). The earthquake, which occurred on September 14, was named "Little Doomsday" (Griffiths *et al.*, 2007). According to the report of the Research Commission of the Turkish Parliament, the magnitude of the earthquake is estimated between 7.6 and 8.0, and human loss was assumed as 13,000 (TBMM, 1999). The same report stresses that following the earthquake, which severely damaged 109 mosques and 1,047 buildings, the Ottoman Emperor (Sultan Beyazıt the Second) prepared and disseminated a mandate in which 50,000 building craftsmen and workers between 14 and 60 years old were assigned to work in rehabilitation and reconstruction of the destroyed city. In addition, the same mandate prohibited construction of buildings on filled grounds of the coastal areas, as well as trying to force the construction of timber-framed housings instead of construction using heavy materials such as stones.

The destruction caused by the earthquake was accepted as an act of God and a kind of punishment for wickedness. However, the response of the Ottoman Emperor, who was believed to stay for ten days in a tent in the garden of his palace (Bayrak, 1996), was a typical rehabilitative approach. That typical post-disaster approach points to two primary objectives: (1) reconstruction of damaged buildings, (2) development of the partial and/or fragmented legal and administrative response taking into account a single hazardous event while excluding the other causes and integrated viewpoint of disaster phenomena.

2.2 The fire threat

The following period generally revealed a very similar response and similar coping strategies during the time of the Ottoman Empire. Fires also threatened the community and caused significant damage to settlements. The suitability of timber buildings during seismic movements, such as the 1509 earthquake, oriented rulers and craftsmen to build timber houses. However, the use of timber increased the danger of fires for the cities of the Empire. Specific examples of such fire hazards are the 1633 Cibali and 1693 İstanbul fires, which destroyed or severely damaged housing and shops (Özgür and Azaklı, 2001).

Governors were forced to develop a new fire brigade system due to deficient coping efforts with fires. The first fire brigade organization, "Tulumbacı Ocağı", was developed in 1720 (Eğilmezer, 2010) as an important post-disaster response approach. As cited by Çelik (1986: p. 52), at least 109 extensive fires took place in İstanbul and Galata region between the years of 1633 and 1839. In addition, the number of fires increased significantly, reaching 229 between 1853 and 1906, indicating the constant threat of fire for nineteenth-century İstanbul (Çelik, 1986: p. 53).

2.3 Return of the ground shaking: 1766 earthquake

In 1766, another intensive earthquake shook İstanbul and a tsunami was experienced as well. Buildings and ports located on the coastal areas of İstanbul and near regions were badly damaged by the tsunami (Hebert *et al.*, 2005; Ambraseys and Finkel, 2006). A similar response to the 1509 earthquake period was observed in the city and in other affected regions; the earthquake and tsunami were believed to be acts of God, which dominated the rehabilitation works.

2.4 The turn of the nineteenth century and the beginnings of more rational approaches

In 1817, the idea of fire-wall construction between adjacent housing had been developed. Based on this idea, a newly published mandate forced the construction of stone fire-walls between houses (Özgür and Azaklı, 2001). This mandate can be seen as an initial idea of a pre-disaster approach. However, recovery and rehabilitation practices still formed the major disaster response policy. Helmuth Von Moltke, a German planner and soldier, was invited to İstanbul by the Ottoman Emperor to develop new planning approaches and projects (in the period 1836–1839) (Ayataç, 2007). Von Moltke prepared plans for the reorganization and development of new measures for the fire hazard. He proposed to eliminate the dead-end streets, which were seen as the main causes of the spread of fire, and barriers for the controlling of fires. In addition, he recommended the use of masonry building materials accepted as fire-resistive, and also the development of city squares as another measure to prevent the spread of fire. Those attempts and planning decisions can be seen as the initial ideas of a mitigation approach proposed in the planning phase. In 1839, the first official development law, called "*İlmühaber*", was published. The main issues in the document were consistent with the pre-disaster understanding and are summarized in Figure 3.1 (Özgür and Azaklı, 2001; Bayrak, 1996).

BUILDING SCALE RELATED ISSUES	URBAN SCALE RELATED ISSUES	LAND USE SPECIFICATION
• Buildings should be constructed with stone or brick (or composite) building materials, and should follow geometrical rules. • Buildings on both sides of the road should not be higher than three stories (or fifteen meters high).	• Dead-end streets should be eliminated and prohibited. • Roads should be wide enough or if possible should be widened.	• New and reserved areas for new housing should be prepared.

Figure 3.1 Major disaster preventive actions in the first development law.

A new building act which was published in 1848 and accepted as a more developed follow-up legislative approach till that time was put into effect. Therein, there were important arrangements such as limiting of timber-framed housing construction, expropriation, building permit development, street and road widths, building inspection and building elevation, etc. (Özgür and Azaklı, 2001; Özcan, 2006; Özyurt, 2007). Although these kinds of legislative documents were trying to regulate building practices and urban planning, they were generally unable to go beyond the partial and fragmented approaches in disaster prevention understanding.

2.5 A very common governmental approach: rehabilitation of disaster-stricken areas

Particularly following the second half of the nineteenth century, re-development of the damaged areas was observed as a common planning and building understanding. One of the first examples of re-development practice following a disaster event is dated to 1856. An Italian architect, Luici Stotari, developed 740 housing units in an area which was destroyed completely by the Aksaray (İstanbul) fire disaster of 1856. This period also saw the beginning of piecemeal development plan applications which were specifically produced for disaster-stricken areas (Tekeli, 2006). That understanding was also consistent with the very usual governmental perception that the state was accepted as the "healer" state but not the "protector" state. Ultimately, the disasters are acts of God and there is nothing to prevent them, and the role of the government was to heal the affected people and rehabilitate the stricken regions.

According to Çelik (1986: p. 49), development and regeneration scope and nature of activity of İstanbul, which was located on the both sides of the Golden Horn in the nineteenth century, were determined by different forces, one of which was fire disaster. In that sense, "the dense, wooden residential fabric of the İstanbul peninsula made the area vulnerable to fires" (Çelik, 1986: p. 49). Çelik asserts that the burned-out or destroyed areas became experimentation and application arenas of "Western-inspired urban planning principles" in terms of being put into practice.

In 1865, a great fire known as the Sirkeci-Hocapaşa fire, which was controlled and extinguished in nearly a day and a half, and believed to destroy more than 2,900 houses, was important in terms of shaping the urban fabric (Özgür and Azaklı, 2001; Çelik, 1986; Bayrak, 1996). Following the disaster, a research commission was established in order to prepare a disaster report to detect the root causes of the disaster and determine the post-disaster activities for the first time (Özcan, 2006; Özyurt, 2007). Subsequently, a new commission called "Islahat-ı Turuk" (a development commission for streets and roads) was established (Bayrak, 1996). This commission was responsible for preparing development plans in the stricken area in terms of producing regional maps, developing new construction regulations, parceling construction sites, construction of infrastructure, etc., which all indicate the rehabilitative approach of post-disaster efforts. The commission specifically worked on the widening of existing roads and opening of new roads, which could all be seen as successful efforts in terms of urban space rehabilitation (Yeşilkaya, 2007).

It is obvious that the 1856 (Aksaray) and 1865 (Sirkeci-Hocapaşa) fires were milestones in terms of improving development ordinances and regulations for urban planning and single building scale. In the post-fire period, a new regulation, Road and Building Legislation, was put into effect in 1865 (Özgür and Azaklı, 2001). Designated legislation covered the enforcement of the following issues of subdivisions, expropriation, road construction, building material choice, fire-wall construction between timber frame buildings and restrictions for new timber building construction.

In 1870, a fire known as the Pera fire destroyed 3,000–5,000 buildings and killed 150 people (Bayrak, 1996; Tekeli, 1999); following this, kargir (brick or stone) construction was made obligatory by the Sixth District administration of İstanbul (Çelik, 1986: p. 46), which can be seen as a similar fragmented solution with the former legal and administrative approaches to prevent fire hazards.

2.6 The first attempt to unify the legislative documents: Development Law of 1882

The date November 5, 1882 has an important place in this chronological approach of legislative and administrative advancements in the Ottoman period. For the first time, a comprehensive law comprising of all development and building issues in a single legislative document was published and put into effect. This law, which can be seen as the first Development Law, was used up until the first years of the Turkish Republic (founded after the demolition of the Ottoman Empire in 1923). With the help of this law, municipal works had started to become widespread across the country in general, and had become particularly common in piecemeal development plan approaches following disasters (Tekeli, 2006).

2.7 Finalizing the nineteenth century with a seismic disaster event: 1894 Marmara earthquake

Ambraseys and Finkel (2006) searched for the historical earthquakes that were observed and recorded between 1500 and 1800 in their study. According to their study, 377 earthquakes were strongly felt and recorded by different sources in that period. Although some were indicated as fake or false records, and could be considered unreliable according to their conclusion (Ambraseys and Finkel, 2006: pp. 167–176), most of them had extensive impact on the built environment and local people.

On July 10, 1894, a very destructive seismic movement occurred in the Marmara region. The earthquake, the focal point of which was in the Marmara Sea and was felt all over the Ottoman land, severely damaged the city of İstanbul (Kundak and Türkoğlu, 2007). The earthquake, with a magnitude of 7.0 (Barış *et al.*, 2005), destroyed not only the city walls surrounding the historical peninsula but also many other buildings, such as mosques, churches and housing, and killed around 5,000 people (Koçak, 2010). It was observed that the masonry buildings constructed without basic seismic-resistant design methods and sufficient load-bearing systems, such as load-bearing walls, floors and roofs, were damaged much more than the timber-framed and wooden structures as well as some other brick buildings (Ambraseys, 2001). The Ottoman Sultan ordered tents to be set up for victims and for first aid to be organized, whereas the city government of İstanbul organized financial and food aid, as well as tent aid for the disaster victims (Bayrak, 1996: p. 125).

In the last decades of the Ottoman State (between 1900–1922), the country continued to experience new and destructive earthquakes, and also some new advancements in coping efforts, all of which were consistent with the "healer state" approach of post-disaster activities.

2.8 Summary

The legal and administrative efforts to cope with the adverse effects of disasters in the Ottoman period (1509–1922) signify a noticeable improvement and enhancement in post-disaster activities which include the rehabilitation approach of stricken areas. However, the common perception and disaster culture among the community had been constructed on the "acts of God" understanding due to socio-cultural, political, intellectual and spiritual characteristics, as well as financial and technical capabilities of the community. Therefore, the struggles and advancements in disaster coping efforts were limited with the response activities of first aid, temporary sheltering (if possible) and reconstruction of stricken areas. Those legal approaches were produced and disseminated following a disaster event (such as fire, earthquake, etc.). In that sense, along with the mandates and orders of the Ottoman Sultans, legal and administrative documents were published specifically in the nineteenth century to regulate and rehabilitate the post-disaster activities. Those typical approaches determine the general framework of the disaster understanding and response cycle of the Ottoman period (Figure 3.2).

3 From acts of God to acts of human: the shift in understanding of disaster coping efforts in Turkey from 1923 to 2011

3.1 Building up of more rational legal documents by the new republic

After the foundation of the Republic of Turkey in 1923 following a painful war period (the Independence War, which started in 1919 and ended in 1922), some important progressions were seen in terms of development and enhancement of

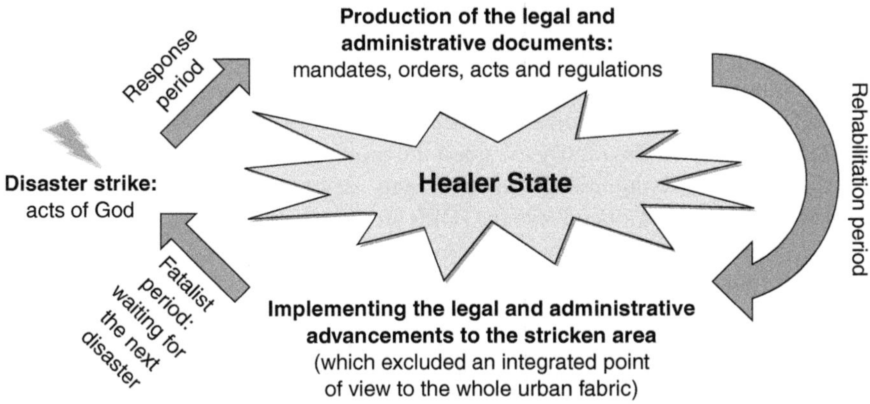

Figure 3.2 A typical post-disaster cycle in the Ottoman Empire period (1509–1922) which reflects the governmental approach and community perception from the legal and administrative point of view.

settlements through the legal and administrative system. In that sense "Village Law" (Law Number 442), which was published in 1924, was one of the first and comprehensive legislative developments of the republic. The law covered various development arrangements (Official Gazette, 1924a: p. 336).[1] Most of the articles are mostly related to the organization of village management and development issues. The thirteenth article organizes the assignments of the villagers, which includes taking precautions before hazards such as floods, epidemics, etc. In the same year, another new law which was published under the name of Law for Arranging Punishments Related to Development and Local Governmental Issues also covered important development regulations, and transferred the responsibility of organizing legislative and construction activities in fire (stricken and/or risky) areas to the municipalities (Official Gazette, 1924b).

3.2 First seismic experience of the new republic: 1924 earthquake

On September 13, 1924, an intensive earthquake shook the Erzurum province and caused extensive damage in many settlements and left hundreds of casualties along with the loss of a great amount of livestock (Kalemli, 2010). Following the seismic event, a law was published in order to arrange the aid and rehabilitation works for the stricken area (Law Number 516) (Egünay, 2011; Official Gazette, 1924c: p. 1). Capacity of the new republic's institutions was so scarce in terms of coping with adverse effects of the seismic event. Law 516 can be considered the first case-specific oriented and rehabilitative approach developed following a disaster event of the newly founded republic.

3.3 Acceleration in developing hazard prevention efforts through legislation in the first half of the twentieth century

The Municipality Law (Law Number 1580), which was put into effect in 1930, involved more detailed issues related to development and inspection activities, as well as disaster preparedness concepts, such as fire prevention approaches. Within article 15, paragraph 4 assigned the municipalities to work with related organizations in epidemic prevention and struggle issues including both human and animal-induced events (Official Gazette, 1930a: p. 8823). Paragraph 18 assumed protection and recovery of the hazard and disaster victims as the responsibility of municipalities. Section 21 (Official Gazette, 1930a: p. 8824) gave the responsibility of natural environment protection within the municipality borders against natural and human-induced hazards to the municipalities. According to paragraph 22 of article 15 within the law (Official Gazette, 1930a: p. 8824), municipalities were assigned to take necessary preventive actions for fire hazards that comprised the control of hazardous material production and storage facilities, construction of water pools in necessary areas in terms of fire preparedness measures, and assurance and maintenance of firefighting tools as well as vehicles, including fire trucks. In addition, organizing and planning of fire-stricken areas according to new development plans were assigned to the municipalities through paragraph 37 of article 15. Paragraph 38 drew attention to the safety of industrial facilities and fabrics in terms of hazardous and risky building components, machinery and boiler systems which have the potential to be harmful to local people and neighboring settlements. Therefore, the responsibility to control and arrange necessary safety rules for those harmful components was also given to municipal organizations as well.

During the first decades of the Turkish Republic, although the country did not face many destructive disaster events other than the 1924 Erzurum earthquake, there were important attempts to develop and improve the legal and administrative system in order to regulate the built environment and secure the health and safety of the communities. In fact, those efforts were consistent with the ideal of the new republic, which was also identified by the founders. That ideal was to re-construct and develop the country on the ruins of the former system of the Ottoman Empire, which was demolished after the Independence War. The Law of Public Sanitation (Law Number 1593) was developed in 1930 to organize and put into order health and sanitation issues all around the country. The law was composed of more than 300 articles, but the most striking point related to the content of the legislation, which included articles related to protective health and how to cope with epidemics and other health disasters (Official Gazette, 1930b).

One of the foremost legal alterations in terms of producing healthy and safe urban areas regarding coping efforts during hazardous events was the development of the Municipality Building and Roads Law (Law Number 2290), which was put into effect in 1933 (Official Gazette, 1933). This law was accepted as the primary law expected to guide the following legal and administrative arrangements in coping with hazardous events and disasters (TBMM, 1999). In addition, this law was also affirmed as an important step in terms of securing the health, safety and orderly production of settlements and buildings, which can be accepted as the development of initial ideas for pre-disaster struggles, although no articles were specifically produced for disaster concepts (METU, 1998: pp. 1–3; TBMM, 1997: pp. 5–6). Paragraph C of article 4 within the law regulates the reduction of harmful effects to the settlements which have the potential to pertain from production and storage facilities, such as military buildings, arsenals, hazardous material depots and production facilities (Official Gazette, 1933: p. 2756). Paragraph D of the same article prohibits dead-end streets. Articles 10–18 cover construction permits and inspection issues, whereas articles 19–42 arrange most of the construction details and rules related to buildings, ranging from window and door standards to fire-wall construction rules (Official Gazette, 1933: p. 2757–2760).

3.4 Beginning of a more planned period: 1930–1945

The period of 1930–1945 can be seen as a planned and organized development period (METU, 1998: pp. 1–2), with new administrative institutions being developed. In addition, local governments were given special importance in terms of improving their capacities and jurisdictions that were determined as prior advancements. However, the central authority also needed new central institutions in order to enforce and regulate the newly developed or developing legal and administrative approaches in order to secure public and built environment safety. In terms of dealing with those works and other development issues, new institutional organizations were established within the Development Ministry in 1939 under Law Number 3611 (METU, 1998: pp. 1–3). According to the law, article 7 organizes the formation of new administrative institutions related to all development and construction activities under both the central and the provincial governmental organizations (Official Gazette, 1939: p. 11833), one of which was named the Building and Development Works Presidency. The main aim of developing this type of organization was to clean up the fragmented view of development issues, and to combine construction activities under a central institution which worked more scientifically and technically in order to secure the safety of the built environment, which was so much vulnerable in terms of natural and human-induced hazards.

3.5 Facing the highest human loss from a disaster event in the period of the Turkish Republic: 1939 earthquake

The newly founded Republic of Turkey was hit by a devastating earthquake which was recorded as the highest seismic movement in magnitude scale in the Turkish Republic's history. Erzincan province was shaken by a 7.8 magnitude earthquake on December 26, 1939. Human casualty numbers exceeded 32,000 and 116,720 buildings were severely damaged. The catastrophic event strongly revealed the fragility of the buildings and vulnerability of the built environmental conditions in Turkey's urban and rural areas. Soon after the earthquake, Law Number 3773 was put into effect (on January 25, 1940), which was published in order to organize assistance and other works for the earthquake victims, and it was a case-specific legislative arrangement. The law was composed of eight articles and almost all articles were related to financial issues, including financial aid to the victims, moratorium arrangements for the victims, organizing foreign aid, etc. (articles 1, 2, 3, 4, 5, 6) (Official Gazette, 1940: p. 13206). The rehabilitative approach was inherited from the former period, along with the traditional and dominant role of the state in disaster events, named the "healer state".

The five-year period (1939–1944) following the Erzincan earthquake was remarkable and showed interesting characteristics in terms of seismological science because, during that period, five intensive earthquakes hit the country (Table 3.1). These earthquakes exposed heavy losses of almost 44,000 casualties, 75,000 wounded and almost 200,000 severely damaged or collapsed buildings.

Following the chain of earthquake disasters recorded between 1939 and 1944, it was clear that post-disaster activities such as first aid and rehabilitation of

Table 3.1 Earthquakes that stuck Turkey in 1939–1944, causing extensive damage to the built environment

Date	*Seismic event*	*Description*
December 26, 1939	Erzincan Earthquake	Magnitude: 7.8; killed: 32,962 people. Erzincan – Kelkit region was the most affected; seismic movement was felt even in Cyprus; some limited tsunami were observed in specific regions of the Black Sea; the earthquake damaged 116,720 buildings.
December 20, 1942	Niksar – Erbaa Earthquake	Magnitude: 7.3; killed: 1,100 people. Earthquake damaged around 32,000 buildings.
June 20, 1943	Adapazarı – Hendek Earthquake	Magnitude: 6.6; killed: 336 people. Earthquake damaged around 2,240 buildings.
November 26, 1943	Tosya – Ladik Earthquake	Magnitude: 7.6; killed: 4,000 people. 75% of the buildings located in the Ladik – Vezirköprü region were destroyed. Total damaged buildings was estimated as 40,000.
February 1, 1944	Bolu – Gerede Earthquake	Magnitude: 7.4; killed: 3,959 people. Earthquake damaged around 20,864 buildings.

Sources: http://earthquake.usgs.gov/earthquakes/world/world_deaths.php (accessed in March 2010), www.koeri.boun.edu.tr/sismo/default.htm (accessed in May 2009).

stricken areas were not sufficient to develop successful and integrated coping strategies for the adverse effects of disasters (METU, 1998: pp. 1–3; TBMM, 1997: p. 6; Ergünay, 2011). It was also realized that better policies and legislative approaches needed to be developed in order to improve the resistance of the built environment against disasters. In that context, a new law (Law Number 4623), "The law for the measures that would be taken before and after earthquakes", was established and put into effect in 1944 (July 22). The basic and important approaches that were given in the law are listed in Table 3.2 (TBMM, 1997: p. 6; Official Gazette, 1944: pp. 7337–7339).

Although the law predominantly consisted of post-disaster activity arrangements through the articles in terms of first aid, temporary sheltering, repair, reconstruction and/or demolishing of damaged buildings in the disaster-stricken areas, it gave some clues related to a shift from fragmented organizational efforts to cope with disasters to more integrated activities, and can also be seen as a shift in disaster perception among the institutions and governments from acts of God to acts of human understanding.

3.6 Facing the flood hazard truth in the first half of the twentieth century

As well as earthquakes, flood disasters were also common in 1941–1943 in different parts of the country (TBMM, 1997: p. 6). A new law, "The law for protection against flood water and floods" (Law Number 4373), was developed and put into effect on January 14, 1943. This law was the first to establish a legislative and administrative approach for flood hazards in Turkey. Specifically, the first articles (articles 1–7) arranged mitigation activities, including the identification of flood hazard areas, the clearing of hazardous buildings and barriers that could cause and/or intensify the flooding from flood-risk areas, and early warning activities (Official Gazette, 1943: p. 4318).

Table 3.2 Law 4623, with specific issues on hazard preparation and prevention

Law 4623: Article 1	*Law 4623: Articles 11, 13, 14, 15, 16, 17, 26*	*Law 4623: Articles 2– 9*
Identification of the zones that face the possibility of seismic hazards in Turkey	Determination of the ordinances and sanctions that should be enforced for construction in earthquake hazard zones	Preparation and keeping available of first aid and SR (search and rescue) plans in cities and towns in case of emergency and/or crises
Initial steps to develop an earthquake hazard map of Turkey	*Primary efforts to establish earthquake-resistant building design and construction approaches in terms of building code development and enforcement among building professionals*	*Initial ideas for disaster preparedness and emergency operation planning*

3.7 Other important advancements in legal and institutional structures in the first half of the twentieth century

Two valuable advancements were developed in 1945, consistent with the successful attempts of pre-disaster legislative and administrative approaches. The first Earthquake Zones Map of Turkey was produced, which can be seen as an initial effort to prepare a Seismic Hazard Map of Turkey. The map was produced in 1:2,000,000 scale, and divided the country into three seismic zones: extensively damaged areas, seismically hazardous zones, seismically safe areas (Pampal and Özmen, 2006). The other striking advancement was the development of a building regulation for earthquake zones in Turkey. This regulation has changed and improved over time, and is still in use under the name "Regulation for the buildings that will be constructed in the disaster zones", which was first enacted in 1997 and revised in 2006. The regulation takes into account three natural hazard concepts: fire, flood and earthquake (Official Gazette, 1997: pp. 191–275). However, earthquakes encompass the majority of the regulation with regards to structural building issues, and mostly excluding the other concepts of hazard and disaster phenomena.

3.8 Shaking the healer state tradition: 1946 earthquake and following advancements

Varto earthquake hit the eastern part of the country on May 31, 1946. Although the magnitude was recorded as 5.9, which can be seen as a mid-size seismic movement, the death toll was considerably high, at 800 people. Many towns and villages were severely damaged, and almost 3,000 buildings were destroyed. In 1948, two laws were enacted, both of which were typical examples of arrangements of post-disaster and case-specific activities. Those laws were "the buildings that would be constructed in Erzincan" (Law Number 5243), which organized the post-disaster reconstruction activities following the Erzincan earthquake, and "the buildings that would be constructed for the flood victims in Eskişehir" (Law Number 5663), which organized the post-disaster reconstruction activities following the Eskişehir flood disaster. The Bingöl-Karlıova earthquake of 1949 (August 17), with a magnitude of 6.7, killed 450 people and destroyed almost 3,500 buildings. Four years after the Bingöl-Karlıova earthquake, an administrative advancement was developed by the establishment of the Earthquake Office in 1953 under the Building and Development Works Presidency of Public Works Ministry, which can also be stressed as a pre-disaster struggle in order to cope with hazardous events (Özden, 2011: p. 73).

However, natural disasters continued to hit the country while the pre-disaster advancements in legal and administrative efforts were going on. On March 18, 1953, Western Turkey was violently shaken. Yenice-Gönen (in Çanakkale province) was hit by a 7.3 magnitude earthquake, resulting in 1,070 casualties and thousands of severely damaged buildings. On the one hand, the central government was trying to develop and implement new legislative and administrative concepts in order to enhance and increase the urban building stocks all over the country. Consistent with that urbanization ideal, local authorities were supported to take responsibility in legal and administrative practices in terms of expanding the building production process. On the other hand, the natural hazards were threatening the insufficient and fragile structures of the settlements which were seen as important causes of failure when faced with natural events. In that sense, a new legal and administrative approach was developed in 1953 which had two aims: on the one hand, to support and increase the building and specifically housing construction in urban areas, and on the other hand, to control, intervene and prohibit illegal building practices which did not comply with the necessary building codes and planning ordinances. The law on building construction encouragement and unauthorized buildings (Law Number 6188) was published in order to achieve the above two main aims of the country's new building approach. Articles 1–11 of the law, in particular, dealt with the appropriation of land to authorized civil building construction, and legal and administrative arrangements for determining the responsibility of the local governmental institutions in terms of construction and financial issues (Official Gazette, 1953: pp. 6844–6845). Article 12 specifically drew attention to enforcing the building codes that construction practices and buildings had to comply with.

Although, there was a growing demand and shifting understanding in safe building production processes to resist hazardous events among institutions and the community, the insufficient legislative and administrative systems interacted with a lack of competent professionals in the building production process, including design, construction and inspection, causing failures during hazardous events. Therefore, the case-specific and rehabilitative legal and administrative approaches continued during this period. Figure 3.3 gives some of those rehabilitative and partial development examples produced for disaster events in terms of arranging legislative efforts.

3.9 Unifying the coping efforts with disaster phenomena: development of DE-SE-YA

The partial and fragmented structure of the legal and administrative system in the country affected the coping efforts and implementation, as well as enforcement of the mitigation activities, negatively. In order to improve the insufficient legal and administrative system, a new institution, the DE-SE-YA (Earthquake-Flood-Fire) Office, was established in 1955. The DE-SE-YA Office was important because it aimed to combine the coping efforts with three major hazards (of earthquake, flood and fire). In this regard, the Earthquake Office, mentioned before, which was established in 1953, evolved into the DE-SE-YA Office. The new organization was important in terms of contributing to the shifting understanding of disaster coping strategies.

The years 1956 and 1958 were important in terms of advancements in legal and administrative developments. One of the first comprehensive legislative publications that comprised identification of natural hazards and hazardous areas as

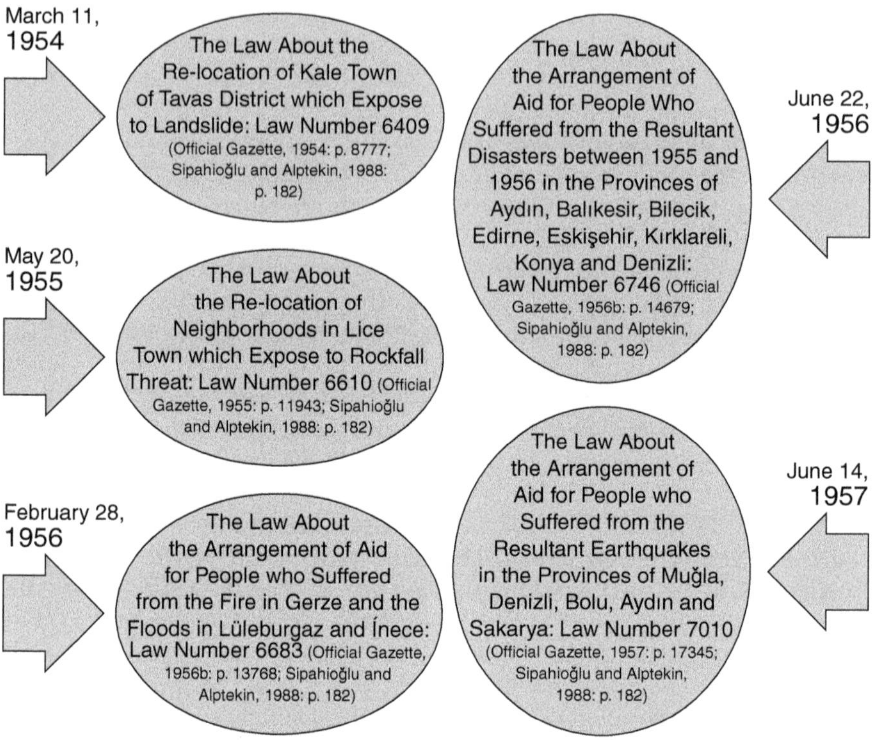

Figure 3.3 Some of the case-specific and rehabilitative disaster coping efforts in terms of legal and administrative approaches between 1950 and 1960 in Turkey.

the criteria for site selection of new settlements, and Technical Application Responsibility system to inspect buildings, was published under the title of "Development Law" (Law Number 6785) in 1956 (Official Gazette, 1956c). This extensive and comprehensive law comprised four sections and 62 articles, all of which arranged building issues conducted in Turkey. Moreover, the law was important in terms of enforcing safe and healthy buildings through the necessary building codes, and this view made the law an important mitigation activity in terms of disaster coping policies. On the other hand, the progression of the legal system in terms of pre-disaster activities needed administrative development as well. In that sense, the Ministry of Development and Settlement was established in 1958 under Law Number 7116. Some of the important and basic responsibilities of the Ministry in terms of producing safe and healthy built environments can be listed as follows: to take necessary measures before and after disasters; to produce plans related to the provinces, towns and villages of the country; to find solutions for the housing and settlement problems; to improve building materials and to prepare the quality standards (Official Gazette, 1958: p. 19305).

3.10 Publishing the first comprehensive disaster legislation: Law Number 7269 – Disaster Law

A major advancement in 1959 related to the disaster coping policy. "The law for arranging measures taken before and assistance after the disasters that are effective on public life" (more commonly known as "Disaster Law", Law Number 7269) was put into effect. The Disaster Law has been in use for many years in Turkey. However, it has been changed many times due to the effects of different disasters in different times and other needs and demands of society. The Disaster Law was the first law to gather all the other published laws and regulations related to hazards and disasters. This law was accepted as an umbrella law and expected to develop an integrated point of view to the disaster phenomena. One of the important contributions of the law was that it proposed a disaster fund (within articles 33–46) (Official Gazette, 1959: pp. 21697–21698). The Disaster Fund regulation was only then put into effect in 1970. In addition, in order to support and increase the extent of the fund capacity, an earthquake fund was put into effect in 1972 (METU, 1998: pp. 1–5).

The 1956–1959 period was very successful in terms of advancements in legal and administrative systems. The development of pre-disaster laws and regulations, as well as newly established, more comprehensive institutions in order to cope with adverse effects of disasters, reveal important clues about the shift from "healer state" to "protector state" understanding.

3.11 The stressful years of the 1960s–1980s: painful steps in disaster coping efforts

The seismic activities between the years 1966 and 1983 revealed the fragility of the built environment once more (Figure 3.4). Moreover, the successful developments through the legal and administrative structures did not fare well in practice due to insufficient application processes and transfer of new developments into practice, as well as a lack of competent building professionals to produce safe and healthy settlements.

In 1970, a new institution was established called the General Directorate of Disasters Research Institute under the Ministry of Development and Settlement. It was converted to the Earthquake Research Institute in 1971 and then evolved as an office of the Building Material and Earthquake Research General Directorate in 1983. Whereas the institute's working area covered all disasters, it was generally organized and oriented to particularly seismic hazards and it did not take into account other types of hazards in detail. The central political authority again turned its focus to earthquake disaster works while excluding the holistic viewpoint.

In order to improve the development and building production process, as well as inspection activities, a new ministry was established (Ministry of Public Works and Settlement) instead of the former Ministry of Development and Settlement (established in 1958) (Official Gazette, 1983). The first article of the law gives the

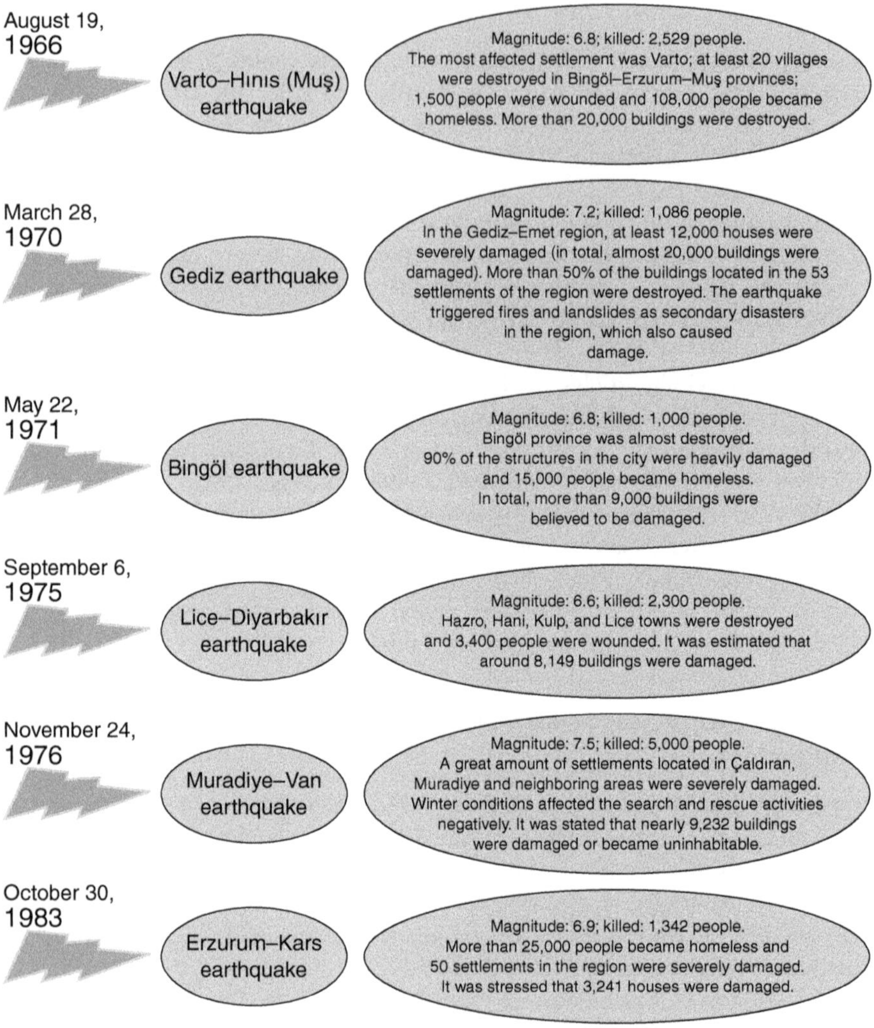

Figure 3.4 Earthquakes that have shaken the different regions of Turkey in the period of 1966–1983 (sources: http://earthquake.usgs.gov/earthquakes/world/world_deaths.php [accessed in March 2010]; www.koeri.boun.edu.tr/sismo/default.htm [accessed in May 2009]).

general aim of the legislation and the new ministry as: "providing and controlling of public buildings' construction and renovation, building materials, earthquake research, and disaster implementation services in terms of meeting the infrastructure needs of the country..." (Official Gazette, 1983: p. 160).

The law has not covered or determined any mitigation and/or disaster risk reduction activities as the responsibility of the ministry and related institutions.

On the other hand, by the establishment of the law and the ministry, a new directorate (General Directorate of Disaster Affairs) was also developed. However, in 2009, this directorate was abolished and became part of the Turkish Republic Prime Ministry Disaster and Emergency Management Presidency.

In 1985, a new development law was established. This law (Law Number 3194) is still in use and effective all over the country. The former development law (Law Number 6785, put into effect in 1956) was insufficient and could not meet the necessary and contemporary needs of building and inspection issues. It was one of the most comprehensive laws related to development issues and building codes. This law has been expected to have the capacity of guiding all professionals participating in building production processes. It has also been expected from the law to achieve best guiding practices on building inspection processes. Former experiences related to legal and administrative concepts as well as coping with disaster efforts have formed a rich source in terms of lessons from past failures. However, the current law (Law Number 3194) has been criticized by building professionals in the country due to its fragmented and partial structure which excludes the integrated approach to coping with disasters.

3.12 Slight movements in the shift from healer to protector state: advancements during the 1990s

Two important rehabilitation and post-disaster intentional legal developments should be mentioned from this period. The first (the Regulation of Disaster Related Emergency Assistance Organization and Planning Fundamentals, Regulation Number 88/12777) was put into effect four years before the devastating Erzincan earthquake of 1992 (March 13, with a magnitude of 6.8, 653 casualties and 8,057 damaged buildings). The regulation was composed of eight sections and 76 articles. In the first article, the aim of the legislation states that the development of emergency assistance organizations is needed to sustain rapid and effective response to disaster areas in terms of first aid and emergency aid to the victims (Official Gazette, 1988: p. 9). The other legislative development was put into effect the same year, after the Erzincan earthquake. That law (the Law for Running the Organization and Application of Services Related to The Damages Which Occurred after the Earthquake in Erzincan, Gümüşhane and Tunceli, as well as for the Damages in Şırnak and Çukurca, Law Number 3838) was again a typical example of a case-specific and rehabilitative approach application for disaster-stricken areas. The 1992 earthquake shook a populated urban area of Erzincan province. This disaster proved that earthquakes damage not only the physical environment but also the socio-economic and psycho-social structures in society in terms of migration, post-traumatic concepts, unemployment, extensive losses in production and stock markets, and interruption of workplace and public sector continuity. The Disaster Law (of 7269), which is still in use, was insufficient to meet most of these needs, and it did not have a holistic view of the disaster phenomenon. That's why Law 3838 was established, as a case-specific law, similar examples of which had been seen following previous disaster events.

Following a mud-flood disaster which caused 74 casualties and left 300 demolished buildings in the town of Senirken (July 13, 1995), another post-disaster intentional law was established on July 23, 1995. The Law for Running Services Related to the Damage and Destruction Due to Natural Disaster (Law Number 4123) was produced after observations and analysis that Law 3838, which was put into effect following the Erzincan earthquake of 1992, had been applied successfully. According to this relative success in post-disaster efforts, the new law was published in order to expand similar successful applications across the country. However, the publication was prepared in a hurry, causing deficiencies within the law. As a result, the law had to be revised after some time with other legislative applications. By this law, it can be observed that the state still placed importance on post-disaster activities without taking account of pre-disaster applications. Specifically, the law organized the material and financial assistance to the disaster-affected areas in terms of credits, loans and debiting issues of the victims, reconstruction works and related issues through articles 1–9 (Official Gazette, 1995: pp. 1–3).

Following the destructive Dinar-Afyon earthquake on January 10, 1995, which killed 90 people, another case-specific law was put into effect. Law Number 4133 was produced to meet the deficiencies of the former disaster-related laws and regulations.

The period of disaster and case-specific legal arrangement was followed by a comprehensive regulation which aimed at enhancing mitigation activities in terms of producing safe and healthy environments. "The Regulation for the Buildings that Will be Constructed in the Disaster Prone Areas" was published in 1997 (February 9). The regulation aimed to guide building professionals and related institutions participating in building production processes that include construction of all public and private buildings in disaster-prone areas. The regulation included three kinds of natural disasters: earthquake, fire and flood, whereas all other types of hazards and disasters were not included (Official Gazette, 1997: pp. 191–275). In addition, earthquakes were covered in detail in terms of technical aspects, such as structural issues among the regulation, while the other two hazard types had limited coverage within the regulation. However, the earthquake concept covered mostly structural issues, while other issues of crucial importance were not covered, such as the constructional, building materials and non-structural components of a building. This regulation did not underline the importance of the building and environment relationship in terms of safety and health concepts. As a result, the regulation cannot be accepted as a holistic approach to risk and safety concepts.

In line with the rehabilitative and "healer state" approach of the governments, the Prime Ministry Crisis Management Center was established in 1997 under the regulation number 96/716 (January 9) in order to organize response and recovery efforts following hazardous events.

3.13 The milestone of understanding disaster phenomena in Turkey: the 1999 Marmara earthquake and its impact

The years 1998 and 1999 were remarkable in terms of destructive effects of disasters. First, the Western Black Sea region of the country was affected by large-scale floods in 1998, which caused severe casualties and damage to the built environment. In the same year, a powerful earthquake struck Adana province, killing 146 people and damaging 31,463 buildings in the region (on June 27, with a magnitude of 6.2).

Unfortunately, 1999 will never be forgotten in terms of the heavy impacts of natural disasters in Turkey. On August 17, 1999, a strong earthquake shook Western Turkey, the Marmara region, with a magnitude of 7.6 (in some sources, 7.4), killing at least 17,118 people. The intensity of the seismic movement was so large that a number of provinces, including Karamürsel, Gölcük, Değirmendere, Yalova, Adapazarı, Kocaeli, Düzce, Bolu, İstanbul, Bursa, Zonguldak and Eskişehir, located in different geographical regions of Turkey, were affected, ranging from severe to slight damage. The earthquake produced a 130 km long surface fault between the Gulf of Izmit and Düzce province. The seismic waves destroyed not only residential areas (such as multi-story apartment blocks) but also many industrial facilities. Just three months later, another strong seismic movement, with a magnitude of 7.2, destroyed a nearby region in Western Turkey, killing almost 1,000 people. The Bolu-Düzce earthquake (of November 12) caused a second trauma among the people of Turkey. In the period between August 1999 and July 2000, following the 1999 earthquakes, many legal and administrative documents were published (38 laws and decree laws, 28 enactments, 6 regulations, 17 statements and 9 circulars). If all of these legislative publications are analyzed, it can be seen clearly that most are legislative arrangements prepared for disaster consequences in order to organize and run services and provide aid following disasters. In that sense, the governmental organizations did not take into account the root causes of the disasters, and instead produced short-term policies in order to find solutions for post-disaster activities. The disasters far exceeded the coping capacity of the state.

On November 15, 1999, a new administrative institution was established under the title of Turkey Emergency Management Presidency by a decree law (Law Number 583). The Presidency was converted to General Directorate in the year 2000 by Decree Law 600.

In the same year (December 27, 1999), another decree law (Law Number 587) was published releasing the establishment of the Mandatory Earthquake Insurance. For the first time, a compulsory insurance system for hazard reduction was to be put into effect by the government. The basic expectations from the law were to develop a pool which could be used not only for post-disaster activities (such as reconstruction) but also for pre-disaster activities (such as risk reduction efforts, including urban regeneration projects). The following year started with the establishment of the Natural Disaster Insurances Institution (on September 27, 2000), which requires homeowners to buy earthquake insurance for their homes.

On March 3, 2000, another decree law (595) related to the re-organization of building inspections was put into effect. According to this remarkable shift in building production processes, it was aimed at enhancing and developing more effective inspection activities in order to secure urban safety and health. Buildings were to be inspected by private building inspection firms according to the new law, meaning building inspection responsibility was to be transferred from public institutions to the private sector. However, the Decree Law Number 595 was canceled by the Turkish court due to legal and administrative insufficiencies within the law. As a result, a new law, the Building Inspection Law (Law Number 4708), was published in 2001. This law has been used all over the country. The expectation from that legal and administrative advancement was very high. On the other hand, the problems and gaps related to the law have been discussed within society for years.

3.14 Important developments in the last decade

Between 2003 and 2010, three major disasters were experienced: the 2003 Bingöl earthquake of magnitude 6.4, which killed 176 people and destroyed almost 6,000 buildings; the 2009 İstanbul–İkitelli–Çatalca flood disaster, which killed 31 people and destroyed urban settlements, including residential and industrial areas; and the 2010 Elazığ–Başyurt–Karakoçan earthquake of magnitude 6.0, which killed 41 people and damaged almost 8,154 buildings.

The last legal and administrative development in this period was the establishment of the Prime Ministry, Disaster and Emergency Management Presidency (Law Number 5902). By this law, three formerly established major institutions working in disaster coping issues were abolished. Those were: the Civil Defense General Directorate, the Disaster Affairs General Directorate and the Turkey Emergency Management Presidency.

4 Implications from the historical analysis of disaster coping efforts in Turkey

The following implications are obtained from the theoretical analysis of legal and institutional development experiences of the Turkish disaster coping approach from a historical perspective.

1. The legal and administrative advancements in terms of coping policies and struggles with disaster phenomena can be organized within six basic periods (Figure 3.5).
2. Following the 1999 earthquakes, the building inspection law is considered the foremost advancement within disaster coping policy change. Until that time, failure in hazardous events was strictly bound to the lack of effective building inspection legislation. However, the new law developed to organize and enforce effective inspection activity still has gaps and deficiencies in terms of legislative and administrative structures. The traditional building

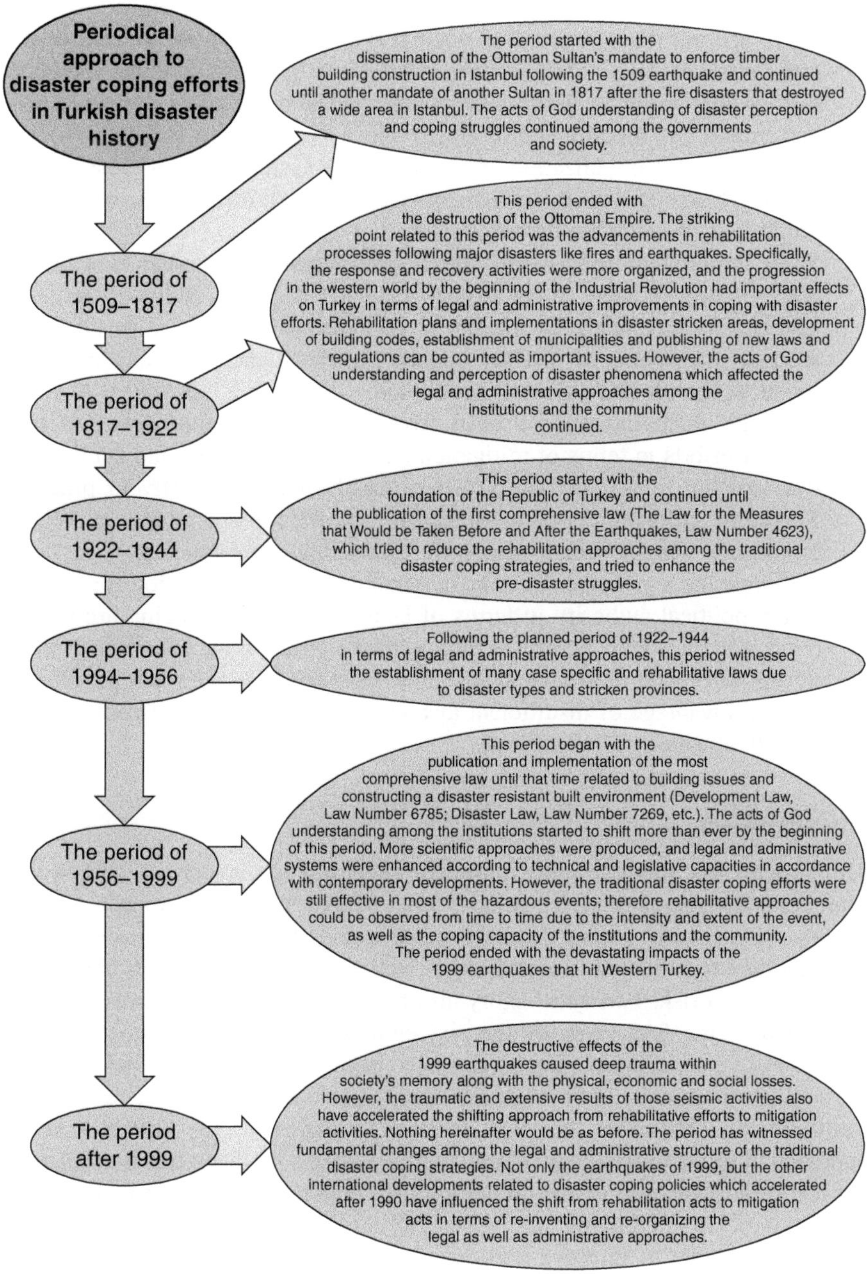

Figure 3.5 Periods of disaster coping efforts in Turkey's 500-year disaster history.

production process still has an effect on the inspection system and this is seen as a barrier to the success of the ongoing inspection efforts.

3 There are too many legislative documents, all of which are related to the disaster issues. Some of those documents cause overlaps, conflicts and complexity that building professionals and other participants cannot easily understand. As a result, those complexities between the legislative documents affect the organization of administrative systems, which causes insufficient efforts and/or misunderstanding among professionals within the production of a safe built environment.

4 There is an urgent need to unify the disaster legislation in order to achieve a holistic point of view of the disaster coping efforts. In addition, the legal framework also needs an integrated administrative structure to take into account all aspects of disaster concepts without excluding any physical, social, economic and environmental issues.

5 Although there has been a shift from rehabilitative approaches to pre-disaster efforts in terms of mitigation among the legislative and administrative structure, that shift has not been conducted consistently in practice. Therefore, enforcement of the necessary knowledge and codes, as well as ordinances, has not been as successful as shifting understanding.

6 Although the legislative structure has changed, the rehabilitation approaches of the political authority in terms of healer state understanding are still in use due to the social, economic and political culture of the community. Politicians still prefer to use the healer state approach from time to time in order to take advantage of insufficient awareness and perception of society, specifically during election periods.

5 Conclusion

This chapter has attempted to explore the legal and administrative shift in disaster understanding and coping policies in a 500-year period of Turkey's disaster history. The disaster coping struggles have changed over the centuries due to scientific and technical advancements, as well as intellectual savings among the communities at risk. Turkey's history also reveals that shift, which was recorded and dated to the first years of the sixteenth century in the Ottoman Empire period. For years, disaster phenomena have been seen as acts of God, and still the Turkish community believes in this fate, which orients the legal and administrative efforts. Therefore, the shift from a "healer state" to "protector state" approach in terms of legal and administrative systems has been transferring very slowly to the daily life of the community. In conclusion, it is not sufficient to develop new laws and regulations specifically following hazardous events, but it is more important to improve and enhance the capacity of the community to understand and internalize those developments within their usual habits and environmental perceptions.

Note

1 Village Law, Law Number 442, acceptance date: March 18, 1924, put into effect on April 7, 1924 (published in the Official Gazette, No. 68, Vol. 5, p. 336).

References

Ambraseys, N.N., 2001. The Earthquake of 10 July 1894 in the Gulf of Izmit (Turkey) and its Relation to the Earthquake of 17 August 1999, *Journal of Seismology*, Vol. 5, No. 1, pp. 117–128.

Ambraseys, N.N. and Finkel, C.F., 2006. *Seismic Activities in Turkey and Neighbouring Areas: A Historical Research, 1500–1800*, trans. M.U. Koçak, Ankara: The Scientific and Technological Research Council of Turkey.

Ayataç, H., 2007. The International Diffusion of Planning Ideas: The Case of Istanbul, Turkey, *Journal of Planning History*, Vol. 6, No. 2, pp. 114–137.

Barış, Ş., Nakajima, J., Hasegawa, A., Honkura, Y., Ito, A. and Üçer, S.B., 2005. Three-Dimensional Structure of Vp, Vs and Vp/Vs in the Upper Crust of the Marmara Region, NW Turkey, *Earth Planets Space*, Vol. 57, pp. 1019–1038.

Bayrak, M.O., 1996. *İstanbul History* (in Turkish), İstanbul: İnkılap Kitabevi.

Çelik, Z., 1986. *The Remaking of Istanbul: Portrait of an Ottoman City in the Nineteenth Century*, California: University of California Press.

Eğilmezer, S.M., 2010. Fire of İstanbul, Epidemic of Anatolia (in Turkish), *Avemeli*, electronic journal, No. 20, pp. 14–18, June. Available from: www.avemeli.com/default.asp (accessed in 2011).

Ergünay, O., 2011. *How the 1999 Earthquakes Changed the Disaster Legislation: Where We Are in Terms of Legislation* (in Turkish), 1st Earthquake Engineering and Seismology Conference of Turkey, October 11–14, METU, Ankara.

Evangelatou-Notara, F., 2001. Natural Disasters in the Greek Sources of Secondary Priority (14th–19th Centuries), in *Natural Disasters in the Ottoman Empire*, ed. Elizabeth Zachariadou, trans. G.Ç. Güven and S. Öztürk, İstanbul: Tarih Vakfı Yurt Yayınları.

Griffiths, J.H.P., Irfanoğlu, A. and Pujol, S., 2007. Istanbul at the Threshold: An Evaluation of the Seismic Risk in Istanbul, *Earthquake Spectra*, Vol. 23, No. 1, pp. 63–75.

Hebert, H., Schindele, F., Altınok, Y., Alpar, B. and Gazioğlu, C., 2005. Tsunami Hazard in the Marmara Sea (Turkey): A Numerical Approach to Discuss Active Faulting and Impact on the Istanbul Coastal Areas, *Marine Geology*, Vol. 215, No. 1–2, pp. 23–43.

Kalemli, H., 2010. The Aid From Abroad in the Earthquake of Erzurum in 1924 (in Turkish), *Journal of Social Sciences Institute*, Atatürk University, Vol. 14, No. 2, pp. 1–19.

Koçak, A., 2010. A Study with a Purpose to Determine Structural Defects and Faults: The Seismic Risks of the Existing Buildings in Various Districts of Istanbul/Turkey, *Scientific Research and Essays*, Vol. 5, No. 5, pp. 468–483.

Kundak, S. and Türkoğlu, H.D., 2007. Evaluation of Earthquake Risk Parameters in the Historical Site of İstanbul, *ARI: The Bulletin of the İstanbul Technical University*, Vol. 55, No. 1, pp. 53–66.

METU, 1998. *Preliminary Report for Sustaining and Developing Revisions for New Inspection and Disaster Resistant Building Measures Through the Development Law and Regulations of Law Number 3194* (in Turkish), Middle East Technical University Earthquake Engineering Research Center, eds P. Gülkan and B. Duygu, Project No: 97–03–03–01–09, project submitted to Republic of Turkey Prime Ministry Housing

Development Administration of Turkey and the Ministry of Public Works and Settlement.
Official Gazette, 1924a. Village Law (Köy Kanunu), *Official Newspaper of the Grand National Assembly of Turkey*, No. 68, p. 336, April 7.
Official Gazette, 1924b. Law for Arranging Punishments Related to Development and Local Governmental Issues (Umur-u Belediyeye Müteallik Ahkam-ı Cezaiye Hakkında Kanun), *Official Newspaper of the Grand National Assembly of Turkey*, No. 70, p. 427, May 17.
Official Gazette, 1924c. Law for Reconstruction and Rehabilitation Financial Activities Arranged for Victims Affected from the Earthquake Occurred in Erzurum and Neighboring Provinces (Erzurum ve Civârı Vilâyetlerde Hareket-i Arzdan Yıkılan Mesâkinin İnşâsı ve Felâketzedegânın Barındırılması İçin Yapılacak Mübâyiâtın Pazarlık Sûretiyle İcrâsına Dâir Kânûn Sûreti), *Official Newspaper of the Grand National Assembly of Turkey*, No. 79, p. 1, November 24.
Official Gazette, 1930a. The Municipality Law (Belediye Kanunu), *Official Newspaper of the Grand National Assembly of Turkey*, No. 1471, pp. 8821–8839, April 14.
Official Gazette, 1930b. Public Sanitation Law (Umumi Hıfzısıhha Kanunu), *Official Newspaper of the Grand National Assembly of Turkey*, No. 1489, pp. 8895–8910, May 6.
Official Gazette, 1933. Municipality Building and Roads Law (Belediye Yapı ve Yollar Kanunu), *Official Newspaper of the Grand National Assembly of Turkey*, No. 2433, pp. 2755–2760, June 21.
Official Gazette, 1939. The Law for Arranging the Organization and Works of Development Ministry (Nafıa Vekâleti Teşkilât ve Vazifelerine dair Kanun), *Official Newspaper of the Grand National Assembly of Turkey*, No. 4219, pp. 11831–11842, May 30.
Official Gazette, 1940. Post-Disaster Assistance Law for the Victims of the Earthquake who Suffered from the Earthquake in Erzincan Province and Other Areas (Erzincan'da ve Erzincan Depreminden Müteessir Olan Mıntıkalarda Zarar Görenlere Yapılacak Yardımlar Hakkında Kanun), *Official Newspaper of the Grand National Assembly of Turkey*, No. 4416, pp. 13205–13212, January 25.
Official Gazette, 1943. The Law for Protection Against Flood Water and Floods (Taşkın Sulara ve Su Baskınlarına Karşı Korunma), *Official Newspaper of the Grand National Assembly of Turkey*, No. 5310, pp. 4313–4328, January 21.
Official Gazette, 1944. The Law for the Measures that Would Be Taken Before and After the Earthquakes (Yer Sarsıntılarından Evvel ve Sonra Alınacak Tedbirler Hakkında Kanun), *Official Newspaper of the Grand National Assembly of Turkey*, No. 5763, pp. 7337–7348, July 22.
Official Gazette, 1953. The Law About Building Construction Encouragement and Unauthorised Buildings (Bina Yapımını Teşvik ve İzinsiz Yapılan Binalar Hakkında Kanun), *Official Newspaper of the Grand National Assembly of Turkey*, No. 8470, pp. 6841–6848, July 29.
Official Gazette, 1954. The Law About the Re-location of Kale Town of Tavas District which Expose to Landslide (Tavas Kazasının Heyelana Maruz Kale Nahiyesinin Yerinin Değiştirilmesi Hakkında Kanun), *Official Newspaper of the Grand National Assembly of Turkey*, No. 8664, pp. 8753–8784, March 22.
Official Gazette, 1955. The Law About the Re-location of Neighborhoods in Lice Town which Expose to Rockfall Threat (Lice Kasabasında Kayaların Tehdidine Maruz Mahallelerin Yerlerinin Değiştirilmesi Hakkında Kanun), *Official Newspaper of the Grand National Assembly of Turkey*, No. 9013, pp. 11929–11952, May 27.

Official Gazette, 1956a. The Law About the Arrangement of Aid for People Who Suffered from the Fire in Gerze and the Floods in Lüleburgaz and İnece (Gerze Yangınından, Lüleburgaz ve İnece'de Su Baskınından Zarar Görenlere Yapılacak Yardımlar Hakkında Kanun), *Official Newspaper of the Grand National Assembly of Turkey*, No. 9248, pp. 13757–13772, March 2.

Official Gazette, 1956b. The Law About the Arrangement of Aid for People Who Suffered from the Resultant Disasters Between 1955 and 1956 in the Provinces of Aydın, Balıkesir, Bilecik, Edirne, Eskişehir, Kırklareli, Konya and Denizli (Aydın, Balıkesir, Bilecik, Edirne, Eskişehir, Kırklareli, Konya ve Denizli Vilayetlerinde 1955–56 Yıllarında Afetlerden Zarar Görenlere Yapılacak Yardım Hakkında Kanun), *Official Newspaper of the Grand National Assembly of Turkey*, No. 9345, pp. 14677–14708, June 29.

Official Gazette, 1956c. The Development Law (İmar Kanunu), *Official Newspaper of the Grand National Assembly of Turkey*, No. 9359, pp. 15109–15124, July 16.

Official Gazette, 1957. The Law About the Arrangement of Aid for People Who Suffered from the Resultant Earthquakes in the Provinces of Muğla, Denizli, Bolu, Aydın and Sakarya (Muğla, Denizli, Bolu, Aydın ve Sakarya Vilayetleri Dahilinde Vukua Gelen Yer Sarsıntısında Zarar Görenlere Yapılacak Yardım Hakkında Kanun), *Official Newspaper of the Grand National Assembly of Turkey*, No. 9638, pp. 17341–17356, June 20.

Official Gazette, 1958. The Law for the Establishment of the Ministry of Development and Settlement (İmar ve İskan Vekaletinin Kuruluşu Hakkında Kanunu), *Official Newspaper of the Grand National Assembly of Turkey*, No. 9906, pp. 19303–19322, May 14.

Official Gazette, 1959. Disaster Law (Umumi Hayata Müessir Afetler Dolayısıyla Alınacak Tedbirlerle Yapılacak Yardımlara Dair Kanun), *Official Newspaper of the Grand National Assembly of Turkey*, No. 10213, pp. 21695–21714, May 25.

Official Gazette, 1983. The Law for the Establishment of the Ministry of Public Works and Settlement (Bayındırlık ve İskan Bakanlığının Teşkilat ve Görevleri Hakkında Kanun Hükmünde Kararname), *Official Newspaper of the Grand National Assembly of Turkey*, No. 18251, pp. 1–432, December 14.

Official Gazette, 1988. The Regulation of Disaster Related Emergency Assistance Organization and Planning Fundamentals (Afetlere İlişkin Acil Yardım Teşkilatı ve Planlama Esaslarına Dair Yönetmelik), *Official Newspaper of the Grand National Assembly of Turkey*, No. 19808, pp. 1–96, May 8.

Official Gazette, 1995. The Law for Running Services Related to the Damage and Destruction Due to the Natural Disaster (Tabiî Afet Nedeniyle Meydana Gelen Hasar ve Tahribata İlişkin Hizmetlerin Yürütülmesine Dair Kanun), *Official Newspaper of the Grand National Assembly of Turkey*, No. 22354, pp. 1–3, July 25.

Official Gazette, 1997. Regulation for the Buildings that Will Be Constructed in the Disaster Zones (Afet Bölgelerinde Yapılacak Yapılar Hakkında Yönetmelik), *Official Newspaper of the Grand National Assembly of Turkey*, No. 23098, pp. 1–576, September 2.

Özcan, K., 2006. Urban Reforms of Tanzimat: Early Planning Practices in the Establishment Process of the Turkish Development System (Tanzimat'ın kent reformları: Türk imar sisteminin kuruluş sürecinde erken planlama deneyimleri (1839–1908)), *Osmanlı Bilimi Araştırmaları*, No. 2, Vol. 7, pp. 149–180.

Özden, A.T., 2011. Building Inspection and Disaster Relation in the History and Today of Turkey: A Log of the Disasters History for Architects (Geçmişte ve Günümüzde Türkiye'de Yapı Denetimi – Afet İlişkisi: Mimarın Afetler Tarihçesi İçin Seyir

Defteri), in *File: Disaster and Architecture*, ed. E.M. Komut, Chamber of Architects of Turkey, Ankara Branch, No. 26, pp. 67–79, September.

Özgür, H. and Azaklı, S., 2001. Fires and Municipal Services in the Ottoman Empire (Osmanlı'da Yangınlar ve Belediye Hizmetleri), Gazi University, *Journal of İİBF*, No. 1, pp. 153–172.

Özyurt, E.D., 2007. *The Changes of the Urban Texture in Galata After Historical Fires Between the Second Half of 19th Century and the Beginning of the 20th Century and Examination of the Situation of Conservation* (*19. Yüzyılın İkinci Yarısı ve 20. Yüzyıl Başındakı Yangınlar Sonrası Galata'da Kentsel Dokunun Değişimi ve Korunmuşluk Durumunun İncelenmesi*), Unpublished Master's Thesis, Graduate School of Natural and Applied Sciences, İstanbul Technical University, November, 127 pages.

Pampal, S. and Özmen, B., 2006. *Earthquake Zone Maps of Turkey (Türkiye Deprem Bölgeleri Haritaları)*, 17th Geophysical Congress and Exhibition Conference, November 14–17, Chamber of Geophysical Engineers of Turkey, MTA Cultural Center, Ankara.

Sipahioğlu, S. and Alptekin, Ö., 1988. Present Appearance of the Earthquake Problem in Turkey, *Journal of Jeofizik*, Chamber of Geophysical Engineers of Turkey, Vol. 2, pp. 151–183.

TBMM, 1997. *Turkish Assembly Research Commission Report for Reduction of Human Casualties and other Losses Pertaining from Natural Disasters*, the Grand National Assembly of Turkey, Report No: 01.1.GEÇ.10/58–72, Number: 345, June 20.

TBMM, 1999. *Report of The Research Commission of The Turkish Parliament*, The Grand National Assembly of Turkey, Report No: 10/66, 67, 68, 69, 70, December 23.

Tekeli, İ., 1999. Yüzyılda İstanbul Metropol Alanının Dönüşümü, in *Modernleşme Sürecinde Osmanlı Kentleri* (original title: *Villes ottomans a la fin de l'empire*), 2nd edition, eds Paul Dumont and Francois Georgeon, trans. A. Berktay, İstanbul: Tarih Vakfı Yurt Publications.

Tekeli, İ., 2006. The Development of the Urban Planning Idea in Turkey (Türkiye'de Kent Planlaması Düşüncesinin Gelişimi), *Yapı Journal*, No. 291, pp. 37–41, February.

Yeşilkaya, N., 2007. İstanbul Beyazıt Square and the Design Traces Oriented to the Urban Space in the Second Half of the 19th Century: Axis, Arcade, Building Facade (19. Yüzyılın İkinci Yarısında İstanbul Beyazıt Meydanı ve Kentsel Mekâna Yönelik Tasarım İzleri: Aks, Arkad, Yapı Yüzü), in *File: Cities and Their Squares* (Dosya: Kentler ve Meydanları), *Journal of Mimarlık*, No. 334, March–April.

4 The legal framework of community-based land administration in tsunami-impacted areas of Aceh

A case study in Baitussalam Sub-District, Aceh Besar District, Indonesia

Taqwaddin Husin and Teuku Alvisyahrin[1]

1 Introduction

The Great 2004 Indian Ocean Tsunami caused a massive loss of lives, destruction of infrastructure and houses, and brought various legal issues in Aceh, one of which concerned land administration. To cope with the problem, the Government of Indonesia, as part of its post-tsunami reconstruction initiative, produced several regulations. This chapter describes the way the local communities reacted to such legal frameworks, with a focus on the implementation of land mapping and registration in resolving land rights issues in the tsunami-impacted areas of Aceh.

As well as the staggering numbers – over 220,000 people dead or missing; 2,618 km of roads destroyed or damaged; 139,000 homes destroyed or damaged; 3,415 schools destroyed or damaged; and over 500 hospitals and health clinics destroyed or damaged (BRR *in* Taqwaddin and Alvisyahrin, 2012) – the mega-disaster also brought about some critical issues in the community that had to be dealt with by the government, one of which was land rights. The 2004 tsunami disaster brought about a negative impact on the management, control, and ownership of lands in Aceh. No less than 7,000 ha of agricultural lands were affected by saline coastal sediments and erosion, significantly reducing soil fertility. Countless land boundary marks, including natural boundaries such as trees and trails, vanished in the disaster. Overall, about 300,000 land parcels were directly affected by the tsunami, 170,000 of which were those in urban areas and 130,000 in suburban village areas, with at least 15,000 of land parcels inundated by sea water (Fitzpatrick, 2010).

To address all post-tsunami reconstruction issues, the Government of Indonesia produced a series of regulations that can chronologically be described as follows:

- Presidential Instruction Number 1/2005 regarding the Emergency Response Activities and Preparations for the Post-Earthquake and Tsunami Disaster

Rehabilitation and Reconstruction in the Regions of Nanggroe Aceh Darussalam Province and North Sumatra Province, issued on March 2, 2005;

- Presidential Regulation Number 30/2005 regarding the Master Plan for the post-Earthquake and Tsunami Disaster Rehabilitation and Reconstruction of the Regions and Communities of Nanggroe Aceh Darussalam Province and Nias Island, North Sumatra Province, issued on April 15, 2005;
- Governmental Regulation in lieu of Law (PERPU) Number 2/2005 regarding the Agency for the Rehabilitation and Reconstruction of the Regions and Communities of Nanggroe Aceh Darussalam Province and Nias Island, North Sumatra Province, issued on April 16, 2005;
- Head of the National Land Agency (BPN) Decree Number 114-II/2005 regarding the Guidelines for Land Registration for Tsunami Impacted Areas;
- Governmental Regulation in lieu of Law (PERPU) Number 2/2007 regarding the Legal Aspect of the Post-Earthquake and Tsunami Disaster Rehabilitation and Reconstruction of the Regions and Communities of Nanggroe Aceh Darussalam Province and Nias Island, North Sumatra Province, issued on September 6, 2007.

In order to implement Article 7 of PERPU Number 2/2007, the national government issued a policy for land mapping and certification that would actively involve land owners and community members. This policy was in line with a program titled *Reconstruction of Aceh Land Administration System* (RALAS) described in the Head of BPN Decree Number 114-II/2005. Although it is often contended that this program was successfully executed as substantiated by more than 220,000 land certificates distributed to tsunami-impacted land owners in Aceh using a community adjudication approach (Multi Donor Fund, Java Reconstruction Fund, and The World Bank, 2012), there are limitations in terms of the treatment of customary land rights in the intersection with the ownership registration as reported by empirical research (Fitzpatrick, 2012). This chapter intends to add further empirical analysis based on the primary information obtained by the author who has, in his status as the Coordinator for the Cash-for-Work program, directly been involved in the support of reconstruction activities of tsunami-affected communities, including the residents of Baitussalam Sub-District, Aceh Besar District (Rinaldi and Taqwaddin, 2011).

This chapter intends to describe, first, the development of unique legal frameworks for the implementation of community-based land administration in the tsunami-impacted areas of Aceh – in this regard, the discussion focuses on the regulations that governed the handling of land issues of tsunami victims; second, the typical land right issues in the tsunami-impacted areas where both formal and customary land regimes have co-existed since the colonial period; and, third, the struggles for the reconstruction of the land administration system to overcome the pluralistic land regime in post-tsunami disaster recovery.

The authors attempted qualitative-descriptive research to employ both normative and sociological approaches to the disaster law. The normative approach involves a chronological review to determine the norms related to land administration. The sociological approach is used to examine the facts on the implementation of land administration in the particular areas (Rinaldi and Taqwaddin, 2011). Empirical research was conducted in 13 *gampong* (villages) located in the Baitussalam Sub-District, Aceh Besar District, Indonesia, i.e. Cot Paya, Klieng Cot Aron, Klieng Meuria, Labuy, Lam Asan, Lambada Lhok, Lampineung, Lam Ujong, Miruk Lamreudep, Baet, Blang Krueng, Cadek, and Kajhu. This sub-district has an area of 36 km^2 or approximately 3652 ha and was one of the most devastated sub-districts of Aceh in the 2004 tsunami disaster. The community members whose lands were affected by the tsunami were used as samples applying purposive sampling technique. Supporting information was also obtained from the head of Baitussalam Sub-District, the Head of the Village, and other community leaders. Data were generated through semi-structured interview and subsequently analyzed using a qualitative approach.

2 Development of the legal framework for community-based land administration in Aceh

As a social asset, land helps maintain social integrity within the community, whereas as a capital asset, land serves as an important economic resource for businesses and investment (Rubaie, 2007). In order to provide legal protection and security for the disaster-affected communities, the blueprint of the Indonesian government for the post-tsunami reconstruction was started with the plan for land administration.

In Indonesia, land administration has been governed under Law Number 5/1960 concerning Basic Regulation on Agrarian Principles (hereinafter referred to as "UUPA 1960"). In this law, it is stated that the national agrarian law is based on adat (customary) law concerning lands which should be simple and should guarantee legal security for all the people of Indonesia without excluding the elements contained in law on religion.[2] This implies that, although the agrarian law is based on the customary law that is simple in nature, its existence should guarantee legal security at all time. Furthermore, with regard to the implementation of the State's power in governing land issues, Article 2 and Article 3 of UUPA 1960 explain that the right to control reserved by the State entitles the government the authority to:

a regulate and implement the designation, utilization, reservation, and maintenance of the earth, water, and airspace;
b determine and regulate legal relations between persons and the earth, water, and airspace; and
c determine and regulate legal relations between persons and legal acts concerning the earth, water, and airspace.

The authority reserved by the State's right to control is basically executed to achieve the highest prosperity of the people in terms of happiness, welfare, and freedom in the community and legal State of Indonesia that is independent, sovereign, and prosperous.

The authority to grant land rights, in principle, is the implementation of the executive power of the government. This authority stipulated in Article 2 of UUPA is executed by the governmental institutions that are concerned with land affairs, i.e. the State Minister of Agrarian Affairs/the Head of the National Land Agency, and the Head of the Provincial Land Agency, and the Head of the District or Municipal Land Agency according to land right category and land size (Ilyas, 2005).

The guarantee of legal security that shall be implemented in land regulation and registration covers the registered right status, subject of right, and object of right. Land registration produces certificates as a proof of the granted land right. Stipulations concerning land registration are described by the Governmental Regulation Number 24/1997 regarding Land Registration.[3]

In the context of the 2004 earthquake and tsunami that ravaged Aceh, land issues were among the most challenging problems that the government faced in the recovery effort. These issues include loss of land due to subsidence in the coastal areas, death of land owners, absence of beneficiaries, loss of land boundaries, and loss of proof of ownership/land certificates (Rinaldi and Taqwaddin, 2011).

There are several regulations that constitute the legal framework for implementing community-based land administration in the tsunami-impacted areas of Aceh. This framework was applied in resolving land disputes among the tsunami victims in Aceh (Taqwaddin *et al.*, 2012). The regulations can be described chronologically as follows.[4]

2.1 The 1945 Constitution of the Republic of Indonesia

The 1945 Constitution of the Republic of Indonesia, which has been amended four times, is the highest form and source of all laws applicable in Indonesia. For this reason, all regulations and laws shall refer to and shall not conflict with the norms described in the Constitution.

In the fourth paragraph of the Preamble of the 1945 Constitution, it is clearly stated "in order to form a government of the State of Indonesia which shall protect the entire Indonesian nation and native land…". This statement provides the constitutional basis for the implementation of the State's responsibility and obligation to protect its entire citizens and prevent its environment from possible degradation or pollution (Asshiddiqie, 2010; Hardjasoemantri, 1993). In this regard, the unitary State of Indonesia is also obliged to protect its entire citizens and native land from disasters, which is a fundamental human right.

The derivative of the above-quoted statement in the fourth paragraph of the Preamble is subsequently described in articles concerning the human right. For example, Article 28C Paragraph (1), "Every person shall have the right to develop him/herself through the fulfillment of their basic needs." Also, Article 28D Paragraph (1), "Every person shall have the right to the recognition, guarantee, protection and legal certainty of just laws as well as equal treatment before the law."

This constitutional norm essentially provided the foundation for the drafting and enactment of Law Number 24/2007 concerning the Disaster Management in Indonesia.

2.2 Law Number 5/1960 concerning basic regulation on agrarian principles (UUPA 1960)

This law provides the primary legal basis for the control, ownership, and management of land. This law also confirms customary (adat) law norms as the legal basis for the National Agrarian Law. Article 5 of UUPA 1960 states that the agrarian law which applies to the earth, water, and airspace is adat law as far as it is not in conflict with the national and State's interests with due regard to the elements based on law on religion.

Furthermore, Article 19 of UUPA 1960 explains that in order to guarantee legal security, the government shall conduct the land registration program throughout the territory of the Republic of Indonesia according to provisions set forth in the Governmental Regulation. The purpose of land registration is to provide legal security in conducting land affairs. The registration of land right will result in the assurance of land right, subject of right, object of right, and the legal security associated with them.

2.3 Presidential Regulation (PERPRES) Number 30/2005 regarding the master plan for the post-earthquake and tsunami disaster rehabilitation and reconstruction of the regions and communities of Nanggroe Aceh Darussalam Province and Nias Island, North Sumatra Province

In essence, the legal basis for the drafting of Presidential Regulation Number 30/2005 is the Presidential Instruction Number 1/2005 regarding the Emergency Response Activities and Preparations for the Post-Earthquake and Tsunami Disaster Rehabilitation and Reconstruction in the Regions of Nanggroe Aceh Darussalam Province and North Sumatra Province. It is explained in this Presidential Regulation that legal issues regarding lands are matters that need to be handled urgently for they concern the civil right of land that needs to be reinstated, guaranteed, and protected. The rehabilitation and reconstruction of land should immediately be started with due regard to elements of culture, religion, customs, and regional condition. This regulation also emphasizes that the reinstatement of land rights is one of the most important parts of the post-tsunami disaster reconstruction effort.

2.4 Governmental Regulation in lieu of Law (PERPU) Number 2/2005 regarding the agency for the rehabilitation and reconstruction of the regions and communities of Nanggroe Aceh Darussalam Province and Nias Island, North Sumatra Province

This regulation, which is equivalent to a law, was drafted to establish the Agency for the Rehabilitation and Reconstruction of Aceh and Nias (BRR) with the main mission of tackling the urgent situation and conditions post-tsunami disaster in Aceh and Nias Island. This agency was charged with implementing specific rehabilitation and reconstruction efforts that were systematic, focused, integrated, and comprehensive by involving and accommodating the aspirations and needs of the community in Nanggroe Aceh Darussalam and Nias Island, North Sumatra Province.

The rehabilitation effort includes the restoration and recovery of:

a infrastructure and facilities for public services;
b infrastructure and facilities for the economic sector, including banking, finance, and businesses, particularly small and medium enterprises;
c infrastructure and facilities for health and psycho-social services;
d infrastructure and facilities for religious and indigenous activities;
e infrastructure and facilities for education and culture;
f land rights and building rights;
g infrastructure for proper temporary shelters for displaced persons; and
h infrastructure and facilities directly related to the revitalization of local governance and life of the community.

The reconstruction activities include:

a spatial planning;
b environmental planning and natural resource management;
c infrastructure and facilities for housing and resettlement;
d infrastructure and facilities for public services;
e infrastructure and facilities for the economic sector, including banking, finance, and businesses, particularly small and medium enterprises;
f infrastructure and facilities for religious and indigenous activities;
g infrastructure and facilities for education and culture;
h job creation to support the rehabilitation and reconstruction efforts;
i infrastructure and facilities directly related to the revitalization of local governance and life of the community;
j other reconstruction activities described in the master and detailed plans.

Referring to the scope of the BRR's tasks described in the above-mentioned PERPU, it is clear that land right issues, including those related to housing development, were among sectors that had to be dealt with in the post-tsunami disaster rehabilitation and reconstruction phase. In this regard, the BRR issued an important policy on spatial planning, i.e. (1) provision of land and resettlement, (2) land certification of properties in marriage, and (3) handling of tenant issues and those occupying lands without legal base.

Land owners who lost their land in the disaster received replacement land at the new relocation sites. This can be observed at several relocated housing sites near Banda Aceh, such as the Jackie Chan Complex, Ujong Batee Neighborhood, Saudi Charity Campaign Housing, Budha Tzu Chi Complex, etc. The disaster-impacted existing lands were properly registered through mapping and certification procedures. The tsunami survivors who previously rented a house that was subsequently impacted by the disaster were also given land to build a new home for free at their respective relocated housing sites.

With regard to the Head of the National Land Agency (BPN) Decree Number 114-II/2005 regarding the Guidelines for Land Registration for Tsunami Impacted Areas, it is stipulated that the land registration process for certification purposes shall be carried out based on the following priorities: (1) areas designated for public housing and resettlement, buildings for public services, and infrastructure, (2) the entire disaster-impacted areas, and (3) areas immediately adjacent to the disaster-impacted areas.

2.5 Law Number 11/2006 regarding the Governance of Aceh

Article 211 of this law regulates the authority of the Aceh government in the subject of land administration. Every citizen of Indonesia residing in Aceh has land rights as described by laws and regulations.

The Aceh (provincial) government and the district/municipal government have the authority to regulate the designation, the utilization, and legal relations regarding land rights by recognizing, respecting, and protecting all established rights, including customary (adat) rights according to the nationally applicable norms, standards, and procedures. Accordingly, the Aceh government can issue right of building and right of exploitation in reference to these norms and standards. Likewise, the Aceh government shall provide legal protection to religiously-endowed land, religious properties, and other sacred needs.

2.6 Governmental Regulation in lieu of Law (PERPU) Number 2/2007 regarding the legal aspect of the post-earthquake and tsunami disaster rehabilitation and reconstruction of the regions and communities of Nanggroe Aceh Darussalam Province and Nias Islands, North Sumatra Province

It is stated in the consideration of this PERPU that the legal matters in the implementation of governmental administration, civil rights, guardianship, land administration, and banking procedure need to be tackled urgently so that the psychological and socio-economic conditions of the community and local governance can be restored through community-based rehabilitation and reconstruction efforts.

This PERPU also stipulates that land owners who lost their lands in the tsunami disaster with or without land registration shall receive replacement land (designated for a new home) through the program executed by the BRR while considering: (1) land availability, (2) proof of ownership or land right, (3) land registers kept by the local land agency, and (4) the spatial planning of the area. Land owners who have been awarded replacement land cannot claim for any type of compensation for their lands lost in the disaster.

The existing identifiable or unidentifiable lands with or without registration shall be resurveyed and their boundary establishment shall be done based on the confirmation by land right owners or legal heirs, along with the community members, village officials, and the Head of the National Land Agency, leading to the issuance of land certificate.

Registered lands whose proof of land right is damaged, lost, or destroyed in the disaster shall be replaced with a new one showing an identity coding system for the land parcel. With this replacement proof of right, the old document shall be considered invalid.

Unregistered lands of customary right origin shall be recognized their land right status by the National Land Agency for the subsequent issuance of proof of land rights and registration using the same land parcel coding system.

Lands whose owners or legal heirs of Islamic faith have passed away shall become religious properties and shall be managed by Baitul Mal (Religious Property Management Agency). Baitul Mal is a unique, non-departmental institution of Aceh regional government, which is authorized to manage and develop religious charity funds, donations, and religious properties with the purpose of establishing people's welfare and serving as the custodian for the orphans and their properties and the properties without legal heirs based on Islamic (*Syariah*) Law. This institution answers to the Head of Aceh regional/local government according to their respective government level, i.e. Governor, Head of District/ Mayor, Head of Associated Villages, or Head of Village. The establishment of Baitul Mal was mandated by Chapters 180, 191, and 192 of Law Number 11/2006 regarding the Governing of Aceh and implemented using the Qanun (Provincial Legislation) of Aceh Number 10/2007 regarding Baitul Mal.

Chapters 36–38 of the Qanun of Aceh Number 10/2007 describe that properties/lands whose owners are unknown or are deceased, including those of tsunami victims, shall be managed by Baitul Mal of the district/municipality in which they are located as confirmed by the Religious Court *(Mahkamah Syariah)*. In this case, Baitul Mal shall request for the custodian status for these properties/lands to the Religious Court. As the custodian for the properties, Baitul Mal may not transfer the ownership of the properties to any other party. The use of these properties is specifically prioritized for religious activities and people's welfare. In addition, lands whose owners or legal heir of non-Islamic faith have passed away shall be managed by *Balai Harta Peninggalan* (Unclaimed Property Management Agency) (Taqwaddin *et al.*, 2012).

In case the owner or legal heir of the property is eventually identified, he/she may request for ownership status confirmation to the Religious Court and subsequently have their right of ownership reinstated. In the event that the Religious Court grants the request, Baitul Mal shall immediately return the property to the owner or legal heir.

2.7 Law Number 24/2007 regarding disaster management

Law Number 24/2007 is the first law in Indonesia that regulates the disaster management effort comprehensively covering the pre-disaster, during disaster, and post-disaster phases. This law provides the legal basis for the implementation of well-planned, coordinated, and integrated disaster management strategies.

This law describes that the implementation of disaster management is the responsibility and authority of the national and regional governments. During a disaster event, the emergency response is entirely executed by the National Agency for Disaster Management (BNPB) and Provincial/Regional Agency for Disaster Management (BPBD).

During emergency response, funding is provided by the national and regional government annual budget (APBN and APBD, respectively) as well as through on-call funds made available through a special accounting mechanism. Disaster management is implemented with due regard to the community's right to receive basic needs, social protection, and education, and to participate in the decision-making process.

Disaster management activities shall also involve business entities and international organizations actively. The supervision of all disaster management activities is conducted by the central government, local government, and the community during each phase of disaster so that discrepancies in the use of the disaster management fund can be prevented.

3 Case studies on post-disaster land administration: land administration in Baitussalam Sub-District

The question arises as to how these legal frameworks for post-disaster land management were implemented by the governmental agencies and the donors, in the interface with the tsunami-affected communities, and how the communities responded to such implementation. The following sections describe the findings from the author's empirical studies.

Quantitative data on the number of land parcels that existed in Baitussalam Sub-District before the tsunami disaster are not exactly known. This is due to the fact that most land owners in the area did not have any document that proved their land rights. Information obtained from the office of the National Land Agency, Aceh Province and the office of Baitussalam Sub-District revealed that only about 20 percent of land parcels in this sub-district were registered with certificates.

Low numbers of land parcels with certificates in this sub-district imply that the land certification and registration program in this area was not optimally implemented, particularly reaching low-income families. In addition, prolonged armed conflict that occurred in Aceh[5] was blamed for the inability of the government to provide public services effectively, which also affected the land registration and certification process.

3.1 Land issues in the tsunami-affected areas

Results of field studies indicate that land issues which surfaced post-tsunami disaster in Aceh can be classified as follows:

3.1.1 Loss of proof of land right (certificate or other proofs)

Most of the tsunami disaster victims lost their proof of land rights, such as land certificates, deeds, or land affirmation letters, which were previously used as proof of land ownership. Loss of proof of right implicates the physical and juridical data concerning lands, which may subsequently result in loss of legal security of land ownership.

3.1.2 Loss of land parcel boundaries

The tsunami disaster damaged or destroyed land boundary marks, which made it very difficult to identify each land parcel in the impacted areas. Most of these boundary marks were washed away by the tsunami wave, while some were still partly visible. However, these visible marks were later accidently destroyed during debris clearing in the disaster-impacted areas.

3.1.3 Death of subject of land right (land owner)

Many of the subjects of right or land owners were killed in the tsunami disaster. Such a situation implicates the issues of protecting the civil right regarding property ownership. In this regard, it was very difficult to properly identify legal heirs to properties left by right owners post-tsunami disaster. Errors in the identification process could disqualify the otherwise true legal heirs of the property. Death of subject of right without identifiable legal heirs also brings another challenge in finding the right solution to the problem.

3.1.4 Loss of physical land

The tsunami disaster also caused the permanent loss of physical lands in several impacted areas with a distance of several tens to hundreds of meters from the coastline due to land subsidence, eventually becoming permanently inundated by sea water and consequently resulting in loss of object of right. These subsided lands were used as farmlands, fish ponds, and/or residential areas. When this study was conducted, no data were available from the provincial or district office of the National Land Agency on the number of land parcels in

Baitussalam Sub-District that disappeared due to land subsidence in the 2004 earthquake and tsunami event.

3.2 Reconstruction of land administration in the post-disaster recovery phase

According to the National Land Agency's terminology, most of the land parcels affected by the tsunami in Baitussalam Sub-District can be classified as customary right land parcels. Although land parcels for this type of land right are not certified, they can be registered through an alternative land registration mechanism (Rinaldi and Taqwaddin, 2011). The registration for these land parcels can be done even by submitting an affirmation letter of ownership signed by the Head of the Village (*keuchik*). This procedure is in line with the national land administration law of Indonesia, which officially adopts customary land law.

In Aceh, land information is usually generated in the form of an affirmation letter recognizing the validity of physical control and customary law ownership of the land. The documents for the legal acts on lands are usually prepared by the Head of the Village or sub-district and attended and signed by witnesses representing parties involved.

The Agency for the Rehabilitation and Reconstruction of Aceh-Nias (BRR) coordinated with the BPN to establish the RALAS (Reconstruction of Aceh Land Administration System) program, which was supported by the World Bank and the United Nations Development Program (UNDP). According to the World Bank (2010), the specific objectives of the RALAS project were: (i) "to recover and protect land ownership rights of people in the affected and surrounding areas"; (ii) "to rebuild the land administration system."

Officers of the national BPN were dispatched to the tsunami-affected areas of Aceh. For every four or five villages, an officer of the national BPN was assigned to implement the RALAS program in these villages. All BPN officers reported directly to their superior at the main office in Jakarta. Meanwhile, officers of provincial and district/municipal BPNs were minimally involved in this program due to the fact that many of them were also victims of the tsunami disaster.

In implementing their tasks, the national BPN officers worked with *gampong* and community leaders, taking measurements of land parcels of tsunami victims while involving land owners or legal heirs. This process was effectively supported by the community. Working with a map, the BPN officers then began the community-based land registration identifying land boundaries and the property owners. The map was subsequently displayed on the public notice board in the village for 30 days. Within this period, any third party may challenge the information posted on the map which shall be considered in a village meeting or by BPN team. If no contest was posted, then the BPN confirmed the land ownership status and a land certificate would be issued within 90 days from the start of land measurements.

Experts or specialists in legal matters, surveying, mapping, economics, information technology, and social works were also recruited to assist national

BPN officers in the RALAS program. These experts were recruited, paid, and supervised by UNDP. Since UNDP received funding from the World Bank to implement this program, they submitted their progress report and work accomplishment to this major global financial institution.

The implementing agent (UNDP) – Donor (World Bank) project management scheme was important in ensuring that all the necessary steps in the RALAS program implementation were properly executed at the ground level. However, the project implementation could have been more effective if work progress had also been communicated to the BPN and other local stakeholders.

3.3 Provision of land for resettlement

The policy regarding the provision of lands for resettlement (relocated housing) was implemented by the government for tsunami-affected villages *(gampong)* whose land areas had partially vanished due to land subsidence and become permanently inundated by sea water. For example, tsunami victims from Kajhu and Mon Singeet villages, Baitussalam Sub-District were relocated to new housing sites in the upland areas of Neuheun village, Mesjid Raya Sub-District, paid for by the government. Similarly, residents of tsunami-affected Dayah Mamplam village, Leupung Sub-District were relocated to Glee Judah in the neighboring Lhok Nga Sub-District. This post-tsunami reconstruction initiative was in line with the stipulation set forth in Article 5 of PERPU Number 2/2007 whereby land owners who lost their lands in the tsunami disaster were entitled to replacement land (intended for a new home) as implemented by the BRR.[6] The implementation of this resettlement program also referred to PERPRES Number 30/2005 regarding the Master Plan for the Rehabilitation and Reconstruction of the tsunami-impacted areas of Aceh and Nias.

Results of research conducted by Darma (2009) revealed that the provision of lands for relocated housing in tsunami-impacted West Aceh District was hindered by land acquisition issues related to the amount of compensation to be paid to land owners by the government. The land owners claimed that the compensation offered was not based on the fair market price for the lands in the region and, therefore, initially decided to turn down the offer. However, after several meetings between the land acquisition committee and land owners to discuss the mutually acceptable price for the lands in reference to the stipulations set forth in the Presidential Regulation Number 65/2006 concerning the Amendment to Presidential Regulation Number 36/2005 concerning the Procurement of Land for the Implementation of Development for Public Interest, an agreement to proceed with the transaction was reached. This agreement was later substantiated by a Decree Number 212/2006 concerning the Confirmation on the Compensation Rate for the Acquisition of Lands Intended for Relocated Housing Program in Leuhan and Blang Beurandang Villages, signed by the Head of West Aceh District.

3.4 Handling of tenants and those occupying lands without legal base

It is important to note that, although the stipulations on the handling of the tenants and those occupying lands without legal base with rented homes having been destroyed by the tsunami were not made either in the PERPRES Number 30/2005 or PERPU Number 2/2007, these tsunami victims were actually entitled to a new home built by donors. For example, tenants whose rented house was destroyed by the tsunami while the contract was still in effect had the right to complete their contract term by moving into a new home built by donors for the landlord. This scheme was implemented in Merduati village, Banda Aceh, whereby the Head of the Village mediated an agreement between the landlords and tsunami-surviving tenants such that upon receiving newly built homes from donors, the landlords shall allow the tenants to occupy the homes for five consecutive years. While this policy was implemented mainly for humanitarian reasons, it also encouraged displaced tsunami survivors to return to their villages.

In another scheme, tenants whose rented house was destroyed by the tsunami received a new home built by donors for free at the relocated housing sites such as in Neuheun Village, Mesjid Raya Sub-District, Aceh Besar District and Panteriek Village, Lueng Bata Sub-District, Banda Aceh. These housing relocations typically have a unique socio-cultural composition in that members of their community are of diverse ethnic, religious, and professional backgrounds living in harmony in the same neighborhood.

3.5 Land certification through the RALAS program

Land certification was basically the main activity of the RALAS program designed to provide legal security for the right of control and ownership of land. The program consisted of land survey and mapping, adjudication, registration of land rights, and issuance of land certificates based on regional priorities (BPN, 2005), namely: "(i) priority 1 – areas assigned for housing and settlement, public service buildings, and infrastructure; (ii) priority 2 – all other areas impacted by the tsunami disaster; and (iii) priority 3 – areas immediately adjacent to the tsunami disaster-impacted areas." The RALAS program was only implemented for a three-year period from 2005 through 2008. The total target for the RALAS land certification program in the entire tsunami-impacted areas of Aceh was 600,000 parcels (World Bank, 2010). For Aceh Besar District, the number of land parcels to be covered through this program was 51,500. Data on the targeted and actual land parcels certified through the RALAS program in Aceh Besar District are presented in Table 4.1.

Table 4.1 shows that not all land parcels affected by the tsunami in Aceh Besar District had their owner's land rights restored with the issuance of a certificate.

The RALAS program was unique in that it did not necessarily involve BPN officers in adjudication matters. In fact, it was a community-driven adjudication

Table 4.1 Completion of land certificate issuance through the RALAS program in Aceh Besar District

Year	*Target (parcels)*	*Completed (parcels)*	*Percentage*
2005/2006	21,500	7,225	33.61
2006/2007	20,000	14,722	73.61
2007/2008	10,000	5,405	54.05

Source: Nazamuddin *et al.* (2012).

process. In contrast, the land certification procedure described in Government Regulation (PP) Number 24/1997 contains no stipulation about the role and function of community-based agreements pertinent to the control and ownership of land as well as confirming land boundaries.

It is described in the RALAS guidelines that the BPN is a government institution that has the authority to conduct land surveys and registration. Furthermore, the confirmation of land boundaries and the control and ownership of land should be executed based on the agreement of the community. In this regard, the role of the BPN is to give legal confirmation for these procedures while setting the requirement for validation against existing government documents.

Using the RALAS community-based adjudication approach, every person claiming to hold a land right must sign a statement of control/ownership of land which has been prior approved by land owners whose land directly borders the claimant's land and validated by the Head of the Village (BPN, 2005). In the event that the land certificate holder has passed away, the RALAS guidelines explain that the Head of the Village (*Keuchik*) and religious leader (*Imeum Meunasah*) shall identify legal heirs (Taqwaddin *et al.*, 2011). *Keuchik* and *Imeum Meunasah* also have the authority to designate a guardian for underaged heirs.[7] Regarding inheritance and guardians, the Religious Court could ratify the decision made by the *Keuchik* and *Imeum Meunasah.*

Essentially, RALAS approach in land certification is quite innovative compared to other land certification programs. Land registration using RALAS works well in disaster-impacted areas because it responds to the urgent need to provide legal security on land rights which subsequently could help accelerate the reconstruction efforts in these areas. This program also responds, at least in part, to appeals to involve the indigenous (adat) community in formalizing land rights (Fitzpatrick, 2010).

3.6 Supporting elements and constraints of the RALAS program

Active participation of the community, direct involvement of national BPN officers, the land certification program being implemented at no charge to land owners, and full support afforded by the village government officials were among supporting elements that defined the success of the RALAS program in Aceh. Within six months of the tsunami aftermath, the survivors, including village officials, along with RALAS project workers and various NGOs were actively conducting community-based land surveys and mapping. In Baitussalam Sub-District, the main supporters of this effort included the Head of Sub-District (*Camat*), *Keuchik*, and village residents. *Imeum Meunasah* and *Tuha Peut* (Village Council) were also involved in identifying the guardians and legal heirs in the implementation of the RALAS program.[8] The fact that the tsunami-affected areas were protected from land grabbing and speculation also contributed to the success of this land certification program (World Bank, 2010).

During the period of the RALAS program implementation (2005–2008), the capacity of the provincial BPN office was very limited. This was attributed to the tsunami disaster impact, i.e. loss of local BPN staff, destruction of local BPN offices and equipment, loss or damage to official land registers, and damage and loss of property right evidence, including witness evidence held in the minds of those who died in the disaster (World Bank, 2010). Staff members of the national BPN were brought in to help with the RALAS program. However, these workers could not perform their tasks effectively due to insufficient facilities, such as transportation, computers, and survey equipment. It is also worth noting that, in the early phase of the RALAS program, it was extremely difficult to identify who controlled and owned which land parcels without the involvement of the village government.

4 Conclusion

The Indonesian government swiftly responded to the 2004 devastating tsunami with disaster management efforts by issuing several important regulatory documents. The issuance of these legal documents was fundamental to resolving many land issues as well as to the reconstruction of the land administration system in Aceh upon which the Indonesian government put a highly important priority in post-tsunami disaster recovery effort.

Challenges in post-tsunami land administration implementation in Aceh were effectively met by the RALAS program with a community-driven approach and strong support from the World Bank and UNDP, which contributed positively to other post-tsunami reconstruction projects.

The specific role and support of village government, i.e. *Keuchik*, *Imeum Meunasah*, and *Tuha Peut*, was instrumental in the implementation of the RALAS program.

Devastating losses afflicted by the tsunami disaster upon land administration human resource, infrastructure, equipment, and facilities were primarily responsible for partial achievement of the RALAS project targeted completion of land certification.

Looking at the positive results and impact of the community-driven RALAS program in the post-2004 tsunami recovery, this land administration model could be implemented in certain areas of the world impacted by mega-disasters.

Notes

1 Lecturer and Researcher, Syiah Kuala University – Tsunami and Disaster Mitigation Research Center, Banda Aceh, Indonesia. The first author was involved in livelihood early recovery while the second author was active in disaster risk reduction initiatives and efforts during the post-tsunami reconstruction of Aceh.
2 Refer to Section on Expressing Opinion in Law Number 5/1960 concerning Basic Regulations of Agrarian Principles.
3 Furthermore, the techniques and procedures for the implementation of land registration are described in the Regulations of State Minister of Agrarian Affairs/Head of National Land Agency Number 3/1997 concerning the Stipulations for the implementation of Governmental Regulation Number 4/1997 concerning Land Registration.
4 The chronological review approach used in this legal framework study was aimed at obtaining the stages of regulation development based on their sequence of ratification. The regulations examined were relevant to and used as the basis for consolidating lands of tsunami victims of Aceh.
5 Aceh conflict started when Dr. Muhammad Hasan Tiro declared Aceh an independent State, seceding from Indonesia in 1976. Refer to Danil Akbar Taqwaddin, *The Roles Of Third Parties In Aceh Peace Process*, Presented at Aceh Development International Conference (ADIC – III), International Islamic University, Kuala Lumpur, 26–28 March 2012.
6 Refer to Articles 5 and 6 of PERPU Number 2/2007 regarding the Legal Aspect of the Post-Earthquake and Tsunami Disaster Rehabilitation and Reconstruction of the Regions and Communities of Nanggroe Aceh Darussalam Province and Nias Islands, North Sumatra Province. This PERPU was later elevated and confirmed to become Law Number 48/2007.
7 This matter is stipulated in Article 16 of Qanun (Supporting Legislation) of Aceh Number 10/2007 concerning Baitul Mal.
8 *Imeum Meunasah* is a religious leader in a village *(gampong)*. *Tuha Peut* is a representative council of the *gampong*/village community. Together with *Keuchik* (head of *gampong*), they conduct the *gampong* government system. Refer to Qanun Nanggroe Aceh Darussalam Number 5/2003 concerning Gampong Government.

References

Asshiddiqie, J. (2010), *The Green Constitution (Nuansa Hijau UUD1945)*, Jakarta: Rajawali Press.

BPN (2005), *Manual of Land Registration in the Tsunami Impacted Areas of NAD and North Sumatra.* Published by the Reconstruction of Aceh Land Administration System (RALAS), Head of BPN Decree No. 114-II.2005.

Darma, S. (2009), *Kajian Yuridis Pengadaan Tanah Untuk Relokasi Korban Tsunami di Kecamatan Johan Pahlawan, Kabupaten Aceh Barat*, Master's Thesis. Pasca Sarjana, Universitas Sumatera Utara, Medan.

Fitzpatrick, D. (2010), "Tatkala Bencana Alam Menghadang: Kelenturan dan Kelemahan Hukum Pertanahan Indonesia," in Myrna A. Safitri and Tristam Moeliono, eds, *Hukum Agraria Dan Masyarakat Di Indonesia*, Jakarta: KITLV Press.

Fitzpatrick, D. (2012), "Between Custom and Law: Protecting the Property Rights of Women after Tsunami in Aceh," in Patrick Daly, Michael Feener, and Anthony Reid, eds, *From the Ground Up: Perspectives Post-Tsunami and Post-Conflict Aceh*, Singapore: ISEAS Press.

Hardjasoemantri, K. (1993), *Environmental Protection Law (Konservasi Sumber Daya Alam Hayati dan Ekosistemnya)*, Yogyakarta: Gadjah Mada University Press.

Ilyas. (2005), *Konsepsi Hak Garap atas Tanah dalam Sistem Hukum Pertanahan Indonesia dalam kaitannya dengan Ajaran Negara Kesejahteraan*, Doctoral Dissertation, Program Pascasarjana, Universitas Padjadjaran, Bandung.

Indirahati, N.S. (2006), "Sertifikasi Tanah dan Permasalahannya," *LEMDIMAS Journal*, Vol. 6, No. 2, November.

Multi Donor Fund, Java Reconstruction Fund, and The World Bank. (2012), *REKOMPAK: Rebuilding Indonesia's Communities after Disasters*, Working Paper 66552, Jakarta, Indonesia.

Nazamuddin, Teuku Alvisyahrin, and Sarah Willis (Eds). 2012. *Indian Ocean Tsunami 2004: Recovery in Banda Aceh*. International Recovery Platform. Recovery Status Report 05. Kobe, Japan.

Rinaldi, Y. and Taqwaddin. (2011), *Pemetaan dan Sertifikasi Tanah Berbasis Partisipatif Dalam Upaya Memperjelas Hak Milik Atas Tanah Di Wilayah Tsunami (Studi Kasus di Kecamatan Baitussalam Kabupaten Aceh Besar)*, Research Report, TDMRC, Universitas Syiah Kuala, Banda Aceh, Indonesia.

Rubaie, A. (2007), *Hukum Pengadaan Tanah Untuk Kepentingan Umum*, Malang: Bayumedia Press.

Santoso, U. (2012), *Hukum Agraria Kajian Komprehensif*, Jakarta: Kencana Press.

Taqwaddin and T. Alvisyahrin (2012), *Governance Issues Learned in the 2004 Tsunami In Aceh, Indonesia*, Paper presented at Rikuzentakata International Disaster Recovery Workshop, 23 December 2012, Japan.

Taqwaddin, Y. Rinaldi, and M.I. Ansari (2011), "Post-Tsunami Strengthening of Village Government: A Case Study of Lambada Lhok," in Nazamuddin, T. Alvisyahrin, and S. Willis, eds, *Indian Ocean Tsunami 2004: Recovery in Banda Aceh*, Kobe, Japan: International Recovery Platform.

Taqwaddin, S. Tripa, M.I. Ansari, and T. Muttaqin (2012), "Penyelesaian Tanah Korban Tsunami Yang Tidak Ada dan/atau Tidak Diketahui Ahli Warisnya," *MEDIA HUKUM Journal*, Fakultas Hukum Universitas Muhammadiyah, Yogyakarta, pp. 251–261.

World Bank (2010), *Implementation Completion and Results Report (TF 055353) on a Multi Donor Trust Fund for Aceh and North Sumatra Grant to Indonesia for a Reconstruction of Aceh Land Administration System Project*, Report No. ICR 00001306. World Bank, East Asia and Pacific Region.

5 Roles of laws relating to post-tsunami management in Thailand

Kanongnij Sribuaiam

1 Introduction

There were two big cases of disaster in Thailand leading to the improvement of laws and policies: the first one was the tsunami on 26 December 2004, which caused serious damage along the coastline of eleven Indian Ocean countries, including six provinces of the Andaman Sea in Thailand: Phuket, Phang Nga, Krabi, Ranong, Satoon, and Trang. The second one was the 2011 floods particularly in and around Bangkok. This chapter mainly focuses on the roles of laws relating to post-tsunami management in Thailand, both immediate reactions after the tsunami through short-term solutions and gradual structural responses through long-term solutions.

After the 2004 tsunami, six provinces in Southern Thailand had severe damage in all dimensions: loss of life of inhabitants and tourists; loss of property of local communities; dislocation of coastal communities; impact on industries: real estate, tourism, and fishing; loss of jobs; land devastation; and ecological destruction. The Thai government had responded to this damage by using policies, administrative instruments, and laws. As an immediate response, existing laws were used to serve different purposes: in terms of emergency management; rehabilitating ecological destruction; repairing and readjusting affected land; or assisting victims and affected communities. However, there was no "disaster management" law at the time.

Compared to some other countries, Thailand has fewer experiences in disaster and disaster law. However, the laws relating to disaster started to develop on a certain level after the 2004 tsunami disaster. The following is an attempt to introduce the development of disaster-related law-making in Thailand from a critical perspective of legal sociology.

2 Legislation responding to emergency

2.1 The 2005 Emergency Decree on Public Administration in State of Emergency

In response to the tsunami, there were only two existing laws to cope with emergencies: the 1979 Civil Defense Act and the 1999 Prevention and Fire Control

Act, which were considered inadequate, inefficient and, in some ways, irrelevant to the case. In taking "immediate action" after the disaster at the end of the year, new emergency legislation was made the following year. The 2005 Emergency Decree on Public Administration in State of Emergency was made to deal with the urgent situation and served as the core legislation for dealing with the tsunami disaster. This Emergency Decree made by the civilian government was considered an exception to the rule of law guaranteeing some provisions in the 1997 Constitution of the Kingdom of Thailand.

Objectives of this Decree were: to permit the expeditious resolution of various forms of situations jeopardizing national security, as well as the handling of problems arising from public calamities and the rehabilitation of the lives of the people injured, and the troubles as to the national security and their seriousness which could not be remedied through ordinary forms of public administration; to repair independence and territorial integrity; and to determine certain special measures for public administration in a state of emergency, so that the State would be allowed to promptly maintain its security and safety, protect the rights and liberties of every person, and restore order. This is such an urgent and inevitable need to preserve national and public safety and to avert public calamities. It is therefore necessary to enact this Emergency Decree.

In this Emergency Decree, "State of Emergency" means a situation which affects or may affect public order, may be adverse to the State security, may expose the nation or any part thereof to a state of crisis, or involves the commission of an offense of terrorism under the Criminal Code, fight or war, and in which certain urgent measures need to be taken for the purpose of maintaining the government under the democratic regime with the King as Head of State pursuant to the Constitution of the Kingdom of Thailand, independence and territorial integrity, national interest, obedience to laws, public safety, peaceful lives of the people, protected rights and liberties, or common peace or interest, or for the purpose of averting or remedying any loss in consequence of an immediate and serious public calamity.

Once it appears that a "State of Emergency" does come to pass and the Prime Minister finds expedient to exercise the combined forces of the administrative or police officers, civil officers or military officers, for the sake of prevention, resolution, withholding, abatement or suppression of the situation, or rehabilitation of or providing of assistance to the people, the Prime Minister, with the approval of the Council of Ministers, may declare a "State of Emergency" throughout the Kingdom or in certain parts thereof, according to the necessity of the circumstances.

The benefit of this Emergency Decree was that powers from relevant authorities were centralized with the Prime Minister to enable easily handling since the scale of the tsunami disaster was at a mega-scale, with serious damage and a great impact on the life and property of the people. In the area where a "State of Emergency" is declared, all the existing legal authority vested in or taken charge of by one Minister or more, only in respect of the giving of approval, endorsement, instructions, commands or support as to the prevention, resolution, withholding, abatement or suppression of the state of emergency, or rehabilitation of or providing of assistance to the people, shall provisionally be transferred to the Prime Minister, for the sake of consistent, expeditious and efficacious administration and resolution of the situation.

2.2 Rule of law questioned

According to Section 9 of the Emergency Decree, in case of the need to put an end to the state of emergency without delay or to prevent the increase of its seriousness, the Prime Minister shall have the power to lay down ordinances. This is considered an exception to the rule of law, and might give rise to the restriction of personal rights and liberties, under the 1997 Constitution of the Kingdom of Thailand. For example:

1 Exception of liberty of dwelling: ordinance on prohibition from staying outside residence during a period of time;
2 Exception of liberty of travelling: ordinance on prohibition from or condition in the use of vehicles; evacuation from or prohibition from entering into an area, building, or place;
3 Exception of liberty of communication: ordinance on prohibition from the use of any means of communication;
4 Exception of liberty of expression: ordinance on prohibition from presentation, distribution or circulation of news, writings, printed materials or any other media, the contents of which are likely to terrify the public, or are intentionally distorted bringing about a misunderstanding;
5 Exception of liberty to assemble peacefully: ordinance on prohibition from meetings or gatherings at any place.

Because the ordinances impose restrictions on the rights and liberty of the people, the execution of any ordinance must be subject to certain a time clause. Therefore, the declaration of "State of Emergency" shall be in force throughout a period of time designated by the Prime Minister but not in excess of three months from its issuance. Upon cessation of the state of emergency, disapproval of the Council of Ministers, or termination of the period of time, the Prime Minister shall lift the declaration of such "State of Emergency".

3 Legislation responding to ecological destruction

3.1 The 1992 Enhancement and Conservation of the National Environmental Quality Act

The tsunami not only caused great loss of life and property but also created losses of coastal resources. For example, mangrove forests, which served as barriers against wind, waves, and erosion, were destroyed. Coral reefs, seagrass beds, and sandy beaches, which served as components of coastal ecosystems, were affected. Immediately after the tragedy, the Prime Minister applied the 1992 Enhancement and Conservation of National Environmental Quality Act (ECNEQA), which has the main objective of providing mechanisms for protecting natural resources and environment.

The government focused on the ecological destruction of the affected areas, and therefore applied Sections 9–10 and Sections 43–44 of the 1992 ECNEQA to apply with the case, the former provision for permitting the Prime Minister power to respond to the disaster, and the latter provisions for applying special measures of areas called "areas designated as environmentally protected areas" within the disaster-affected areas.

3.2 The role of the Prime Minister in taking action under Sections 9–10 of the 1992 ECNEQA

Section 9 stipulates that, in case of an emergency or public danger arising from natural disaster or pollution caused by contamination and spread of pollutants which will, if left without any remedial actions, seriously endanger the safety of life, body, or health of the people, or cause damage to the properties of the people or the State, the Prime Minister shall have the power to order, as deemed appropriate, government agencies, State enterprises, or any persons, including the persons who are or may be the victims of such danger or damage, to take prompt action, individually or jointly, in order to be able to control, extinguish, or mitigate the adverse effects of such danger or damage. The Prime Minister may delegate the power to the Changwat Governor (or Provincial Governor) to exercise such power and act on his behalf within the territorial jurisdiction of that Changwat (province).

The said delegation of power shall be made by a written order and published in the Government Gazette. When any order is given by the Prime Minister, or by the Changwat Governor acting on behalf of the Prime Minister, such order shall be published in the Government Gazette without delay. The Minister on Environment shall determine preventive measures and prepare a contingency plan to rectify the situation in advance, in order to prevent, remedy, extinguish, or mitigate the emergency or danger of pollution envisaged by Section 9 (Section 10).

3.3 Special measures for areas designated as environmentally protected areas under Sections 43–44 of the 1992 ECNEQA

In order to restore and rehabilitate the affected areas providing ecological functions, the Ministry on Natural Resources and Environment, through the Office of Natural Resources and Environmental Policy and Planning, declared the affected areas as "environmentally protected areas" as a measure to support the restoration and conservation of natural resources and the environment. Under this Act, in Chapter III Environmental Protection, Part 3 Conservation and Environmentally Protected Areas, there are Sections 43 and 44, which are mainly applied to the tsunami areas. In case of any area characterized as a watershed area, a unique natural ecosystem, naturally composed of fragile ecosystems, or worthy of being conserved due to its natural or esthetic values or amenities, and such area is yet to be designated as a conservation area, the Minister on Environment has the power to designate such area as an environmentally protected area (Section 43). It was discovered that some tsunami areas have some of these requirements. Once such areas are declared as environmentally protected areas, there will be strictly protective measures specially applied – for example, land use prescription, prohibition or conditions of activities, determination of management, etc. (Section 44). In coping with the tsunami, the Thai government applied set-back measures, construction set-backs, green-belt barriers, and construction-free zones, in order to establish long-term security for inhabitants, as well as rehabilitate the coast from coastal erosion. These measures are elaborated by the Ministerial Regulation of the Ministry for Natural Resources and Environment.

3.4 The 2006 Ministerial Regulation of the Ministry for Natural Resources and Environment on Designation of Conservation Areas with Conservation Measures in Tsunami Areas of Six Provinces (Kra Bee, Pang Nga, Pu Ket, Ra Nong, Sa Toon, and Trang)

This Ministerial Regulation covers the following conditions:

- *Land use control of coastline areas* with permission for certain objectives of land use: activities for maintaining safety on the sea and the coast, sports on the coast without using vehicles or engines, and land excavation, land filling or changing of natural factors of the coastal areas by governmental organization for rehabilitation of areas from natural damage.
- *Land use control of sand dune areas* with permission for certain objectives of land use: planting of local trees or coastal plantations, and land filling or changing of natural factors of the sand dune areas by governmental organization for rehabilitation of areas from natural damage.
- *Control on activities* which cause pollution and negative impacts on natural resources and the environment, including catching ornamental fish and other living things in the coral reef and sea grass.
- *Control on buildings and other construction* in order to restore damage, prevent deterioration, and control development, by setting rules on set-back from the coastline, limitation on the height of buildings, distance from ancient buildings, including rules for hotels or resorts, especially those with fewer than eighty rooms.
- *Promote operations for environmental quality control*, by ordering relevant governmental bodies restore coral reef, sea grass, quality of sea water, mangrove plantation, and restore and conserve peat swamp forest, in order to prevent coastal erosion in the coastal zone.
- *Stipulate each province to appoint a committee* for monitoring the result of environmental protection.

This Ministerial Regulation was in place for one year. After that, there were four other Ministerial Regulations announced in a similar manner, covering more specific areas on the Andaman Sea, in order to increase effectiveness and continuity of the prevention and protection of natural resources and the environment in such areas. These Ministerial Regulations are: the 2007 Ministerial Regulation of the Ministry for Natural Resources and Environment on Designation of Conservation Area with Conservation Measures in Tsunami Areas of Five Districts in Kra Bee Province, and Seven Districts in Pang Nga Province; the 2010 Ministerial Regulation on Designation of Conservation Area with Conservation Measures in Tsunami Areas of Kra Bee Province; and the 2010 Ministerial Regulation of the Ministry for Natural Resources and Environment on Designation of Conservation Area with Conservation Measures in Tsunami Areas of Pu Ket Province. Among these, only the last one is still effective with certain conditions, as follows:

1 *Prohibition on the construction of factories* with the exception of small-scale industrial operations producing dirty waste water after treatment of no more than 20 kilograms per day; or the exception of the building of gas stations.
2 *Conditions on maintaining space:building ratio* by specifying different parts of the island for different rates of density in the construction of buildings; and conditions on providing empty space within each type of area.
3 *Prohibition on construction within particular areas* above 80 meters height from sea level, with the restricted exception in certain cases relating to national security, public interest, or public welfare.
4 *Prohibition on construction within particular areas* with high slope levels of more than 50 percent, conditions on construction on land with slope levels between 20 and 50 percent only for single buildings not higher than 6 meters, and other conditions on having green-belt with local plantations.

4 Legislation responding to affected land

Besides the ecological destruction, land and land use were also affected by the tsunami. In coping with the land problems, the government used two legal mechanisms: making a "general plan" for the Andaman coast through town planning by the Office of Town Planning; and restoring and developing the affected areas through "land readjustment" by the Department of Public Works and Town and Country Planning. These two mechanisms come under two existing legislations: the 1975 Town Planning Act and the 2004 Land Readjustment Act.

4.1 Making a "general plan" for the Andaman Coast through town planning under the 1975 Town Planning Act

The "general plan" is a type of town planning. Under Section 4 of this Act, "town planning" means the preparation, making, and implementation of a "general plan" and a "specific plan" in the area of a town and related areas or in the country in order to build or develop a new town or a part thereof or to replace a damaged town or a part thereof for the purpose of providing or improving sanitation, amenity and convenience, orderliness, beauty, use of property, public safety, and social security, of improving economy, social affairs, and environment, of preserving a place and an object of interest or value in the field of art, architecture, history or antiquity, or of preserving natural resources, landscape of beauty, or natural interest. The Director of the Office of Town Planning or the Local Office is the authority who prepares and makes the general plan.

Under this definition, the plans can be divided into two types:

- "General plan" means a plan, policy, and project, including a measure of general control, to be used as guidance in the development and maintenance of a town and related areas, or of the country in the fields of use of property, communication and transport, public service, and environment, for the purpose of achieving the objective of town planning.
- "Specific plan" means a plan and operation project for the development or maintenance of a specific area, or related affairs in a town and related areas, or in the country, for the benefit of town planning.

Upon the preparation and making of a general plan in any locality, the Office of Town Planning shall notify the local officer of such locality of it, and such local officer shall give the Office of Town Planning his opinion (Section 19, paragraph 1). In the preparation and making of any general plan, the Office of Town Planning or the local officer, as the case may be, must advertise the plan in order to inform the public (Section 19, paragraph 2), as well as arrange at least two public meetings in order to listen to public opinion and expression. The meeting place must be set in the locality where such general plan is to be prepared and made. In this public hearing, certain representatives of the public who will be allowed to attend the meetings will be identified. Other rules, methods, and conditions for the advertisement, the meeting, and the expression of opinions shall be prescribed by a Ministerial Regulation (Section 19, paragraph 2).

In this case, people in the locality can have the right to participate with the government by giving some information and expressing their opinions that are useful for the preparation and establishment of the plan. In particular, they can share their opinions and additional information during the meetings. These opinions and information will be brought into consideration by the government in order to make the general plan more suitable for the nature of local conditions, as well as the needs of the communities in the area.

When the general plan is prepared and made, the Changwat Governor shall appoint a "General Planning Advisory Board", which is composed of a representative of the local administrative authority, a representative of the Office of Town Planning, and no fewer than ten but no more than fifteen representatives of other government units, and other persons as deemed appropriate, with the duty to give advice and opinion concerning the general plan to be prepared and made by the Office of Town Planning or the local officer (Section 21, paragraph 1). The Office of Town Planning shall submit the plan to the "Board of Town Planning" for consideration and approval (Section 22).

After the Board approve the plan, the Office of Town Planning or the local officer must post a notice of the map showing the area of the general plan at the open space of the Sub-District or District Office, and a public place within the area of such general plan for no less than sixty days (Section 23, paragraph 1). Such notice shall contain an invitation to interested persons to examine the general plan and its prescriptions at the Office of Town Planning or the office of the local officer who prepared and made such plan (Section 23, paragraph 2). The interested persons can submit written rejection, alteration, or cancellation of the conditions in the use of land under the plan.

4.2 Restoring and developing affected areas through "land readjustment" under the 2004 Land Readjustment Act

The 2004 Land Readjustment Act was made to serve land use and land planning which can be used as long-term post-tsunami reconstruction. The Ministry of the Interior, through the Department of Public Works and Town and Country Planning, is responsible for the enforcement of this Act. The Ministry established a center to facilitate the construction of buildings for tsunami victims, while the Department developed a map of tsunami-affected areas for planning and developing a community town plan and infrastructure. The objective of this Act is to promote the private sector in participating with the State for readjusting land as a contribution to infrastructure development, improvement of residential areas, business areas, industrial and agricultural sources, and solving environmental problems in both urban and rural areas. The term "land readjustment" is defined as the implementation of development of many plots of land by land replotting, improving or constructing infrastructure, and jointly bearing the burdens and equitably distributing the returns (Section 3). Public–private cooperation in utilizing land more appropriately with regard to transportation, economics, society, environment, communities, and in line with urban planning, is also promoted.

Under this Act, there are two levels of Committee. The first one is the Land Readjustment Committee at the Ministerial level, having powers and duties to formulate policies, goals, and measures; approve master plans and target areas for readjustment; establish standards for readjustment; issue regulations on criteria and procedures for readjustment, and for project approval procedures; set rules on related matters, etc. (Section 6). The second one is the Provincial Land Readjustment Committee at the Provincial level, having powers and duties to approve establishment and oversee operation of the Association; determine measures and guidelines for promotion and support of readjustment; propose the Provincial Readjustment Master Plan and target areas for approval; appoint Association Inspectors and members; harmonize Land Readjustment Projects with other local projects; approve Readjustment Projects in the provinces;

provide opinion on financial support from the Fund; provide opinion on the use of public land and land expropriation to the Committee, etc. (Section 13).

There is also the so-called Land Readjustment Association, prescribed under Chapter 3 of this Act, which is meant to be an association to be established for the purpose of Land Readjustment following certain rules under this Act. Its main objective is implementation of the Land Readjustment Project (Section 15). In applying for registration of the Association, there must be at least three land owners who will be promoters and members of the association. The application must be submitted to the Provincial Committee (Section 16). After registration, the Association shall be a juristic person (Section 20). However, the Provincial Committee still have power to dissolve the Association if the Association fails to commence its operation, ceases its operation, or operates against law or public good morals or may be harmful to public peace or State security (Section 32). Without having status as the Association under this Act, the private sector cannot directly be involved in the land readjustment process.

In brief, main actors who can implement land readjustment are (Section 35):

1 The Land Readjustment Association;
2 The Department of Public Works and Town and Country Planning, National Housing Authority, and local administrative organizations;
3 Government agencies or any other juristic person established by the Government for Land Readjustment;
4 Any other government agency as prescribed by the Ministerial Regulation.

Another main instrument for the implementation of land readjustment is the Land Readjustment Project, which means a project which is initiated for the purpose of land readjustment (Section 3). Proposal of the Land Readjustment Project must be submitted to and approved by the Provincial Committee (Chapter 5). In some special cases, the Land Readjustment Project can also be used to develop and restore particular areas which have fire or any other catastrophe (Section 45). For example, in case of fire or any other catastrophe which causes great damage to buildings, if the local competent authority finds it necessary to implement the Land Readjustment Project, he shall propose his opinion together with a map showing the area of fire or any other catastrophe to the Provincial Committee within thirty days from the date the fire or catastrophe took place. If the area of fire or catastrophe is in more than one jurisdiction of a local competent authority, the local competent authorities concerned shall jointly consider and propose their opinions to the Provincial Committee. This provision is therefore very helpful for post-tsunami management (Section 45, paragraph 1).

4.3 Implementation of land readjustment

The following projects are examples of the implementation of the Land Readjustment Project. After the tsunami, the Department of Public Works and Town and Country Planning implemented four Land Readjustment Projects for developing and restoring the areas which were impacted by the tsunami. These projects are:

1 Land Readjustment Project for Tsunami Impacts in Pee Pee Islands, Kra Bee Province;
2 Land Readjustment Project for Tsunami Impacts in Kao Luck Community, Bang Niang Village, Kug Kug Sub-District, Ta Kua Paa District, Pang Nga Province;
3 Land Readjustment Project for Tsunami Impacts in Moo 5 Village and Moo 6–7 Village, Kug Kug Sub-District, Ta Kua Paa District, Pang Nga Province;
4 Land Readjustment Project for Tsunami Impacts in Kaew Jai Area, Num Kem Village, Bang Muang Sub-District, Ta Kua Paa District, Pang Nga Province.

Under the fourth project in Num Kem Village, there are certain adaptations to the general Land Readjustment Project which usually applies for land development in general. The unique manner of this project takes into consideration more sensitive issues suitable for that terrain, socio-cultural conditions, touristic factors, and the particular needs of land owners and the emergency of the problems. The four projects not only apply the process of land readjustment in general, but also focus on the improvement and increase of lanes for emergency evacuation from areas next to the coast to main roads. This also adds more value to these areas, at the same time, reducing the risk to life and reducing damage to inhabitants' property as much as possible if any disaster would happen again in the future.[1]

As mentioned earlier, the objective of this Act is to promote private sector involvement with the State for readjusting land. Although the word "private" mainly focuses on land owners, there are some provisions in the Act which can be interpreted as being beneficial for people who are not land owners but make use of the land for their living. Sections 3 and 37 can be read together to support the final goal of land readjustment as being for both "private" and "public" interests. Section 3 emphasizes that the goal of land readjustment is to use land more appropriately with regard to transportation, economics, society, environment, and communities, as well as to be in line with urban planning, while Section 37 prescribes that land readjustment must be in conformity with the principle of town and country planning, and must operate for the benefit of the public which is suitable for conditions of community and town development in the future.

Besides "land owners", other people can join the land readjustment process through the Land Readjustment Association as "members" of the Association (Section 20, paragraph 2), or as "interested persons" who may be called by the Provincial Committee to give an explanation on certain facts relevant to consideration on registering the Association (Section 17).

As a matter of fact, on the land along the coastline around tsunami areas, there are not only land owners but also ordinary land-users in the affected communities who live there. These people are basically fishermen who live on the coastal land which belongs to the State. According to the 1954 Land Code Section 2, land which has no ownership always belongs to the State. Under the Civil and Commercial Code of Thailand, Section 1304 prescribes that "the Domaine Public of State" includes every kind of State property which is in use for the public interest or reserved for the common benefit, such as: (a) waste land and land surrendered or abandoned; (b) property for the common use of people, e.g. foreshores, waterways, highways, lakes; and (c) property for special use of the State. Under the 1947 Fishery Act, Section 16, "Land for Common Interest" is where "everyone has the right to catch fish and do aquaculture…". In other words, the land under the Fishery Act is the Domaine Public of State under the category of the property for the common use of people. Therefore, these people in the communities affected by the tsunami and the Land Readjustment Projects, although they are not "land owners", can be counted as "interested persons" under paragraph 4 and paragraph 5 of Section 43.

According to Section 43, paragraph 4, if it is necessary to change Domaine Public of State under the category of the property for the common use of people in the Land Readjustment Project, "interested persons" may propose their opinions in writing to a competent authority within thirty days from the date of posting the announcement of the Land Readjustment Project, according to the regulations and procedures as provided for by the Committee. Paragraph 5 of this section provides that facts and opinions proposed by the "interested persons" must be brought into consideration by the Provincial Committee in using discretion for approval of registration on the Land Readjustment Project.

During the management of the Land Readjustment Project, if it is necessary to use land and immovable property belonging to the State for land readjustment, whether or not it is the Domaine Public of State under the category of the property for the common use of people, the Land Readjustment Project implementer needs to ask for permission to use such land from the Readjustment Committee at the Ministerial level (Section 55, paragraph 1). Once the Committee approves the use of such property in the Land Readjustment Project, such approval shall withdraw the status of State property. As a result, the Land Readjustment Project implementer can use such land under following conditions (Section 55, paragraph 3):

1 The land which is Domaine Public of State under the category of the property for the common use of people *but the people stop making use of that land*, or which has been transformed from being the land for common use by citizens, and such land does not belong to any person;
2 The land which is Domaine Public of State under the category of the property for the common use of people *and the people still make use of that land, another land plot must be provided as replacement for common use by people*, after an announcement in the Government Gazette etc.

5 Core legislation on disasters

5.1 The 2007 Disaster Prevention and Mitigation Act

The Disaster Prevention and Mitigation (DPM) Act was made in 2007 as a lesson learned from the 2004 tsunami, expected to be an integration law having more efficiency, consistency, and unity of disaster risk reduction management, and meant to replace the two former laws: the 1979 Civil Defense Act and the 1999 Prevention and Fire Control Act. The Act integrated public work on emergency incidents, prevention and mitigation for fire, and disaster to strengthen capacity of implementation. It also established the Department of Disaster Prevention and Mitigation (DDPM) as the core government department with primary roles on prevention, mitigation, and recovery for both disasters and emergency incidents. Although this Act was not applied to the tsunami case, it was used substantially during the 2011 floods in Bangkok.

The DPM Act defines the term "disaster" as any of the following: fire, storm, strong wind, flood, drought, epidemic in humans, epidemic in animals, epidemic in aquaculture, epidemic in plants, and other public disaster, either natural disaster or human-made disaster, accident or all other incidents that affect life, body, or properties of the people, or of the government. And in this regards, air threats and sabotages are also included. While "air threat" means any disasters affected from strikes or attacks in the air by terrorists or alien nations, and "sabotage" means any disasters affected from any activities that aim to destroy private or government properties, public utilities, or activities of offensive, deterrence, delay to any operations, including of any harmful actions toward persons which will create a political, economic and social disturbance or damage to national security as a whole.

Since the meaning of disaster is very broad, in practice, there are twenty-four governmental agencies responding to different types of disaster, although the DDPM serves as the main authority. Different disasters can be grouped and specifically handled by four main institutions attached to different ministries:

- *DDPM, Ministry of Interior*: responsible for flood, drought, storm, and tsunami;
- *Department of Mineral Resources, Ministry of Natural Resources and Environment*: responsible for landslide;
- *Department of Livestock Development, Ministry of Agriculture and Cooperatives*: responsible for epidemic (animal and human);
- *Department of Disease Prevention Control, Ministry of Public Health*: responsible for epidemic (animal and human).

It is noticeable that in the definition part of the DPM Act, most of the key words are governmentally oriented; for example, "Government agency", "Local administration", "Province", "District", "District governor", "Local governor", "Commander in Chief", "Director", "Officer", "Director-General", and "Minister".

There is only one term referring to non-governmental people, "Volunteer", which means any disaster prevention and mitigation volunteers. Another key word, "Victims", is also missing from the definition part of this Act.

Under the DPM Act, disasters are categorized into four levels or scales, matching with the hierarchy of authorities responsible for each category of disaster as follows:

- *Small-scale disaster*: under the control of local administration – Chief District Officer acts as District Director; and Tambon (Sub-District) Mayor acts as Local Director;
- *Medium-scale disaster*: beyond control of local administration, but under control of the Provincial Governor – Provincial/Bangkok Governor acts as Provincial Director;
- *Big-scale/serious disaster*: beyond control of Provincial Governor, which requires experts, technology, and equipment from other stakeholders for response and mitigation – Director-General of the DDPM acts as Central Director, while the Minister of Interior acts as Commander in Chief;
- *Mega-scale/extremely serious disaster*: where greater impacts on life and property of people exist: Prime Minister will be responsible.

In terms of central–local relationship of governmental authorities, the DPM Act arranges the division of power and connectivity between the two levels by establishing two levels of committees. At the national level, the National Disaster Prevention and Mitigation Committee (NDPMC) was set up with functions to formulate National Disaster Prevention and Mitigation Plans; to authorize local governments to take responsibility of disaster management in their respective areas; and to recommend or support any disaster prevention and mitigation activity.

At the local level, two committees are formed: the Provincial Disaster Prevention and Mitigation Committee, and Bangkok Metropolitan Committee. Their duties are to formulate Provincial Disaster Prevention and Mitigation Plans in accordance with the national plan; to oversee and train all volunteers of local administration in the province; to oversee and investigate all local administrations on preparing disaster prevention and mitigation equipment, materials, vehicles, and other related hardware for their own use in accordance with the Provincial plan; to operate as a government service unit at the local administration level to provide basic support to disaster-affected people, and other activities related to disaster prevention and mitigation; to support local administrations on any related activities of disaster prevention and mitigation; and to perform any other duties as may be required by the Commander in Chief or the Central Director.

The relationship between the central and local governments is also secured by Section 31 of this Act, which stipulates that, in case of severe disaster occurring, the Prime Minister or designated Minister shall have the power to demand the Commander in Chief, Directors, government agencies and related local administrations to deploy disaster prevention and mitigation, including providing support to people in the affected areas. If any government employees abandon their duties or deny to comply with any commands from the Prime Minister or designated Deputy Prime Minister, such persons shall be charged with the highest disciplinary violation or improper operation at the highest degree.

5.2 Implementation of the 2007 Law in the 2011 Bangkok flood

During the 2011 floods in Bangkok, there was political conflict in the administration between the Prime Minister, who came from one party, and the Governor of the Bangkok Metropolitan, who came from the opposition party. This conflict led to the disunity in the commanding system of the administration during the flood, leading to unnecessary severe damage in many affected areas. In the end, the Prime Minister exercised her power under Section 31 of this Act.

From the people's perspective, both were under heavy criticism for sending mixed messages to the public, closing water gates, building floodwalls to protect inner Bangkok, causing water directions to other provinces, and ending with water levels staying higher than two meters for several months in surrounding provinces. The flooding came in late July 2011 and lasted until late November 2011, killing more than 600 people and affecting about 2.4 million more in a third of the country's provinces. Such industrialized provinces as Pathum Thani, Nonthaburi, and Ayutthaya on the northern fringes of Bangkok were the worst affected, with farmland, homes, and industrial estates deluged, causing huge damage to homes, businesses, and factories, and disruptions in global supply chains.

In giving feedback to the government concerning the 2011 flooding management, the Stop Global Warming Association (SGWA) took legal action against relevant authorities and officials, including the Prime Minister, on behalf of the flood victims over the flood crisis, at the Central Administrative Court in Bangkok. The main grounds of the accusation were mismanagement, negligence, delayed delivery of services, and committing actions that caused damage.

In the lawsuit, the defendants were accused of mismanagement by closing water gates and obstructing natural waterways, causing flooding in parts of Nakhon Pathom Province and damage to life and property of the victims. Mr. Srisuwan, the lawyer in this case, said that the government had the Disaster Prevention and Mitigation Act in place, but failed to enforce it, for the flood-prevention and flood-relief operations, and that the government was too slow in sending relief items to flood victims. In addition, it was believed that the construction of big-bag floodwalls also hurt many people who then have had to face prolonged flooding.

The Central Administrative Court ruled that the former Prime Minister and her government had done its best to handle the flooding and prevent the water entering inner Bangkok. The court dismissed the case on the grounds that, between June and October 2011, the northern part of Thailand was hit by many tropical storms and the monsoon, which was also augmented by high tides;

therefore, massive flooding occurred in many parts of the country. Moreover, all of the country's dams held a record-high level of water. Despite careful discharging of water from the dams' reservoirs, a huge volume of water still flowed from the north to the central region, flooding nearly all industrial estates and vast areas of rice fields. Measures were taken to prevent the inner part of Bangkok, which is the country's economic center, from flooding.

The Court said that the government had taken every possible measure to prevent and mitigate the flooding indiscriminately. Households affected by the floods were paid 5,000 baht each in compensation. Necessary assistance was provided for the affected people. The plaintiffs' lawyer said he would consult his clients as to whether to take the case to the Supreme Administrative Court.

6 Regulations responding to victims and affected communities

During the 2004 tsunami, the Prime Minister refused financial support from abroad. Rather, he depended on the government budget and internal donation. In spending the money for assisting the tsunami victims and affected communities, there was a principal Regulation on how to use this money: the 2003 Regulation of the Ministry of Finance on Official Advanced Budget for Assisting Disaster Victims under Emergency. During the 2011 floods, there was a similar Regulation for compensating the flooding victims: the 2011 Regulation of the Ministry of Interior on Criteria and Procedure for Compensating to People Having Damages from Disaster Mitigation.

However, the two are only examples of by-laws relating to the financial aspects directly responding to victims and affected communities. There is other financial support available for specific issues, such as:

- Tax exemption by the Ministry of Finance;
- Soft loan by financial institutions and the Bank of Thailand;
- Flexibility in reimbursing governmental budget and increasing budget to the provinces;
- Rehabilitation measures for affected tourism spots by the Tourism Authority of Thailand.

6.1 The 2004 tsunami case: the 2003 Regulation of the Ministry of Finance on Official Advanced Budget for Assisting Disaster Victims under Emergency

The objective of the 2003 Regulation is to alleviate the immediate suffering of disaster victims, but does not intend to provide compensation to any person. Beneficiaries from this Regulation are affected persons from the tsunami. According to this Regulation, the term "affected person" means a person who has suffered loss or damage from a disaster emergency, including governmental agencies that have suffered from the disaster emergency in the area.

Under this Regulation, "financial assistance" can be divided into three groups:

- "Agricultural Assistance" includes assistance to victims of disasters relevant to damage to livestock and fisheries;
- "Assistance on Social Welfare and Rehabilitation to Victims" means short-term assistance only for the victims who can help themselves, such as helping children, the elderly, or handicapped members when the head of the family has died or been injured from the disaster, moving houses, promoting short-term professional skills to families, giving advice to disaster victims, and referring the victims to responsible agencies as soon as possible to bring their life back to normal;
- "Assistance on Medical and Public Health" means assisting disaster victims both physically and mentally, which includes medical care, sanitation, disease control and prevention, rehabilitation, and public health, to bring their life back to normal.

The Permanent Secretary of the Ministry of Finance was in charge of the implementation of this Regulation.

6.2 The 2011 floods case: the 2011 Regulation of the Ministry of Interior on Criteria and Procedure for Compensating to People Having Damages from Disaster Mitigation

This Regulation was made according to the 2007 DPM Act to elaborate on its principle by providing certain rules to protect people. If the operations performed with properness and carefulness upon the officers' authorities and functions cause any direct damage to properties of people, the government shall compensate for that damage as provided by the Ministerial Regulations and Procedures (Section 43). The Committee on Compensation for Damaged Property is established by the Regulation to identify cause of damages and determine compensation for the victims. It is particularly observed that, while the 2007 DPM Act does not provide the term "victim", this Regulation does define the word clearly. According to the Regulation, "victim" means a person whose property has been damaged by the operation of officers in preventing and mitigating disaster, but not a person who gains benefit from such prevention or mitigation.

7 Conclusion

The development of public administration and legislation of the Thai case on post-tsunami management in connection to the rule of law and legal sociological perspectives can refer to the following observations:

- *Adhoc or temporary actions vs. long-term or permanent structure*: at the early stage of development, adhoc or temporary measures were used mainly due to lack of knowledge, skills, manpower, systematic plans, appropriate laws, etc. This leads to the legitimacy in using centralized power, even by the civilian government, following the use of some exceptions of the rule of law, and ending up with the fragmentation of laws and policies. At the later stages, it is necessary to develop long-term or permanent structural change to respond to the more frequent disasters, based on the knowledge and technology on disaster management.

- *National security or safety vs. rights and liberties of individuals*: although it is common to put priority on public interest through claiming national security or safety over private interest through rights and liberties of individuals, it is still necessary to be aware of providing certain conditions in applying such a claim as they are regarded as exceptions to the rule of law that must be interpreted and used strictly. This should not be abused or distorted by governments, particularly those who have conflicts of interest.
- *Centralized power vs. delegation or decentralized power and public participation*: while working in chaotic situations needs clear and determined command – and many laws thus preferred to authorize centralized power to one single authority, for example, the Prime Minister – it is still necessary to be aware of sharing or delegating such power to other governmental bodies and/or citizens according to each one's expertise and appropriateness based on different factors: size and type of disaster, location, experience, etc. This can be seen under decentralization, public–private partnership, public participation, and integrated legislation.
- *Integration as managing the management through laws*: good disaster law must maintain the quality of integration both vertically through central, regional, and local government, and horizontally through government, business, developers, communities, NGOs, academics, media, and volunteers. The objective on public interest illustrated in several legislations can be harmonized and can be connected in the structure of disaster law.

Note

1 Land Readjustment Office, Pilot Land Readjustment Project, B.E. 2548 (2548). P. 59–72.

6 Building back a better nation

Disaster rehabilitation and recovery in the Philippines

Ebinezer R. Florano, Joe-Mar S. Perez, and Abel Táiti Konno Pinheiro

1 Introduction

One of the main highlights of the Philippine Disaster Risk Reduction and Management System (PDRRMS) is the thematic area of "Disaster Rehabilitation and Recovery" (DRRE).[1] DRRE generally involves the rebuilding of infrastructure and settlements devastated by disasters and the restoration of livelihoods to bring back normalcy to the affected communities.

The need to institutionalize DRRE as a thematic area in the PDRRMS was brought about by the fact that disasters, whether natural or human-induced, frequently occur in the country. Examples of natural hazards are tropical storms or typhoons accompanied by heavy rain and/or strong winds, earthquakes, tsunamis, and volcanic eruptions (National Disaster Risk Reduction and Management Plan [NDRRM Plan], 2012: 3–4). There are also human-induced disasters brought about by political and socio-economic factors (NDRRM Plan, 2012: 10). Furthermore, the worsening condition of the climate due to global warming aggravates the occurrences of natural calamities. Combining all of these, thousands of Filipino lives and properties are affected every year. Given the magnitude and scope of damages, it has always been a challenge for the government to restore the normal living conditions of the communities and start all over again. Hence, a comprehensive approach to rehabilitation and recovery was developed.

To have a better understanding and appreciation of DRRE, this chapter explores its operationalization in the Philippines context. It is divided into four sections. The first section discusses the origins and development of DRRE as a thematic area. It highlights the paradigm shift in the PDRRMS, which was brought about by the enactment of the Republic Act 10121 (RA 10121), also known as the "Philippine Disaster Risk Reduction and Management Act of 2010" as its legal framework. The second section explains the design principles of DRRE. It explains how DRRE is carried out through the National Disaster Risk Reduction and Management (NDRRM) Plan. It also describes the involvement of the communities in rehabilitation and recovery programs. It also discusses the Post-Disaster Needs Assessment (PDNA) as a specific DRRE tool. To further illustrate the use of PDNA, the third section presents the case of Davao Oriental, a province in the131Mindanao region, which was heavily devastated by Typhoon "Pablo"

(International Name: “Bopha”) in December 2012. It also explains how civil property rights serve as among the major considerations in the aftermath of a disaster and how the PDNA takes into account the civil property rights of the victims.

2 Origins and development of disaster rehabilitation and recovery

RA 10121 is the overall legal framework that provides the holistic and comprehensive Disaster Risk Reduction and Management (DRRM) approach. It was signed into law on May 10, 2010. Prior to RA 10121, the Philippine government used to focus on intensifying and strengthening disaster response operations. Whenever disaster strikes, the government agencies convene to plan and prepare for the necessary rescue and relief activities. However, such approach revealed pre- and post-disaster gaps. In particular, past rehabilitation and recovery practices have not ensured that better and safer structures are built on safer locations (NDRRM Plan, 2012: 12). Overall, the reactive stance was concentrated on disaster response, which was not enough to comprehensively manage the consequences of disasters.

Because of the identified pre- and post-disaster gaps, the Philippines took a paradigm shift from a reactive disaster response and coordination to a proactive DRRM stance through RA 10121. As defined in Section 3(o) of RA 10121, DRRM is “the systematic process of using administrative directives, organizations, and operational skills and capacities to implement strategies, policies and improved coping capacities in order to lessen the adverse impacts of hazards and the possibility of disaster”. To operationalize DRRM, four thematic areas were introduced:

1 Disaster Prevention and Mitigation;
2 Disaster Preparedness;
3 Disaster Response; and
4 Disaster Rehabilitation and Recovery.

The paradigm shift gave birth to DRRE as a specific DRRM thematic area. Section 3 of RA 10121 further expounds on DRRE through the following terminologies:

> (aa) “Post-Disaster Recovery” – the restoration and improvement where appropriate, of facilities, livelihood and living conditions. of disaster-affected communities, including efforts to reduce disaster risk factors, in accordance with the principles of “Build Back Better”.
>
> (ee) “Rehabilitation” – measures that ensure the ability of affected communities/areas to restore their normal level of functioning by rebuilding livelihood and damaged infrastructure and increasing the communities’ organizational capacity.

The enactment of RA 10121 also led to the formulation and approval of the NDRRM Framework on June 16, 2011. The NDRRM Framework provides for the comprehensive, all hazards, multi-sectoral, inter-agency, and community-based approach to DRRM (NDRRM Plan, 2012: 12). It explains that the DRRE, together with the other three thematic areas, should work together to achieve the vision of "safer, adaptive and disaster resilient Filipino communities toward sustainable development" (NDRRM Plan, 2012: 12).

In summary, it is through the RA 10121 that the DRRM approach was established. There was a paradigm shift from a reactive stance to a proactive stance, which entails a much more holistic management of disaster impacts. Such paradigm shift led to the institutionalization of DRRE as a distinct DRRM thematic area.

3 Design principles: operationalizing disaster rehabilitation and recovery through the NDRRM Plan

To put DRRE into action, the NDRRM Plan was formulated. It serves as a fulfillment of the requirements of RA 10121. It is basically a road map from 2011 to 2028 on how DRRM shall contribute to gender-responsive and rights-based sustainable development, promote inclusive growth, build adaptive communities, increase resilience of vulnerable sectors, and optimize disaster mitigation opportunities to promote people welfare and institutions (NDRRM Plan, 2012: 17). The NDRRM Plan covers the four thematic areas, with a total of 14 objectives, 24 outcomes, 56 outputs, and 93 activities. It pinpoints the key agencies and the participating institutions involved, their vertical and horizontal mechanisms for coordination, and the operational timelines of completion.

According to the NDRRM Plan (2012: 37), DRRE covers concerns related to employment and livelihoods, infrastructure and lifeline facilities, and housing and resettlement. The head agency for all activities under this thematic area is the National Economic and Development Authority (NEDA), which is the central socio-economic planning and policy coordinating agency of the Philippines.

The goal of DRRE is to restore and improve the facilities, livelihoods, living conditions, and organizational capacities of the affected communities, and reduce disaster risks in accordance with the "Build Back Better" principle (NDRRM Plan, 2012: 37). To achieve the said goal, the NDRRM Plan (2012: 37) emphasizes four objectives:

1 To restore people's means of livelihood and continuity of economic activities and business;
2 To restore shelter and other buildings/installation;
3 To reconstruct infrastructure and other public utilities; and
4 To assist in the physical and psychological rehabilitation of persons who suffered from the effects of disaster.

For each objective, the NDRRM Plan (2012: 36–40) specifies the corresponding outcomes, outputs, and activities, together with the lead agencies involved, their implementing partners, and the projected operational timelines, as shown in Tables 6.1–6.4.

Table 6.1 DRRE to restore livelihood and continuity of economic activities and business in the Philippines[1]

Outcome 20	**Damages, losses and needs assessed**				
Indicators	• % of livelihood activities restored/reviewed through government/LGU support • % increase in livelihoods established through government/LGU support • % of approved credit for affected sectors				
Lead agency	OCD				
Implementing partner	National government agencies, regional line agencies, and local offices				
Outputs	*Activities*	*Operational timeline*			
		Within 1 year	*Within 1–3 years*	*Within 3–6 years*	*Beyond 6 years*
1 Post-Disaster Needs Assessment	1.1 Conduct Post-Disaster Needs Assessment (PDNA)	X			
2 Strategic Action Plan	2.1 Coordinate the formulation of the Strategic Action Plan for disaster-affected areas	X			

Outcome 21	**Economic activities restored and, if possible, strengthened or expanded**				
Indicators	• % of livelihood activities restored/revived through government/LGU support • % increase in livelihoods established through government/LGU support • % of approved credit for affected sectors				
Lead agency	Agency to be determined based on the sectors affected				
Implementing partner	AFP, CSO, DA, DBM, DLIG, DSWD, DTI, LGU, MINDA, OP, Congressional Development Authorities				
Outputs	*Activities*	*Operational timeline*			
		Within 1 year	*Within 1–3 years*	*Within 3–6 years*	*Beyond 6 years*
1 Livelihood programs and projects	1.1 Identify the needed assistance and formulate/ implement appropriate programs	X			
2 Credit facilities for affected sectors	2.1 Identify/mobilize funding sources	X	X		

Note

1 "National Disaster Risk Reduction and Management Plan: 2011–2028", 2012: 32.

Table 6.2 DRRE to restore shelter and other buildings/installations in the Philippines[1]

Outcome 22	**DRRM/CCA elements incorporated in human settlement**				
Indicators	• % of affected LGUs implementing appropriate safety codes • % of affected LGUs providing safe relocation and resettlement areas • Relevant government housing cum livelihood programs developed or implemented • % of affected families involved in the construction of Core Shelter/Modified Shelter, Cash for Work/Food for Work and Sustainable Livelihood				
Lead agency	NHA				
Implementing partners	AFP, DAR, DENR, DILG, DOST, DPWH, DSWD, HLURB, LGU, NEDA, PAGIBIG				
Outputs	*Activities*	*Operational timeline*			
		Within 1 year	*Within 1–3 years*	*Within 3–6 years*	*Beyond 6 years*
1 Safe relocation sites	1.1 Identify and provide suitable relocation sites for affected population	X	X		
2 Disaster-resilient housing designed and reconstructed	2.1 Design/construction of disaster resilient housing	X	X	X	
3 Self-sufficient communities with access to basic social services	3.1 Conduct training for social preparation of host communities and those that will be relocated to reduce conflict	X	X		
4 Empowered informal settlers/ affected families	4.1 Organize NASA/construct Core Shelter/engage in Cash for Work/Food for Work/organize SEA-K groups	X			

Note
1 "National Disaster Risk Reduction and Management Plan: 2011–2028", 2012: 32.

Table 6.3 DRRE to reconstruct infrastructure and other public utilities in the Philippines[1]

Outcome 23	**Disaster and climate change-resilient and infrastructure reconstructed**				
Indicators	• % of disaster-resilient transport infrastructure facilities rehabilitated/reconstructed • % of constructed/reconstructed social infrastructure (hospitals and schools) following safety standards • % of applications approved within the prescribed time (linked to risk transfer mechanism and anti-red tape act RA 9485)				
Lead agency	DPWH				
Implementing partners	AFP, ASEP, CSC, DENR. DepEd, DILG, DOJ, LGUs, PICE				
Outputs	*Activities*	*Operational timeline*			
		Within 1 year	*Within 1–3 years*	*Within 3–6 years*	*Beyond 6 years*
1 Infrastructure facilities restored/ rehabilitated according to safety and resiliency standards	1.1 Identify the needed assistance and formulate/ implement appropriate programs		X	X	X
	1.2 Implement building code and promotion of green technology		X	X	X
2 Development permits approved within prescribed timeline	2.1 Close monitoring and/or tracking of approval of infrastructure projects and permits		X	X	X

Note
1 "National Disaster Risk Reduction and Management Plan: 2011–2028", 2012: 33–34.

Table 6.4 DRRE to assist in the physical and psychological rehabilitation of persons who suffered from the effects of disaster in the Philippines[1]

Outcome 24	**A psychologically sound, safe, and secured citizenry that is protected from the effects of disasters able to restore to normal functioning after each disaster**				
Indicators	• % of vulnerable population provided with adequate and appropriate risk protection measures				
Lead agency	DOH and DSWD				
Implementing partners	AFP, CSOs, DILG, NBI, PNP, PRC, OPAPP				
Outputs	*Activities*	*Operational timeline*			
		Within 1 year	*Within 1–3 years*	*Within 3–6 years*	*Beyond 6 years*
1 Vulnerable population provided with adequate and appropriate risk protection measures	1.1 Develop systems for appropriate risk protection measures	X			
	1.2 Conduct of post-disaster/conflict needs analyses with affected communities	X			
	1.3 Develop systems of support and communication among key stakeholders	X			
	1.4 Build capacities of psychosocial care providers	X	X		

Note
1 "National Disaster Risk Reduction and Management Plan: 2011–2028", 2012: 34.

As seen in the tables above, the NDRRM Plan generally works by maximizing together the mandates and expertise of the various national and local agencies in conducting rehabilitation and recovery programs for a specific timeframe. Overall, the NEDA supervises these institutions to ensure a holistic and sustainable economic development while undertaking rehabilitation and recovery programs for affected communities.

3.1 Disaster rehabilitation and recovery: a cross-cutting thematic area

Although DRRE is a distinct thematic area in the PDRRMS, the NDRRM Plan (2012: 18) emphasizes that it cannot stand alone and that it has no clear starting and ending points. Instead, it mutually reinforces the other thematic areas, which are all focused towards reducing people's vulnerabilities and increasing their capacities (NDRRM Plan, 2012: 18). Hence, it generally follows the "Build Back Better" principle, which indicates the comprehensiveness of the PDRRMS. In the aftermath of a disaster, rehabilitation and recovery programs are intended not just to restore normalcy but also to ensure that the communities will no longer experience the same devastation in the future. In other words, it "builds" "back" the communities in "better" conditions. For example, under Disaster Prevention and Mitigation, it recommends the installation of early warning systems and flood control structures. Under Disaster Preparedness, it proposes the completion of comprehensive land use plans and recommends the conduct of regular training. Under Disaster Response, it highlights the need to establish predetermined evacuation centers and to pre-position resources for emergencies. Overall, the "Build Back Better" principle is a cross-cutting feature of the DRRE, which integrates all DRRM thematic areas to effectively capacitate the communities.

3.2 Community participation in disaster rehabilitation and recovery

To cascade the implementation of the NDRRM Plan at all levels, from the regional, provincial, city, and municipal levels down to the barangay level, all local government units (LGUs) are tasked to create their own Local DRRM (LDRRM) Plans. The LDRRM Plan is microcosm of the NDRRM Plan, with its own specific objectives, outputs, outcomes, and activities that are intended to complement those of the NDRRM Plan. Its provisions are set to be implemented in the respective jurisdiction and area of responsibility of the LGU.

It is through the LDRRM Plan that community participation plays a vital role in DRRE. The LDRRM Plan provides specific programs and activities that invite the participation of the community members, including women, children, and persons with disabilities. Hence, the concept of community-based DRRM (CBDRRM) was institutionalized, with "gender-mainstreaming" as the core feature. Gender-mainstreaming in CBDRRM is about reducing the vulnerabilities of men and women to disasters and encourages a balance in their participation and decision-making in community-based DRRM (Victoria, 2012). Examples of CBDRRM activities involved in DRRE are the following (Victoria, 2012):

- Involving of women on planning "how to build better";
- Strengthening livelihood and community health;
- Ensuring that socio-economic projects do not add to women's multiple burden;
- Increasing capacities and reducing vulnerabilities of the communities; and
- Increasing livelihood options and access to resources.

In addition to the involvement of community members, civil society organizations (CSOs) and private institutions also play a role. CSOs engage in various volunteer works and conduct information campaigns to introduce alternative means of livelihood. Private institutions facilitate Corporate Social Responsibility (CSR) programs, such as provision of donations for restoration of facilities and mobilization of private volunteer groups. These are among the many examples of how the entire community participates in DRRE.

3.3 Post-Disaster Needs Assessment: a tool in disaster rehabilitation and recovery

To ensure an efficient, effective, and well-organized DRRE, the Philippine government begins by conducting an aggregate but detailed assessment of the disaster impacts and identifying the critical needs of the affected sectors. Such strategy is particularly achieved through the Post-Disaster Needs Assessment (PDNA). To further understand how PDNA works, this section provides an overview of the PDNA, its conceptual framework, initiation and timing, the organization of assessment teams, and the steps involved. This section summarizes the "PDNA Guidance Notes",[2] a document prepared by the World Bank (2014) for the Philippine government, together with the PDNA reports and references by the Office of Civil Defense (OCD),[3] the country's primary government agency that coordinates and orchestrates all DRRM activities.

3.3.1 What is PDNA?

PDNA[4] is defined as a multi-sectoral and multi-disciplinary structured approach for assessing disaster impacts and prioritizing recovery and reconstruction needs. It is led and undertaken by the government agencies in collaboration with international development partners and the private sector. The purpose of PDNA is generally to estimate two important factors: (1) the short-term interventions to initiate recovery from the damages and losses; and (2) the financial requirements to achieve a holistic post-disaster recovery, reconstruction, and risk management.

PDNA was initially developed by the United Nations Economic Commission for Latin America and the Caribbean, which has been increasingly recognized as the standard for reconstruction processes at the national level. As of now, it is the internationally accepted approach in post-disaster damage, loss, and needs assessment. In the Philippines, PDNA, as a tool for DRRE, is institutionalized through the enactment of RA 10121. Its utilization is spearheaded by the OCD. As stated in Section 9(m) of RA 10121, one of the powers and functions of OCD is to "conduct early recovery and post-disaster needs assessment institutionalizing gender analysis as part of it". Furthermore, in Outcome 20 of the NDRRM Plan, the OCD is specifically identified as the lead agency in PDNA to assess the damages, losses, and needs.

Figure 6.1 shows the conceptual framework for PDNA. It basically starts with Damage and Loss Assessment (DALA), an assessment of the post-disaster damages based on baseline data. Baseline data or pre-disaster data are the complete information about a certain community, such as the number of buildings, infrastructure, residential houses, and population. DALA works by identifying how much the disaster has caused changes in the baseline data in terms of damages and losses.

From the DALA, PDNA moves on to the analyses of disaster impacts. The analyses entail in-depth assessment of the disaster impacts at the personal, social, and macro-economic perspectives.

Based on the outputs of the analyses, PDNA then proceeds to the Human Recovery Needs Assessment (HRNA) to determine how the people can recover from the disaster. It specifies the strategies and programs for reconstruction, recovery, and disaster risk reduction activities.

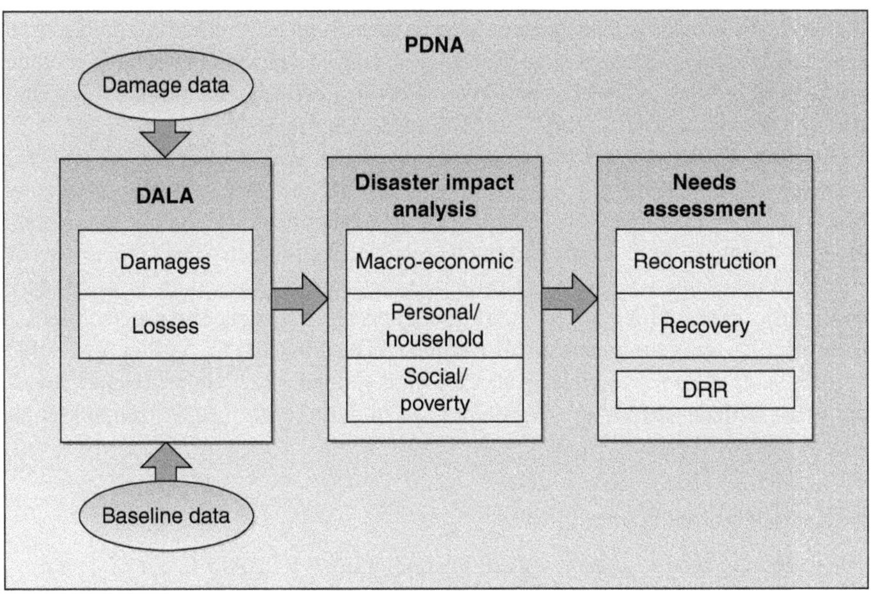

Figure 6.1 Conceptual framework of PDNA in the Philippines (source: "PDNA Guidance Notes – Introduction by World Bank", Draft 2012 Version, 2012: 2).

3.3.2 Initiation and timing

The need to initiate PDNA is decided by the government by following certain criteria. These include the number of affected provinces and people, the scope and extent of damages on certain sectors, and a declaration of a state of calamity or emergency by the Philippine President. Whatever the criteria are, the conduct of PDNA should not commence while humanitarian assistance and initial recovery programs are still at work. This is because resources and efforts of the government should first prioritize the provision of emergency assistance to the affected people. However, PDNA should not be unnecessarily delayed because there is also an urgent need to seek support from the international community. Furthermore, the government must have an overview of the funding and resources required for reconstruction and recovery.

The indicative time schedule for the conduct of PDNA is shown in Table 6.5.

In carrying out PDNA, there is a need to balance speed and accuracy. Speed is much more important than accuracy in order to immediately facilitate rehabilitation and recovery programs and to take into account the support from international agencies. Nevertheless, a PDNA should still aim for the highest possible accuracy by combining the best professionals and technical experts, the best available information, and a reliable and adequate methodological tool for assessment.

3.3.3 Organization and composition of the assessment team

The assessment process is conducted in teams composed of professionals and technical experts. The composition of the assessment teams depends on the sectors to be covered. They generally include architects, engineers, sociologists, economists, statisticians, and the respective sectoral experts. They also include professionals who are well acquainted with the assessment methodology and with the socio-economic conditions of the affected areas.

From the government's side, the respective roles and tasks of the government agencies in PDNA are based on their institutional mandate and official agency functions. For example, the Department of Agriculture undertakes the assessment of the agriculture sector and the analysis of the impacts. The Department of Public Works and Highways assesses the devastation caused to infrastructure and public roads. OCD, as the lead agency in PDNA, consolidates the assessment reports by these government agencies. The final PDNA is then presented by the OCD to the National DRRM Council (NDRRMC),[5] international development partners, and other stakeholders to undertake the needed rehabilitation and recovery programs.

3.3.4 Steps in conducting a PDNA

The following are the steps involved in conducting a PDNA:

1 *Collect and/or validate the baseline data*: Baseline data cover all the assets of the locality and the related replacement and repair costs. Examples are

Table 6.5 Indicative schedule for PDNA in the Philippines

Activities	*Month 1*				*Month 2*			
	Week				*Week*			
	1	*2*	*3*	*4*	*5*	*6*	*7*	*8*
Emergency stage	X	X						
• Search and rescue	X							
• Evacuation	X	X						
• Food supply	X	X						
Post-emergency phase								
• Decision to conduct PDNA (by NDRRMC)		X						
• Organizational arrangements (by NDRRMC and RDRRMC)		X						
Activities of participating agencies								
• Organizing of assessment team		X						
• Step 1. Collecting/updating baseline information at regional level		X	X					
• Coordination with and briefing of regional offices and LGUs			X					
• Step 2. Start field visits for damage and loss assessment				X	X			
• Assessment of government assets				X	X			
• Assessment of private assets				X	X			
• Summarizing overall damages and losses						X		
• Step 3. Validation of results to avoid duplication with other sectors						X		
• Step 4. Impact analysis						X		
• Step 5. Provide impact analysis to:								
• Macroeconomic impacts to NEDA						X		
• Social impact analysis to DSWD						X		
• Environmental impacts to DENR						X		
• DRRM impacts to OCD						X		
• Step 6. Estimate recovery and reconstruction needs							X	
• Step 7. Provide NEDA with list of recovery and reconstruction projects							X	
• Step 8. Analyze financing options							X	
• Step 9. Draft implementation plans for the projects							X	
• Step 10. Draft the sectoral PDNA report and submit to OCD							X	X
• Draft overall PDNA report by OCD								X

physical structures (office buildings, garages, warehouses, and other buildings) together with the equipment, supplies, and other assets. It is important to note that baseline data should be compiled by the LGU prior to the occurrence of a disaster.

2 *Estimate damages and losses*: Using the baseline data, the damages and losses can now be estimated. Assessment teams will be organized and deployed in the affected areas and sectors to conduct data gathering and assessment.

3 *Validate the information on damages and losses*: To ensure the integrity of the data collected, OCD will convene a meeting to be attended by the assessment teams. The meeting will enable the assessment teams to validate and reconcile the data collected from the field and prevent double counting.
4 *Analyze the impacts of the damages and losses to affected population*: From the validated and consolidated data, the assessment teams will begin the analysis of the potential impacts of the damages and losses in relation to the delays in the socio-economic activities, the losses in government revenues, and any other disaster-related issue.
5 *Forward the impact assessment to the appropriate agency for aggregate analysis*: The results of the analysis will be part of an aggregate assessment by the concerned agencies and technical experts. For example, the social impact assessment must be consolidated by the Department of Social Welfare and Development. DRR-related concerns must be reported to OCD. Environmental-related impacts must be communicated with the Department of Environment and Natural Resources. Macro-economic effects or impacts should be relayed to NEDA.
6 *Estimate recovery and reconstruction needs*: Based on the damages and losses of the agency together with their aggregate analyses, the needs will then be identified. Examples of the possible recovery needs are immediate repairs of structures, procurement of vital equipment needed, and cash assistance, if necessary.

    There are also the reconstruction needs that are long-term in nature, usually three years or more. Examples of the possible reconstruction needs are reconstruction and repair of damaged structures, replacement of the destroyed equipment, machinery, and furniture, structural retro-fitting of undamaged or partially damaged structures, and relocation to safe areas, if necessary.
7 *Provide NEDA with the list of identified programs and projects for recovery and reconstruction*: NEDA consolidates the list of identified programs and projects for recovery and reconstruction. NEDA undertakes macroeconomic impact analysis of the programs and projects for the current and future years as well as preparing a strategic action plan (SAP) for recovery and reconstruction in consideration of the Philippine Development Plan.
8 *Analyze financing options*: The assessment must also suggest the possible sources of financing, such as Quick Response Fund, National DRRM Fund, existing funds that can be re-directed to the present needs, grants from international development partners and the private sector, etc.
9 *Write the draft of the implementation plan of the identified programs and projects*: The identified needs should have a rough schedule of implementation outlining timing and budget required and other needed information.
10 *Write the draft of the PDNA report*: With all the information gathered and analyzed, a PDNA report of the each agency should be drafted. The report should show the following:

- Total value of destroyed physical assets and of changes (losses) in the flows of production of goods and services;
- Ownership of the above: public and private sectors;
- Identification of most affected sectors;
- Spatial or geographical distribution of disaster effects;
- Impact of disaster at macro-economic, sectoral and personal/household levels; and
- Estimation of post-disaster needs for recovery, reconstruction, and disaster risk reduction measures.

The draft PDNA report of the participating agencies is submitted to the OCD for consolidation and inclusion in the overall PDNA report and the disaster recovery plan. Based on the PDNA, all government agencies and other development partners can now proceed with the implementation of rehabilitation and recovery projects and activities.

4 Case analysis: PDNA for Typhoon Pablo – the livelihood sector of Davao Oriental

This section presents a case analysis on the use of PDNA in Davao Oriental following the aftermath of Typhoon Pablo in December 2012. Typhoon Pablo was among the recent disasters that hit several provinces in the Philippines, with Davao Oriental among the most affected provinces. A summary of the PDNA Report "Davao Oriental Province: Post Disaster Needs Assessment for Typhoon 'Pablo': February 2013", highlighting the livelihood sector, is presented in this section. The said report was prepared and consolidated by the Office of Civil Defense-Regional Disaster Risk Reduction and Management Council (OCD-RDRRMC) XI[6] (2013) in collaboration with the local and national government agencies and other partners.

4.1 Background of the disaster

Typhoon Pablo was the second typhoon that affected Mindanao in the last two years and the sixteenth tropical cyclone that entered the Philippine Area of Responsibility (PAR) in 2012. On December 4, 2012, Typhoon Pablo made landfall over Baganga, Davao Oriental, with maximum sustained winds of 185 kph near the center and gusts of 220 kph. The strong winds damaged houses, roads, bridges, school buildings, churches, covered courts, and public and private infrastructure. It also uprooted trees, coconut and banana trees, and lifted light materials. As of March 1, 2013, a total of 537 fatalities, 2,271 injured, and 51 missing were recorded in Davao Oriental.

PDNA was conducted starting with the field assessment on January 21–30, 2013 in Davao Oriental, covering its seven municipalities. The assessment teams and partners conducted a series of data-gathering activities, sectoral visits, write shops, and consultative meetings until the PDNA report was drafted. The PDNA report was then completed in February 2013.

4.2 Summary of damages and reconstruction needs

Based on the PDNA findings, the total estimated damages in Davao Oriental was PHP12,802,604,657.17 and the amount needed for recovery and reconstruction was PHP14,350,733,106.33. The breakdown of the damaged sectors and recommended funding for recovery and reconstruction are shown in Table 6.6.

4.3 The livelihood sector

The assessment of the livelihood sector of Davao Oriental covered the sub-sectors of Agriculture, Tourism, Mining, and Industry, Trade, and Services (ITS). Based on the assessment, the needs for the Agriculture sub-sector accounted for 70 percent of the total recovery needs. The breakdown of the damages and reconstruction needs for the livelihood sector is shown in Table 6.7.

In the Agriculture sub-sector, assessments on damage were based on the reported areas of crops, fishery, and forestry affected by the disaster multiplied by the pre-disaster market value of the specific crop, fishery, and forestry lands. Subject-matter specialists from the municipal and provincial agriculturists' offices provided evaluation on a province-wide perspective, employing near-to-the-actual value of the agricultural area.

Table 6.6 Cost of damage and reconstruction in Typhoon Pablo (in PHP)[1]

Sector	*Estimated damage*	*Reconstruction needs*
Infrastructure	4,166,813,356.17	5,387,919,153.33
Livelihood	6,683,692,681.00	2,448,761,698.00
Social	261,080,720.00	483,177,255.00
Resettlement	1,691,017,900.00	6,030,875,000.00

Note
1 "Davao Oriental Province: Post-Disaster Needs Assessment for Typhoon 'Pablo': February 2013", 2013: i–ii.

Table 6.7 Cost of damage and reconstruction, livelihood sector in Typhoon Pablo (in PHP)[1]

Livelihood	*Reported damages*	*Recommended recovery/ reconstruction needs*
Agriculture	469,772,115.00	1,440,161,698.00
Tourism	5,528,200,000.00	5,200,000.00
Mining	0.00	3,400,000.00
Industry, Trade, and Services	685,720,566.00	1,000,000,000.00
Total	**6,683,692,681.00**	**2,448,761,698.00**

Note
1 "Davao Oriental Province: Post-Disaster Needs Assessment for Typhoon 'Pablo': February 2013", 2013: 43.

In the Tourism sub-sector, assessments were made on beach resorts, guest houses/lodging houses, municipal tourism guest houses, cultural sites, trees, and plants of the natural formations. There were also assessments based on the revenue losses by the private beach owners and the public local earnings. Data were based on the interviews with the Local Tourism Officers and owners of the lodging houses and resorts.

In the Mining sub-sector, the assessment was based on the foregone income and the cleaning up of debris needed. In the Industry, Trade and Services sub-sector, the affected private establishments were assessed.

4.4 Recommendations

Using PDNA, the teams were able to recommend concrete actions to undertake rehabilitation and recovery of the different sectors. The final PDNA report provided a list of all the recommended programs and activities, target locations, the reported damages, funding requirements, implementing agencies, and the operational timelines. The recommendations were also ranked according to urgency or priority.

Table 6.8 gives a few examples of the recommended programs and actions under the Agriculture sub-sector.

4.5 Implementation framework

To undertake the recommended programs and projects, the teams generated an implementation framework by identifying the possible fund sources, implementing bodies or agencies, as well as the teams responsible for monitoring and evaluating the implementation process.

In totality, the PDNA report proposed 69 strategies for recovery and reconstruction as well as 16 policy recommendations to complement the proposed programs and activities. The strategies are anchored on the "Build Back Better" principle. Furthermore, they are geared on restoring the capacity and capability of the livelihood sector.

4.6 Protection of civil property rights during Typhoon Pablo

Civil property rights are among the major considerations in the aftermath of a disaster. For example, private business groups and entrepreneurs suffered losses and damages in their facilities and equipment. Ordinary residents lost their homes, properties, and their means of livelihood. In the aftermath of a disaster, all of these rights remain with the victims. Hence, the government undertakes measures to help the affected victims start all over again until they are able to bring back their lost properties and assets. The government cannot provide the exact value of their lost properties nor bring back everything that was lost, hence, the victims are taught how to help themselves and restore their normal living conditions.

Table 6.8 DRRE programs and actions for the Agriculture sub-sector in Typhoon Pablo[1]

Rank	*Priority projects/activities (description)*	*Location/sites*	*Amount*		*Implementing agencies*	*Timeline*	*Remarks*
			Reported damage	*Recommended for funding*			
1	A. Crop production		212,438,975.00	175,000,000.00	DA	2013	
	Provision and distribution of seeds and planting materials (rice certified/inbred), corn-OPV legumes (soybeans and peanut) and root crops	Boston, Cateel, Baganga, Caraga, Manay, Tarragona		25,000,000.00			Annual crops including saba-banana as staple food and could produce in short-term months and is a source of livelihood. Legumes are best source of protein and nitrogen-fixing bacteria.
	Provision and distribution of saba-banana plantlets						
	Distribution of cassava cuttings (food/feeds)					2013	As staple food substitute in all seasons
	Provision of high-value crops and industrial crops (durian, mango, rubber, coffee and cacao)					2013–2015	

	Provision and distribution of abaca plantlets				FIDA	2013	Immediate rehabilitation for value adding product as source of livelihood of farmers
	Distribution of seednuts			150,000,000.00	PCA	2013–2016	Restore coconut areas by providing new variety where is the champion commodity
2	B. Pre-post production equipment and machinery			10,000,000.00	DA, PhilMech	2013–2016	Ensure postharvest losses and quality of produce
1	C. Livestock and poultry, production	Boston, Cateel, Bananga, Caraga, Manay, Tarragona	133,487,300.00	200,000,000.00			
	Restocking of breeders (Cattle/Carabao)				DA-BAI, PCC	2014	Restore breeder stock due to mortality caused by Typhoon Pablo. This will help enable farmers to sustain livestock production as source of livelihood.
1	Forage and pasture development				LGU	2013	
4	Reconstruction of slaughter					2014–2015	

continued

Table 6.8 Continued

Rank	*Priority projects/activities (description)*	*Location/sites*	*Amount*		*Implementing agencies*	*Timeline*	*Remarks*
			Reported damage	*Recommended for funding*			
5	Establishment of Artificial Insemination Center (native pigs)					2014–2015	
4	Establishment of native chicken hatchery					2013	
2	Animal health program, drugs and biologics					2014	
	D. Fishery		64,965,180.00	71,461,698.00	DA, LGUs, BFAR, LGU		
2	Rehabilitation of mangrove	Boston, Cateel, Baganga, Manay					Immediate rehab of sanctuaries as shelter to enhance biodiversity of marine and other aquatic species
2	Rehabilitation of fish sanctuaries						

1	Communal fish seeding			Immediate source of food and livelihood for inland farmers and fisher folks and restore the annual earnings and production of 43,723,000 & 301MT respectively
1	Fingerling dispersal		2013	
1	Provision of fishing banca, engines and gears			
3	Establishment/rehabilitation of Aquasilvi (mudcrab project)	Cateel, Baganga		
1	Rehabilitation of fishpond (freshwater tilapia)	Boston, Cateel, Mati		
3	Establishment/rehabilitation of seaweeds project	Cateel, Baganga		Immediate rehabilitation of projects stated to restore livelihood of fisher folk
	Establishment/rehabilitation of lobster production in pen project	Baganga		
	Establishment/rehabilitation of fishcages (saline tilapia) project	Cateel, Baganga		

continued

Table 6.8 Continued

Rank	*Priority projects/activities (description)*	*Location/sites*	*Amount*		*Implementing agencies*	*Timeline*	*Remarks*
			Reported damage	*Recommended for funding*			
	E. Forestry		58,880,660.00	5,000,000.00	DENR, LGU		Reforestation
1	Bamboo production	Boston, Cateel, Baganga, Manay					
1	Reforestation project						
2	F. Extension, education and training			4,410,000.00			
	Capability building of farmers on the different Package of Technology (POT) on rice, corn cassava, HVCC livestock and poultry production and disease management (native animals) SALT for upland areas	Boston, Cateel, Baganga, Manay, Tarragona			ATI, LGU	2013–2015	Institutionalize capability building to enhanced technical knowhow for farmers, especially on marginal areas, to sustain productivity and profitability
2	G. Establishment of technology demonstration/ commercialization on diversified farming	Boston, Cateel, Baganga, Manay, Tarragona		550,000.00	RFU-LGU	2013–2016	To be established in the identified production zones for market promotion

2	H. Research and development		370,000.00			
	On-farm review of technology on crop-soil adaptability/suitability	Boston, Cateel, Baganga	270,000.00	RFU-LGU	2013	To determine the specific crop and type of soil that crops are more suitable and resilient to
	Conduct of market research on champion commodities	Boston, Cateel, Baganga, Manay, Tarragona	100,000.00	RFU-LGU	2015	To determine domestic and international markets
1	I. Agricultural land debris management (Cash for Work) a. Forest trees and coconut trunks		798,000,000.00	DA-PCA, DENR, LGU, Development Partner	2013	Obstruction to development, pollution of waterways health hazard, siltation and flooding as well as damage to infrastructure. Other incidentals (tools, equipment, fuel for transport, etc.) will be shouldered by the concerned agencies

Note

1 "Davao Oriental Province: Post-Disaster Needs Assessment for Typhoon 'Pablo': February 2013", 2013: 59.

Box 6.1 Implementation of PDNA for Typhoon Pablo disaster

Possible fund sources

- National Calamity Fund
- Local Calamity Fund
- International Donors
- Local Donors
- National Programs

Implementing bodies/agencies

- Department of Agriculture
- Department of Tourism
- Department of Natural Resources – Mines and Geosciences Bureau
- Department of Trade and Industry
- Local Government Units
- Respective Sectoral Agencies

Monitoring and evaluation team

- Department of Budget and Management
- Commission on Audit
- Department of Agriculture
- Department of Tourism
- Department of Natural Resources – Mines and Geosciences Bureau
- Department of Trade and Industry
- Local Government Units
- Respective Sectoral Agencies

Source: "Davao Oriental Province: Post-Disaster Needs Assessment for Typhoon 'Pablo': February 2013", 2013: 59.

In the case of Davao Oriental, PDNA also accounted for the civil property rights of the victims by assessing the affected private properties. All of the affected establishments under the Industry, Trade and Services sub-sector were purely private owned. The recommended measure identified by the PDNA teams was the provision of financial assistance through soft loans. The affected micro entrepreneurs were also given the option to engage in other types of livelihood together with the necessary assistance in the form of training or grants. The breakdown of the recommendations in the PDNA report is shown in Table 6.9.

5 Case analysis: post-disaster recovery after Super Typhoon Yolanda and the No-Build Zone policy

This section presents a case analysis on the post-disaster recovery in the Philippines after Super Typhoon Yolanda (International Name: "Haiyan") in November

Table 6.9 DRRE programs and actions for the Industry, Trade and Services sub-sector in the Philippines[1]

Rank	*Priority projects/activities (description)*	*Location/sites*	*Amount*		*Implementing agencies*	*Timeline*	*Remarks*
			Reported damage	*Recommended for funding*			
1	Credit Facility (soft loans with lenient requirement and considerable amortization scheme; for the reconstruction/repair/rehab and starting capital of business establishments)	Province of Davao Oriental	685,720,566.00	822,000,000.00	DTI	Mar 2013	LGUs covered are Boston, Cateel, Baganga, Manay, Caraga, Tarragona
2	Shared Service Facility (Equipment and Machinery)	Province of Davao Oriental		60,000,000.00 20,000,000.00 20,000,000.00	DTI DAR DOLE	May 2013	
3	Entrepreneurial and Capability Training and Seminars with Starter	Province of Davao Oriental		28,000,000.00 20,000,000.00 10,000,000.00 20,000,000.00	DTI	Apr 2013	
Total			685,720,566.00	1,000,000,000.00			

Note
1 "Davao Oriental Province: Post-Disaster Needs Assessment for Typhoon 'Pablo': February 2013", 2013: 58.

2013, based on the field research conducted in the islands of Leyte and Samar, with a focus on safety and efficacy issues related to the establishment of the No-Build Zone policy in coastal regions, including areas devastated by a storm surge during Yolanda landfall.

5.1 Research background

Typhoon Yolanda was one of the most intense and deadliest tropical cyclones ever observed in Southeast Asia, with a wind speed up to 300 km/h, resulting in at least 6,300 causalities in the Philippines. Reports reveal that the disaster affected 12,122 barangays in 44 provinces, 591 municipalities and 57 cities, located in 9 out of the 17 administrative regions in the Philippines (Commission on Audit, 2014). During Yolanda landfall, many places in coastal areas registered catastrophic damage by storm surges up to 6 meters. The east coast of Samar and Leyte were most severely stricken, and flooding also extended for 1 km inland in some regions. Particularly in the eastern part of Tacloban City, with a large population living in low lying areas, many buildings were completely washed away by the storm surge, making it the major cause of causalities. In the weeks after the typhoon, the Department of Environment and Natural Resources (DENR) declared the establishment of a No-Build Zone policy along the coast of Eastern Samar and Leyte to prevent casualties from storm surges, prohibiting the construction of permanent structures within 40 meters from the shoreline as outlined in the Water Code.

In this research, site visits were conducted in March 2015, through interviews with barangay officers and local residents in coastal areas of Tacloban, Tanauan, and Dulag in Leyte Island and Basey in Samar Island, and aimed to investigate the evacuation efforts during Yolanda landfall and efficacy of establishment of the No-Build Zone as safety and recovery strategies. The following research results were presented in Kobe University, Japan (Pinheiro, 2015).

5.2 Evacuation efforts during Typhoon Yolanda

Through interviews conducted in coastal areas damaged by the storm surge, it was observed in general that the massive efforts to evacuate the population living in the risk area began a day before the typhoon made landfall, with barangay officers announcing the evacuation door-to-door, under ordinance of Municipal or Barangay Level Disaster Risk Reduction Management Council (MDRRMC or BDRRMC). Hazards related to the storm surge were also announced days before by local media and authority, and some barangays officers who were well aware of storm surges could inform the population that it would be like a tsunami or a tidal wave, calling them to evacuate more effectively. However, in most cases, its meaning had not been highlighted or fully understood by the population. In fact, a great majority of families living in low-lying areas took evacuation measures as they had done during strong typhoons in the past: husbands and men of the family tended to be left behind to take care of the house, while children, the elderly, and women were evacuated to relatives' houses or designated shelters such as schools, usually located within the same barangay or in the next barangay.

According to the survey, the early evacuation (day before landfall) tends to be completed on average by 60–90 percent of the population in coastal barangays. Some of those who remained decided to escape in imminence of the typhoon landfall, or were hit by the storm surge, in which case few survived. Furthermore, some designated shelters such as schools were not only compromised by strong winds, but were also partially flooded by storm surges whose height was higher than expected. After Typhoon Yolanda, local authorities under MDRRMC/BDRRMC reported in the survey that, in case of the announcement of a strong typhoon, the risk perception and concern with storm surges by the population has been rising, contributing to higher early/voluntary evacuation rates, as reported in following typhoons, such as Typhoon Ruby (international name "Hagupit") in December 2014. Currently, mixed strategies for evacuation against storm surges are being adopted by coastal barangays, including the designation of shelters located farther from the coast and not necessarily within the same barangay, or construction of stronger buildings, such as multi-purpose halls up to three or more floors in coastal areas. In any case, the evacuation routes tend to become larger, and factors such as transportation of vulnerable people and logistics to ensure provision of relief supplies are being discussed by barangay officers and the local population.

5.3 Safety and efficacy of the establishment of the No-Build Zone

The efficacy of the No-Build Zone policy as a strategy to prevent causalities by storm surges is questionable in terms of evacuation safety. Established along the coast of Eastern Samar and Leyte, most of the areas under this policy tend to have lower elevation extended for hundreds of meters inland, allowing storm surges to reach beyond the 40-meter buffer zone. Depending on the topographic situation, even structures outside the No-Build Zone would be damaged, and the difference of damage within or outside the 40-meter zone could be irrelevant in low-lying areas.

Furthermore, assuming that the average walking speed to perform evacuation is 1.0 m/sec. for adults, a 40-meter buffer zone would theoretically gain at most 40 seconds in an inland evacuation route. However, this time difference would be insignificant if the evacuation is delayed and starts in the imminence of a storm surge strike, in which the incoming tidal speed could be faster than walking speed. Staying inside the No-Build Zone or immediately outside the zone, the evacuee would have the same few seconds to escape from the imminent inundation by storm surge. In fact, considering the increasing awareness about risks related to the storm surge, especially in post-Yolanda evacuation planning, the tendency to perform early and voluntary evacuation days before landfall of a strong typhoon became more pertinent in low-lying areas.

According to the survey, the establishment of a 40-meter No-Build Zone in coastal areas could create a false sense of security, suggesting to populations living in low-lying areas that they are safe, when in fact they may be vulnerable and still exposed to the risks of storm surges. Instead to strictly establish the No-Build Zone, it would be necessary to evaluate the topography to identify local vulnerabilities, contributing to managed resettlement of disaster-affected populations, including fisher folk communities, under mitigating measures and better distribution of evacuation places.

6 Conclusions

Following the enactment of RA 10121, the Philippines is now undertaking a holistic approach to DRRE by involving multi-agency participation. Through the NDRRM Plan, DRRE is much more strategized by identifying the objectives, outcomes, and outputs that are laid out until 2028. Together with the other thematic areas, it envisions the achievement of "safer, adaptive and disaster resilient Filipino communities toward sustainable development". Furthermore, community participation is also given emphasis in rehabilitation and recovery through the LDRRM Plan and the gender-mainstreaming approach. Overall, DRRE aims to bring back a better nation not only by restoring normalcy in the living conditions but also by strengthening the resiliency of the communities.

To facilitate DRRE, the government starts by conducting PDNA to assess the disaster impacts, estimate damages, and identify the needed reconstruction and recovery programs. As exemplified in the case of Davao Oriental, PDNA enabled the government to estimate the total damages of Typhoon Pablo for each critical sector and recommend the programs together with their corresponding implementation frameworks and strategies. Using the findings of the PDNA, rehabilitation and recovery programs are now being undertaken in Davao Oriental by government agencies, other institutional partners, and communities.

Notes

1 In this paper, DRRE is used as an acronym for Disaster Rehabilitation and Recovery, instead of DRR, which is popularly used for Disaster Risk Reduction.

2 The PDNA Guidance Notes are a draft compilation of guidelines prepared by the World Bank for the perusal of the OCD in the conduct of PDNA. Although these are still draft documents, they are already being used by OCD for PDNA, with some modifications and customizations when applied on the actual ground assessment.

3 OCD is the Executive Arm and Secretariat of the National Disaster Risk Reduction and Management Council. It is the lead agency that spearheads the implementation of the provisions of RA 10121.

4 The PDNA Guidance Notes refer to the assessment process as "Post Disaster Assessment". For OCD, it is called Post-Disaster Needs Assessment. Consistent with OCD, the paper refers to the process as PDNA.

5 The NDRRMC is a council of government agencies in the Philippines, together with the CSOs and private sector, which collectively formulate and implement DRRM policies and programs nationwide.

6 OCD-RDRRMC XI is the Regional Council chaired by OCD Region XI, which oversees all DRRM activities in Southern Mindanao, including Davao Oriental province.

References

Commission on Audit (2014). "Assessment of Disaster Risk Reduction and Management (DRRM) at the Local Level", September, Republic of the Philippines.

"National Disaster Risk Reduction and Management Plan: 2011–2028" (2012), Republic of the Philippines.

Office of Civil Defense – Regional Disaster Risk Reduction and Management Council (OCD-RDRRMC) XI. (2013). "Davao Oriental Province: Post-Disaster Needs Assessment for Typhoon 'Pablo': February 2013", Republic of the Philippines.

Pinheiro, Abel Táiti Konno (2015). "Case Study of Evacuation Response in Islands of Leyte and Samar in Typhoon Yolanda", Presentation for the 199th Kobe University Research Center for Urban Safety and Security Open Seminar, July.

Republic Act 10121. "An Act Strengthening the Philippine Disaster Risk Reduction and Management System, Providing for the National Disaster Risk Reduction and Management Framework and Institutionalizing the National Disaster Risk Reduction and Management Plan, Appropriating Funds Therefor, and for Other Purposes", Republic of the Philippines.

Victoria, Lorna P. (2012). "Gender in Community Based Disaster Risk Reduction and Management", Presentation for the RESILIENCE PROJECT in partnership with OCD.

World Bank. (2014). "PDNA Guidance Notes", Washington: World Bank.

Part II

Aid, compensation, or insurance?

In search of an effective institutional basis for early recovery

7 Legislation to support disaster victims in Japan

Eichi Yamasaki

1 Introduction

The current legislation to support disaster victims in Japan originates from the Disaster Relief Act (hereinafter, "DRA") enacted immediately after World War II. The DRA played the central role in the provision of support to disaster victims up until the Great Hanshin-Awaji Earthquake in 1995 (hereinafter, "GHAE"). The legislation to support disaster victims was reviewed following The GHAE. A good example of this is the enactment of the Act on Support for Livelihood Recovery of Disaster Victims (hereinafter, "ASLRDV"). Extensive review of the legislation was also undertaken following the Great East Japan Earthquake in 2011 (hereinafter "GEJE"), and the revision of the Disaster Countermeasures Basic Act (hereinafter, "DCBA") is one example of this.

This chapter will introduce the legislation to support disaster victims in Japan and look at the problems associated with each piece of legislation. What are the problems facing Japan, one of the world's most disaster-prone nations that should be at the forefront of legislation to support disaster victims? Earthquake-related deaths, gaining an understanding of disaster victims, personal information, and instability of disaster victim livelihood recovery support are issues that Japan is currently facing.

2 Basic principles of disaster victim support – DCBA (1961)

The DCBA was enacted in the wake of the Ise Bay typhoon of 1959, and a significant volume of provisions concerning disaster victim support were subsequently added in amendments to the DCBA in 2012 and 2013. This chapter will now introduce the provisions concerning the basic principles of disaster victim support. Other provisions concerning disaster victim support will be introduced later as appropriate.

Article 2–2 of the DCBA prescribes the following provisions concerning disaster victim support:

1 Disaster countermeasures shall carry out the following matters as the basic principles:

2 Ensure the appropriate division of roles and mutual collaboration and cooperation between the State, local governments, and other public institutions, as well as promote disaster prevention activities carried out by each resident and disaster prevention activities voluntarily carried out by voluntary disaster prevention organizations (voluntary disaster prevention organization based on the spirit of neighborly cooperation of residents; the same shall apply hereinafter) and by various regional entities.

4 Gain an understanding of the disaster situation as accurately as possible, even immediately after a disaster has occurred or any other times when the collection of information is difficult, and place the utmost priority on the protection of human life and physical safety through the appropriate distribution of personnel, supplies, and other necessary resources.

5 Provide appropriate relief to disaster victims based on the disaster victim's age, gender, presence/absence of any disorder, and any other information in accordance with the timing and so as not to inhibit the proactive efforts of disaster victims.

6 Promptly restore facilities and provide relief to disaster victims after a disaster has occurred with the aim of recovering from the disaster.

Article 8, paragraph 2 of the DCBA also mandates the following considerations:

2 In the interest of preventing a disaster from occurring and of blocking the spread of a disaster that has occurred, the local government as well as the State shall particularly endeavor to carry out matters listed below:

14 Matters related to ensuring the physical and mental health of disaster victims, securing a place for disaster victims to live, and other protection of disaster victims.

15 Matters relating to necessary disaster prevention measures for the elderly, the handicapped, infants, and others requiring special care (hereinafter, "persons requiring special care").

17 Matters relating to the provision of accurate information to disaster victims and consultation from disaster victims.

The provisions of the DCBA are expected to function as legislative and operational guidelines for the disaster victim support legislation described below.

3 Emergency disaster response (refuge life): DRA (1947)

3.1 Positioning of the DRA

The DRA was enacted in the wake of the Nankai Earthquake (1946). The act is intended to provide direct relief to disaster victims immediately after a disaster, and it plays an important role in emergency disaster response. In the past, the Ministry of Health, Labor and Welfare had jurisdiction under the DRA; however, this jurisdiction was transferred to Cabinet Office in 2013 after the GEJE. Below

I would like to provide an overview of the DRA and outline the problems, particularly those associated with refuge life.

3.2 Implementation structure and expenses

Relief under the DRA is carried out as a statutory entrusted function by the prefectural governor (Article 2 of the DRA, Article 18 of the Ordinance for the Enforcement of the DRA). Statutory entrusted functions are matters that should be carried out by the State, but are instead entrusted to local governments. Mayors of municipalities are either mandated to carry out some of these functions by the prefectural governor or instead assist the relief provided by the prefectural governor (Article 30 of the DRA).

Essentially, almost all functions are delegated to mayors of municipalities to achieve rapid and competent relief. For instance, in the event of a wide disaster area, the construction of emergency temporary housing, emergency housing repair, and provision of emergency medical care and midwifery are carried out by the prefectural government. But if the disaster is localized, these functions are delegated to municipal government (Article 18, paragraph 1 of the DRA). In the event some functions related to the provision of relief have been delegated to the mayor of a municipality, that municipality will temporarily pay for the necessary expenses related to the provision of the delegated relief on behalf of the prefecture (Article 29 of the DRA). The State will also bear a portion of the expenses related to the provision of relief in excess of one million yen (Article 21 of the DRA, Article 19 of the Ordinance for the Enforcement of the DRA).

The DRA can be positioned as legislation on funding required for the relief of disaster victims. The application of the DRA means that the State and prefectural government pays the expenses for the relief actually provided following a disaster. Therefore, the application of the DRA allows the mayors of disaster-affected municipalities to devote themselves to actual disaster relief without worrying about costs.

3.3 Types of relief, the degree of relief, methods of relief, and the period of relief – general standards

Specifically, the following relief menus are provided (Article 4, paragraph 1 of the DRA, Article 2 of the Ordinance for the Enforcement of the DRA):

- Establishment of evacuation centers and the provision of emergency temporary housing;
- Provision of food through the emergency distribution of boiled rice and other methods, and the supply of drinking water;
- Supply or lending of clothing, bedding, and other necessities;
- Medical care and midwifery;
- Rescue of disaster victims;
- Emergency repair of disaster-affected housing;

- Supply or lending of funds, equipment, or materials required for subsistence;
- Supply of school supplies;
- Burial;
- Search and handling of corpses;
- Removal of rubble.

Of these relief menus, the "supply or lending of funds, equipment, or materials required for subsistence" is not performed under the DRA. This is because it is performed under another system.

The law allows the provision of relief in kind or the payment of cash (Article 4, paragraph 2 of the DRA), but in reality, relief is only provided in kind.

The degree of relief, methods of relief, and the period of relief are determined in advance by the prefectural governor in accordance with the standards prescribed by the Prime Minister and are set within the scope necessary for emergency relief (Article 4, paragraph 3 of the DRA, Article 3, paragraph 1 of the Ordinance for the Enforcement of the DRA).

The "Standards for the Degree of Relief, Methods of Relief, the Period of Relief and Reimbursement of Actual Expenses under the DRA (Public Notice of the Cabinet Office #144, dated October 1, 2013)" are standards prescribed by the Prime Minister. They are so-called "general standards" which prefectural governors follow. However, page 90 of the "Guidelines for the Handling of Disaster Relief affairs" (Cabinet Office, June 2014) states that the general standards are "merely concepts expressed as general rules" and asks that "care be taken so as not to fall into rigid operation".

Although the "Standards for the Degree of Relief, Methods of Relief, the Period of Relief and Reimbursement of Actual Expenses under the DRA" are general standards, they specifically prescribe the opening period and daily operating costs of evacuation centers, daily food expenses, and temporary housing construction costs, etc.

3.4 Flexible operation – the establishment of special standards

In the event that it is difficult to provide appropriate relief under the general standards prescribed by the Prime Minister, a prefectural governor may determine the degree of relief, methods of relief, and the period of relief after first consulting with the Prime Minister and obtaining his consent (Article 3, paragraph 2 of the Ordinance for the Enforcement of the DRA). Standards established in this manner are referred to as "special standards".

Pages 89–90 of the "Guidelines for the Handling of Disaster Relief Affairs" (Cabinet Office, June 2014) states that:

> disasters and the response thereto significantly differ according to the scale, situation and region, etc., so it is necessary to respond flexibly from the perspective of providing full relief by coordinating with the Cabinet Office and establishing special standards in consultation with the Prime Minister if necessary, etc.

So, the actual procedure is that municipalities providing relief will, depending on the needs of each case, consult with the prefecture to establish special standards, and prefectures providing relief will consult with the State to establish special standards.

3.5 Realities of special standards – operation and issues following the GEJE

The Ministry of Health, Labor and Welfare had jurisdiction under the DRA at the time of the GEJE. The Ministry of Health, Labor and Welfare issued numerous notifications to local governments encouraging the proactive establishment of special standards following the GEJE.

The specific content of these notifications was as follows:

- Encouragement of active acceptance of disaster victims by prefectures of non-disaster-affected areas;
- The opening period of evacuation centers and the period for the provision of meals is seven days or less, but this may be extended up to two months (and further extension is also possible);
- Evacuation center partitioning, air conditioning, temporary laundries/baths/showers/toilets;
- Consideration of the elderly and infirm in the provision of meals;
- Establishment of welfare evacuation centers;[1]
- Specifications for emergency temporary housing in cold regions;
- 5,000 yen per person for day for accommodation in private inns and hotels etc. (including meals);
- Private rental or rental of vacant housing: approx. 60,000 yen per month.

Rather than the acknowledgment of special standards that had not been recognized in the past, these notifications were more a "reminder" or "confirmation" of special standards that had been recognized in the past. However, it can be inferred from the frequent issue of these notifications that municipalities were not even establishing special standards that had been recognized in the past.

Sometimes local government officials in areas not usually affected by disaster are not particularly familiar with the DRA. If that is the case, they will provide disaster relief without knowledge of the special standards described above. That could result in the vulnerable, such as the elderly and the handicapped, dying without being able to get the support they should have been able to receive. Even in the GEJE, there were many "disaster-related deaths" that occurred in evacuation centers. According to the Reconstruction Agency's "Report on Disaster-Related Deaths in the GEJE" (August 21, 2012), there were a total of 1,632 disaster-related deaths that occurred during or after evacuation as of March 31, 2012. Approximately 90 percent of those deaths were persons aged 66 and older, and approximately half of the victims died within a month of the earthquake. The cause of death in approximately 30 percent of these cases was the physical fatigue of life in the evacuation center. The use of special standards is required to improve the living environment of disaster victims following evacuation. So, what should be done to ensure the flexible operation of the legislation?

3.6 Proposals for the proactive utilization of special standards

Although flexible operations such as the establishment of special standards are indeed possible, their establishment is quite difficult in reality due to (1) local (municipal/prefectural government) officials being unaware of the right to establish special standards, (2) local government officials being aware of the right to establish special standards, but unsure of what special standards to establish, (3) local government officials wanting to establish special standards, but being unable to persuade the higher-ranking administrative institution (the prefectural government in the case a municipality wants to establish special standards, and the State in the case a prefecture wants to establish special standards), (4) the emotional burden for local government officials to negotiate with higher-ranking administrative institutions, and (5) the extra financial burden for prefectures to establish special standards.

It is necessary to examine institutional reforms in the future such as (1) allowing the establishment of special standards that have been recognized in the past without the need for consultation with a higher-ranking administrative institution, (2) allowing the establishment of special standards at the discretion of the prefectural governor, (3) making special standards that have been recognized in past general standards, (4) having the State bear the full amount of costs that exceed a certain limit, and (5) adding "reminder provisions" to encourage flexible operation under the DRA.

In order to prevent such disaster-related deaths from occurring, it is also necessary to make the DRA well known to local government officials before a disaster occurs. The usual situation of having officials that have never seen operational documents related to the DRA suddenly implement disaster relief operations following a disaster is untenable. To depart from this, it is necessary to develop measures such as "periodic examinations" and a "qualification system" in order to spread knowledge of the DRA to officials. If knowledge of the DRA is not spread to local government officials, the support that should be provided under the legislation will continue to go unprovided and lives could be lost.

3.7 A system to lease existing private housing – privately-rented temporary housing

If a disaster has destroyed homes, temporary housing is provided to ensure a temporary residence for disaster victims. However, after the GEJE it was impossible to ensure a residence for all disaster victims solely with temporary housing. Therefore, a system of "privately-rented temporary housing" whereby the prefecture leases existing private rental housing and provides it to disaster victims was utilized.

Although privately-rented temporary housing is temporary housing provided under the DRA, the leasing of the private rental housing by the prefecture creates a complex legal relationship. Essentially, privately-rented temporary housing is provided to disaster victims through the conclusion of a three-party agreement between the prefecture (lessee), the lessor, and the disaster victim.

The privately-rented temporary housing system has the advantages of (1) being able to rapidly provide housing to disaster victims, (2) being cheaper than constructing temporary housing, and providing housing from which a certain level of quality can also be expected, and (3) being able to meet the diverse lifestyle needs of disaster victims (such as commuting to work and school).

However, there are also some problems. Persons living in temporary housing can be clearly identified as disaster victims and can easily receive a variety of support. Persons living in privately-rented temporary housing, however, live in ordinary apartments and condominiums, etc. and cannot immediately be recognized as disaster victims. Support organizations may want to provide support to disaster victims living in privately-rented temporary housing but find it difficult to approach them because of this. In addition, as disaster victims living in privately-rented temporary housing are separated from the disaster-affected area in which they previously resided, they find it difficult to continue their pre-disaster community and communications. Therefore, disaster victims living in privately-rented temporary housing can be considered prone to suffering from feelings of isolation. Although the prefecture possesses information about disaster victims living in privately-rented temporary housing, the creation of a system whereby this information can be provided to groups such as support organizations is required. However, this also poses problems related to the protection of personal information.

3.8 Gaining an understanding of and supporting wide-area evacuees

One of the features of the GEJE was that it resulted in many wide-area evacuees evacuating their disaster-affected municipalities. According to a Cabinet Office survey, evacuees were present in over 1,100 municipalities in 47 prefectures as of July 14, 2011, and approximately 56,000 of these evacuees had fled from the three disaster-affected prefectures.

Generally, the disaster-affected prefectures provide relief to disaster victims. However, after a huge disaster such as the GEJE, disaster victims flee to other prefectures not affected by the disaster. The provisions of Article 35 of the DRA state that "prefectures that have provided disaster relief to other prefectures may be reimbursed by the prefecture in which the disaster relief was provided for the costs associated with its provision of the disaster relief". So there is indeed a framework for prefectures to provide relief to evacuees from other prefectures under the DRA.

Questions were raised as to the method of gaining an understanding of and supporting wide-area evacuees following the GEJE, and the Ministry of Internal Affairs and Communications commenced operation of the "National Information

System for Refugees" on April 25, 2011 to gain an understanding of wide-area evacuees. As evacuee registration is voluntary, there is a risk that the National Information System for Refugees will be unable to provide disaster victim support information to disaster victims who have not registered on the system. Although this is a system to support wide-area evacuees, wide-area evacuees are difficult to recognize as disaster victims in refuge and face the same problems as disaster victims living in privately-rented temporary housing.[2]

4 Disaster victim consultation service – disaster victim directory

4.1 Overview of the disaster victim directory

The disaster victim directory is created in order to facilitate the provision of smooth livelihood reconstruction support to disaster victims. Generally, the disaster victim directory includes information about the damage suffered by disaster victims, the support being received by disaster victims, and the concerns of the disaster victims.

The disaster victim directory can be traced back to the GHAE (1995), and there were also local governments that introduced a disaster victim directory following the Niigata Chuetsu Earthquake (2004), Noto Peninsula Earthquake (2007), and Chuetsu-oki Earthquake (2007). Some local governments also introduced a disaster victim directory following the GEJE.

Provisions related to the disaster victim directory were newly set forth in Article 90–3 and 90–4 of the DCBA in the revision following the GEJE. The key points are as follows:

1. Municipal mayors may create a disaster victim directory when a disaster has occurred.
2. Existing personal information can be used for purposes other than for which it was provided in the creation of the disaster victim directory, and requests can also be made to relevant local government leaders for the provision of information.
3. Information in the disaster victim directory may be used for purposes other than for which it was provided, or provided to third parties such as other local governments with the consent of the individual or to the extent necessary to support the disaster victim.
4. Information in the disaster victim directory may also be provided to support organizations with the consent of the individual.

Disaster victim directories were also created following the 2013 Izu-Oshima mudslides and 2014 Fukuchiyama floods. It is likely that many municipalities will create disaster victim directories following disasters in the future. However, it is more desirable if disaster victim directories are created in advance before a disaster actually occurs.

4.2 Problems associated with the disaster victim directory

The following problems are associated with the disaster victim directory. First, the whereabouts of disaster victims must always be known in order to utilize the disaster victim directory. If a disaster produces wide-area evacuees, how can municipal mayors that have created disaster victim directories gain an understanding of wide-area evacuees? As mentioned earlier, the Ministry of Internal Affairs and Communications' "National Information System for Refugees" cannot fully grasp the situation of wide-area evacuees. Given that, construction of a nationwide information network that forcibly keeps track of disaster victims is desirable. However, problems related to the protection of personal information are a major barrier to the realization of such a system. The State should manage an integrated disaster victim directory system envisioning wide-area evacuees, as the limitations of the system of disaster victim directory creation and management by municipalities have been exposed.

The problems associated with privately-rented temporary housing, wide-area evacuees and the disaster victim directory can be summarized as personal information-related problems.

5 The ASLRDV (1998) and the Act on Earthquake Insurance (1966)

5.1 Overview of the ASLRDV

The ASLRDV is the legislative framework to support housing reconstruction. This act was enacted in the wake of the GHAE. It has been amended twice, in 2004 and 2007, and the Cabinet Office has jurisdiction under this act.

The ASLRDV applies to the following households: (1) households whose home has been completely destroyed, (2) households whose home has been partially destroyed, or who suffered damage to their land which necessitated demolition of their home, (3) households whose home is uninhabitable for a long period of time due to danger associated with a disaster, and (4) households whose home has been partially destroyed and would be difficult to live in unless large-scale repairs are carried out (households with large-scale damage).

The ASLRDV provides financial support of up to 3 million yen to affected households – "basic grants" paid according to the extent of the damage, and "supplementary grants" paid according to the manner in which the housing is reconstructed (Table 7.1).

5.2 Problems associated with the ASLRDV

The grants are funded from a fund established by the prefecture based on the spirit of mutual assistance and an equal amount which is provided by the State. 107.2 billion yen had been pooled as funds at the time the GEJE struck; however, the enormous number of disaster-affected households quickly depleted the fund.

Table 7.1 Applicable households and grant amounts

Classification	*Home reconstruction method*	*Basic grant*	*Supplementary grant*	*Total*
Completely destroyed Demolished Uninhabitable for a long period	Construction/ purchase	1 million yen	2 million yen	3 million yen
	Repair	1 million yen	1 million yen	2 million yen
	Rental	1 million yen	500,000 yen	1.5 million yen
Large-scale damage	Construction/ purchase	500,000 yen	2 million yen	2.5 million yen
	Repair	500,000 yen	1 million yen	1.5 million yen
	Rental	500,000 yen	500,000 yen	1 million yen

Note
Single-person households will be paid 75 percent of the amount of multi-person households.

The State then had to specially top up the fund. A similar situation can be envisioned if another major disaster occurs, so designing a system that can cope with major disasters is a challenge.

There has also been criticism that not enough households are eligible for the grant. That is to say, no support is provided for partially destroyed households, households flooded above floor level, and damaged ground which households stand on. However, these households may be supported through measures implemented by local governments that will be described below.

There is also criticism of the fact that support is limited to housing reconstruction despite the name of the act itself suggesting support for the livelihood recovery of disaster victims. In other words, no support is provided to guarantee income and support subsistence. There are no measures in place to provide grants to support the livelihood of households whose income has been reduced as a result of disaster or grants to support the resumption of an occupation, for instance.

5.3 Independent measures implemented by local governments to complement the ASLRDV

Local governments (prefectures and municipalities) often establish an independent disaster victim support system in the event the national disaster victim support system is not sufficient. These independent measures go some way to overcoming the problems associated with the ASLRDV mentioned earlier. These so-called "independent measures implemented by local governments" cannot be ignored when analyzing disaster victim support systems.

Looking at the historical background, we can see that independent measures implemented by local governments came to be recognized following the enactment of the ASLRDV. The ASLRDV was enacted in 1998, and independent measures implemented by local government were established to make up for some of the problems associated with the ASLRDV. A prime example of an independent measure implemented by local government was Tottori Prefecture's system to pay grants of up to 3 million yen for housing reconstruction and 1.5 million yen for housing repairs following the Western Tottori Earthquake (2000). This was a breakthrough independent measure, as grants under the ASLRDV could not be used for housing reconstruction and repairs at the time. Similar independent measures came to be implemented by local governments following subsequent disasters. Japan suffered a great deal of storm and flood damage nationwide in 2004, and many local governments implemented independent measures in that year to really establish the system.

Independent measures were also implemented by local governments following the GEJE to supplement the ASLRDV and the DRA. Independent measures in relation to earthquake orphans and the livelihood recovery of wide-area evacuees have also been established.

The factors behind the establishment of such independent measures implemented by local governments can be considered: (1) the discretion of the heads of local governments, (2) the fiscal situation of local governments, and (3) trends amongst surrounding local governments, etc. In some cases, a "recovery fund" is established to promote independent measures implemented by local governments following a large-scale disaster.

The establishment of independent measures implemented by local governments can also affect national disaster victim support systems and promote the amendment of legislation. In fact, the impact of independent measures implemented by local governments was one of the factors behind the amendment of the ASLRDV.

However, there are also problems associated with independent measures implemented by local governments. A situation may arise in which the victims of the same disaster can receive different grant amounts depending on the local government to which they belong. Essentially, the total amount that a disaster victim can receive will differ depending on whether or not their local government has implemented independent measures. In addition, the content of the independent measures implemented may differ between local governments. So, issues of equality between disaster-affected areas arise in this respect.

5.4 Overview of the Act on Earthquake Insurance (1966)

Earthquake insurance also exists in Japan as a system to support housing reconstruction. Earthquake insurance is public insurance provided under the Act on Earthquake Insurance (1966) (hereinafter, "AEI"), which was enacted in the wake of the 1964 Niigata Earthquake.

The AEI prescribes a limit on total insurance benefits paid out by the government and insurers for a single earthquake. This limit is based on the characteristics of earthquake disasters, which have the potential to cause huge amounts of damage. The limit was established to limit the liability of the government. However, the limit has been determined so as not to interfere with the payment of insurance benefits even in the event of another Great Kanto Earthquake. In the event the total amount of insurance benefits to be paid exceeds the total payment limit, the amount of the insurance benefits to be paid under each agreement may be reduced. The current limit is 7 trillion yen as of April 1, 2014 ("Statistics compiled by Non-Life Insurance Rating Organization of Japan, 2013"). The limit on the insurance benefits to be paid out by the government is 6.7386 trillion yen and the limit on the insurance benefits to be paid out by insurers is 261.4 billion yen (Non-Life Insurance Rating Organization of Japan, "Overview of earthquake insurance standard rates", July 2014).

Earthquake insurance covers buildings for residential use and household goods (personal property for daily living). Earthquake insurance assumes enrollment in fire insurance. The risks of earthquakes are not covered by fire insurance alone. And the amount insured under earthquake insurance can be determined within a range of 30–50 percent of the amount insured under fire insurance. Buildings can be insured for a maximum of 50 million yen, and household goods can be insured for a maximum of 10 million yen. One hundred percent of the insured amount is paid out in the event of complete destruction, 50 percent is paid out in the event of partial destruction, and 5 percent is paid out in the event of partial damage.

The following organizations have established systems to cover earthquake risks in addition to earthquake insurance. These systems act as an alternative to earthquake insurance (Zenrosai, the National Mutual Insurance Federation of Agricultural Cooperatives [JA Kyosai]) or supplement earthquake insurance (Hyogo Prefecture):

- Zenrosai: Natural disaster guaranteed fire mutual aid;
- The National Mutual Insurance Federation of Agricultural Cooperatives (JA Kyosai): Building reconstruction mutual aid;
- Hyogo Prefecture: Hyogo Mutual Aid Fund for Housing Reconstruction;

5.5 Problems associated with the AEI

Earthquake insurance is not compulsory in Japan. In the financial year 2013, only 27.9 percent of households were subscribed to earthquake insurance, with the earthquake insurance attachment rate (with fire insurance) being 58.1 percent ("Statistics compiled by Non-Life Insurance Rating Organization of Japan, 2013"). In designing legislation on housing reconstruction, a choice must be made on whether to design on the assumption of subscription to earthquake insurance. However, it cannot be said that a national consensus on whether this assumption should be made has been reached. Consequently, the incompleteness of the design of systems for housing reconstruction can also be noted. Compulsory earthquake insurance was debated following the GHAE, but the debate died down after problems such as the burden of operating the system, the possibility of bankruptcy of the system, and the constitutionality of the system were highlighted. As this stage, there is no choice but to assume optional subscription to earthquake insurance and devise measures to increase the subscription rate.

The insurance premiums and benefits of insurance systems are designed based on the "law of large numbers". However, the "law of large numbers" may not be appropriate for earthquake insurance. As risk calculation relying on the "law of large numbers" is impossible, a scientific and rational system design should also be recognized as impossible. If that is the case, system design must be reduced to a political decision, and procedural legitimacy of the system design must be sought.

6 Compensation for human casualties and a loan system for the reconstruction of livelihoods – The Act on Payment of Solatia for Disasters (1973)

6.1 Overview of the Act on Payment of Solatia for Disasters

The Act on Payment of Solatia for Disasters (1973) (hereinafter, "APSD") was enacted in the wake of the Niigata Prefecture Uetsu floods (1967). The Ministry of Health, Labor and Welfare previously had jurisdiction under this act, but jurisdiction was transferred to the Cabinet Office in 2013 after the GEJE.

Article 1 of the APSD prescribes the following financial support:

- Solatia paid to bereaved families of victims who died as a result of a disaster;
- Ex-gratia payments paid to persons sustaining significant physical or mental disorder as a result of a disaster;
- Disaster relief funding loaned to households whose homes have been damaged by a disaster.

Persons eligible to receive disaster solatia and disaster disorder ex-gratia payments, and the amount of these payments are as follows:

- Disaster solatia:
  (Persons eligible to receive disaster solatia)
  - Spouse, child, parent, grandchild, grandparent
  - Siblings (if living together with the deceased or sharing the same subsistence)

  (Amount paid)
  - When the deceased was the primary income provider: 5 million yen
  - When the deceased was a person other than the primary income provider: 2.5 million yen.
- Disaster disorder ex-gratia payments:
  (Persons eligible to receive disaster disorder ex-gratia payments)
  Persons sustaining the following disorders:
  - Severe disability
  - Blindness in both eyes, damage necessitating constant nursing care, both arms severed above the elbow joint

- Disorder equivalent to class #1 under the Industrial Accident Compensation Insurance Act or multiple severe disabilities

(Amount paid)

- When the person suffering the disorder is the primary income provider: 2.5 million yen
- When the person suffering the disorder is a person other than the primary income provider: 1.25 million yen.

Disaster relief funding is a system under which a maximum of 3.5 million yen is loaned to households suffering injury or damage to their home and household goods as a result of a disaster.

6.2 Problems associated with The APSD

Disaster solatia are paid to bereaved families of victims who "died as a result of a disaster". If disaster victims have died some period after the disaster, is this death "a result of a disaster"? Sometimes it is hard to tell, and the courts are forced to hear disputes to determine this question.

The major problem of disaster disorder ex-gratia payments is that the eligibility criteria to receive them are too stringent. In addition, the provision of regular long-term payments can be considered more desirable than lump-sum payments given that the disorders covered by ex-gratia payments are ones that remain for a long period.

Many disaster victims who were loaned disaster relief funding following the GHAE were unable to repay the loan. This poses a dilemma – if the lending conditions are relaxed in order to support the livelihood reconstruction of as many disaster victims as possible, then there will inevitably be disaster victims who are unable to repay the loan. On the other hand, if the lending conditions are tightened, there will be an increase in disaster victims that cannot access the system.

7 Conclusion

An overview of the legislation to support disaster victims in Japan has been provided above. The legislative problems still facing Japan, one of the world's most disaster-prone nations, were also identified. The problems associated with the design and operation of legislation, as well as those associated with disaster victims' personal information, are deeply interesting. We hope this chapter can be used as material for the comparative study of legislation related to disaster victim support and serve as a reference when developing legislation to support disaster victims in foreign countries. This chapter was written based on Yamasaki (2013).

Notes

1 Welfare evacuation centers/welfare temporary housing: Welfare evacuation centers are evacuation facilities for persons such as the elderly and handicapped requiring nursing care, pregnant women, infants, and the infirm, etc. for whom special consideration is required in evacuation center life. Welfare evacuation centers have support staff on hand, are equipped with portable toilets, and feature universal design including handrails and temporary slopes. This kind of facility utilizes existing buildings. There is also welfare temporary housing. It is necessary to gain an understanding of the buildings that could potentially be used as welfare centers and register and designate them as such before disasters occur. Welfare evacuation centers are expected to function as an important tool to prevent disaster-related deaths.

2 Provisions of the DCBA concerning refuge life: The following provisions were established by revision to the DCBA. Municipal mayors are obligated to assign designated emergency shelter areas (Articles 49–4 through 49–6 of the DCBA) and designated evacuation centers (Articles 49–7 through 49–8 of the DCBA). Furthermore, designated emergency shelter areas must be assigned for "each type of abnormal phenomenon". The duty is also imposed upon municipal mayors to take measures to disseminate the necessary information to residents etc. to facilitate their smooth evacuation.

The DCBA also obligates emergency disaster response personnel to maintain living conditions for disaster victims in their post-evacuation refuge life (Article 86–6) and make considerations for disaster victims that cannot stay in evacuation centers (Article 86–7).

Provisions concerning "temporary wide-area evacuees" have also been added to the DCBA. Namely, the obligation of municipal mayors to coordinate with other municipalities and prefectures with regard to the acceptance of disaster-affected residents (wide-area evacuation) has been newly established (Articles 86–8 through 86–13 of the Act), and this obligation has led to such consultation with other municipalities and prefectures and coordination by the prefecture or State to achieve the acceptance of disaster victims by other municipalities and prefectures.

Reference

Yamasaki, E. (2013), *Natural Disasters and Support for Victims* (originally published in Japanese as "Shizen saigai to hisaisha shien"). Tokyo: Nippon Hyouron Sha Co., Ltd.

8 Compensation or assistance?

Law and policy for post-disaster housing recovery in the U.S. and Japan

Tamiyo Kondo

1 Introduction

This chapter will discuss the law and policy surrounding housing recovery in the United States and Japan. Housing is an essential function for human-centered recovery for the simple reason that it serves as the basis for human living and community. Based on a comparison of the U.S. and Japanese systems, this chapter examines the characteristics and philosophy of housing recovery law and policy in each country. It is common to both countries that housing policy in general is market-driven, which shapes the philosophy and design of post-disaster housing recovery policies and programs.

The first section of this chapter explains the law and policy surrounding housing recovery in the U.S. in the case of a flood disaster. The systems that address recovery after flooding and earthquake are quite different because the risk of each disaster occurring (which consists of four parameters: probability, severity, time period, and location) differs between seismic hazards and water-related hazards. Policies, laws, and insurance systems for housing recovery following a flood are more systematically designed and developed compared to that of seismic risk. Therefore, this chapter will focus on flooding. The second section explains the intent and design process of programs for housing recovery through a case study of Hurricane Katrina, the most expensive and severe disaster in U.S. history.

After explaining the U.S. system and experience, the third section describes the historical development process and philosophy of Japanese law and policy for housing recovery programs. This section explains in more detail the historical background of the law concerning assistance for victims of natural disaster in Japan, focusing on the design and implementation of a housing recovery subsidy program for homeowners after the Great East Japan Earthquake in 2011. The law and systems for housing recovery have evolved since the Great Hanshin-Awaji Earthquake in 1995.

The questions to consider are as follows: What kinds of programs are in place for housing recovery? What shapes the characteristics of government assistance policy? Who pays housing reconstruction costs and why? When government subsidies are provided for homeowners after a disaster, is it "compensation for loss" or "assistance for victims"?

2 U.S. law and policy for housing recovery for flooding

2.1 Federal law and programs for individuals

There are three major federal agencies that have jurisdiction over assistance programs following disaster in the U.S.

One is the Federal Emergency Management Agency (FEMA). FEMA describes disaster assistance as "financial or direct assistance to individuals and families whose property has been damaged or destroyed as a result of a federally-declared disaster, and whose losses are not covered by insurance". The agency emphasizes that "the assistance is not intended to restore damaged property to its condition before the disaster. But it is meant to help people with critical expenses that cannot be covered in other ways." From this description, we can understand that disaster insurance is designed as a function for transferring disaster risk and that it is considered to be the major method of meeting housing reconstruction costs. The Individual and Households Program (IHP) provides financial help and direct services to those who have unavoidable expenses and serious needs, including housing assistance amongst other needs.

Another federal institution is the Small Business Administration, which provides loans, loan guarantees, contracts, advice, and other forms of assistance to small businesses. Housing assistance funds, known as SBA loans, are available through disaster assistance from the SBA. However, it is frequently pointed out by studies that "poor homeowners typically did not meet the SBA credit requirements for government low-interest loans" (Comerio, 1998: 76).

The main source of disaster recovery assistance in the U.S. is funding from the Department of Housing and Urban Development (HUD) in the form of Community Development Block Grants for Disaster Recovery (CDBG-DR), which is allocated to disaster-affected jurisdictions based on their respective Action Plans that outline recovery projects. The CDBG program is a flexible program that provides communities with resources to address the wide range of development needs that are unique to each community. These grants have been utilized to provide assistance subsidies for homeowners to reconstruct their housing after a disaster.

2.2 National Flood Insurance Program: its effectiveness and problems as a system

Although 90 percent of all disasters in the U.S. involve flooding, homeowner insurance policies that cover damage from wind, fire, and theft do not usually cover flooding; because of the "catastrophic nature of flooding and inability to adequately predict risks, private insurance companies have been unwilling to underwrite and bear the risk that results from providing primary flood insurance coverage" (U.S. Government Accountability Office, 2014: 3). In response to multiple severe hurricanes and flood disasters, and the accompanying rising cost of providing disaster assistance to uninsured residents, the National Flood Insurance Program (NFIP) was created by the National Flood Insurance Act of 1968, with the intention of reducing future losses from disasters. This Act prompted one of the largest federal flood-mapping efforts, as "the government promised local governments that they would provide them with the technical tools to determine where the floodplains were in their communities so they could steer development away from these areas" (Haddow *et al.*, 2013: 73).

One of the most important characteristics of the NFIP is that it is designed to function not only as compensation for loss but also to promote mitigation. To be eligible for compensation through the NFIP after a disaster, homeowners are required to comply with building codes that are based on flood risk assessments by FEMA when constructing their home. This system is similar to Japanese earthquake insurance, which is offered by the national government and private insurance companies, in the sense that insurance premiums are calculated based on disaster risk and the building's reliability. Neither country's insurance policy is compulsory; however, the difference is that the NFIP requires the purchase of federal flood insurance as a prerequisite for any federally backed loan. This system enhances the ability of homeowners to pay for housing reconstruction costs and reduces the cost of post-disaster recovery funding by investing public funding toward mitigation and preparation ahead of disaster.

3 Housing recovery assistance subsidies after Hurricane Katrina

3.1 Difference in damage between Louisiana and Mississippi

Hurricane Katrina is the most severe destructive disaster in U.S. history, which brought catastrophic damage to human life and economic losses region-wide. In Louisiana, much of the damage occurred in the southeastern portion of the state. It is said that "the homogeneity of destruction provided a clearer starting point for identifying damage and structuring subsequent compensation policy" (Norcross and Skriba, 2010: 5). In greater New Orleans, some neighborhoods experienced more than ten feet of water that washed away everything, while other neighborhoods had only scattered damage. In Mississippi, damage caused by the storm surge completely erased many houses along the beachfront. Damaged housing in Mississippi included privately owned and rental vacation cottages, while the severe damage that New Orleans experienced mainly affected principal residences.

3.2 Disaster recovery funding for states from federal government: CDBG for housing recovery

It is commonly accepted that Louisiana and Mississippi targeted a majority of funds towards homeowner assistance (U.S. Government Accountability Office, 2009: 8). When the HUD and state government officials started considering the design of housing assistance through CDBG-DR, there was a discussion about whether the objective of subsidies should be rehabilitation or compensation for loss.

Louisiana initially created a program that incorporated certain elements from two different housing recovery program models: compensation and rehabilitation. Generally, in a rehabilitation program funds are used explicitly for repairs or reconstruction projects. In contrast, a compensation program disburses grant payments directly to homeowners for the damage they suffered regardless of whether they intend to repair or rebuild (U.S. Government Accountability Office, 2009: 9). Finally, both states selected compensation. There are two main reasons that the decision was made to provide housing recovery subsidies as compensation.

First is that the flood damage spread across not only the NFIP pre-designated floodplain areas but also beyond the floodplains. The Federal Coordinator for Gulf Coast Rebuilding testified to a Senate hearing during the First Session of the 110th Congress that

> the truly unique nature of the storms of 2005 and the driver of Federal Government to get involved was the flood damage caused by the storm surge and levee breaches. This is damage for which there is no private insurance market, damage that in many cases was experienced by those who lived outside of the federally identified floodplains and/or those who lived inside Federal levees. Therefore, despite the original intent and purpose of the CDBG funding, the State utilized the autonomy available to them to push through their own program design to compensate damaged homes, whether by wind or flood, unlike any other Gulf Coast State.

This statement does not totally acknowledge the culpability of the government, which lay in the failure of the levees and the NFIP-designed flood maps; however, it can be said that the government sector decided to compensate homeowners because it was the system of government-designed and constructed systems and physical infrastructure that led to the severe flooding in New Orleans.

Second, the regulations governing CDBG influenced the states in their decision about whether to provide rehabilitation or compensation. When CDBG funds are used to rehabilitate a property, the state is required to conduct site-specific environmental reviews. A U.S. Government Accountability Office report found that "officials in both states said this was a key factor considered when deciding whether or not to adopt the rehabilitation model" (U.S. Government Accountability Office, 2009: 9).

The maximum funding provided to homeowners in either state was equal at $150,000, although the intent and design of the respective housing recovery programs was quite different.

The first difference was in the eligibility requirements. While Mississippi's Homeowner Assistance program covered only flood-related damage, Louisiana's program extended eligibility to residents that sustained wind damage, an event typically covered by homeowners insurance. In Mississippi, the homeowners' assistance program was designed by the Mississippi Development Authority to award compensation grants to homeowners "located outside the 100-year flood plain" who experienced damage due to hurricane-related flooding (Norcross and Skriba, 2010: 6). In Louisiana, the amount of compensation homeowners were eligible to receive depended upon which of the three options available to them under the program they chose to pursue: (1) stay and rebuild their damaged housing, (2) sell and relocate within Louisiana, or (3) sell and relocate outside of Louisiana. Higher payments under option (1) gave incentive for people to repopulate Louisiana. This is different from Mississippi, where the amount of compensation did not depend upon the decisions of whether to rebuild or where to relocate to.

The second difference was in the goal and objective of each program. "Road Home", Louisiana's program, was designed to serve as more than a disaster compensation program; it was designed to function as both planning and housing policy (Norcross and Skriba, 2010: 1). Road Home departed from Mississippi's more concrete compensation-for-losses approach (Norcross and Skriba, 2010: 6). Louisiana initially adopted a plan that tied federal funds to home reconstruction and controlled the flow of funds to homeowners while Mississippi paid homeowners for their losses regardless of their intentions to rebuild (U.S. Government Accountability Office, 2009: 9). In Louisiana, recovery was about rebuilding housing stock and bringing people home. For that reason, it gave people incentive to return to Louisiana by providing funding eligibility based on the full-market value of their property if they came back to the state, but only 60 percent of market value if they decided to sell their home to the program and move outside of the state. The compensation was based on either Road Home's estimated cost of damage to the house minus other assistance received by the homeowners, or the pre-storm value of the home minus other assistance, whichever amount was lower. This demonstrates the characteristics of the Road Home program, including rebuilding assistance and compensation.

3.3 How has housing recovery assistance in New Orleans functioned in reality?

Regardless of how it was designed, it is especially important to evaluate how the system has functioned in practice. How has Louisiana's housing recovery subsidy program, the Road Home program, contributed to human-centered recovery in New Orleans? There have been three major problems in the design and operation of the program that caused negative impacts upon the human-centered housing recovery.

First, the design of the program has been criticized in that the policies of Road Home adversely affected minority race homeowners since there is a relationship between neighborhood racial characteristics and housing values. The Road Home program has functioned to "help the wealth great and the wants small". Finger (2008) identifies the problem that CDBG's target is at variance with the people who received benefit from Road Home. While CDBG generally requires that at least 70 percent of its funding be used for the benefit of low- and middle-income persons, post-Katrina the U.S. Congress authorized a general waiver of the CDBG's requirement. As a result, the mandatory minimum amount of funding to be spent on low- and middle-income people for all combined disaster recovery programs was lowered to 50 percent. The Additional Compensation Grant is supposed to add up to $50,000 to an applicant's grant when there is a "gap" between the estimated cost of damage and Road Home's actual compensation (Finger, 2008: 64).

Second, buyouts by the state have not been implemented at a neighborhood-wide level, but on an individual basis that has triggered "checker-board housing recovery". This is defined as residents returning to formerly densely populated neighborhoods in an uneven fashion, leaving some very sparsely populated areas (Kondo, 2015b: 287). This leads to many unmanaged vacant lots and blighted properties which reduce the level of public safety, a lack of amenities such as grocery stores, falling real estate prices, etc. At the same time, the continuing existence of blighted and vacant properties causes the deterioration of the residential environment and residents become hesitant about returning to the neighborhood, which falls into a negative spiral.

Third, there are many operational and procedural issues that applicants have encountered in Road Home. Homeowners did not receive any assistance from CDBG funds until 2007 or 2008, two to three years after their losses occurred (Seidman, 2013: 45). Its underlying valuation formula and problems with home-valuation policies; insufficient funding for low- and middle-income families; nondisclosure of critical information; problems with its appeal system; inadequate written information and documentation; and expedited program deadlines have unduly burdened applicants (Finger, 2008: 60).

Green and Olshansky evaluated the Road Home program as being "successful in funneling billions of dollars to homeowners for rebuilding and mitigation, but the unresolved tension between its role as a rebuilding program and a compensation program created significant barriers to recovery" (Green and Olshansky, 2012: 76).

After the Superstorm Sandy that hit the east coast of the U.S. in 2012, New York City prepared a housing recovery assistance program called the "Build it Back program". Its designers paid close attention to the failures of the Road Home program, namely: (1) poor overall management and oversight of the program itself; (2) the issue of contractor fraud – residents hired private contractors with money from Road Home, who took the money and subsequently disappeared; and (3) the checker-board pattern of land use and the difficulties that resulted from the Road Home buyouts that were scattered throughout the city and neighborhoods (Maly *et al.*, 2016). The objectives of buyouts after Katrina and Sandy were not the same; the former compensated for loss while the latter sought risk-based land use control for disaster risk reduction, which is similar to the response to the Great East Japan Earthquake that is explained in the next section.

4 Japanese law and policy for housing recovery

4.1 Government funding for housing recovery

As will be explained in this section, Japanese government assistance for survivors of natural disasters has evolved dramatically since the Great Hanshin-Awaji Earthquake in 1995. The Act on Support for Reconstructing Livelihoods of Disaster Victims, which requires government funding support for survivors to restore their livelihood after a disaster, was an achievement of the civic movement. When the law was legislated, there were restrictions on the use of funding for housing rehabilitation and reconstruction, because the national government had a strong stance that public funding should not be used for the improvement of private property. However, several earthquakes occurred country-wide in the years after the Great Hanshin-Awaji Earthquake, and local governments prepared subsidies for survivors to enable housing rehabilitation and reconstruction. Local governments realized that government assistance for housing recovery of victims is essential for regional recovery. These responses by local government proved that the national government's support for homeowners was too limited. In parallel with local movements, the national law was revised in 2007 to permit use of the money for housing rehabilitation and reconstruction. The national government established a committee to examine the revision of the law, and the committee stated the policy basis for permitting the use of funding for housing recovery as

> individual housing is surely a private asset, however, when a large number of houses are destroyed, housing recovery is strongly related to the recovery of the region's society. This is why government funding for survivors has a certain element of public benefit.

This means that the use of public funds is justified by the severity of housing damage, and if housing damage is low, the government does not necessarily have to provide funding for housing recovery. Murosaki (2014) pointed out that "public help and self-help do not exist in parallel, but public help should promote self-help by survivors". This interpretation means that the life and livelihood of people should be "guaranteed" by government funding. In sum, Japanese government disaster assistance for survivors is intended to achieve public sphere (i.e. welfare) objectives rather than respecting human-centered recovery.

4.2 Case study: the Great East Japan Earthquake

The Great East Japan Earthquake triggered an unprecedented tsunami that washed away many cities and towns along the Pacific coastline. One of the major national government policies for recovery and mitigation is to designate high-risk tsunami areas as buffer zones with restrictions on building, and to promote the relocation of communities to higher ground. Private lots in designated buffer zones have been bought out by the government. The value paid for the buyout of land is based on the standard amount for land expropriation for public use, which is post-tsunami property value determined by the Ministry of Land, Infrastructure, Transport and Tourism.

The buffer zones consist of approximately one third of the area inundated by the tsunami (Masuda, 2014: 77), an unprecedented area that used to be home to vibrant communities before the disaster, but has now become deserted due to this strict control of land use. Collective relocation is based on the Act on Special Financial Support for Promoting Collective Relocation for Disaster Mitigation. Its objective is to protect human lives and property from disaster by promoting relocation "as a group". This project provides funding for the development of reclaimed land, buyouts in buffer zone areas, and loans for housing and land purchases by survivors. This is essentially government funding that supports private properties; however, it is justified by the public sphere benefit that contributes to the formation of a lower disaster-risk environment.

Local governments also prepared rebuilding subsidy programs for homeowners whose property was located outside of the buffer zones. The motivation for providing these programs is to address the gap between survivors whose properties are inside and outside of the buffer zones. This is based on the achievement of fairness with support from the government sector, and exposes the instability of the national government's rebuilding assistance system and philosophy, which encourages self-help by survivors during housing reconstruction (Kondo, 2015a: 141). This philosophy is quite different from the law and programs developed by the government sector since the Great Hanshin-Awaji Earthquake.

Local governments prepared the subsidy programs based on locality, but at the same time this caused gaps between local governments, which meant that the amount that people received was decided not by the damage they suffered, but the municipality they resided in before the disaster and where they choose to live.

5 Conclusion

It is seen that the philosophy and system of laws and programs for housing recovery assistance and compensation are different between the U.S. and Japan. The main objective of the NFIP is to reduce the loss of life and property, which functions not only as compensation for loss after disaster, but also as promoting mitigation before disaster hits. This can be called a "pre-disaster housing recovery" approach that is not incorporated in the Japanese system. Government subsidies for housing recovery after disaster are justified in Japan by the benefit to the public good, which is "regional-wide" recovery that differs from human-centered recovery.

Whatever the differences are, it is true that both countries' law and policies for housing recovery are fragile in the sense that they each lack the theoretical basis for assistance and compensation for housing recovery via government subsidy and insurance. The housing recovery program after Hurricane Katrina differed by having two sides: compensation for loss and assistance for people to reconstruct their housing.

On the other hand, housing recovery subsidy programs prepared after the Great East Japan Earthquake seek the achievement of fairness for survivors, which is distinct from the national law and local government programs that have evolved since the Great Hanshin-Awaji Earthquake.

The fragility has both positive and negative issues. The positive aspect is that even when the theoretical basis is not written in rules and policy, there has been sufficient flexibility for national and local governments to design programs after a disaster based on the experience and characteristics of the disaster and the strategies for post-disaster recovery planning. At the same time, it is ideal when local governments compete with each other to improve the level of assistance, which enables the establishment of programs that better suit local needs. Local governments after the Great East Japan Earthquake prepared housing recovery assistance subsidy programs based on "local needs" for post-disaster human-centered recovery (Kondo, 2015a: 141), which is nearly impossible for the national government to assess or define in pre-written legislation. It seems that the philosophy has to be defined more clearly before disaster strikes, but at the same time, we should not expropriate the role of local government policy for housing recovery after disaster. On another front, the negative aspect is that governments can exploit their position to design and plan a program that neglects human-centered recovery based on the strength of the "public good" that provides political cover. Global society has to reconsider and redesign the philosophy and design of housing recovery assistance laws, policies, and programs from a perspective of human-centered housing recovery, in preparation for the next mega-disaster.

References

Comerio, Mary C., *Disaster Hits Home: New Policy for Urban Housing Recovery* (California: University of California Press, 1998).

FEMA, *The Disaster Process & Disaster Aid Programs*. www.fema.gov/disaster-process-disaster-aid-programs.

Finger, Davida, "Stranded and Squandered: Lost on the Road Home", *Seattle Journal for Social Justice*, 7, pp. 59–100, 2008.

Green, Timothy F. and Robert B. Olshansky, "Rebuilding Housing in New Orleans: The Road Home Program after the Hurricane Katrina Disaster", *Housing Policy Debate*, 22: 1, pp. 75–99, 2012.

Haddow, George, Jane Bullock, and Damon P. Coppola, *Introduction to Emergency Management*, 5th edition (Waltham, MA: Butterworth-Heinemann, 2013).

Kaneko, Yuka, "Loss Compensation and Judicial Access in Post-Disaster Recovery in Asia", *Journal of International Cooperation Studies*, 22: 2, 3, pp. 1–42, January 2015, Graduate School of International Cooperation Studies, Kobe University.

Kondo, Tamiyo, "The Founding Background and Characteristics of Housing Rebuilding Assistance Subsidy Programs by Local Governments After the Great East Japan

Earthquake: Discussion on Housing Rebuilding Assistance Subsidy after Mega Disaster", *Journal of Architecture and Planning*, 80: 707, pp. 135–144, 2015a (in Japanese).

Kondo, Tamiyo, "Clustered and Community-Driven Housing Recovery: Lessons Learned from Hurricane Katrina to the Great East Japan Earthquake", in *Cities and Disaster*, ed. Davia C. Downey (Boca Raton, FL: CRC Press, 2015b), pp. 269–296.

Maly, Elizabeth, Tamiyo Kondo and Michiko Banba, "Post-Disaster Land Use Management after Hurricane Katrina and Superstorm Sandy in the U.S.", in *Land Use Management and Disaster Risk Reduction*, eds Michiko Banba and Rajib Shaw (New York: Springer, July 2016).

Masuda, Satoru, "The Issues for Buffer Zone and Group Relocation Projects", *Disaster Recovery and Revitalization Review*, 5: 3, pp. 73–79, March 2014.

Murosaki, Yoshiteru, "Verification of Act on Support for Reconstructing Livelihoods of Disaster Victims", Kwansei Gakuin University Publishing (in Japanese), pp. 235–240, 2014.

Norcross, Eileen and Anthony Skriba, "The Road Home: Helping Homeowners in the Gulf after Katrina", in *The Political Economy of Hurricane Katrina and Community Rebound*, ed. Emily Chamlee-Wright (Cheltenham, Glos: Edward Elgar Publishing, 2010), pp. 185–214.

Seidman, Karl F., *Coming Home to New Orleans: Neighborhood Rebuilding After Katrina* (Oxford: Oxford University Press, 2013).

The Road Home? An Examination of the Goals, Costs, Management, and Impediments Facing Louisiana's Road Home Program, Hearing before the ad hoc Subcommittee on Disaster Recovery of the Committee on Homeland Security and Governmental Affairs, United States Senate, 110th Congress, First Session.

U.S. Government Accountability Office, *Report to the Committee on Homeland Security and Government Affairs, U.S Senate, Gulf Coast Disaster Recovery Community Development Block Grant Program Guidance to States Needs to Be Improved* (GAO-09–541), June 2009.

U.S. Government Accountability Office, *Flood Insurance* (GAO-14–297R), April 2014.

9 Lessons from the Canterbury earthquakes

Adequacy of a first loss insurance scheme for natural disasters

Michael J.V. White

In September 2010 and February 2011, Christchurch, New Zealand's second largest city, suffered major earthquakes ("Canterbury earthquakes"). The Canterbury earthquakes resulted in significant personal injury and trauma, and the destruction of homes, jobs, businesses and infrastructure. The effects were compounded by continuing, and often powerful, aftershocks. The February 2011 earthquake killed 185 people, making it New Zealand's second deadliest natural disaster.

In the immediate aftermath of the 22 February 2011 earthquake, the Government (along with other humanitarian agencies and volunteers) responded quickly and provided a variety of support and services to assist those affected. Together with local authorities and communities, they responded as best they could to the chaos of the day.

As the dust settled, affected people refocused their attention on compensation for physical loss and damage. This chapter does not consider the Government's response to physical injury and death which was subject to New Zealand's unique no fault accident compensation scheme and its public health system.[1] Nor does it focus on loss of income or other welfare needs which were dealt with under New Zealand's social welfare system.[2] Instead, it focuses on how the longer-term response to claims for damage to property has affected the rights of vulnerable groups and individuals.

Over one-third of the buildings in the Central Business District ("CBD") were damaged beyond repair. The worst affected part of the city was designated the "red-zone", being land that the Government concluded had been so badly damaged that it was unlikely it could be rebuilt for a prolonged period.[3] The loss of property was unprecedented and continues to challenge New Zealand's natural disaster insurance compensation framework.

1 The context

Before considering New Zealand's natural disaster insurance compensation framework, it is important to consider the particular circumstances surrounding the Canterbury earthquakes.

At 4.35 am on Saturday 4 September 2010, Canterbury was struck by a 7.1 magnitude earthquake. The quake caused significant damage to the Canterbury region with power outages, ruptured pipes, falling masonry, collapsed buildings and liquefaction across the region. While Canterbury faced a massive clean-up and long recovery, it was fortunate that no lives were lost.[4]

The September earthquake was followed by almost continuous aftershocks – over 1,400 in the month following the quake. The ongoing impact and stress from these aftershocks was telling. However, the devastation thrust upon Canterbury did not stop there and on 22 February 2011, at 12.51 pm, a shallow 6.3 magnitude earthquake shook Christchurch again. *GeoNet*[5] recorded the highest shaking at 220 per cent of the acceleration of gravity – the highest ever recorded in New Zealand.

The February earthquake struck right in the middle of the day when the CBD was alive with activity. As a result, 185 people were killed.[6] Over one-third of the buildings in the CBD were damaged beyond repair. Despite many residential buildings not being directly damaged by the shaking from the earthquakes, losses flowed from the process of liquefaction. This is a process by which the compressed sandy soil on which much of Christchurch is built broke up, allowing pressurised water to escape. This resulted in much of the soil being converted into sludge and mud. Matters were made worse by the fracturing of sewer pipes, releasing large quantities of sewerage into the streets of Christchurch. The mixture of sewage and sludge submerged whole streets and had a devastating effect on the foundations of houses.

Again the impact of the February earthquake was compounded by significant and ongoing aftershocks. Two large aftershocks on 13 June 2011, of magnitudes 5.6 and 6.3, brought further damage. By mid-January 2012 Canterbury had experienced 9,500 quakes. This equated to approximately one quake over magnitude 3.0 every four hours.

Experts predict that aftershocks are likely to continue for several decades.[7] In the meantime, the people of Canterbury continue to live in a state of uncertainty with ongoing financial, emotional and psycho-social stress. It is against this backdrop that New Zealand's disaster insurance framework has been tested.

2 Disaster insurance

New Zealand operates a first loss insurance scheme[8] for natural disaster recovery. The legislative framework is unusual in that New Zealand is one of the very few countries in the world that insures residential land.

2.1 History of the New Zealand Disaster Insurance Framework

Prior to 1859, when the New Zealand Insurance Company was established, individuals were left to carry the risk of disasters and other hazardous events themselves. From 1859, earthquake insurance on residential and commercial properties was available. However, whether or not to take out earthquake insurance on a given property was entirely voluntary.[9] Very few people availed themselves of the opportunity to insure their properties against earthquake damage and loss at this time.

In the early 1900s, a series of catastrophic events highlighted New Zealand's vulnerability to earthquakes and other natural disasters.[10] It was clear that there was a need for the Government to provide access to affordable insurance to mitigate the devastating social cost of leaving such matters entirely to the private insurance industry. In 1942, a War Commission was set up which provided those who had insured their property against fire cover for damage resulting from war-related acts. Subsequently the Government extended cover to earthquakes.[11]

Eventually war damage cover was abolished and the Earthquake Commission ("EQC") was established. EQC is a Crown entity that operates under the Earthquake Commission Act 1993 ("EQC Act"). The EQC Act restricted cover to residential property. Commercial property owners were left to make their own decisions about insurance protection. This distinction between residential and commercial property owners remains to this day.

2.2 EQC scheme

EQC's primary objective is to administer New Zealand's first loss national disaster insurance scheme through the Natural Disaster Fund ("Fund"). The Fund is backed by private reinsurance and a Government guarantee. The Government guarantee applies in the event that the Fund and the reinsurance are exhausted. The viability and sustainability of the Fund is obviously critical for the effective operation of New Zealand's scheme.

EQC levies are collected by insurance companies and forwarded to EQC, which does not receive or have direct access to the details of the people and properties it covers. All premiums are paid into the Natural Disaster Fund and claims are paid from it. The fund is invested primarily in New Zealand Government securities with about half of the sum through the Reserve Bank in Foreign Bond Linked Notes. A substantial amount of catastrophe insurance is carried with some 150 separate entities. The total amount of reinsurance protection is NZ$1.5 billion ($1.43 billion) once the total claims from a single event exceeds NZ$750 million ($716 million). If the Fund is exhausted, the Government steps in to pay the remaining claims.

The EQC Act provides coverage for damage to insured buildings caused by a natural disaster. The sum recoverable in relation to buildings is based on the terms of the fire policy in the insured's private insurance policy, being the lesser of any specified replacement value, the sum insured (if there is no specified replacement value) or $100,000 plus GST[12] for each dwelling disclosed to the insurer prior to entering into the insurance contract.[13] An excess of $200 applies for each event, being damage occurring within any one 48-hour period – or seven days in the case of a fire.[14]

The cover for land damage offered by EQC is unique internationally.[15] The cover provided for damage to residential land is determined based on the value of a portion of that land, being the lesser of the minimum allowable size for residential use, the portion of the land actually damaged, or 4,000 square metres.

It was held in *Earthquake Commission v Winch*[16] that the land includes a right of way over neighbouring land which does not belong to the insured themselves. Any bridges, culverts and retaining walls necessary for the support of buildings is included in this assessment for their indemnity value (taking into account their age and state of repair). A per dwelling excess of $500 or 10 per cent of the value of the land applies. This excess is capped at $5,000.

Finally EQC provides cover for personal property[17] for its replacement value up to a maximum of $20,000, subject to an excess of $200. Cover excludes any personal property used for business purposes.

2.3 Limits of EQC cover

The deemed insurance sums are based on 1994 values. When inflation is taken into account this means that cover is about 50 per cent in real terms. Private insurance is left to cover the shortfall. Furthermore the compulsory insurance does not extend to: intangible property, motor vehicles, vessels, animals, roads, paths and bridges that are not an integral part of the building, drains, swimming pools, tennis courts, jewellery, money, works of art or documents.[18] Of particular concern is that there is no universal coverage – only those whose properties are privately insured can avail themselves to EQC coverage.

There is no contractual relationship between EQC and the insured. Rather it is a statutory arrangement. Practically this means that the protective measures in respect of insurance contracts as set out in the Insurance Law Reform Act 1977 do not apply.[19] Nor is EQC a member of the Insurance and Savings Ombudsman ("Ombudsman"). The Ombudsman is a voluntary organisation set up to resolve disputes between insurers and consumers.[20]

3 Protecting the rights and dignity of Canterbury residents

The importance of human rights in the Government's response to the Canterbury earthquakes has been emphasised by the United Nations supervisory bodies to whom New Zealand reports. For example, the concluding observations by the United Nations Committee on Economic, Social and Cultural Rights ("CESCR") on New Zealand's third periodic report stated:[21]

> The Committee notes the challenges caused by the recent earthquakes on the enjoyment of Covenant rights by persons affected, especially their right to housing.
>
> (art. 11, 2(2))
>
> The Committee recommends that the State party adopt a human rights approach to reconstruction efforts, ensuring thereby appropriate consideration to availability, affordability and adequacy of housing, including for temporary housing. In this regard, the Committee refers the State party to its general comment No. 4 (1991) on the right to adequate housing…

The Government has acknowledged the human rights implications of its response to the earthquakes in its statements to these bodies, and confirmed its commitment to respect and protect those rights. For example, the Government stated – in the recent second Universal Periodic Review – to the United Nations Human Rights Council that "ensuring any human rights impacts of the Canterbury earthquakes are accounted for in the ongoing decisions around the rebuild" was a "key priority" for New Zealand.[22] The Government has "accepted in full" the recommendation made in response that it "facilitate the realization of economic, social and cultural rights through the reconstruction of the areas affected by earthquakes in 2010 and 2011".[23]

Disaster insurance, and more specifically the EQC scheme, is pivotal to the Government's response. If effective, Canterbury residents will be in a better position to realise their rights, and to move forward with dignity. If not, some residents – invariably those who are already most vulnerable – will be further marginalised. The unintended consequences can be dire for certain groups and lead to significant and ongoing psycho social harm.

3.1 Relevant human rights obligations

New Zealand is party to a range of international human rights instruments, including the Universal Declaration of Human Rights ("UDHR"),[24] the International Covenant on Civil and Political Rights ("ICCPR")[25] and the International Covenant on Economic, Social and Cultural Rights ("ICESCR").[26] New Zealand has undertaken obligations to implement and protect these rights domestically.[27] The two Covenants allow for very limited exceptions to compliance.[28]

Natural disasters raise complex and significant human rights issues, both in the initial response and in the recovery phase. These issues have been recently outlined in the 2011 revised Inter-Agency Standing Committee ("IASC") operational guidelines for the protection of persons in situations of natural disasters.[29] The guidelines emphasise the importance of adopting a human rights based approach to the response to natural disasters:[30]

> Often, negative impacts on the human rights concerns after a natural disaster do not arise from purposeful policies but are the result of inadequate planning and disaster preparedness, inappropriate policies and measures to respond to the disasters, or simple neglect.
>
> ...
>
> These challenges could be mitigated or avoided altogether if the relevant human rights guarantees were taken into account by national and international actors, in all phases of the disaster response: preparedness, relief and recovery.

A wide range of human rights will obviously be engaged in the context of the response to a natural disaster.[31] However, the rights to housing, home and property are particularly relevant to New Zealand's unique response to property loss arising from a natural disaster. It is therefore worth considering the scope of these particular rights in more detail.

3.1.1 Right to housing: Article 11 ICESCR

The right to housing is part of the right to an adequate standard of living recognised in Article 11 of ICESCR. The right to adequate housing is described by the CESCR as being of "central importance for the enjoyment of all economic, social and cultural rights", and:[32]

> the right to adequate housing cannot be viewed in isolation from other human rights contained in the two International Covenants and other applicable international instruments. Reference has already been made in this regard to the concept of human dignity and the principle of non-discrimination. In addition, the full enjoyment of other rights – such as the right to freedom of expression, the right to freedom of association (such as for tenants and other community-based groups), the right to freedom of residence and the right to participate in public decision-making – is indispensable if the right to adequate housing is to be realized and maintained by all groups in society. Similarly, the right not to be subjected to arbitrary or unlawful interference with one's privacy, family, home or correspondence constitutes a very important dimension in defining the right to adequate housing.

The Committee has confirmed that Article 11 recognises the right to live somewhere in security, peace and dignity, and that it incorporates rights to security of tenure, availability of services, facilities and infrastructure, and affordability. This requires New Zealand to respect, protect and fulfil (including, where appropriate, provide), the right to adequate housing, including security of tenure, affordability, access to services and infrastructure, and habitability. Any retrogressive step must be clearly justified.

3.1.2 Right to home: Article 17 ICCPR

Article 17 of the ICCPR provides:

> 1 No one shall be subjected to arbitrary or unlawful interference with his privacy, family, home or correspondence, nor to unlawful attacks on his honour and reputation.
> 2 Everyone has the right to the protection of the law against such interference or attacks.

The European Court of Human Rights describes this right as "of central importance to an individual's identity, self-determination, physical and moral integrity, maintenance of relationships with others and a settled and secure place in the community".[33] The Court has confirmed that the importance of this right to the individual must be taken into account when considering the margin of appreciation allowed to national authorities,[34] and stressed the importance of procedural safeguards and a fair process for affected individuals when assessing whether interference is justified.[35]

The concept of "interference" is less than total negation, and includes any action that interferes with a person's enjoyment of their home. "Home" is understood as the place where a person resides or carried out his or her usual occupation.[36] Only unlawful or arbitrary interference will contravene the right.

Whether interference is "arbitrary" requires an assessment of whether it is reasonable, proportionate and consistent with the Covenant.[37] The test is similar to that laid down in section 5 of New Zealand's Bill of Rights Act 1990 ("BORA").[38] The provision of procedural safeguards and a fair process for affected individuals will be an important part of that assessment. In this regard, Article 2 of the ICCPR requires New Zealand to ensure that there is an effective remedy available through competent judicial, administrative or legislative authorities, and to "develop the possibilities of judicial remedy" for any violation of this right.

3.1.3 Right to property: Article 17 UDHR

Article 17 of the UDHR provides:

1 Everyone has the right to own property alone as well as in association with others.
2 No one shall be arbitrarily deprived of his property.

The right to property is not reflected in either of the ICCPR or ICESCR, principally as a result of the intractable differences that arose out of the ideological division between the capitalist and socialist countries during the Cold War. However, non-inclusion does not equate with a denial of the right, as recorded for example in the ICCPR *travaux preparatoires*:[39]

> no one questioned the right of the individual to own property … it was generally admitted that the right to own property was not absolute and there was wide agreement that the right … was "subject to some degree of control by the State" while "certain safeguards against abuse must be provided…

4 EQC resolution of earthquake claims

The scale of the Canterbury earthquakes and the complexity of the circumstances were far greater than any event EQC had foreseen. Prior to September 2010, EQC's experience was limited, typically to events resulting in around 5,000 claims.[40] In 2011, the Canterbury earthquakes represented the second largest insurance event in the world.[41] The total number of claims as of 9 September 2013 was 467,839.[42]

Through the course of the claims resolution process significant issues arose causing delays in settlement and significant discrepancies in the quantum paid out. These issues have invariably resulted in additional undue stress and burden on individual property owners, impacted on the rights of Canterbury residents and undermined their dignity. This does not imply any criticism of EQC and their intentions to help Cantabrians to move on with their lives and ensure a safe and sustainable rebuild. As the Christchurch Press noted:[43]

> EQC's persistent line has been that its procedures are as good as can be, its settlement of claims as speedy as possible and fair, and any problems it does have are being put right – and all that in the face of a civil emergency unprecedented in New Zealand's history.

That may very well be the case. However, what is clear is that the EQC system was put under significant stress and a number of fragilities in the system have been highlighted that need to be addressed if EQC is going to be able to respond to future "large scale" events.

4.1 Assessment discrepancies: repair or replace

One of the most common complaints about the recovery process has been about the rate at which insurance payouts have been made and repairs completed. Many discrepancies have arisen between assessments made by EQC and those made by private insurers. Sarah Miles notes that "there are many accounts of the assessment gaps between insurers and EQC of between $200,000 and $500,000".[44]

An overarching issue has been where one of the parties has classified the damage as a *repair job* and the other considered it a *rebuild.* It was not uncommon for EQC to deem the house a repair job worth under $100,000 and the private insurer to assess it as a rebuild. Homeowners were left waiting and wondering. Canterbury Communities' Earthquake Recovery Network ("CanCERN")[45] aptly summarised the situation as follows: "There is no set standard for repair or replacement. Every assessor and every insurer has different ideas about costings and methodologies, and as people discuss and compare costings, this ultimately generates confusion, mistrust, anxiety, and sleepless nights."[46] There is no doubt an imperative for insurance companies, and the EQC, is to get this assessment right to satisfy any reinsurance obligations. AMI Insurance earthquake recovery executive manager Peter Rose described the situation as follows:[47]

> Our policy says we will reinstate the property "as new". There's not much wriggle room there. [The EQC Act] says "substantially the same as when new". "Substantially the same as when new" isn't the same as "as new" … We are talking about humans here who are making assessments and … it's possible they simply have a difference of opinion.

Even where there has been no dispute over whether a rebuild or repair is required the approach to costings of this work has been variable. This has meant that estimates for repairs or replacement have varied significantly between private insurers and EQC. Some insurers have been relying on "reasonable equivalence" provisions in policies, thereby minimising costs. Relying on this method is artificial and in some circumstances impracticable – for example, materials that were used in an original home may no longer be suitable and/or not meet modern building standards and codes.

EQC is bound by its Act to repair, or pay for the repair of earthquake damage, or to restore a property to a condition substantially the same as, but not better or more extensive than, its condition when new. Although it has been argued that EQC has, at least in substance, the same obligations as a private insurer, this has not played out in practice. The intricacies of the interpretation of policy wording has led to a failure to agree liability and quantum. Many disputes have ultimately ended up in the courts, increasing delay.

Adopting a strict interpretation to its Act, the EQC asserts that claimants are required to prove loss. Private insurers adopt a similar approach, although based on the contractual relationship with their clients. Therefore, where there is a dispute as to the value of an assessment, it is the customer who is responsible for seeking independent evidence and presenting this to the EQC for consideration. The New Zealand Human Rights Commission recalls the experience of one resident in his dealings with EQC in this regard:[48]

> We have had huge upheaval in our lives and that of our school age children, and we still have not had any hint of resolution. We are paying thousands in independent reports which our insurer ignores. We have not had our over cap payment from EQC – despite our house's obvious structural and land slip problems we struggled to get over the EQC cap – with intervention of our MP we got another assessment – the damage assessment went from approx $60k to $484k. The incompetence of the first assessment was truly eye watering. It was then that our faith in the system started to change.

4.2 Dealing with multiple events

The scale of the earthquakes and the fact that there were significant aftershocks on 13 June and 23 December 2012 magnified the complexity of the insurance response. It meant that many homes were damaged by multiple events which, although linked for EQC insurance purposes, needed to be treated as separate events. Treating the different events separately is necessary for the purposes of quantification of liability as between EQC and private insurers and their respective reinsurers.

The system of having EQC as a first loss insurer working with other insurers to determine these multiple losses has added a further layer of complexity. For example, it has meant that for approximately 25,000 of the 172,000 properties covered by EQC in the Canterbury earthquakes, homeowners have had to negotiate with two insurers instead of one, and EQC has had to negotiate with both a private insurer as well as a client.

4.2.1 The application of the doctrine of merger

In relation to private insurers, damage from multiple events raised significant questions of whether claims from earlier earthquakes could be merged with the "final earthquake". Some analogies can be drawn with the marine insurance framework which assumes that an assured should not be able to recover both the amount necessary to make good the first loss and then full reinstatement cost from a second loss. This is referred to as the doctrine of merger. Section 77(2) of the Marine Insurance Act 1908 provides that an unrepaired partial loss merges into a subsequent total loss in the same policy year.[49] In circumstances where repair has been made, an insured may recover for a series of partial losses even though in aggregate the amount would exceed policy limits.

The application of the doctrine of merger to the Canterbury earthquakes was considered by the High Court in *Ridgecrest NZ Ltd v IAG New Zealand Ltd.*[50] *Ridgecrest* concerned a commercial building in Christchurch that was insured by IAG NZ. The policy provided repair/replacement cover under the following provisions:

> **C1:** This insurance will pay the amount of loss or damage or the estimated cost of restoring your Business Assets as nearly as possible to the same condition they were in immediately before the loss or damage happened using current materials and methods.
> **C2:** Where Replacement cover has been agreed by us and specified in the Schedule and following loss or damage you restore or replace the lost or damaged Business Assets this insurance will pay
>
> (a) For Buildings
>
> (i) Where repairable, the cost of restoration of damage to the same condition as new,
> or
> (ii) If unable to be repaired because of such damage, the cost of replacement by an equivalent building which meets your requirements at any site provided we shall not pay more than the cost of replacement at the site stated in the Schedule.

The building suffered damage in four earthquake events. It was damaged in the first two earthquakes, and partially repaired, before becoming a total loss from the third and fourth events. Ridgecrest – the building owner – sought to recover the full amount for each repair as well as the full sum insured on total loss. IAG took the position that once the building was irreparable, it was only required to pay the cost of replacement.

The High Court dismissed the claim and found in favour of IAG. The High Court implied a term that discharged IAG from paying for losses arising from the earlier earthquakes. In relation to the doctrine of merger, the Court concluded that it did not have wider application beyond marine insurance. It ruled that marine and non-marine insurance differed in two respects. First, marine insurers were liable for damage to the insured vessel only when the policy came to an end. Second, marine insurance policies contemplated that after a vessel became a constructive loss it was to be abandoned to insurers. This was contrasted with non-marine insurance where insurers:

a are liable from the moment the loss occurs; and
b remain liable for damage after total loss in certain circumstances.

Professor Rob Merkin has suggested that the assessment by the High Court of the application of the doctrine of merger is incorrect.[51] In his view the categorisation of the differences between marine and non-marine insurance made by the Court are inaccurate. Professor Merkin considered that the approach taken by the High Court was unsupported by authority and "incorrect as a matter of principle".[52] In his view, "the doctrine of merger applies alike to marine and non-marine insurance unless it is ousted by agreement".[53] Even if the doctrine of merger did apply, Professor Merkin acknowledges that it may be ousted in certain circumstances depending on the policy wording. Justice Dobson was of a similar view noting that "per happening" coverage would have ousted merger had it been applicable.[54]

On appeal, the Court of Appeal reached the same conclusion but by a different route – preferring to draw a distinction between clauses C1 and C2 of the policy.[55] By reaching its conclusion in this way, the Court of Appeal was not required to consider the doctrine of merger.

On appeal to the Supreme Court a middle ground was forged.[56] The Supreme Court held that under the policy wording, Ridgecrest was entitled to be paid in respect of the damage caused by the earlier earthquakes (up to the policy limit in respect of each earthquake) as well as in respect of the final earthquake. The Court also held that the merger principle did not apply given that:

a in contradistinction to the position under marine insurance policies, the wording of IAG's policy provides for independent causes of actions in respect of the partial and unrepaired losses and the subsequent total loss; and
b the application of the merger principle would be inconsistent with the insurance policy and in particular the resetting of the liability limit after each happening.

However, despite these findings the Court concluded that, by reason of the indemnity principle, Ridgecrest was not entitled to recover more than the replacement value of the building and may not double count the losses.

4.2.2 Seeking clarity: multiple events and the respective liability of EQC and private insurers

There has been a particular problem with regard to properties damaged in the Canterbury earthquakes where a single policy was in place for a period covering both earthquakes and associated aftershocks. EQC was unsure whether the EQC Act provided for $100,000 plus GST for the aggregate damage in a 12-month period, or whether there would be multiple aggregates available in 12-month renewal periods. This was significant as it could have meant private insurers would have been required to pick up significantly larger losses.

In 2011, EQC, the Insurance Council of New Zealand, Vero and IAG applied to the High Court for declarations to clarify how EQC cover responds to home-owners who have made more than one claim for damage suffered in more than one earthquake.[57]

The issue was described by the High Court as follows:[58]

> when multiple events cause natural disaster damage to the same property during the term of a fire insurance contract and EQC has not, at the time of later natural disaster damage, made a payment in respect of the earlier natural disaster damage is EQC liable to pay either (1) up to $100,000/$20,000 for each occurrence of natural disaster damage, or (2) up to $100,000/$20,000 in total for the aggregate of all natural disaster damage caused by multiple events?

The private insurers asserted that there was a separate indemnity for each of the claims. By contrast, EQC argued that there was one limit of indemnity per policy period, and that its cover reinstated only on the renewal of the cover. In practice this would mean that any liabilities in excess of $100,000 were for the insurance market.

The High Court rejected the EQC's argument and expressed a preference for option 1 – the continuing cover approach. This meant that for any natural disaster big enough for EQC to class as an event, EQC is liable for the first $100,000 plus GST[59] worth of damage. EQC therefore needed to revise its process to determine how much and when damage occurred on properties that EQC was unable to assess between each event. There were 13 earthquake events between September 2010 and the end of June 2011, generating 400,000 claims.

4.2.3 Apportionment – a pragmatic solution?

In response the insurance industry, along with EQC, devised an apportionment process. This process seeks to determine how much damage each event caused, and thus determine EQC's liability *vis à vis* private insurers. If possible, EQC uses information from house damage assessments after the event. When a current assessment from an event is unavailable, EQC uses other sources of information to estimate the damage from each event.

EQC refers all claims to the homeowner's private insurance company if the apportionment process shows that the cost of repairing damage to the house will be more than the cap for any one event. If the apportionment process shows that the cost of repairing damage to the house will be less than the cap for each relevant event, the house is repaired as part of the Canterbury home-repair programme ("CHRP").[60]

The complexity of this task has resulted in a significant slowing in claims processing. Many had more than four visits from EQC to consider how damage was to be apportioned. Earlier assessments were modified, often downwards. Many who had houses that were originally deemed a total rebuild discovered their homes were now able to be repaired. The uncertainty for Canterbury homeowners was compounded by lack of prompt information from insurers and EQC. CANcern summed the situation up nicely stating:[61]

> The issue now is that EQC and the insurers have to work out what their relationship is with one another. While they hash that out, the residents are stuck in limbo and from their perspective, it's neither here nor there who's paying for what. As long as they know a payment is going to be made soon, or they're going to be able to get the information they need, the residents will be in a position to make decisions and move on.

4.3 The Canterbury home-repair programme

In response to the need for a coordinated response, EQC took on the role of managing the undertaking of repairs for which it was responsible. It engaged Fletcher Construction ("Fletcher") to project manage the repair of earthquake damaged homes with damage between $15,000 and $100,000 per claim.

It is possible for residents to choose their own builder and to *opt out* of the programme. However, if they do so they must meet any costs over and above the EQC assessed value of repairs. The *opt out* process has worked well for some. However, the overwhelming response from homeowners has been that it has been an onerous, uncertain and slow process. Most have had to wait about six months for reimbursement of payments they have made to contractors. This is symptomatic of the fragility of the EQC framework, where a small agency has been required to take on additional and complex roles in the recovery.[62]

More worrying, however, is that in some instances EQC has made payments in instalments. Whether this is an attempt to stagger liability and thus insulate the National Disaster Fund which is under significant stress is unclear. What is clear is that, regardless of the motives, it shifts the short-term financial burden from EQC to homeowners – homeowners who have lost a lot through the earthquakes and continue, in most cases, to live in difficult and stressful conditions.

The CHRP is an agency-driven approach to reconstruction where homeowners have little control and autonomy over their own rebuilding and repairs. Although this may be expedient in the circumstances, the World Bank has identified a people centric, owner-driven approach as more effective. Such an approach has "proven to be the most empowering, dignified, sustainable and cost-effective reconstruction approach".[63] In its 2013 Report of the Canterbury earthquakes,[64] the New Zealand Human Rights Commission clearly identified six key benefits of an owner-driven approach:[65]

- Homeowners have control over the reconstruction of their homes. This has the associated benefits of owners being able to supervise the process often to a greater extent than when the process is controlled by an external agency.
- There are clear lines of accountability for the work of homeowners.
- It encourages recycling and use of sustainable solutions with households being more likely to use salvaged and local building materials.
- It encourages people to be resourceful and recognises the rights of people to privacy and sanctity in their own homes.
- It helps preserve continuity in local building and architectural style.
- It allows people the flexibility to top-up State funding to re-build or repair homes to reflect their specific needs, such as wall insulation, universal design and retrofitting for accessibility.

Acknowledging the positive aspects and potential of the CHRP, the New Zealand Human Rights Commission suggests that expanding and improving the existing provisions for *opting out* could provide Cantabrians with more choice, control and flexibility.[66]

It seems that the need for change was also acknowledged by EQC with a streamlining of their customer-managed repairs (*opt out*) process. EQC now meets with the customer and confirms the damage and repair scope. Customers then get an updated statement of works and a cash settlement. Customers have full control of this cash settlement and can undergo repair work with flexibility. This is a vast improvement from the way the process was initially managed.

4.4 Disputes resolution

Schedule 3 of the EQC Act contains a number of provisions that allow EQC to limit its liability, decline claims or cancel coverage. In normal circumstances, these decisions are subject to review by the courts (and legal aid would be available in some cases). However, the extent of the damage caused by the Canterbury earthquakes has to a large degree nullified the possibility of review, and where it is available the delays undermine the appropriateness and adequacy of any remedy. The realisation of rights (particularly housing and an adequate standard of living) can be severely compromised while awaiting the outcome of court proceedings.

The absence of a suitable alternative independent review and appeal authority has resulted in appeal and review rights being effectively denied and has created an environment within which EQC has been able to operate, to a large degree, in the absence of independent oversight.

5 The red zone[67]

Although there is no legislative prohibition against rebuilding in the red zone, in practical terms this is not a reality. Owners of property in the red zone are left with no other real alternative but to sell to the Government because the Council will not install new or maintain existing services, nor issue any building or resource consents within the red zone. Similarly, insurers will not repair or rebuild properties in the red zone.

In light of this reality it is useful to consider whether EQC and/or insurance companies are adopting the correct approach to this unprecedented zoning decision.

5.1 Traditional approaches to insurance law

Residential insurance policies generally provide cover, in respect of damage caused by earthquake, for one (or a combination) of the following:

a loss; or
b physical loss; or
c damage; or
d physical damage.

5.1.1 Loss

Where a property may not satisfy the test for physical damage there is the possibility of it being "lost". Loss can refer to both losing possession and use of something, and also to loss in the sense of something being destroyed. In a number of cases it has been decided that it is unnecessary to show that recovery of possession is "unlikely", merely that there is some uncertainty about repossession.[68]

While loss in the traditional sense will apply to situations where the owner is unable to find an insured item, it has also been applied to situations where the owners are unable to access or use property effectively. Some have suggested that there is an argument that owners of houses in the red zone have been effectively deprived of possession and therefore the houses have been lost. This assertion is made on the basis that deprivation is a function of the fact that continued occupation of the home is untenable as a result of decisions made by Government, Council and insurers.

Where policies apply a "physical loss" test the situation is more complicated. Residential insurance policies provide cover for the house, not the land. This means that loss or damage to land and surrounding infrastructure – which led to the red zoning decisions – can result in an effective loss of the house without any apparent physical damage to the house itself. EQC cover for damage to land does not provide any indemnity for effective loss of a house due to zoning decisions.

5.1.2 Damage

The leading decision on what constitutes "damage" in the context of an insurance policy is *Ranicar v Frigmobile Pty Limited.*[69] In *Ranicar*, the insured was a seafood processor and exporter. It entered into a contract to sell frozen scallops to a Canadian company. While waiting to be loaded in Melbourne, Australia, the scallops were found to be at a temperature outside the regulatory range and were rejected for export. However, they were sold on the Australian market for an amount less than they would have been sold to the Canadian company. The insurance policy provided cover for "all risks of loss or damage to the subject matter insured". The insurer denied liability on the grounds that the scallops were not lost or damaged, claiming that the inability to sell them under the original export contract was merely a matter of regulation.

The Court in *Ranicar* confirmed that property is damaged when it is rendered imperfect or inoperative, or when there is physical alteration or change, not necessarily permanent or irreparable, that alters the value or usefulness of the property because it affects its quality and saleability.

Drawing on this case some have suggested that by reason of the red zone there has been a physical alteration to a property. This is on the basis that prior to the earthquakes the house was located on land zoned suitable for residential use. Following the Canterbury earthquakes, the environment of the houses has changed to the extent that they are no longer located in an area deemed suitable for residential use. Although some analogies can be drawn to *Ranicar* it would seem to me – if it is accepted, as asserted by the Government, that the red zoning had no legal effect on actual residential zones and was merely the provision of information[70] – that the zoning decisions did not result in a change/physical alteration to the red zoned houses. However, if the zoning decisions did have a legal effect on the rights of homeowners then the situation may very well be different.[71]

In March 2015, the Supreme Court[72] concluded that the Government's red zone decisions were not merely the provision of information. The majority stated:

> The fact that decisions are based on information and that some or all of the information on which the decisions are based is communicated to the public at the same time as the decisions, does not mean that the decisions are subsumed in the information upon which they are based. Nor does it mean that communication of the decisions is merely communication of information.[73]

In light of this decision the *Ranicar* approach may have wider application to the red zone situation in some cases. It could be argued that the decisions to designate properties red zone effectively rendered them "inoperative" as the area was deemed inhabitable and no services or infrastructure were maintained or repaired. Residents had no real option but to leave their homes and communities. Invariably these circumstances altered the "value of usefulness" of the property and affected their saleability.

The impact of the red zone decisions on property values can clearly be seen by the Christchurch City Council's 2014 property re-evaluation.[74] In conducting this re-evaluation it was determined that:[75]

> Due to the impact of the earthquakes, Red Zoned properties have been treated as unsuitable for residential occupation. The land value was initially assessed with regard to rural land sales evidence. A premium was then applied taking into account the city location and the possibility that at some time in the future the land may be suitable for residential occupation with remediation work undertaken…

This methodology has resulted in red zoned properties being valued at around $30,000 to $40,000,[76] significantly less than the previous 2007 valuations. For example, one person has had their property in the red zone re-valued at $44,000. In 2007 this same property had a valuation of $645,000.[77]

5.1.3 Physical damage

In order to establish physical damage, there must be evidence of some physical alteration having occurred to the insured property.[78] It would be reasonable to assume that all the houses in the red zone have suffered some degree of physical damage. That is damage that were the house not located in the red zone is capable of being repaired. However, the effects of the red zone on the ability to continue to live in a red zoned house and on the ultimate value of property, although significant, would not meet the criteria for physical damage. There has not been physical change to the house by the red zoning per se.

5.2 The approach being taken by EQC and private insurance companies

The approach most insurers are adopting is to conclude that the insured loss comprises only that actual physical damage done to the property. Under such an approach where the property is only moderately damaged it will not constitute a total loss and the liability of the insurer is calculated as the amount it would take to repair the damage. This has been the case even though this could never practically take place because of the designation of the areas as red zones, resulting in less compensation for homeowners whose house is not considered to be damaged beyond repair.

EQC is taking a similar approach with respect to compensation for damage to land and is assessing the cost of repairing land even though such repairs will never actually take place in practical terms. In many cases this has led to a calculation of liability less than the maximum amount payable under the EQC Act.

The approach taken by EQC and private insurers in this regard is arguably at odds with the traditional approach to insurance law and raises significant concerns in relation to the realisation of social, economic and cultural rights of residents in the red zone. Without fully considering the implications of the zoning decisions on the habitability of property, EQC and private insurance companies effectively compel those with minimal damage to their house who unfortunately find themselves in the red zone to leave their home and their communities.

6 Dangerous properties

The Building Act 2004 sets out the requirements that must be complied with when building work is undertaken and confers a wide range of powers on territorial authorities in relation to building work and the safety of buildings generally. Section 124 of the Building Act provides for a territorial authority to require work to be carried out on an earthquake-prone building by issuing a notice requiring the building owner to "reduce or remove the danger". Section 124 provides:

> **124 Powers of territorial authorities in respect of dangerous, earthquake prone, or insanitary buildings**
>
> (1) If a territorial authority is satisfied that a building is dangerous, earthquake prone, or insanitary, the territorial authority may –
>
> (a) put up a hoarding or fence to prevent people from approaching the building nearer than is safe;
> (b) attach in a prominent place on, or adjacent to, the building a notice that warns people not to approach the building;
> (c) give written notice requiring work to be carried out on the building, within a time stated in the notice (which must not be less than 10 days after the notice is given under section 125), to –
>
> (i) Reduce or remove the danger; or
> (ii) Prevent the building from remaining insanitary.

The definition of dangerous was modified by clause 7 of the Canterbury Earthquake Building Act Order 2011. This Order applied only to the districts of those territorial authorities within Canterbury that were affected by the earthquakes. The applicable definition of "dangerous", as amended by the Order, includes the position where "there is a risk that adjacent, adjoining, or nearby buildings or land could collapse (including collapse by way of rockfall, landslip, cliff collapse, or subsidence) or otherwise cause injury or death to any person in the building".[79] The February earthquake caused widespread rockfalls in an area of the city called the Port Hills. Thousands of rocks and boulders dislodged and rolled down the hills. As a result, five people died. In the immediate aftermath, Civil Defence was responsible for the assessment of risk and evacuation of homes in the area. A number of properties were "red carded" under Civil Defence's emergency powers.[80] This meant that occupants of these properties were required to leave and were not allowed to re-enter their homes until they were deemed safe.

In July 2011, the Council established a Port Hills Geotechnical Group ("PHGG") to carry out a review of red carded properties. The PHGG made recommendations to the Council about the ongoing status of properties and the need for a notice under s124 of the Building Act 2004. As a result of these recommendations the Council issued notices under s124 of the Building Act 2004 that prevented some people from using or occupying their homes. These notices may remain in place for many years – legally they can apply on an indefinite basis until hazards are removed or the property is made safe.

Practically this means that homeowners with s124 notices remain in a state of limbo. Insurance assessments are unable to be completed, insurance funded repairs progressed or payouts made to enable them to purchase a new property. The New Zealand Human Rights Commission has noted the case of one individual who has been told that there may be a wait of at least another two years until a determination can be made.[81] It should be noted that a s124 notice does not necessarily prevent repairs to a house being carried out. In certain circumstances temporary access can be granted to property owners and their agents and contractors. However, people feel that there is little point in carrying out repairs if a s124 notice remains in place preventing them from living in the property.

The Council will remove a notice if it is satisfied that there is no longer a risk and evidence suggests that the risk from rockfall will decline over time – this decline being in direct correlation to the decline in the aftershock sequence. However, in order to make any real difference to the safety of the property this change would have to be significant. In real terms the risk of rockfall is not anticipated to dissipate to pre-earthquake levels until 2021. Accordingly GNS Science has recommended that the risk be re-evaluated in 2022.

These issues were examined in the recent case of *Kraal v The Earthquake Commission and Allianz New Zealand Ltd.*[82] This was a test case which would have a profound impact on Port Hills residents – it provides some clarity and information to enable residents to make informed decisions about their future.

Kraal related to a red zoned property in the Port Hills. The Government offered to purchase the property but not at its replacement value. Kraal brought a claim against EQC and her insurer, Allianz, for replacement cover under the EQC Act and top up cover for her full rebuild costs under her insurance policy. The case concerned whether there is cover under the EQC Act, and in turn insurance cover, for a homeowner's loss of the right to occupy their home.[83]

The case hinged on whether the property had suffered "natural disaster damage" within the meaning of the EQC Act. "Natural disaster damage" is defined under s2 of the EQC Act as:

(a) Any physical loss or damage to the property, occurring as the direct result of a natural disaster; or
(b) Any physical loss or damage to the property occurring (whether accidentally or not) as a direct result of measures taken under proper

> authority to avoid the spreading of, or otherwise to mitigate the consequences of, any natural disaster, but does not include any physical loss or damage to the property for which compensation is payable under any other enactment.

"Physical loss or damage" is also deemed to include "any physical loss or damage to the property that (in the opinion of the Commission) is imminent as the direct result of a natural disaster which has occurred".[84] Under the EQC Act a residential building is insured for its "replacement value" (that is the cost of replacing or reinstating the building to the prescribed standards).[85] EQC may settle the claim by payment, replacement or reinstatement – the choice as to how to settle the claim being EQC's.[86] The term natural disaster damage includes "any physical loss or damage to the property occurring as the direct result of a natural disaster". Kraal argued that her property had suffered physical loss because the house could not be physically used or occupied for the foreseeable future.

EQC and Allianz argued that the EQC Act covered loss or damage to the physical integrity of the house and needed to be contrasted with non-physical effects on the house (such as loss of use) which may reduce its value or usefulness. Justice Mallon agreed with the interpretation put forward by EQC and Allianz and held that the ordinary meaning of the words physical loss was loss to the physical materials or structure of the house. Kraal had suffered an economic not a physical loss. Accordingly the Judge dismissed the claim against both EQC and Allianz.

The decision has been received with concern by homeowners in the Port Hills red zone who are yet to settle their insurance claims or sell their properties to the Government. Although this decision appears to be correct as a matter of legal interpretation, natural disaster damage in the EQC Act can include physical loss or damage that has not occurred but is imminent. The evidence before the Court in Kraal was that the s124 notice had been issued because there was a risk of damage to the property from rockfalls for many years to come. That risk arose as a result of the natural disaster that was the Christchurch earthquakes. On this basis it is arguable that there is a threat of imminent physical loss or damage, in relation to these properties and there are suggestions in the judgment of Justice Mallon that she may have been receptive to an argument along those lines.

7 Concluding remarks

Earthquake insurance can help relieve the financial burden on the Government to fund relief and recovery of the affected population by spreading risk and cost. The Asian Development Bank has suggested four key aspects for successful earthquake insurance:[87]

a affordability to the insured;
b universal coverage;

c financial sustainability; and
d incorporation of measures to limit or avoid damage.

The EQC Act provides for some restitution. It provides affordable disaster cover to property owners in New Zealand. This cover is guaranteed by the Government. The EQC framework and process is consistent with comparative international approaches and broadly reflects human rights norms and principles. However, the Canterbury earthquakes have shown that, in the face of such a massive and destructive series of events, the EQC Act is inadequate in some respects.

The situation has been far from straight forward and the ongoing aftershocks have added extra strain on the framework. As noted by Bruce Emson, General Manager Customer Services at the Earthquake Commission:[88]

> the series of multiple events complicated both our assessment programme, and the way we apportion costs across claims. In most cases this has meant multiple visits to houses from our teams. We know that this has been frustrating for some of our customers, and at times confusing.

However, it remains clear that in the aftermath of the Canterbury earthquakes the EQC scheme has not adequately delivered for the people. It is underfunded, it provides compensation based on unrealistically low measures of land value and there is too much room for dispute as to the interaction between EQC cover and that proffered by the private insurance market. The scheme is also iniquitous, in that it benefits only those who have taken out fire insurance on their properties.

Under the EQC Act framework the interface between the private insurer and the EQC is critical. This has proved problematic in practice given the lack of overall leadership and accountability – ultimately impacting on effective and timely settlement. For example, there has been uncertainty about who has the role of assessor in certain circumstances. In the absence of any suitable complaints and disputes resolution mechanism litigation has been rife – adding to the cost and delay for affected individuals.

Matters have been further complicated by EQC's role in the rebuild process. Stretching EQC's mandate in this way has required some innovative solutions, such as the CHRP. However, it has not been without its problems, with many people facing uncertainty over the cost and quality of remediation and rebuild work on their properties. Many remain stuck in negotiations with EQC – continuing to live in inadequate, and in some cases unsafe, housing.

The Canterbury experience also suggests that a number of private insurers are unable or unwilling to fulfil their obligations in a timely fashion, in part because they await the outcomes of EQC assessments and because their profitability increases by delaying pay outs. Without their insurance pay outs many homeowners are unable to repair the damage to their homes and to move on with their lives.

The role of private insurance in the disaster insurance framework has proved to be deficient, in that policy wordings are at best loose or ambiguous and in that many of the issues that have arisen – although foreseeable – have been left for *ex post facto* resolution. Furthermore, despite a recognised duty of good faith in relation to handling of claims, private insurance companies behaviour has failed to meet this standard – with delays in payments, undervaluation of claims and a continued failure to provide information to policyholders.

States are required to ensure that private entities or individuals within their jurisdiction do not deprive individuals of economic, social or cultural rights and are liable for violations that result from the failure to exercise due diligence in controlling the behaviour of non-state actors, such as insurance companies.[89] The behaviour of insurance companies has had a significant impact on the economic and social rights of people in Canterbury and the EQC framework failed to provide the platform to ensure the continued realisation of the rights of affected people in the aftermath of a natural disaster.

There is an emerging consensus amongst the affected population in Canterbury that the first priority after a natural disaster should be the re-establishment of communities: keeping as many people in the affected area as is possible, followed quickly by a return into homes, with the provision of temporary or transitional accommodation.[90] The New Zealand insurance disaster insurance scheme, which provides a limited cash settlement for the replacement of personal possessions and a contribution to the cost of rebuilding, is unable – in its current form – to meet this objective.

In order to be able to respond to future events of the same, or bigger scale, serious consideration must be given to how to ensure the adequacy of funding from both insurers and reinsurers. Any scheme must also be flexible enough to respond to the needs of a particular event, ensuring a return to adequate housing as soon as possible. Perhaps most importantly, however, it must be premised on a principle of good faith, be designed to ensure the protection of human rights – prioritising those who find themselves the most vulnerable – and subject to accessible and efficient complaints and dispute resolution systems.

Notes

1 www.acc.co.nz/index.htm.
2 The Government made some amendments to the standard welfare system, including, for example, by providing specific welfare programmes such as Temporary Accommodation Allowances.
3 See Chapter 14.
4 This was largely because the majority of residents were in bed, the location of the sparsely populated epicentre and – to a lesser degree – the quality of New Zealand's comparatively stringent building code.
5 GeoNet is a project to build and operate a modern geological hazard monitoring system in New Zealand. http://info.geonet.org.nz/display/geonet/About+GeoNet.
6 The majority of these deaths occurred in the collapse of two multi-storey, central city office buildings, the Canterbury Television and Pyne Gould Corporation buildings where, respectively, 115 and 18 people lost their lives.

7 But the aftershocks should become undetectable over time.
8 A first loss scheme is a scheme where cover is limited to an agreed amount – smaller than the full value.
9 War insurance, by contrast, was compulsory.
10 The Murchison earthquake of 1929, the Hawke's Bay earthquakes of 1931, the Pahiatua earthquakes in 1934 and two earthquakes in Wairarapa in 1942. Today GeoNet records more than 15,000 earthquakes per year in New Zealand.
11 In 1945, the Earthquake and War Commission was set up under the Earthquake and War Damage Act 1944.
12 GST is New Zealand's Goods and Services Tax. GST is currently set at 15 per cent.
13 Earthquake Commission Act 1993, s18.
14 Earthquake Commission Regulations 1993 (as amended), regulation 4.
15 Supra note 13, s19.
16 [2008] NZHC 1721.
17 Supra note 13, s20.
18 Supra note 13, s21
19 *AMP Fire and General Insurance Company (NZ) Ltd v Earthquake and War Damage Commission* (1983) 2 ANZ Ins Cas 78,016; *Earthquake and War Damage Commission v Waitaki International Ltd* [1992] 1 NZLR 513; *Earthquake Commission v Disputes Tribunal* [1997] NZAR 115; *Coughlan v Earthquake Commission* [2007] NHC 178.
20 www.iombudsman.org.nz/.
21 Concluding observations from the Committee on Economic, Social and Cultural Rights in response to New Zealand's third period report considering New Zealand's obligations under ICESCR, E/C.12/NZL/CO/3, 18 May 2012 at [21].
22 New Zealand's Universal Periodic Report, *National Report Submitted in Accordance with Paragraph 5 of the Annex to the Human Rights Council Resolution 16/21, New Zealand* A/HRC/WG.6/18/NZL/1, 8 November 2013 at [4].
23 United Nations Human Rights Council, *Report of the Working Group on the Universal Periodic Review* A/HRC/26/3, 7 April 2014 at page 18, recommendation 53; Government's response at page 7 at www.justice.govt.nz/policy/constitutional-law-and-human-rights/human-rights/international-human-rights-instruments/universal-periodic-review/upr-documents-relating-to-new-zealand-1/second-report-2014/new-zealand-government-response-to-2014-upr-recommendations.
24 UN General Assembly, *Universal Declaration of Human Rights*, 10 December 1948, 217 A (III).
25 International Covenant on Civil and Political Rights 999 UNTS 171 (adopted 16 December 1966, entered into force 23 March 1976). NZ ratified on 28 December 1978.
26 International Covenant on Economic, Social and Cultural Rights 993 UNTS 3 (signed 16 December 1966, entered into force 3 January 1976). NZ ratified on 28 December 1978.
27 Art 2 ICCPR, art 2 ICESCR.
28 Art 4 ICCPR, art 4 ICESCR. Art 27 of the Vienna Convention on the Law of Treaties (done at Vienna on 23 May 1969) also confirms that "a party may not invoke the provisions of its internal law as justification for its failure to perform a treaty". New Zealand has not lodged any relevant reservations to the ICCPR or ICESCR in terms of Article 21 of the Vienna Convention.
29 Inter-Agency Standing Committee, *Human Rights and Natural Disasters. Operational Guidelines and Field Manual on Human Rights Protection in Situations of Natural Disaster*, January 2011. The Inter-Agency Standing Committee was established in June 1992 in response to the UN General Assembly Resolution 46/182 on the strengthening of humanitarian assistance, and is an interagency forum for coordination, policy development and decision-making involving the key UN and non UN humanitarian partners. The Office of the High Commissioner for Human Rights is a standing invitee to the

Committee. The first guidelines were published in 2006. The guidelines are primarily aimed to help international and NGO humanitarian organisations (see page 7), but they also provide a useful guidance for government actors on the implementation of a rights-based response to natural disasters, and record that they may also inform national policies and laws (page 8), recognising that (at page 13 [II.2]): "States have the primary duty and responsibility to provide assistance and protection to persons affected by natural disasters. In doing so, they are obliged to respect the human rights of affected persons…" The guidelines are based on the relevant human rights instruments (see fn 8 on page 9) but are not of course in themselves binding on any group or government.

30 Inter-Agency Standing Committee, *Human Rights and Natural Disasters. Operational Guidelines and Field Manual on Human Rights Protection in Situations of Natural Disaster*, January 2011 at page 2.

31 Ibid. at pages 10–11.

32 United Nations Committee on Economic, Social and Cultural Rights (1991), General Comment No. 4. *The Right to Adequate Housing: Article 11(1) CESCR* at [1] and [9].

33 *Connors v United Kingdom*, (2004) 16 BHRC 639 at [52].

34 *Gilllow v United Kingdom*, (1989) 11 EHRR 335 at [55].

35 *Connors v United Kingdom*, (2004) 16 BHRC 639 at [83]. See also *Chapman v United Kingdom* (2001) 33 EHRR 399 at [92], and by way of example *R v North & East Devon District Health Authority ex p Coughlan* [2001] QB 213, [2000] 3 All ER 850 at [90]–[93].

36 United Nations Human Rights Committee (1988), General Comment No. 16: *The Right to Respect of Privacy, Family, Home and Correspondence, and Protection of Honour and Reputation (Art. 17)* at [5].

37 See, for example, *Mohammed Sahid v. New Zealand*, CCPR/C/77/D/893/1999 (11 April 2003) at [4.13], and *Toonen v Australia* No. 488/92, U.N. Doc CCPR/C/50/D/488/1992 (1994) at [8.3].

38 The approach to s 5 was recently discussed in *CPAG v AG* [2013] NZCA 402, see in particular [79]–[103].

39 Annotations on the text of the draft International Covenants on Human Rights, 1/7/95 UN Doc. A/2929 at [197], [202] and [206].

40 Its previous biggest claim event was the Inangahua earthquake in 1968, which generated 10,500 claims.

41 Behind the Japanese tsunami for which public and private insurance losses were estimated at over $30 billion.

42 Human Rights Commission, *Monitoring Human Rights in the Canterbury Earthquake Recovery*, December 2013 (Wellington), www.hrc.co.nz/files/2114/2427/8929/HRC-Earthquake-Report-2013-final-for-web.pdf.

43 www.stuff.co.nz/the-press/opinion/editorials/6553936/EQC-admits-some-of-its-errors-but-does-not-say-how-it-will-correct-them.

44 Sarah Miles, *The Christchurch Fiasco; The Insurance Aftershock and its implications for New Zealand and Beyond*, dunMore Publishing (2012).

45 Canterbury Communities' Earthquake Recovery Network is a network of Residents Association and Community Group representatives from the earthquake-affected neighbourhoods of Canterbury.

46 CanCERN media Release, 27 March 2012. See www.mpcc.org.nz/wp-content/uploads/earthquake-info/CanCERN-Media-Release.pdf.

47 www.stuff.co.nz/the-press/news/christchurch-earthquake-2011/6648753/Confusion-over-fixing-homes.

48 Supra note 42.

49 *Kusel v Atkin, The Catariba* [1997] 2 Lloyd's Rep 749.

50 [2012] NZHC 2954.

51 Rob Merkin, *The Christchurch Earthquakes Insurance and Reinsurance Issues*, Canterbury Law Review [Vol. 18, 2012].

52 Ibid. at 130.
53 Ibid.
54 Supra note 50.
55 [2013] 3 NZLR 618.
56 [2014] NZSC 129.
57 *Re Earthquake Commission* [2011] 3NZLR 695 (HC).
58 Ibid.
59 Plus $20,000 for loss or damage to contents.
60 See section 4.3.
61 Supra note 75.
62 EQC has recently reported improvements in the process with reimbursements being paid, in the most part, on the 20th of the following month.
63 Jha, Abhas K, Barenstein, J.D., Phelps, P.M., Pittet, D., Sena, S. *Safer Homes, Stronger Communities; A Handbook for Reconstructing after Natural Disasters* (2010) Washington DC.
64 Supra note 46.
65 Ibid.
66 Ibid.
67 See Chapter 14.
68 *Hampson & Others Syndicate 1204 v Mining Technologies Australia Pty Ltd* (1998) 10 ANZ Insurance Cases 61–389; *Holmes v Payne* [1930] 2 KB 301, 310; *Webster v General Accident* [1953] 1 QB 520, 532; *Kuwait Airways Corp SAK v Kuwait Insurance Co* [1996] 1 Lloyd's Rep 664, 686.
69 (1983) 2 ANZ Insurance Cases 60–525.
70 See discussion below on the effect of the zoning decisions.
71 Ibid.
72 *Quake Outcasts v The Minister for Canterbury Earthquake Recovery* [2015] NZSC27.
73 Ibid. at 108.
74 The Rating Valuations Act 1998 (RVA), administered by LINZ, requires that rating valuations be reviewed at least every three years through a general revaluation. A general revaluation aims to provide territorial authorities with an accurate and equitable rating valuation for revising rates and rating policy, in accordance with the Local Government (Rating) Act 2002.
75 http://qvgroup-assets.s3.amazonaws.com/CCC%20Revaluation%20FAQs%20May-63b9a07edc7c5a5713018e988a83e33df537b1af.pdf.
76 Ibid.
77 www.ccc.govt.nz/CCC.Web.RatesInfo/homeliving/ratesvaluations/ratesinfo/index.aspx.
78 *Technology Holdings Ltd v IAG NZ ltd (2009)* 15 ANZ Insurance Cases 61–786.
79 Canterbury Earthquake (Building Act) Order 2011, cl 7.
80 Civil Defence Emergency Management Act 2002, Part 5.
81 Supra note 42.
82 [2014] NZHC 919 at [21].
83 Because of the wording of the insurance policy it was accepted by Kraal that if there was no EQC cover then there was no insurance cover.
84 Supra note 13, s2.
85 Ibid.
86 Ibid, s29, sch 3, cl 9.
87 Asian Development Bank, *Earthquake Insurance: Lessons from International Experience and Key Issues for Developing Earthquake Insurance in the PRC*, 2008.
88 Bruce Emerson at www.eqc.govt.nz/news/assessment-phase-complete.
89 Maastrict Guidelines, 16 & 18.
90 Supra note 44, at 96.

10 Divided fates of victims after the Fukushima nuclear power plant accident

Wakana Takahashi

1 Introduction

A phenomenon that was a combination of a great earthquake and a large tsunami, the Fukushima nuclear power plant accident triggered by the Great East Japan Earthquake became an "enormous" disaster of "historical proportion" (Imai, 2014). According to the Reconstruction Agency, as of 2015, four years after the accident, over 110,000 Fukushima residents remained displaced from their homes. Even to this day, the nuclear disaster greatly affects Fukushima and its surrounding areas and forces its residents to make sacrifices.

How has the Fukushima nuclear power plant accident affected its victims? What kind of legal measures have been taken to relieve them? Have such legal measures been sufficient and comprehensive enough to relieve all of the victims? In summation, the nuclear disaster victims are truly diverse, and this diversity has caused friction among the victims as well as a lack of understanding among the people (Yamashita *et al.*, 2013), amplifying the social damage as a whole. Nuclear compensation and support for the victims remains rigidly one-sided. Compensation and support have been applied to a limited number of victims. The victims' intentions have not been sufficiently considered. On the other hand, disaster victims outside the evacuating zones who do not qualify for nuclear compensation and support have been partially aided by ordinal disaster relief, but this relief has been far from complete.

The next section will summarize the current status of victims by reviewing existing studies and media reports. The third section will discuss how victims are recompensed in the context of nuclear disaster compensation. The fourth section will discuss how nuclear disaster victims who do not qualify for nuclear compensation and support are aided in the context of ordinal disaster relief.

2 Diverse victims

In the last four years, quite a few studies on nuclear disaster victims and their compensation and aid have been published in Japanese. While they are all called "victims," their situations vary greatly depending on their place of residence, belongings, gender, and generation, among others.

Residents who lived in the government-designated evacuation zones were forced to leave their houses, and many of them remain displaced in temporary housing. In addition to the houses, many of them have faced loss of employment and/or significant decrease of income. More than 50 percent of residents have been forced to live apart from their families because of the fathers' job location, the relocation of their children to different schools for safety reasons, and other reasons. As refuge life is prolonged, elderly residents decline significantly both physically and mentally, and while more of them need assistance, they lack access to medical services. Coming from an agricultural area, many residents have lost opportunities to cultivate plants and flowers, chat with their neighbors, and visit their ancestors' graves, losing their connection with the local community. Some of them blame themselves for exposing their children and grandchildren to radioactive substances. Having lost their happiness, some of them have committed suicide. Others feel sad about the jealousy over receiving compensation. Many victims' notes describe a financially immeasurable amount of suffering (Yamashita *et al.*, 2013; Hasegawa, 2012).

On the other hand, residents outside the evacuation zones have faced various suffering in another context. Agriculture and fishery workers have suffered financially as consumers stopped buying products from Fukushima and its surrounding prefectures. This kind of damage is called "damage caused by harmful rumor (*fuhyo higai*)." However, it is not accurate to describe the damage as being the result of harmful rumors alone. Areas that are radioactively contaminated as much as the evacuation zones are scattered inside and outside the Fukushima Prefecture. According to the International Commission on Radiological Protection (ICRP), the annual radiation exposure dose limit for the public in normal time should be 1 mSv, but the Japanese government raised it to 20 mSv after the Fukushima nuclear power plant accident, which remains the same even to this day, four years after the accident.[1] This eased limit has caused anxiety among residents in the radioactive contaminated areas both inside and outside the Fukushima Prefecture, especially families with children and pregnant women, who are said to be highly vulnerable to radioactive exposure.

There exists scientific uncertainty regarding radiation exposure risk, and, thus, there are certain gaps among people over the radiation threat and the countermeasures depending on generation, gender, personal disposition, and personal experience, among others. It has been pointed out that most Fukushima residents feel tired of the media focusing too much on radiation as well as the stereotypical image of "poor Fukushima" (Kainuma, 2015). On the other hand, a survey shows that a high percentage of mothers with infants living in Fukushima have feelings of anxiety about the health effects on their children, and there is widespread distrust of the government and local medical authorities (Sung *et al.*, 2015).[2] Many mothers try to decrease internal and external radioactive exposure, for example, by avoiding their children touching the outside air and natural environment, which causes some adverse effects, such as infant obesity.

Some residents in such contaminated areas have decided to evacuate. Evacuees from outside the designated evacuation areas are called "*jishu hinan sha* (voluntary evacuees)," who are scattered throughout Japan. More than 40,000 persons from outside the government-designated evacuation zones in the Fukushima Prefecture have registered as evacuees, but it is believed that more people have been away from their homes.[3] Many such evacuee families have lived apart after the disaster; typically, mothers evacuate with their children while fathers remain in Fukushima for work and travel to their families on the weekends. Surveys conducted by local governments and/or research institutions have revealed that many "voluntary evacuees" lose their peace of mind, face financial hardship, and suffer mental and physical disorders (Takahashi *et al.*, 2014).

Regardless of such hardship, both those who keep living in radioactive contaminated areas outside the evacuation zones and "voluntary evacuees" have a tendency not to speak out about their situation, keeping silent. That is partially because they are afraid of "discrimination" and partially because they know they will be accused of generating harmful rumors and preventing reconstruction efforts.[4]

In summary, there are various nuclear disaster victims who have lost their previously happy, peaceful lives, and their suffering continues. Many evacuees lead unstable existences having been unable to reconstruct their lives. Furthermore, the social damage has been amplified because there is discord and friction among the various victims and a lack of understanding from people regarding evacuation orders, compensation, and compensation level.

3 Victim relief in the context of nuclear damage compensation

This section investigates what kind of compensation and aid has been given to the aforementioned victims since the day of the nuclear disaster. The first subsection describes the Nuclear Damage Compensation Act as well as the Committee for Nuclear Damage Compensation. The second subsection will deal with other related legislation.

3.1 The Nuclear Damage Compensation Act and the Committee for Nuclear Damage Compensation

Nuclear damage is supposed to be primarily compensated for in accordance with the 1961 Nuclear Damage Compensation Act. According to this act, the nuclear operator (in the case of Fukushima Daiichi nuclear power plant accident, the Tokyo Electric Power Company [TEPCO]) is held liable for damage with no compensation amount limit. However, once a disaster strikes, the compensation reaches an amount that is considered too tremendous for the nuclear operator to cover entirely. Thus, the Japanese government is required to offer necessary funding (Article 16). In August 2011, the nuclear damage support mechanism was established as a system that allows the government to pay for compensation.

The compensation scope for damage is decided by the Committee for Nuclear Damage Compensation, which was set up by the Ministry of Education, Culture, and Sports (Article 18). The "intermediate guidelines" issued by the Committee in August 2011 decided that victims in evacuation zones, which total about 80,000 residents, were eligible for a relatively wide range of compensation, which includes radiation inspection costs, evacuation costs, temporary housing costs, return costs, physical damage, psychological damage, financial damage, unemployment compensation, inspection costs, and property damage/value loss, among others. On the other hand, except for damage due to the shipping limitation of agricultural and marine products and harmful rumors, it hardly mentioned compensation for residents in non-evacuation zones.

Based on the Committee's guidelines, TEPCO decided upon specific compensation criteria and became responsible for assessment of the claim contents. This mean that the offending enterprise itself sets up the compensation criteria and determines the actual amount of the compensation fee (Yokemoto, 2013). As for the actual amount, items for individual cases and lump-sum payment items both exist. For instance, it was decided that each person in evacuation areas would receive 100,000 yen monthly for psychological damage from living in temporary housing.

On the other hand, there is hardly any compensation for "voluntary evacuees" from non-evacuation zones. This fact has invited criticism by evacuees and lawyer organizations. Subsequently, in November 2011, the Committee granted 400,000 yen per child under 18 and per pregnant mother and 80,000 yen for others for the residents of 23 cities and towns around the evacuation zones. Approximately 1.5 million people were compensated. However, this decision did not consider volunteer evacuation to be "reasonable," and kept the compensation amount much lower than that for victims in evacuation zones.

Based on the above-mentioned criteria, each victim was expected to apply for the compensation fee. However, in some cases, the compensation amount decided by TEPCO tends to fall far short of the actual damage. This is particularly true with "voluntary evacuees." However, it is difficult for them to negotiate directly with TEPCO, let alone fight in court. For those victims, the Nuclear Damage Dispute Resolution Center was opened in September 2011. By May 2015, 16,237 claims had been filed, and 11,008 of them had been settled. About 1,000 cases concerned voluntary evacuation, mainly paying for psychological damage, evacuation costs, unemployment compensation, etc. However, most of the settled cases showed that victims received a much smaller amount than the one originally claimed. On the other hand, lawyer groups in evacuation places have initiated class action lawsuits on behalf of voluntary evacuees. Not only voluntary evacuees in Fukushima but also voluntary evacuees living in other parts of Japan have started to speak out. It is likely that litigation over compensation will continue in the future.

Incidentally, the evacuation zones have been rearranged and restricted several times with the initiative of the Ministry of Economy, Trade, and Industry. In May 2015, the Liberal Democratic Party (LDP) submitted a proposal to cancel the evacuation zones by accelerating further decontamination except for the "difficult-to-return zone (*kikan konnann kuiki*)" where the radiation level remains extremely high and has about 24,000 residents. The LDP and the Nuclear Damages Dispute Committee have been discussing plans to discontinue compensation for psychological damage after one year in the previous evacuation area. However, many evacuees in such areas, especially young ones, do not wish to return for the sake of their children, and this group has increased over the passage of time, as resident surveys have revealed.[5] Some critics have questioned the effectiveness of decontamination and the validity of discontinuation of compensation. Many residents prefer to prolong evacuation life, and the governmental proposal seems to be against the intentions of the evacuees.

3.2 Other compensation and relief methods

As aforementioned, the Nuclear Damage Compensation Act was mainly applied to a limited geographic area, mostly the government-designated evacuation area. The victims outside evacuation areas remained unqualified for nuclear disaster compensation regardless of their actual damage. Many victims and their supporting lawyer groups as well as NGOs have spoken out against this and insisted on establishing "evacuation rights," in particular for children and pregnant women, who are said to be vulnerable to radiation exposure (Kawasaki *et al.*, 2012). In response to such criticism, the Nuclear Accident Child Victims' Support Law was enacted as a House member-initiated legislation in June 2012. This law establishes the principle that victims are supposed to choose freely options such as "move to a refuge place," "return from a refuge place," and "continue living in Fukushima," and requires the government to make policies and take measures to support victims regardless of their choices (E Shift, 2014). The law, however, did not materialize for about a year, which invited criticisms from victims and supporters. Meanwhile, the regime change from the Democratic Party to the LDP took place in December 2012. In August 2013, the Reconstruction Agency made public basic policies regarding the promotion of the disaster victims' life assistance. The policies limited the relief area to the zones with a relatively high level of radiation (the areas are called Nakadori [middle area] and Hamadori [coastal area]) in Fukushima Prefecture only, which discouraged victims in high-radiation areas outside the Fukushima Prefecture. Also, the law gives jurisdiction to the Reconstruction Agency, but different governmental agencies are in charge of various areas: the Ministry of Education, Culture, and Sports for radiation investigation; the Ministry of the Environment for decontamination and heath management; and the Ministry of Land, Infrastructure, Transport, and Tourism for housing. Given the compartmentalized government structure and the lack of the LDP administration's leadership, it is doubtful whether measures to relieve children and their families in accordance with the principle to respect personal choices will be sufficiently implemented (Hino, 2014).

On the other hand, the LDP administration shows strong leadership in implementing the Act on Special Measures for Fukushima Reconstruction and Revitalization enacted in 2012. The specific plans were immediately developed in accordance with the law, and budgeting has steadily progressed. However, the principal axis of the law is the reconstruction of Fukushima, including the development of regional infrastructure, decontamination,[6] and the revitalization of industry. As for improvement of the living environment, health management investigations have been focused upon, such as estimates of the radiation dose and testing for thyroid cancer among children; measuring radiation in agriculture, forestry, and fishery products; decontamination; and large indoor facilities where children can play without worrying about being exposed to radiation. It also focuses on improvement of the living environment for those who return to the previous evacuation and decontaminated zones. In other words, while the policy encourages residents to continue living and returning to the previous evacuation zones, it lacks any policy to attend to those who want to prolong their evacuation.

In addition to these two laws, it is worth mentioning the Special Law on Administrative Procedure for the Nuclear Disaster, which is supposed to support nuclear disaster evacuees. As stated above, reportedly 110,000 Fukushima residents inside and outside the evacuation zones have been displaced from their homes. Many of them decided not to transfer their resident cards[7] because they wanted to maintain their connections with Fukushima Prefecture both practically and mentally. However, without their resident cards, they will face difficulties in the refuge place, as they may not be able to receive administrative services such as infant immunizations and health checks or send their children to daycare facilities. Thus, this law allows them to receive administrative services regarding education and welfare, as the government bears the cost of such services. However, this law only applies to very limited municipalities. For instance, voluntary evacuees from Fukushima's two biggest cities, Koriyama City and Fukushima City (with a population of about 300,000), both of which are located outside evacuation zones but have scattered areas with high radiation contamination and thus many residents who opt to voluntarily evacuate, are not eligible. This case is only one instance among many wherein voluntary evacuees are unqualified to receive aid regardless of their damages and needs.

4 Victim relief in the context of disaster reconstruction assistance

As seen above, nuclear disaster compensation has provided "poor victims" who were forced to leave their home in the evacuation zones with generous compensation and assistance (Yamashita and Kainuma, 2012). On the other hand, those from outside the evacuation zones hardly received any compensation. It has been ordinal disaster reconstruction assistance that relieved those who were not included under the umbrella of nuclear disaster compensation.

As mentioned in the introduction, the Great East Japan Earthquake was a complex disaster involving an earthquake, tsunami, and nuclear disaster, and it is characteristically difficult to categorize damages and victims. Right after the disaster, emergency response was carried out without distinguishing natural disaster from nuclear disaster or evacuation zones from non-evacuation zones. For instance, after the Great East Japan Earthquake, temporary shelters around the country were open to all kinds of evacuees. Three days after the earthquake, the Ministry of Education, Culture, and Sports issued a notice to all education boards in Japan. This notice asked them to provide the costs of school materials and lunches to school-aged children who needed assistance as soon as possible and in the most flexible way possible.

This flexible response, which does not distinguish victims, partially continued in the early stages of reconstruction. Several months after the disaster, one temporary shelter after another was closed. Instead, evacuees were given public housing and privately leased temporary housing. The privately leased temporary housing system is a policy based on the Disaster Relief Act. The system allows each prefecture to make available private housing for evacuees with expenses covered by both the national government as well as the evacuees' home prefectures. Those eligible for housing assistance are defined as "disaster victims currently in need of relief."[8] Usually, only those who have a government-issued Afflicted Certification are eligible to receive housing assistance.[9] However in the case of Fukushima, evacuees who do not hold Afflicted Certification were considered qualified for housing.

5 Conclusion

This chapter examined whether diverse victims of the nuclear plant disaster have been sufficiently compensated and assisted. Section 3 analyzed how compensation and support measures that were specifically intended for nuclear accident victims remain rigidly one-sided and in many cases do not meet the victims' requirements. Many victims outside the evacuation zones have been excluded regardless of their actual damages and needs. Alternatively, the initial emergency response and early reconstruction assistance in the context of ordinal disaster reconstruction assistance were implemented in a flexible manner and relieved the voluntary evacuees. In addition, local governments and civil societies that received evacuees from Fukushima have extended various assistance, which often meets the evacuees' needs and thus contributes to their partial relief.[10] Still, it should be noted that this assistance are far from being complete relief.

However, as time goes on, the government's ordinal disaster relief is tending to separate natural disaster and nuclear disaster and move toward not supporting nuclear disaster victims. For instance, Japan has the Law on Support for Reconstruction of Living of Natural Disaster Victims that is designed to assist natural disaster victims. The law was enacted in 1998, three years after the Kobe earthquake in 1995. It financially supports long-term evacuee families. At first, Fukushima Prefecture requested that this law apply to nuclear disaster evacuees. However, eventually, it was not applied to long-term evacuees from the Fukushima Daiichi nuclear power accident because it is not a natural disaster, and its victims should be compensated by TEPCO.

Furthermore, four years after the disaster, the disaster management cycle has passed the emergency response/early reconstruction stage and is moving toward the next stage, the mid-to-long term reconstruction stage. In the midst of this, nuclear disaster victims who face an uncertain future are left alone without compensation and assistance. For instance, the privately leased temporary housing system that became a lifeline for voluntary evacuees has been repeatedly a discussion topic regarding its renewal each year. As of May 2015, at the time of writing this chapter, it has not been publicly announced whether or not the system will be renewed after March 2016. If the system is discontinued, voluntary evacuees who desire long-term evacuation but lack financial means will be forced to return to their homes, which are radioactively contaminated, or left on the streets. The same thing applies to residents of the decontaminated former evacuation zones. It is said that many worry about the health impact of radiation. If they return to their original addresses, they have no choice but to live with this anxiety. If they do not return, they will suffer the same hardship as voluntary evacuees. As reconstruction is made a priority, the victims' desires and ways to reconstruct their lives are gradually being disregarded.

As Kaneko (2014) points out, Japan is currently facing a situation in which "disaster reconstruction imposed by the public authority" is inappropriate and in fact discourages the "victims' life reconstruction," but it is "inclined to the neoliberalism that favors the business community." We are urgently required to determine how to implement human-oriented reconstruction efforts.

Notes

1 Caldicott (2014) estimates that if the conventional 1 mSv criteria is strictly applied, a few million residents will be affected as they live in a broad part of the Tohoku and Kanto areas that will be evacuation zones.

2 According to the survey conducted by Sung *et al.* (2015), more than half of the mothers continue to have concerns about the health effects on children. In addition, 30 percent of mothers suffer a serious recognition gap regarding the health risks of radiation exposure with their spouses and parents. More than 70 percent of the mothers regard it as unfair that the government offers cordial compensation to evacuees from the government-designated evacuation zones.

3 The evacuee registration system is run not on a mandatory but on an ad hoc basis, and it does not distinguish between the refugees from the earthquake, tsunami, or nuclear accident. It is said that many have been displaced from their homes without the registry. There have been no official statistics that indicate a number of "*genpatsu hinansha* (nuclear power plant disaster evacuees)" nor a number of "*jishu hinan sha*."

4 Many evacuees think that they must not speak out about contamination and evacuation, as it could be offensive to those who still live in the area (Kawasaki *et al.*, 2012, 30–31; Takahashi, 2014).

5 A survey of residents from a certain evacuation zone revealed that the factor that keeps residents, especially young ones, from returning is worry over their children's health and futures (Oura, 2014).

6 Decontamination means reducing the radiation level in a living environment by removing radioactive materials and covering them with dirt.

7 The resident card is a record made by a local government regarding a resident's name and address.

8 See the Notice issued by the Director on Assistance, Ministry of Health, Labor, and Welfare to the Governor of the Fukushima Prefecture, No 0430–01 on April 30, 2011,

titled *Higashi Nihon Daishinsai ni Kakaru Okyuu Kasetsu Juutaku toshiteno Minkan Chintai Juutaku no Kariage no Toriatsukai ni Tsuite* (*Regarding Private Rental Housing as Emergency Temporary Housing Related to the Great East Japan Earthquake*).

9 An Afflicted Certificate is a certificate indicating that the holder's home was damaged by a natural disaster, such as a tsunami or earthquake. First, citizens apply for the certificate through the local government, then city officials check the damage situation and issue the certificate. With the certificate, citizens will be qualified to receive a variety of support measures.

10 For example, Niigata Prefecture, one of the top three local governments that received many evacuees, has repeatedly conducted evacuee surveys, has grasped their needs, and has taken some original and creative assistance measures. One instance is to offer to cover the travel costs for evacuee families who lived apart for the sake of their children (Takahashi and Taguchi, 2014). Civil societies in Niigata Prefecture have played a significant role in relieving individual refugees (Takahashi, 2012). Nishikido and Harada (2013) also discuss how local governments in collaboration with civil societies in Saitama Prefecture have contributed to relieving the nuclear disaster victim in a creative manner.

References

Caldicott, Helen ed. (2014) *Crisis Without End: The Medical and Ecological Consequences of the Fukushima Nuclear Catastrophe*, New York: The New Press.

E Shift (2014) *Genpatsu Jiko Kodomo Hisaisha Sienho to Hinan no Kenri (Nuclear Accident and Nuclear Accident Child Victims' Support Law-Evacuation Rights)*, Tokyo: Godo Shuppan.

Hasegawa, Shinichi (2012) *Genpatsu ni Furusato wo Ubawarete – Fukushima Ken Iitate Mura Rakunoka no Sakebi (Being Deprived of "Hometown" by Nuclear Power – Cry Farmers in Iitate Village, Fukushima Prefecture)*, Tokyo: Takarajima sha.

Hino, Kosuke (2014) *Fukushima Genpatsu Jiko Hisaisya Sien Seisaku no Giman (Deception of Fukushima Nuclear Accident Victim Assistance Policies)*, Tokyo: Iwanami Shoten.

Imai, Akira (2014) *Jichitai Saiken: Genpatsu Hinan to Ido suru Mura (Reconstruction of Local Government: Nuclear Disaster Evacuation and Migrating Village)*, Tokyo: Chikuma Shobo.

Kainuma, Hiroshi (2015) *Hajimete no Fukushima Gaku* (*The Initial Fuskuhima Study*), Tokyo: East Press.

Kaneko, Yuka (2014) "Saigai Fukko niokeru Sanka no Tetsuduki Hosho – nihon, Thai Indonesia no Hikakukento" ("Participatory Procedures in Post-Disaster Recovery: A Comparative Legal Approach to Japan, Thailand and Indonesia"), *Journal of International Cooperation Studies* 21(2&3), 1–40, Graduate School of International Cooperation Studies, Kobe University.

Kawasaki, Kennichiro, Suganami, Kaori, Takeda, Masahiro, and Fukuda, Kenji (2012) *Hinan Suru Kenri, Sorezore no Sentaku – Hibaku no Jidai wo Ikiru (Right to Evacuate, Each Choices – Surviving the Age of Radioactive Exposure)*, Tokyo: Iwanami Shoten.

Nishikido, Makoto and Harada, Shun (2013) "Saitama Ken niokeru Kengai Hinansha to sono Sienn no Genjo to Kadai" ("The presence of evacuees from Fukushima prefecture and its support in Saitama prefecture"), *The Hosei Journal of Humanity and Environment* 15(1), 69–103, The Faculty of Humanity and Environment, Hosei University.

Oura, Hirokuni (2014) "Text Mining niyoru Genpatsu Jiko Hinansha no Kikan Ito Yoin Bunseki" ("Text mining analysis of return intention factors of nuclear plant disaster evacuees"), *Teikyo Journal of Sociology* 27, 1–19, The Department of Sociology, Faculty of Liberal Arts, Teikyo University.

Sung, Woncheol, Ushijima, Kayo, Matsutani, Mitsuru, and Sakaguichi, Yusuke (2015) *Owaranai Hisai no Jikan- Genpatsu Jiko ga Fukushimaken Nakadori no Oyako ni Ataeru Eikyo (No Ending Time of the Disaster – Influence (Stress) on Parent and Child of Fukushima given by the Fukushima Nuclear Accident)*, Fukuoka: Sekifusha.

Takahashi, Wakana (2012) "Niigata niokeru Fukushima Nyuyo-ji Ninsan-pu kazoku to Chiiki Chakai no Juyo-Fukushima Genpatsu Jiko Go no Simin Shakai wo Kangaeru" ("Fukushima refugee mothers and infants evacuation to Niigata and the acceptance of those families by local communities in Niigata – a study of 'civil society' after the Fukushima nuclear accident"), *Asia-Africa Kenkyu (Asia Africa Studies)* 52(3), 16–47, Afro-Asian Institute of Japan.

Takahashi, Wakana (2014) "Fukushima Kengai niokeru Genpatsu Hinansha no Jitsujo to Ukeire Jichitai niyoru Shien- Niigata Ken niyoru Koiki Hinansha Ankeito wo Daizai nishite" ("Situation of the nuclear evacuees outside Fukushima Prefecture with assistance by a hosting local government – an analysis of Fukushima evacuee surveys conducted by Niigata Prefecture"), *Journal of the Faculty of International Studies, Utsunomiya University* 38, 35–51, Faculty of International Studies, Utsunomiya University.

Takahashi, Wakana and Taguchi, Takumi eds. (2014) *Okaasan wo Sasae Tsuduketai-Genpatsu Hinan to Niigata no Chiiki Shakai (The Desire to Support Mothers – Nuclear Power Plant Disaster Evacuees and Local Communities in Niigata)*, Tokyo: Honnoizumi-sha.

Yamashita, Yusuke and Kainuma, Hiroshi (2012) *Genpatsu Hinan Ron – Hinan no Jitsuzo kara Second Town, Kokyo Saisei made (Nuclear Power Plant Disaster Evacuee Study – From Actual Situation, Second Town to Home Recovery)*, Tokyo: Akashi Syoten.

Yamashita, Yusuke, Ichimura, Takashi, and Sato, Akihiko (2013) *Ningen naki Fukko Genpatsu Hinan to Kokumin no Furikai wo Megutte (Reconstruction without Human Beings – Nuclear Power Plant Disaster Evacuation and a Lack of Understanding among the People)*, Tokyo: Akashi Syoten.

Yokemoto, Masafumi (2013) *Genpatsu Baisho wo Tou- Aimaina Sekinin, Honro sareru Hinansha (Questioning Nuclear Damage Compensation – Ambiguous Responsibility, Evacuees Tossed about)*, Tokyo: Iwanami Shoten.

11 The role of legal services after the 2011 Great East Japan Earthquake and Tsunami

Takayuki Ii

1 Introduction

There are many earthquake zones around the world. Japan is frequently hit by earthquakes due to its location near the boundaries of major tectonic plates. The Great East Japan Earthquake and Tsunami (hereinafter GEJET) in 2011 brought multiple dangers that were large in scale. The earthquake was big, the tsunami which followed was relatively high and radioactive material was dispersed due to the Fukushima nuclear power plant accident (Carpenter 2012, Oshima and Yokemoto 2012).

The disaster brought by the tsunami and other factors caused great loss of life and property. Around 20,000 people were left dead or missing, and 300,000 buildings were completely or partially destroyed. The power of the tsunami was so massive that even big ships were thrown on to the land. The damage was similar to that seen in Indonesia and the Philippines following the tsunami and typhoon that affected those countries in the first decade of the twenty-first century. The recovery is obviously slow and there are many evacuees who are living outside and inside the affected areas, and some of them face the risk of radiation exposure.

It is important to note that, whilst the trigger was a natural earthquake, the damage has been escalated by human errors and social conditions. So how has the legislature, legal services and jurisprudence responded to the disaster in Japan? Many statutes addressing disaster have been newly enacted and revised; however, most of them are concerned with changes to government structures to cope with future disasters (Ii 2013b: 19–21). On the other hand, statutes that advance the recovery of the lives of those who were affected are inactive. The legal service industry is expected to play an important role after a disaster, but is in short supply in the region.

To date there have not been many judicial decisions related to the disaster. Jurisprudence on disaster in general is developing (e.g. Farber and Chen 2006, Malloy 2009) but is a late-comer (Butt *et al.* 2014: 16–17). It does not even form a chapter in the *Handbook of Disaster Research* (Rodriquez *et al.* 2007). The role of lawyers following a disaster was considered after Hurricane Katrina in 2005 (Morse 2011), but has not been extensively discussed. While the legal treatment of the GEJET is partly discussed in some English writing (Leflar *et al.* 2012, Feldman 2013), this chapter focuses on the role of legal services after the GEJET, which has rarely been touched on. In this chapter, inequality under the law after the GEJET (section 2) and the shortage of legal services (section 3) will be examined and the role of attorneys (section 4) and the courts (section 5) will be considered.

2 Inequality in legal treatment

The history of the Tohoku region in northeast Japan, where agriculture, fishing and cattle breeding have been the main industries, goes back to a time before the Christian era called the Jomon period. This area has suffered from big tsunamis in the past, including ones recorded in 869, 1896 and 1933. Three prefectures of Tohoku (Iwate, Miyagi and Fukushima) face the Pacific and were greatly damaged by the GEJET.

Sociologists point out many inequalities in Japan in relation to education, income, labor and inequality among regions (Shirahase 2014). In terms of the area, Yamashita considers that northeast Japan has been a persecuted area for a long time. It is a part of what he calls the "wide area system", in which the periphery (regions) takes risk for the benefit of the center (Tokyo) (Yamashita 2013).

Among others, Fukushima is said to be a sacrifice of the national policy of promoting nuclear power plants, whereas Okinawa, with its many US army bases, is a sacrifice of the US–Japan security treaty (Takahashi 2012). These views on northeast Japan imply an inequality towards the affected areas in the country, which has partly influenced the government's and citizens' indifference to the victims of the GEJET.

Among those affected by the disaster, complaints are often voiced that some have received considerable compensation while others have not. There are various types of compensation and condolence money which have been supplied by the central and local governments and the Tokyo Electric Power Company. The criteria for these payments make some victims feel that they are not being treated equally. This can be seen as the segmentation of victims by arbitrary criteria, which has previously been witnessed in environmental pollution cases, including Minamata (Iijima 1984: 173–204).

Incidents between evacuees and local residents have been reported in Iwate city. Iwaki is a southern coastal city in Fukushima Prefecture that many displaced people have migrated to from other areas because it is relatively uncontaminated by radioactive material. Both evacuees and the local residents of Iwaki have been affected by the nuclear plant accident, but the former have tended to receive larger amounts of compensation than the latter. This is a sad story partly brought about by the criteria, which are often determined by the government and prescribed in law.

From a legal perspective, constitutional rights and freedoms, including the freedom to choose and change one's residence (Article 22) and the right to maintain the minimum standards of wholesome and cultured living (Article 25), are not necessarily being guaranteed to evacuees and others who have been affected. They are facing a situation of inequality before the law, contrary to Article 14 of the Constitution.

As is widely known, the law can be a powerful tool for rulers to govern, and statutes are relatively hard to change in Japan once they are enacted. In gender studies, the law is seen to have an ambivalent character in regards to gender (Ehara 2001). Through its various functions, the law makes people aware of and reduces sexual discrimination, yet in other ways it also promotes, creates and stabilizes sexual discrimination. This ambivalent feature of the law in terms of inequality also applies to the law in response to disaster and should be kept in mind.

3 Shortage of attorneys in the affected areas

Then, let us focus on legal services and issues of access to justice. There are some traditional characteristics of Japanese attorneys and their business practices. Attorneys, as the legal profession in Japan, have a monopoly over the provision of legal services (Article 72 of the Attorney Act) but mainly deal with trials. Therefore, law firms tend to cluster around the seats of the courts (including branch offices). The fact that most courts are stationed in urban areas results in an uneven geographical distribution of law firms.

Attorneys tend not to be specialized in their practice and most of them are generalists. Attorneys often consider government agencies as adversaries in litigation and not as partners to cooperate with. They are not comfortable with being hired as staff by the government or governmental organizations. Attorneys are not entitled to practice law unless they are registered with the Japan Federation of Bar Associations (hereinafter JFBA) and the local bar association, which has jurisdiction over the law firms practicing in a given area. The local bar has a strong influence on attorney registration.

The attorney's main market is litigation. There are high entry barriers for attorneys who are not under the jurisdiction of the local bar or those involved in other law-related jobs. Legal education, which includes education, examination and training, is also designed and administered on the assumptions of traditional attorney business practices, which is centered on trial practice. The image of attorneys has evolved in big cities, but it remains virtually unchanged in regions including the areas devastated by the GEJET.

According to Yamamoto, there are four barriers which hinder citizens from access to justice – namely, distance, money, information and mentality (Yamamoto 2006). The issue of access to justice is partly related to features of Japanese attorneys. Japan has relatively few attorneys per capita[1] and, in addition, they are disproportionately located in major metropolitan cities. In particular, the areas affected by the GEJET are regions with relatively few attorneys.

Measures have been taken to address the scarcity of attorneys in regional areas (Ii 2009). The bar started to address the scarcity problem in the 1990s by making what is called the "zero-one" map, which identified district court branches with zero or only one attorney practicing in the area. In addition, it set up legal consultation centers and bar association-funded Himawari (sunflower) law firms, in which attorneys work in regions for a term of several years supported by the bar association. Around that time, the number of attorneys doubled. In the 2000s, at last, the government showed an interest in access to justice and set up the Japan Legal Support Center (JLSC).[2]

In 1993, Pacific coastal areas in the northeast, which were affected by the disaster in later years, had few attorneys. However, zero-one areas gradually decreased and have now almost disappeared. The Japanese legal aid system had also been in short supply, but has seen some improvement. The JLSC has administered the system since 2006, though the redemption system, in which users of legal aid must repay their expenses afterwards, has not changed.

At the time of the disaster, thanks to these reforms on access to justice, the affected areas in northeast Japan (excluding the large cities Sendai and Iwaki) had around thirty attorneys. Most of them had been working in the region for a period of several years to cope with the attorney scarcity problem (Ii 2013a). However, contrary to expectations, there have not been many legal consultations or litigation. The cause of the low level of legal consultations is hard to discern, but might be partly caused by residents' attitudes toward the law and legal profession.

According to a legal needs survey conducted by an attorney, Takiue, around half of the evacuees residing in temporary housing had legal problems (Ii and Takiue 2012). However, they do not necessarily consult attorneys due to concerns about attorney fees and their lack knowledge of what type of cases might be suitable for legal consultation. This survey result implies that victims are not accustomed to using lawyers due to the shortage of legal services in the region for a long period of time. Attorney Takiue, who opened his own law firm in the area, received around 500 legal consultations over two years, but had to close his firm due to there being few profitable cases.

Other surveys of victims show similar results. According to a JLSC survey in late 2012, 27 percent of victims have consulted attorneys or judicial scriveners. Reasons given for not seeking legal advice included "seeking advice is pointless" (28.1 percent), "it may take time and effort" (26.2 percent), "it may cost money" (26.2 percent), "the problem is not important enough to consult an attorney or judicial scrivener" (15.8 percent), "I do not know any attorneys or judicial scriveners" (12.3 percent) and "my problem is not within the scope of their service" (12.0 percent) (Japan Legal Support Center 2013: 33–34).

The problems victims have faced include debts, housing and accessing disaster recovery services, amongst others. Some of these problems could be relieved with legal assistance; however, they seem to hesitate to use lawyers. Legal consultation for people living in the affected areas has been free from the year 2012 under a special law on legal aid, but in view of their continuing concerns about legal costs, this information might not have completely reached the victims.

4 Legal assistance by attorneys

Backed up by the reforms to legal access, attorneys seem to have tried to support victims relatively well, including an outreach approach and campaigns for necessary legal amendments (Japan Federation of Bar Associations 2014: 32–58, Japan Federation of Judicial Scrivener Associations 2014: 129–138).

According to a comparison of the activities of attorneys following the Hanshin Awaji Earthquake of 1995 and the GEJET (Nagai 2005, 2012), their common features are basically the same; the provision of legal advice, defending victims using legal aid, making proposals for necessary legal changes and assisting community reconstruction. In addition, following the GEJET, attorneys have been seen to be performing new functions, which include supplying information to and from victims in the place of ruined local governments, providing services for the ADR, responding to the nuclear power plant accident and supporting evacuees from Fukushima.

The JLSC started a “Great East Japan Earthquake telephone counseling” service in cooperation with the JFBA and the three bar associations in Tokyo. The counseling was also conducted in cooperation with Sendai bar association, Iwate bar association, the Japan Federation of Judicial Scrivener Associations and other local judicial scrivener associations. It ended in mid-October 2011 after providing over 13,000 instances of legal advice. From November 2011, a free-dial service was set up at the Sendai call center. The JLSC also prepared a Q&A brochure addressing the disaster in November 2011, which contained 172 questions in 260 pages with 100,000 copies being printed.

Whilst the JLSC has only one local office in the affected area, in Miyako city, by the end of March 2013 it had set up seven branch offices; two each in Iwate and Fukushima and three in Miyagi Prefecture. These branch offices do not have permanent legal professionals. Instead, attorneys and other law-related professionals (judicial scriveners, tax accountants, land and house investigators, architects, administrative scriveners, public consultants on social and labor insurance, social workers) come from adjacent cities on a daily basis to give free legal advice.

In 2012 the five branch offices in operation[3] provided a total of 4,486 legal consultations and 2,235 other consultations (Japan Legal Support Center 2013: 21–27), while nationwide there were another 40,000 legal consultations related to the disaster provided free of charge in the first one and a half years following the earthquake. It seems to be largely due to grassroots advertising and the hard work of the teams of three staff employed at each JLSC branch office, most of whom are former local government employees. The staff visit local houses, mainly temporary housing, to make the branch office known to the public. They make routine contact with persons in charge of counseling in municipal and administrative agencies. The branch offices have automobiles for circuit counseling and routinely conduct counseling at temporary housing sites and other community centers.

The JLSC has also dispatched lawyers to local government offices and the Dispute Reconciliation Center for Nuclear Damage Compensation (hereinafter "the nuclear ADR") in cooperation with the Ministry of Justice and the JFBA.

Attorneys and the JFBA began conducting legal consultations immediately after the disaster. On-site consultation in the devastated areas was conducted by attorneys nationwide, who were dispatched from bar associations outside the devastated areas. Free telephone legal consultation for victims was administered by bar associations in the Tokyo area.

There was some successful lobbying activity by lawyers, which included the enactment of the Act to Support Children and Victims of the Nuclear Power Plant Accident, which was established on June 21, 2012. Although scientific research is yet to clarify the risks of long-term exposure to low doses of radiation, the legislation is intended to support each individual who was living in the affected area in their own decision whether to continue to live in an area subject to support, move to another area or return to the area they lived in before the disaster (Article 2(2)). In particular, the government is responsible for health care, with the act specifying that victims who have lived in a prescribed area while they were a child (or their mother lived there while pregnant) will be eligible for free medical checks for their entire life (Article 13 (2)). If they require medical treatment, the fee for such treatment is to be waived or reduced (Article 13 (3)).

In order to draft and pass the bill, a group of lawyers named the Save Fukushima Children Lawyers Network (SAFLAN) in particular did a lot of work. Since the risks of long-term, low-dose radiation exposure are not yet scientifically established, at first the government would not agree to the bill. SAFLAN collected data and voices from the area, researched in order to prepare an argument in support of the theoretical ground to "the right to evacuate", drafted the bill and lobbied lawmakers. As a result, the bill was passed on June 21, 2012. As the act stipulates basic ideas rather than concrete rights, it will be quite important to have groups continuing the commitment to the enrichment of rights, especially those of children and expectant mothers (Kawasaki *et al.* 2012).

Lawyer groups also advanced the enactment of the Act on Special Measures Concerning Countermeasures for Large-Scale Earthquakes. This was backed by the fact that the Comprehensive Legal Support Act, which is the legal basis of JLSC, stipulates that "citizens or foreign nationals lawfully residing in this country who are not financially capable of paying the necessary expenses incurred in the preparation and performance of the exercise of their own rights in civil judicial decision proceedings, etc." are eligible for legal aid.

However, victims in the region who have received a temporary payment such as condolence money, support money, charity or insurance may become ineligible to receive legal aid. Local governments in the affected area said that it was hard to ask victims about their financial circumstances. The JFBA collected these opinions from the area and lobbied for the enactment of special measures for the victims.

The Act on Special Measures was enacted to administer the Great East Japan Earthquake legal support project for residents in the devastated areas as of March

11, 2011. The eligibility requirements for legal aid were relaxed. Under the new system, people can use legal counseling without passing a means test. Additionally, the scope of legal aid was broadened to include ADR and administrative complaint procedures as well as civil litigation, and obligations to repay the advanced money at the end of the legal procedure have been suspended. However, even in light of the special scheme introduced after the Hanshin Awaji Earthquake, under which most victims could receive legal help virtually free of charge (Legal Aid Association Foundation Hyogo Prefecture Chapter 2003: 176), further relaxation of the rules was needed following the GEJET.

On the other hand, there have been some deficiencies in the treatment of the disaster by the legal service industry. The bar-funded Himawari law firms were expected to be set up in the affected areas, but only two eventuated. It has also been reported that some local attorneys opposed newcomers entering their area of business. Some attorneys have worked hard to deal with the disaster, but others seem to have stuck to their own interests. Attorneys, judicial scriveners and other law-related occupations as well as local governments should work together to help reconstruct the lives of victims and affected communities, which is the most important goal and should be continually kept in mind.

5 Legal treatment by the courts

The legal response to the disaster is not limited to attorneys and other law-related occupations. It is known that the courts conducted on-site mediation circuits after the Kanto Great Disaster of 1923. However, this example seems to be an exception. After the Hanshin Awaji Earthquake of 1995, the courts in the Kobe area, which were partially damaged themselves, dealt with an increase in mediation cases but did not take such outreach approaches (Kitazawa 1995). Instead, the Federation of Kinki Bar Associations set up the Afflicted City Private Settlement Services Arbitration Center (Sakamoto 1995: 192), which over a period of approximately three years accepted 385 applications that mainly concerned leasehold issues.

After the GEJET, some courthouses in northeast Japan were also partially damaged. The courthouse of Ofunato town in Iwate Prefecture was struck by the tsunami and was not operational (Ujimoto 2011: 130). Courts in the affected areas tried to supply victims with information on court procedures and to cope with disaster-related cases, such as succession cases and appointments of guardians for minors. However, the courts did not conduct the on-site mediation which was seen in 1923. The courts instead appear to be busy, with relatively few staff available to deal with a moderate caseload that did not increase after the disaster.

Traditionally there has been a shortage of legal services in Japan. As stated before, attorneys tend to cluster around big cities, but the situation is similar in respect of the courts. In northeast Japan, the number of courthouses has decreased since the 1980s. The decline was brought about by a policy of the Supreme Court that focused on efficiency, according to which courthouses and staff are clustered in big cities with larger caseloads. The policy resulted in a scarcity of courthouses in regions including areas affected by the GEJET.

There was an attempt by attorneys in Sendai city to solve disaster-related disputes after the GEJET via ADR. The resolution of disputes using ADR worked relatively well (Sendai Bar Association 2012: 64–79) and applications amounted to 509 as of the end of 2013, which exceeded the number of those accepted by the ADR system operated by the Kinki Federation of Bar Associations after the Hanshin Awaji Earthquake. The aforementioned nuclear ADR also received around 14,371 applications by the end of 2014, in which 35.0 percent were represented by attorneys (Nuclear Damages Compensation Dispute Resolution Center 2015: 4). It has virtually taken over the role of the courts in determining compensation for damage caused by the nuclear power plant accident.

If the courts had been more adequately staffed and widely distributed across the country, including the smaller cities and towns of northeast Japan, they could have performed a more active role in ADR. Therefore, in order to advance legal assistance to victims, the number of courthouses and staff levels should be further increased. Court-annexed mediation and litigation cannot increase without courts which are readily available to claimants.

6 Conclusion

The lessons for the legal service industry in Japan after the GEJET to be taken from this chapter are as follows. The first is that attention is to be paid to inequalities after a disaster as well as in daily lives. The disaster is considered to be a function of a natural hazard and social vulnerability. Socio-legal studies should note the latter element because it deals with society. The second is that the law and attorneys should take the issue of disaster seriously. There are many socio-legal topics relating to disaster response. The third is to remember the power of the law and to reconsider the law, legal practice and jurisprudence based on the actual circumstances of victims. We should defer to the words of Suehiro, a father of Japanese socio-legal studies, who said that the law must be built on the concept washed by the fact (Suehiro 1929: 5).

The last lesson is to reconsider legal services by equating ordinary clients with victims after a disaster. There have been devices to advance legal access to victims, which include circuit visits by car, an outreach program for victims and the special provision of legal aid without means testing. These devices are worth developing in respect of regular legal services.

Japanese attorneys have been a profession relatively small in number and clustered around courthouses, which are distributed in big cities. They are largely hard to find and expensive; therefore, citizens have consulted attorneys only when they need to sue or defend. The view of the court and legal profession as service providers has been improving following the judicial reform in the early twenty-first century, which proposed a gradual increase in the number of legal professionals, public participation in justice (the "saiban-in" lay judge system), advancements in legal access (the JLSC) and other initiatives (Ii 2005). The relatively devoted response of the legal service industry after the GEJET should be praised in light of their past stance of portraying an air of importance, but there seems to be further potential legal needs that are yet to be met.

Notes

1 The population per one attorney is 3,632 (Japan), 1,128 (France), 495 (Germany), 411 (England and Wales) and 266 (the United States). Within the country, the number varies from 820 (Tokyo) to 13,462 (Akita Prefecture) (Japan Federation of Bar Associations 2014: 80, 70).

2 The JLSC is a public corporation established according to the framework of an incorporated administrative agency under the Comprehensive Legal Support Act (promulgated on June 2, 2004). It provides legal information services, legal aid, court-appointed criminal defense counsel and criminal victim support, as well as support for areas with insufficient legal services.

3 The five branch offices operational in 2012 are situated in Minami Sanriku, Yamamoto, Higashi Matsushima, Nihonmatsu and Otutsi. Nihonmatsu was only operational for half of the year. Two other branches have since been opened in March 2013.

References

Butt, Simon, Hitoshi Nasu and Luke Nottage, eds. (2014), *Asia-Pacific Disaster Management: Comparative and Socio-legal Perspectives*, Berlin, Heidelberg: Springer.

Carpenter, Susan (2012), *Japan's Nuclear Crisis: The Route to Responsibility*, Basingstoke, New York: Palgrave Macmillan.

Ehara, Yumiko (2001), *Gender Chitsujyo (Order)*, Tokyo: Keiso Shobo.

Farber, Daniel A. and Jim Chen (2006), *Disasters and the Law: Katrina and Beyond*, New York: Aspen Publishers.

Feldman, Eric (2013), "Fukushima: A Catastrophe, Compensation and Justice in Japan", *Depaul Law Review*, 62, 335–355.

Ii, Takayuki (2005), "Judicial Reform in Japan: Its Outline and Characteristics", *Waseda University Faculty of Education Gakujyutsu Kenkyu (Geology, History and Social Sciences)*, 53, 13–23.

Ii, Takayuki (2009), "Young Migrants from Big Cities: Measures for Dealing with the Shortage of Legal Services in Japan", *Zeitschrift für Japanisches Recht*, 27, 59–80.

Ii, Takayuki (2013a), "Horitsu Senmonka to Hisaichi Shien (Legal Professionals and the Support of Affected Area)", *Sogo Horitsu Shien Ronso*, 2, 105–124.

Ii, Takayuki (2013b), "Saigai ni Taiou Shiuru Ho, Shiho, Hogaku no Arikata: Higashinihon Daishinsai o Tsujite (Law, Judiciary and Jurisprudence which can Respond to Disaster: Through the East Japan Great Earthquake and Tsunami)", *Ho no Kagaku*, 44, 18–28.

Ii, Takayuki and Akira Takiue (2012), "Higashinihon Daishinsai Go no Iwateken Enganbu ni okeru Bengoshi to Ho no Yakuwari (The Role of Attorney and Law after the East Japan Great Earthquake and Tsunami)", *Jimbun Shakai Ronso (Jimbun Kagaku Hen)*, 27, 11–35.

Iijima, Nobuko (1984), *Kankyo Mondai to Higaisha Undo (Environmental Problems and Victims' Movements)*, Tokyo: Gakubunsha.

Japan Federation of Bar Associations, ed. (2014), *Bengoshi Hakusho 2014 Nen Ban (Attorney White Paper of 2014)*, Tokyo: Japan Federation of Bar Associations.

Japan Federation of Judicial Scrivener Associations, ed. (2014), *Shiho Shoshi Hakusho 2014 Nen Ban (Judicial Scrivener White Paper of 2014)*, Tokyo: Japan Federation of Judicial Scrivener Associations.

Japan Legal Support Center, ed. (2013), *Hou Terasu Hakusho Heisei 24 Nendo Ban (Law Terrace White Paper of the Year 2012)*, Tokyo: Japan Legal Support Center.

Kawasaki, Kennichiro, Kaori Suganami, Masahiro Takeda and Kenji Fukuda (2012), *Hinan suru Kenri, Sorezore no Sentaku (The Right to Evacuate, Each Person's Selection)*, Tokyo: Iwanami Shoten.

Kitazawa, Akira (1995), "Hanshin Awaji Daishisai to Saibansho (Hanshin Awaji Great Earthquake and the Courts)", *Jurist*, 1070, 179–181.

Leflar, Robert B., Ayako Hirata, Masayuki Murayama and Shozo Ota (2012), "Human Flotsam, Legal Fallout: Japan's Tsunami and Nuclear Meltdown", *Journal of Environmental Law & Litigation*, 27, 107–124.

Legal Aid Association Foundation Hyogo Prefecture Chapter, ed. (2003), *Horitsu Hujo Jigyou eno Tenbou: Hanshin Awaji Daishinsai Hisaisha Horitsu Hujo Jigyo no Bunseki kara (Prospects for the Legal Aid Project: From the Analysis of the Hanshin Awaji Great Earthquake Victim Legal Help Project)*, Hyogo: Legal Aid Association Foundation.

Malloy, Robin Paul, ed. (2009), *Law and Recovery from Disaster: Hurricane Katrina*, Farnham: Ashgate.

Morse, Reilly (2011), "Come On in This House: Advancing Social Equity in Post-Katrina Mississippi", in Amy Liu, Roland Anglin, Richard Mizelle and Alisson Plyer, eds., *Resilience and Opportunity: Lessons from the U.S. Gulf Coast after Katrina and Rita*, Washington: Brookings Institute Press, 131–147.

Nagai, Kouju (2005), "Saigai Ji ni okeru Bengoshi no Yakuwari (Role of Lawyers in the Case of Disaster)", *NBL*, 820, 51–61.

Nagai, Kouju (2012), "Higashinihon Daishinsai deno Bengoshi Kai no Higaisha Shien Katsudo (Support Activities by the Bar Association in the East Japan Great Earthquake and Tsunami)", *NBL*, 974, 12–20.

Nuclear Damages Compensation Dispute Resolution Center (2015), *Genshiryoku Songai Baishou Hunsou Kaiketsu Center Katsudou Jyoukyou Houkokusho: Heisei 26 Nendo ni okeru Jyoukyou ni tsuite (Report of the Activity Condition of the Nuclear Damages Compensation Dispute Resolution Center: On the Condition of the Year 2014)*, Tokyo: Nuclear Damages Compensation Dispute Resolution Center.

Oshima, Kenichi and Masafumi Yokemoto (2012), *Genpatsu Jiko no Higai to Hosho: Fukushima to "Ningen no Hukko" (Damage and Compensation of the Nuclear Power Plant Accident: Fukushima and "Human Recovery")*, Tokyo: Otsuki Shoten.

Rodriguez, Havidan, Enrico Quarantelli and Russell Dynes, eds. (2007), *Handbook of Disaster Research*, New York: Springer.

Sakamoto, Hidehumi (1995), "Hanshin Awaji Daishinsai ni okeru Houritsu Soudan: Hisaisha Kyuen Katudou no Hitotsu to shite (Legal Counseling in the Hanshin Awaji Earthquake: As One of the Sufferers Help Activities)", *Jurist*, 1070, 182–186.

Sendai Bar Association (2012), *Sendai Bengosi Kai Kaihou Higashinihon Daishinsai Totkushugou (Sendai Bar Association Magazine Special Issue on the East Japan Great Earthquake)*, Sendai: Sendai Bar Association.

Shirahase, Sawako (2014), *Social Inequality in Japan*, London: Routledge.

Suehiro, Izutaro (1929), *Bukken Ho Jyokan (Real Rights Part I)*, Tokyo: Yuhikaku.

Takahashi, Tetsuya (2012), *Gisei no Sistem (System of Sacrifice): Fukushima and Okinawa*, Tokyo: Shueisha.

Ujimoto, Atsushi (2011), "Higashi Nihon Daishisai to Saibasho (East Japan Great Earthquake and the Courts)", *Jurist*, 1427, 130–135.

Yamamoto, Kazuhiko (2006), "Sogo Horitsu Shien no Rinen: Minji Shiho no Shiten kara (Ideal of the Comprehensive Legal Support: From the Perspective of Civil Justice)", *Jurist*, 1305, 8–15.

Yamashita, Yusuke (2013), *Tohoku Hastu no Shinsai Ron: Shuhen kara Koiki Sistemu o Kangaeru (Discussion on the Disaster from Northeast: Considering Wide Area System from Periphery)*, Tokyo: Chikuma Shobo.

Part III

Redefining the recovery

Law for human-centered recovery vs.
Build Back Better

12 Lessons learned from a comparison of the 2011 Great East Japan Earthquake and the 1995 Great Hanshin-Awaji Earthquake

Yuichi Honjo

1 Introduction

Three years after the Great East Japan Earthquake occurred on March 11, 2011, the disaster-affected areas have begun to make progress step-by-step towards recovery from the earthquake, tsunami and nuclear damage. Taking a brief look at the progress of reconstruction projects in the literature of the Reconstruction Agency "Current Status and Path Toward Reconstruction (updated on November 29, 2013)", some infrastructure and industrial facilities have recovered more than 60 percent of their original state before the earthquake. On the other hand, however, while the number of large-scale projects, such as the construction of housing and coastline, are generally increasing, most such projects are still incomplete. In addition, it has become difficult to grasp the actual condition of affected areas as they have been segmented and diversified over time. Under such circumstances, a widening disparity in terms of reconstruction has become apparent between districts and industries within the affected areas.

In order to develop prospects for reconstruction, it is important to understand the full picture from various aspects concerning earthquake reconstruction efforts in the past and the current status and challenges. As will be mentioned later, while being aware that there are fundamental differences between the Great Hanshin-Awaji Earthquake, which occurred on January 17, 1995, and the Great East Japan Earthquake, the author believes that in terms of the management of reconstruction of the affected areas, we can make use of the experience and lessens acquired during the course of recovery from the former, which recently passed the milestone of its twentieth anniversary.

The first section of this chapter outlines the damage of the Great East Japan Earthquake. The following section introduces the lessons learned during the recovery process of the Great Hanshin-Awaji Earthquake which are considered relevant, in order to study ways to efficiently achieve recovery from the Great East Japan Earthquake as soon as possible. Finally, reconstruction efforts for the Great East Japan Earthquake are explained as well as the status of the implementation of its reconstruction measures, while comparing them with those of the Great Hanshin-Awaji Earthquake.

2 Damage from the Great East Japan Earthquake

The Great East Japan Earthquake disaster in 2011 started with the earthquake off the Pacific coast of Tohoku, followed by tsunami and subsequent aftershocks. According to the Japan Meteorological Agency, the seismic center was in the vicinity of 130 kilometers east/southeast off the coast of the Oshika Peninsula of Miyagi Prefecture, at a depth of approximately 24 kilometers. Measuring 9.0 on the Richter magnitude scale (i.e. a unit of destructive force at the point of a seismic source), it was recorded as the fourth most powerful earthquake in the world since 1900. The hypocentral region spread extensively approximately 500 kilometers from north to south and 200 kilometers from east to west, from the coast of Iwate Prefecture to Ibaraki Prefecture. The released energy was approximately 1,000 times more than that of the Great Hanshin-Awaji Earthquake. It created giant tsunami waves with a height of more than 10 meters and a maximum runup height of 40.5 meters in some places. Furthermore, the Tokyo Electric Power Company's Fukushima No. 1 nuclear power plant lost control of several nuclear reactors due to the loss of its entire power source, which caused a meltdown of reactor cores, resulting in a serious nuclear reactor accident, releasing a vast amount of radioactive material.

The damage caused by the Great East Japan Earthquake was the worst since the end of World War II and far exceeded that of the Great Hanshin-Awaji Earthquake, while the affected areas spread throughout a wide area centered on the Tohoku region. According to the damage count as of February 10, 2015 by the National Police Agency, the death toll reached 15,890 (6,434 in the case of the Great Hanshin-Awaji Earthquake), those missing 2,590 (3 in the Great Hanshin-Awaji Earthquake) and fully- and half-destroyed buildings combined approximately 400,000 housing units (250,000 buildings in the Great Hanshin-Awaji Earthquake).

With respect to the amount of direct financial damage suffered from the Great East Japan Earthquake concerning stock such as buildings, real estate and social infrastructure, the Japanese Cabinet Office (Economic Research) announced on March 23, 2011 that, based on certain assumptions, it was estimated to be approximately 16 to 25 trillion yen. According to another estimation announced by the Cabinet Office (Disaster Management) on June 24 the same year, the damage directly resulting from damaged social capital, housing and private company facilities was approximately 17 trillion yen. This is about 1.7 times greater than that of the Great Hanshin-Awaji Earthquake, which is estimated at approximately 10 trillion yen (Table 12.1).

A breakdown of the economic damage of the Great East Japan Earthquake shows that damage to buildings is the largest, accounting for 61.5 percent of the total, followed by social infrastructure facilities at 13 percent and agriculture/forestry/fisheries facilities at 11.2 percent. When compared with the Great Hanshin-Awaji Earthquake, the ratio is higher in terms of agriculture/forestry/fisheries facilities and lower in social infrastructure facilities. This is probably because the Great Hanshin-Awaji Earthquake was an urban disaster while the

Table 12.1 Comparison of estimated financial damage

	Great East Japan Earthquake: Japanese Cabinet Office (Disaster Management)	*Great East Japan Earthquake: Japanese Cabinet Office (Economic Research)*		*Great Hanshin-Awaji Earthquake (National Land Agency)*
		Case 1	*Case 2*	
Buildings (housing, shops, offices, factories, machinery, etc.)	Approx. 10.4 trillion yen [61.5%]	Approx. 11 trillion yen	Approx. 20 trillion yen	Approx. 63 trillion yen [65.6%]
Lifeline utilities (water services, gas, electricity, communications and broadcasting facilities)	Approx. 1.3 trillion yen [7.7%]	Approx. 1 trillion yen	Approx. 1 trillion yen	Approx. 600 billion yen [6.3%]
Social infrastructure (rivers, roads, ports/ harbors, drainage, and airports, etc.)	Approx. 22 trillion yen [13.0%]	Approx. 2 trillion yen	Approx. 2 trillion yen	Approx. 2.2 trillion yen [22.9%]
Agriculture, forestry and fisheries	Approx. 1.9 trillion yen [11.2%]	Approx. 2 trillion yen	Approx. 2 trillion yen	Approx. 500 billion yen [5.2%]
Others	Approx. 1.1 trillion yen [6.5%]			
Gross total	Approx. 16.9 trillion yen [100%]	Approx. 16 trillion yen	Approx. 25 trillion yen	Approx. 9.6 trillion yen [100%]

Source: estimated financial damage of the Great Japan Earthquake by the Cabinet Office (Disaster Management).

Note
Divisions of the stocks are based on those used for estimation by the Cabinet Office (Disaster Management).

Great East Japan Earthquake involved much more in terms of devastated and flooded farmland and fishery bases by tsunami.

As the above damage from the Great East Japan Earthquake excludes damage resulting from the Fukushima nuclear disaster, the direct total damage is anticipated to be greater.

3 Lessons from the Great Hanshin-Awaji Earthquake

This section introduces helpful lessons from the Great Hanshin-Awaji Earthquake learned during the process of its reconstruction, in order to study how fast and effectively reconstruction from the Great East Japan Earthquake can be achieved.

3.1 Thematic outlines

In order to swiftly formulate measures towards recovery in Kobe, on January 26, 1995, just nine days after the earthquake, the mayor announced his basic vision for recovery. The basic principle as indicated in "The New Kobe City Basis Concept" was that Kobe "shall build a disaster-safe model city where citizens can live and work in a safe and secure manner through the swift recovery of the urban infrastructure, civic life and urban development" and that Kobe "shall create a new Kobe that will become a civic-minded creative city interacting with the world." Based on this basic principle, the Kobe City Recovery Plan, which covered a ten-year period, was formulated in June 1995.

The recovery plan consists of approximately 1,000 recovery projects. These projects can be roughly grouped into six categories, as seen in Figure 12.1:

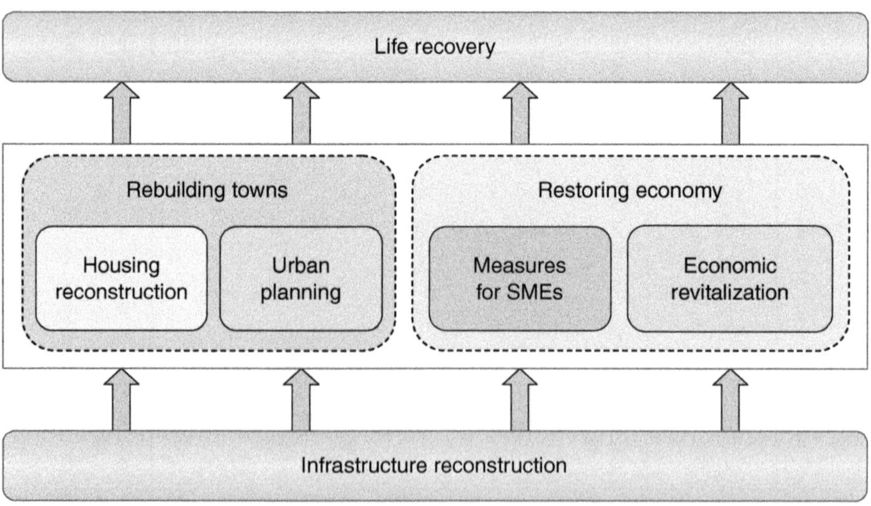

Figure 12.1 Basic structure of the Kobe City Recovery Plan (source: "Earthquake Prevention Methodology for Protecting Lives" by Haruo Hayashi).

(1) infrastructure reconstruction, (2) housing reconstruction, (3) urban planning, (4) economic revitalization, (5) measures for SMEs, and (6) life recovery.

The formulated plan will be meaningful only when the visions described in the plan are actualized. Therefore, to proceed steadily with recovery in the affected areas, it is important to continually evaluate the progress of recovery and to review and revise the measures in order to make the plan more feasible. Based on this management concept, Kobe assessed the progress of recovery and reviewed and then revised the plan based on the results.

This chapter describes the lessons learned through the author's experiences as a city official promoting the Kobe City Recovery Plan. Specifically, the author wishes to use the results of the Comprehensive Recovery Assessments conducted in 1999, before the fifth anniversary of the earthquake, and 2003, before the tenth anniversary, to suggest strategies for promoting a recovery plan, and to convey the importance of adopting "self-governance and community solidarity" as values in the recovery process and expanding "social capital" to support those values.

3.2 Management of the recovery plan

3.2.1 PDCA cycle

In reality, it is difficult to foresee the economic situation ten years after a disaster when planning a process of recovery under the situation where the social situation is changing drastically. Moreover, in the recovery process for a large-scale disaster, issues to be tackled are changing as time goes by. Starting from emergency response to search and rescue and then relief followed by full-fledged recovery, the focal point shifts from recovery in structural aspects to enrichment in nonstructural aspects.

To flexibly handle the change in issues due to the impact of socioeconomic situations, the progress of recovery or citizens' awareness, the Kobe City Government decided to adopt the PDCA management principle when implementing the Kobe City Recovery Plan. The PDCA management cycle is one tool used to help implement projects smoothly. This cycle adopts the following concepts for project implementation and management: **P**lan it; **D**o it; **C**heck it; **A**ct upon the results; and repeat these four processes continuously (Figure 12.2).

Based on the PDCA cycle concept, Kobe monitored the progress of each recovery project and reviewed and revised the plan when required. In fiscal year 1999, the last year of the first half (five years) of the recovery plan, the city conducted a Comprehensive Recovery Assessment. This was to assess what had been done in the recovery process to date by checking the progress of each project and examining effective measures for the next five years in the areas of daily-life recovery, safe and secure city development, housing and urban reconstruction and economic/port recovery. By taking the proposals based on the results into consideration, Kobe formulated the "Kobe City Recovery Plan Promotion Program" where the recovery measures to be dealt with in the latter term of the recovery process were indicated.

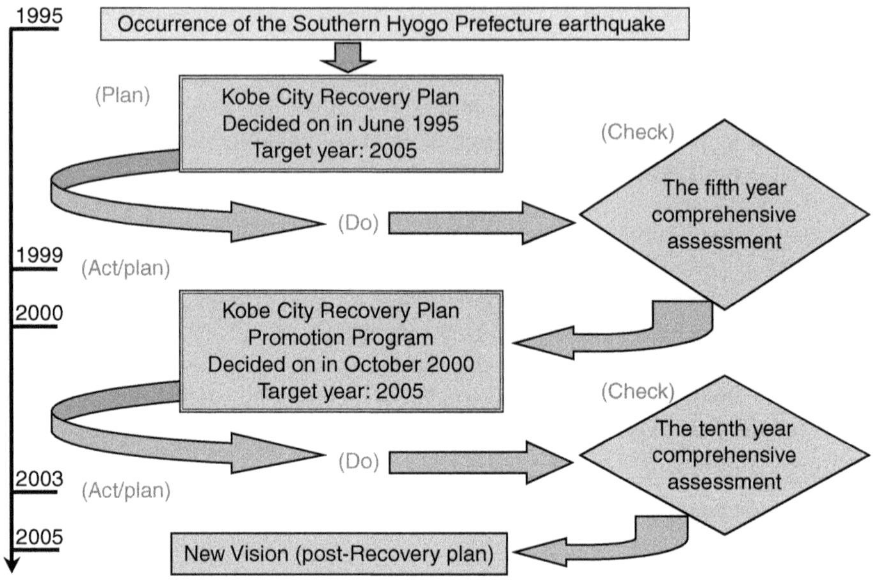

Figure 12.2 Progress of the implementation of the Kobe City Recovery Plan.

In fiscal year 2003, one year before the final year of recovery plan implementation, a second comprehensive assessment of recovery based on civic life, urban activities, housing and community development and a safe and secure city was conducted to examine "Kobe Now (the current situation in Kobe)", which had been rebuilt through the recovery process. The results were presented to the mayor of Kobe.

On the basis of the results, in fiscal year 2005, after the recovery plan implementation period was over, the "New Vision (mid-term plan)" was formulated (target year: 2010). This aims at finding solutions for issues raised in the recovery process and at being a guideline for future Kobe development through utilizing the experiences and lessons learned from the earthquake and the recovery process. In this way, after recovery plan implementation, the remaining recovery issues continued to be tackled within the framework of the city government's general measures and policies.

3.2.2 System and organization for management

The Kobe City Government set up the "Kobe City Recovery Promotion Council" in 1996 to examine comprehensive progress control, necessary measures, issues concerning implementation of the recovery plan, and smooth and effective management. The objectives of this council were (1) to fully understand the progress of the recovery plan, (2) to clarify the remaining issues, (3) to examine potential measures to solve the issues, and (4) to submit proposals to the mayor of Kobe.

For the council, members were selected based on the idea that opinions from a wide range of fields should be absorbed; as a result, 19 academic experts and 14 representatives divided among private organizations and citizens in light of promoting collaboration with citizens (33 in total) were selected. For 18 months after the council was set up, the members discussed a wide range of topics to prepare proposals for the mayor.

As time went by after the earthquake, many members voiced opinions that they should handle not only urgent issues for recovery but future-oriented issues in light of the coming of the twenty-first century and long-term structural issues Kobe had long before the earthquake. To cope with this, the council was disbanded at their sixth meeting. In its place, the Kobe City Recovery and Rejuvenation Promotion Council was established in June 1998 to handle long-term issues as well as recovery issues. Similar to the previous council, the city government chose the members from among academic experts, representatives of private organizations, and citizens.

As mentioned before, the Kobe City Recovery and Rejuvenation Promotion Council conducted Comprehensive Recovery Assessments in fiscal years 1999 and 2003. The purpose of these assessments was to absorb opinions from various citizens to achieve a so-called grassroots assessment. The measures taken were workshops for Kobe citizens, questionnaires for 10,000 citizens, interviews with concerned people, and so on. In particular, the workshop methodology was found to be an effective measure to obtain opinions and proposals from all the participants. This methodology does not take a unilateral knowledge transmission style like a lecture but takes a meeting style featuring bilateral learning and creative thinking; this means that in the workshop participants actively engaged in discussions voluntarily to learn from each other and create something together through group synergy.

In the second Comprehensive Recovery Assessment, the council solicited public comments to absorb citizens' opinions for their interim report and proposal to the mayor. By taking all opinions into consideration, the council finalized the proposal.

3.2.3 Evaluation index for recovery

In the Comprehensive Recovery Assessment conducted by the Hyogo Prefectural Government, it was indicated that there were no numerical targets in their recovery plan, and a strong desire to reach the targets was beginning to wane. There were other observations that it was difficult to monitor the recovery plan with policy evaluation methodology to assess the outcomes, because there were no numerical targets in the plan.

One reason clear numerical targets could not be set in the recovery plan is that, although it is rather easy to quantify the progress of structural development, there were no established evaluation methods for nonstructural measures, let alone benchmarks. Under such circumstances, the Kobe City Government received the proposal from the Kobe City Recovery and Rejuvenation Council saying that Kobe should create an easy-to-understand index with citizens to share community development targets with them and to evaluate the achievements with them for implementing the "Kobe City Recovery Plan Promotion Program" (formulated in October 2000) through collaboration between citizens and the government. This triggered the city government to adopt the administrative evaluation methodology to formulate the outcome index to measure the recovery targets and achievements. Kobe is probably the first administrative body to use the above index to monitor the progress of a recovery plan. The outcome index was named Citizen-Happiness Index.

The Citizen-Happiness Index covers 16 prioritized measures called the 16-point Plan of Action under the "Kobe City Recovery Promotion Program." The index consists of 45 individual indices with the following characteristics.

1 Represented the targets to be reached through partnerships and the comprehensive results of the partnerships;
2 Could be represented numerically;
3 Could be compared with the index of other cities;
4 Represented changes in the daily lives of the citizens;
5 Reflected the citizens' awareness of the creation of communities as well as the needs of the citizens;
6 Utilized existing data, involved understanding information in daily business and represented changes over time;
7 Represented the characteristics of Kobe.

Each index has "the value at the determination" when it was initially created and the goal value which is set to be reached through cooperation among citizens, businesses and the government called "the target value to be reached through partnerships" (see Figure 12.3).

Citizens, stakeholders and the city government officers cooperated to select the individual indices. The selection processes were (a) index draft creation workshop by citizens (127 participants) and workshop with experts and academic experts (47 participants), (b) questionnaire survey for citizens to evaluate the index draft (637 replies), and then (c) citizens' workshop to narrow down the draft index to produce the draft bill (41 participants). In this way, the creation procedure itself is a form of cooperation: discussing matters to make decisions on an equal level between citizens and the government.

As for how to set the target value to be reached through partnerships, the following methods were adopted. If there were goal values for the above target values in the various Kobe plans or national plans, these values were adopted for the index as well; if not, the pre-earthquake values were adopted in case the values were related to the earthquake recovery, while values based on trend estimation from historic data development were adopted in some cases. In addition, the indices and the target values were reviewed and revised according to changes in social and economic conditions.

- Kobe City strives to be a city where volunteers, non-profit organizations (NPOs) and non-governmental organizations (NGOs) play an active role.

Index	Value at the determination (Time)	Target value to be reached through partnerships (Time)
Proportion of the population who are involved in volunteer activities, NPOs or NGOs	14.5% (FY2001)	20% (FY2005)
Number of individuals and organizations that are registered at the Volunteer Information Center or the Volunteer Center in each ward	Individuals: 2,202 Organizations: 1,088 (End of FY2000)	Individuals: 2,900 Organizations: 1,700 (FY2005)
Number of organizations that participate in the campaign called "Volunteers for the creation of a beautiful city full of trees and flowers"	Organizations: 588 (End of FY2001)	Organizations: 700 (FY2005)

Figure 12.3 Example of the Citizen-Happiness Index.

The progress of each individual index in the Citizen-Happiness Index was uploaded onto the Kobe City Government's website and updated as needed. The city government also prepared leaflets to distribute to the public to enable everyone to monitor the progress at any time.

3.3 Fifth year Comprehensive Recovery Assessment

3.3.1 Overview of recovery situation

The Kobe City Recovery and Rejuvenation Promotion Council overviewed the recovery conditions in Kobe five years after the earthquake. The council observed that urban infrastructure like port facilities and roads were restored to the original state in two to three years; infrastructural relief and recovery together with public housing constructions were completed; and all the victims were moved out from the temporary housing. Therefore, they concluded that structural bases in civic life were almost recovered within five years after the earthquake. On the other hand, the council pointed out that the remaining issues for the latter half of the recovery plan should be: (1) citizens' life recovery, (2) economic recovery, and (3) safe and secure housing and community development.

The citizens' efforts for the recovery at that time were highly evaluated, because even under the severe economic conditions and with their anxieties in life, each of the citizens had a strong spirit focused on complete recovery on their own and made the utmost effort to achieve it, starting from calm attitudes and mutual help right after the earthquake through the early resumption of their businesses to their community development activities.

3.3.2 Seven critical elements of life recovery

Life recovery has a very large scope and is ambiguous. Therefore, the assessment of life recovery as one of the recovery projects started by clarifying the definition. Twelve workshops were conducted in Kobe to find out the following: (1) what life recovery means to earthquake victims; and, (2) what are the factors that citizens feel are helpful to the promotion of life recovery? In the workshops, a total of 269 victims and supporters participated and filled out 1,623 opinion cards. After sorting and categorizing these cards, it was clarified that a real sense of life recovery consists of seven elements. The following are the seven elements in descending order based on the number of opinions submitted: (a) housing, (b) social ties, (c) community rebuilding, (d) physical and mental health, (e) preparedness, (f) economy, livelihood and economic and financial situations, and (g) relationship to government (Figure 12.4). In terms of housing, many homes were lost in the earthquake, and victims indicated the importance of efforts to provide housing, a daily necessity for life recovery.

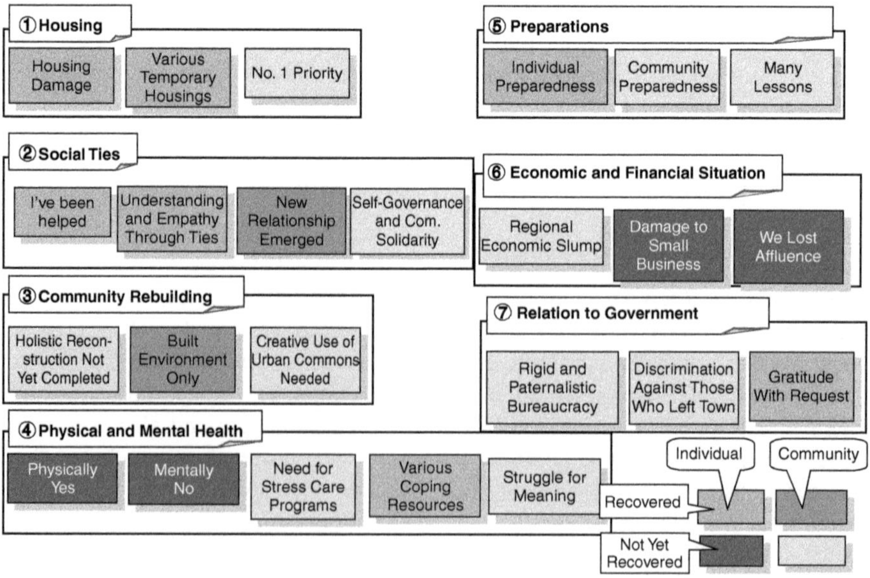

Figure 12.4 Seven critical elements for life recovery (July to August 1999).

All of the city's residents identified social ties as an important component in life recovery. When a disaster strikes, existing personal relationships are dissolved, and people are forced to create new ones from scratch. This change in personal relationships is a major source of stress. Victims were reminded of the importance of social ties as they continued to face unfamiliar living situations.

Although the public infrastructure was restored within about two to three years after the earthquake, the overall recovery of communities seemed to still be a work in progress. Physical and mental health are important preconditions for moving forward in life, and even five years after the earthquake, victims were still feeling a heavy toll on their mental health. Those who lived through the earthquake developed an interest in earthquake preparedness as a result of their desire to avoid the recurrence of such a horrible experience. In the fifth year after the earthquake, the prolonged stagnation of economic recovery and the wave of economic recession nationwide put additional pressure on victims who were already experiencing financial hardship as a result of the earthquake.

As for citizens' relationship to government, services often failed to meet the victims' expectations. This forced them to learn how to interact with their government.

3.3.3 Self-governance and community solidarity

Out of the seven critical elements of life recovery, two elements, housing and social ties, covered more than 50 percent. Especially notable was the fact that the percentage related to social ties stuck out in comparison with the other elements (see Figure 12.5).

Focusing on this fact, academic experts and experts in administration verified the cause-and-effect relationships and other factors in terms of social ties. As a result, the opinions regarding creation of New Kobe through these cause-and-effect relationships were divided into three types: self-sustainable individuals, mutual help (coexistence/solidarity) and establishment of attitude in daily social ties. An individual takes actions by him/herself first. This means "you do first and don't wait for somebody to do something for you." Another aspect is the sense of a main player in community development. Self-sustainability often starts with self-help.

Even though self-governance and self-sustainability is important, a single individual has limited capability. To compensate for the limited capability of each individual and enhance mutual benefits of all individuals, coexistence and solidarity are the answers. What is important to recognize is that there are many people who have lost their assets in various ways and have difficulties making ends meet in the case of earthquake disasters.

However, mutual help has its limits, and it does not mean an individual can get any kind of help.

Regardless of the situation, individuals should not feel that they are special and that others should do everything for them.

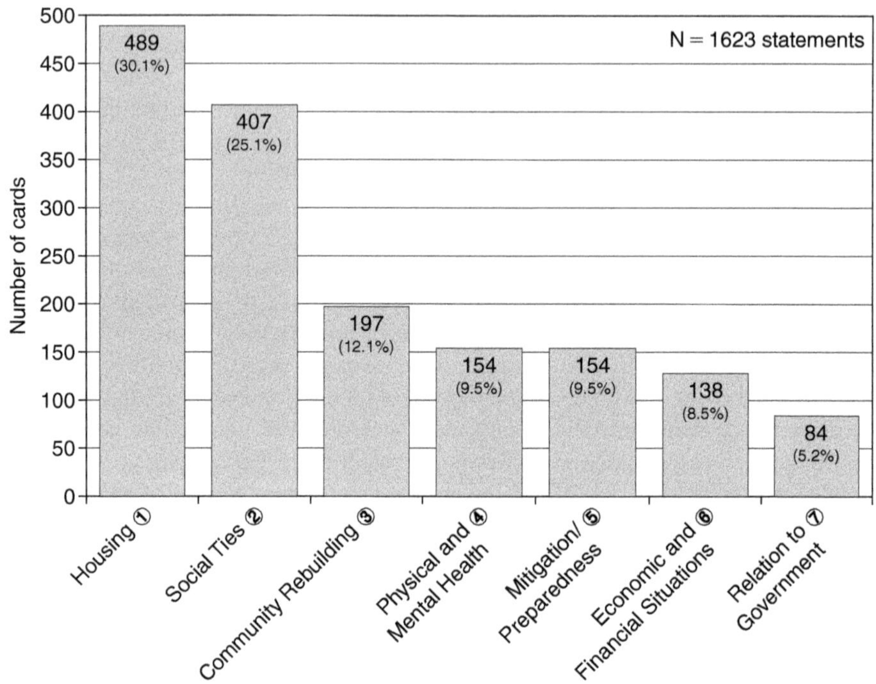

Figure 12.5 Number of opinion cards for each life recovery category.

In the fifth year comprehensive assessment, the key social ties for individual life recovery were integrated into two values and norms: self-governance and community solidarity.

This self-governance and community solidarity was shown in a multidisciplinary way beyond the field of life recovery. Specifically speaking, community development promotion with self-governance and community solidarity was shown in the field of a safe and secure city, housing and community development with self-governance and community solidarity in the field of housing and urban reconstruction, and self-governing recovery and community economy in economic and port recovery (Figure 12.6).

3.4 Tenth year Comprehensive Recovery Assessment

In 2003, the year before the final year of the plan, the Council conducted another Comprehensive Recovery Assessment to examine "Kobe Today," which means the state of the city as it had been rebuilt through recovery efforts taken up to that point.

The city government examined to what extent "Kobe Now" and the earthquake experience were correlated. This was based on the results of 10,000

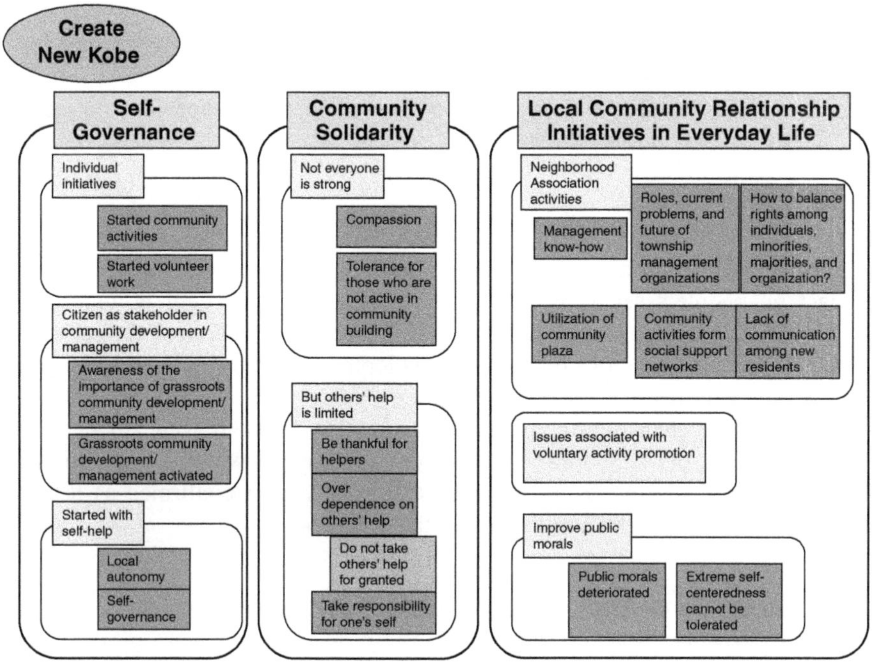

Figure 12.6 Stories told in the 1999 grassroots workshop on social ties (July to August 1999).

questionnaires and economic-related data, etc. Through the examination, it was found that the correlation between "Kobe Now" and the earthquake was gradually waning under the prolonged recession and socioeconomic changes in the post-earthquake period.

"Kobe Now" (from the 2003 Comprehensive Recovery Assessment):

1 Measures should be continuously taken to tackle earthquake-related issues.
2 At the point when eight years had passed since the earthquake, the national and structural issues had bigger effects than the earthquake itself.
3 Some achievements from new efforts and projects in recovery were observed.
4 New challenges emerged as time passed following the earthquake.

In the Comprehensive Recovery Assessment, the direction of these efforts and projects was grouped by the administrative field; among them the following were raised as major remaining issues:

1 As for civic life, set up a permanent, local, friendly visitation program and take care of mental health issues.

2 As for urban activities, continue the disaster recovery loan system and extend the Kobe Enterprise Zone Ordinance.
3 As for housing and community development, finalize the urban development projects for reconstruction in earthquake-stricken areas.
4 As for a safe and secure city, increase seismic-resistant capacities for public facilities and housing structures.

3.5 Lessons learned from the earthquake and the recovery process

The earthquake not only caused severe damage in Kobe but also had a great impact on people's sense of value, their way of life and their attitude. It is important to confirm what was learned from the earthquake and the recovery process to be utilized for community development in light of considering the future direction of Kobe.

In the Comprehensive Recovery Assessment, the lessons were divided into two categories: those lessons learned from the earthquake and those lessons learned from the recovery process. These lessons were reconfirmed as lessons looking towards the tenth anniversary of the earthquake.

3.5.1 Lessons learned from the earthquake disaster management includes a disaster reduction concept

According to the Kobe City Recovery and Rejuvenation Promotion Council, all the lessons learned from the earthquake can be integrated into one phrase: the concept of disaster reduction should be included in disaster management.

In the earthquake, much urban infrastructure like housing and port facilities was destroyed, and it was found that those structures that were supposed to protect human lives or their assets were not perfectly safe or secure. From that fact, the lessons have shown that consideration of disaster management should be taken on the assumption that a disaster will occur. Thus, they said it was important that the concept of disaster reduction, protecting what should be protected, such as life, while minimizing damage, should be included in future disaster countermeasures.

Based on the above idea, enhancement of the capacity of safe and secure city development while utilizing the lessons learned from disasters through the total disaster management process, starting from preventive measures such as damage prevention and damage mitigation to the post-disaster countermeasures like emergency response and relief and recovery is required.

Specifically, the following three lessons were indicated:

1 The earthquake reminded people of the severity of nature. Natural disasters will definitely occur in the future.
2 Local community protects people's lives. Things should start from the place closest to the people.
3 Actions people do not take in their daily lives cannot be undertaken in a disaster situation.

Community development activities should be continuously ongoing in normal times.

When the Hanshin Earthquake hit, citizens' houses became lethal weapons, and many victims were crushed to death. In this context, it was important for individuals or households to increase seismic-resistance capacity and safety of their own homes, which are closest to them. At the same time, the importance of local communities and regular community development activities was recognized because many of the victims trapped under the debris of destroyed houses were rescued by their neighbors.

3.5.2 Lessons learned from the recovery process from self-governance and community solidarity

Following the earthquake, citizens recognized the importance of human-to-human ties, and this was recognized again during the recovery process. Each individual is self-sustainable by one's own responsibility, and one's presence should be positioned as a local community member; this recognition was enhanced during the recovery process. However, each individual's capability has a limit, and each individual needs to give help and consideration to others. This also creates an opportunity to generate human-to-human solidarity.

In the recovery process, unique individuals got together, and these social ties generated a new type of uniqueness. In this way, it was revealed that human-to-human solidarity generates self-governance.

Thus, self-governance and community solidarity are not unilateral factors but are enhanced by each other due to synergistic effects. As a lesson learned from the recovery process, this should be utilized in the future, and be pivotal to the creation of a civic society where self-sustainable citizens are unified through solidarity.

Specifically, the following five lessons were emphasized:

1 The meaning of recovery changes with the passage of time.
2 Recovery should be tackled flexibly through interrelated recovery fields.
3 Community development is accomplished or enhanced by individual self-governing activities.
4 Community development can be advanced by daily collaboration and individual participation.
5 Recovery means moving towards a new system.

During the recovery process, while the issues were changing with time, citizens, businesses and the city government provided their own wisdom to learn from each other to try to find solutions for the challenges they still faced. After the earthquake, things started from scratch. Under these circumstances, the city government firmly believes that Kobe proposed and created various new systems. In terms of administrative policies, the best examples are community-friendly visit programs and the Kobe enterprise zone. In addition, from the community side, payment with autonomy and other examples have been cited. Regarding the creation of the future Kobe, it is essential to utilize the lessons learned: the importance of proposing and creating new systems and attitudes to implement them.

3.5.3 Basic attitude towards creation of the future Kobe by utilizing lessons learned from collaborative community development

In Kobe, since the earthquake changed people's sense of value and way of life, the attitude of self-governance and community solidarity was enhanced, which led to new efforts and actions in the recovery process. The point is that these efforts and actions have been advanced by both people power and community power. It is considered that collaborative and participatory community development has contributed a lot to this achievement.

Comprehensive Recovery Assessment shows why collaborative community development has been advanced in Kobe. According to the assessment, it was notable that not only individual power (human capital) but also the existence of social organizations (so-called social capital), whose features are the ability to enhance collaboration and networking, produced the driving force for advancement. The assessment also pointed out the following important issues for the future: collaborative community development made great achievements in handling individual issues during the recovery period; in light of moving on to the second stage, in order to implement this idea in a sustainable and comprehensive manner, social capital should be nurtured to eventually create a horizontal and highly open network globally as well as locally.

3.6 Important points

As mentioned above, the following is the main feature of management concerning the Kobe City Recovery Plan: ever-changing issues were observed calmly, and the PDCA cycle was then adopted to control the progress by collaboration with citizens in order to cope with issues flexibly. This shows that citizens, businesses and the city government got together to share wisdom and learn from each other how to implement the plan in the recovery process where the issues and challenges were changing day by day after the earthquake.

For the assessment of recovery, the city government adopted administrative evaluation methodology to create the Citizen-Happiness Index as an outcome index. In the process of creating the index, even from the examination phase for each index, the city government solicited citizens' opinions and proposals; as a result, citizens and the city government could create the index through partnerships. These activities further efforts and activities; therefore, this seems to be one of the opportunities for victims and the government to work together to reach common goals.

They themselves have led to nurturing the citizens' awareness towards their own recovery, and the progress of the proposals from the fifth and tenth year Comprehensive Recovery Assessments show that the following are important to proceed with recovery: self-governance and community solidarity, collaborative community development and social capital. Based on this, Kobe formulated the New Vision (mid-term plan) in 2005. In the plan, Kobe aims to proceed with collaboration and participation among private, academic, industrial and administrative sectors to become a new city model ahead of the times. In this way, it is necessary to pass on the concepts of self-governance and community solidarity, collaboration and participation, and social capital to the next generation and beyond, since their importance was made clear during the recovery process.

4 Efforts regarding the Great East Japan Earthquake reconstruction

This section examines the progress concerning the system formulation for reconstruction by the national government, and recovery plans by the prefectures and municipal governments. Immediately after the Great East Japan Earthquake, there was no legal position regarding recovery plans, and the plans drawn up by prefectures and municipalities according to the disaster conditions were said to be voluntary master plans. With an absence of legal guidance concerning reconstruction, each disaster has been individually dealt with by special legislation, causing a delay in taking action. Based on the lessons reflected by this, the Act on "Large-Scale Disaster Reconstruction" of June 2013 sets forth that "municipalities shall formulate recovery plans in order to achieve smooth and prompt recovery in accordance with the Basic Guidelines for Reconstruction and other national legislations", thereby establishing legal support for recovery plans.

4.1 National efforts

The Basic Act on Reconstruction in response to the Great East Japan Earthquake was adopted on June 24, 2011, more than three months following the earthquake. It stipulates the national government's basic concept and measures/policies (securing of funds and establishment of special reconstruction zones) and the organization (basic policy concerning the establishment of the Reconstruction Headquarters and the Reconstruction Agency). Although a draft law had been proposed modeled on the method employed at the time of the Great Hanshin-Awaji Earthquake on May 13 in the same year, it was opposed by the opposition party concerning the scope of the Agency's authority, and was finally enacted following acceptance of their demand. In the case of the Great Hanshin-Awaji Earthquake, the Basic Act on Reconstruction was enacted a little over one month after the earthquake.

In accordance with the Basic Act on Reconstruction, the national government decided the Basic Guidelines for Reconstruction in response to the Great East Japan Earthquake at the meeting of the Reconstruction Headquarters in Response to the Great East Japan Earthquake held on July 29, 2011, which shows the entire picture of measures to be taken by the national and local governments, while taking into consideration the report "Towards Reconstruction – Hope Beyond the Disaster," compiled on June 25, 2011 by the Reconstruction Design

Council in response to the Great East Japan Earthquake. The Basic Guidelines set forth that the reconstruction period is to be ten years and the initial five as the concentrated rapid reconstruction period. In order to implement the reconstruction measures, the national government specified the scale of measures and projects to be implemented during the concentrated rapid reconstruction period to be at least at the level of 19 trillion yen combining those by the national and local governments, and for the entire ten-year restoration/reconstruction period to be at least 23 trillion yen. Later, on January 29, 2013, the 19 trillion yen budget quota for the first five years was increased to 25 trillion yen with the aim of expediting reconstruction.

As one of the implementation acts for the Basic Act on Reconstruction, the Act on Special Zones for Reconstruction relaxing regulations and providing tax incentives for the affected areas was adopted on December 7, 2011. The Special Zone for Reconstruction Systems under the said Act grants 222 municipalities which suffered from the earthquake preferential measures, provided that such municipalities prepare a reconstruction promotion plan, land restructuring plan and other plans, and obtain approval/consent from the national government. The preferential measures include: (1) simplified procedures concerning licensing and zoning and easing of requirements for permissions, (2) utilization of new business methods for the integrated exchange/development of dwelling and farming land, (3) easing of occupancy criteria for public housing, and (4) allocating severely affected municipalities grants for reconstruction in a lump sum for wide-ranging projects required for the affected municipality to reconstruct its area. The grants are described as being relatively well-funded and highly flexible to allow their use for the various recovery plans of each municipality.

As another implementation act, the Act for Establishment of the Reconstruction Agency as a "control tower" for reconstruction from the Great East Japan Earthquake was adopted on December 14, 2011. In response, the Reconstruction Agency was established in the Cabinet Office and made its debut in February 2012. The Agency requests and secures all budgets necessary for reconstruction projects, and distributes them to each ministry and agency, while earmarking execution plans at its discretion. At the same time, it plays a role in approving special zones for reconstruction, distribution of the grants for reconstruction and direct implementation of preparations for the resumption of public facilities located around the Fukushima No. 1 nuclear power plant. On January 29, 2013, the government decided to establish the Fukushima Bureau of Reconstruction and Revitalization by centralizing its branches and assigning senior executive officers of the Reconstruction Agency on a full-time basis for the purpose of accelerating the reconstruction of Fukushima, thereby undertaking overall control of reconstruction projects of Fukushima. At the same time, the Fukushima Headquarters for Reconstruction and Revitalization was established in Tokyo, which assembles director-general level officials of government ministries and agencies, including Land, Infrastructure, Transport and Tourism; Agriculture, Forestry and Fisheries; and Economy, Trade and Industry, with the Minister of the Reconstruction Agency at the top.

In parallel with the above legislation, additional consolidation of earthquake-related legal systems in terms of the government financial assistance as part of preferential measures was adopted, such as the Act on Special Fiscal Aid and Subsidy for Recovery from the Great East Japan Earthquake, the Act on Special Provisions concerning the Total Amount of Local Allocation Tax for Fiscal 2011 and the Act to Amend the Local Taxation Act to alleviate the burden of those affected. In response to this, a supplementary budget was compiled in three stages in 2011, and in 2012 financing regarding the reconstruction was covered under the Great East Japan Earthquake Special Account for Reconstruction. The reconstruction-related budgets were 15 trillion 169.7 billion yen (FY 2011), 4 trillion 93.1 billion yen (FY 2012) and 4 trillion 384 billion yen (FY 2013) respectively, with a total of 23 trillion 646.8 billion yen. The resources for these have been financed by cuts in expenditures/non-tax revenue (850 million yen), a tax increase for reconstruction (10.5 trillion yen), stock sales of Japan Post Holdings (4.5 trillion yen) and surplus account (2.9 trillion yen) with a total of 25 trillion yen. While in the case of the Great Hanshin-Awaji Earthquake, the government compiled supplementary budgets of 3.2 trillion yen in total, three times within one year following the quake (second supplementary budget of 1 trillion yen for FY 1994, first supplementary budget of 1.4 trillion yen for FY 1995, and second supplementary budget of 0.8 trillion yen for the same year). With the several hundreds of billions of yen level related budgets thereafter allocated, the national budgetary measures represent a total of 5 billion yen, including the expenses allocated for the initial and supplementary budgets for about five years until the second supplementary budget of FY 1999 was implemented. This demonstrates that the scale of the national budgetary measures for the Great East Japan Earthquake has become significantly larger compared with that of the Great Hanshin-Awaji Earthquake.

As shown above, the national government's response to reconstruction at the initial stage was slow, reflecting the issue of an over 1,000 trillion yen deficit as well as the confusion of the political process resulting from the divided Diet. On the other hand, however, the level of the government's support this time has been generous compared with that of the Great Hanshin-Awaji Earthquake. For example, systems which remained unrealized, which the disaster victims and areas of the Great Hanshin-Awaji Earthquake had also proposed in the aftermath, such as the establishment of special zones for reconstruction, grants for reconstruction, a special local allocation tax for recovery, a tax increase for reconstruction, special account for reconstruction and a reconstruction agency. The concept of special zoning goes back to the Enterprise Zone which the Hyogo Prefecture, Kobe City and the business community proposed to the government as a recovery measure following the Great Hanshin-Awaji Earthquake. Although aimed to find a way out for the economy through the advancement of existing industries, it was opposed and rejected by ministries who would not grant special exceptions.

The government gave its support in the case of the Great East Japan Earthquake on a level exceeding that of the Great Hanshin-Awaji Earthquake in all aspects of legislation, organization and administration/finance. The reasons are as follows. As mentioned earlier, the Great East Japan Earthquake resulted in a complex and mega-scale disaster far greater than that of the Great Hanshin-Awaji Earthquake. In addition, the municipalities who were supposed to have been at the forefront of support activities for the disaster victims suffered seriously from damage to their administrative functions as their staff members themselves fell victim, and damaged government buildings and facilities, or through being obliged to move their office functions, as well as the fact that the financial capability of the municipalities was more vulnerable than that of Kobe City and Hyogo Prefecture. Further, many of the disaster-stricken municipalities were those which had been suffering from both depopulation and an aging population with fewer children.

Now, with respect to the lower financial strength of the affected municipalities compared to Kobe City and Hyogo Prefecture, there follows an outline of the financial capability of three prefectures: Iwate, Miyagi and Fukushima and their municipalities which suffered particularly severely. First of all, regarding the level of independent financial resources of the municipalities of the above three prefectures before the earthquake based on the financial index (FY 2009), there are many affected municipalities where they were lower than the national average (0.55), except for Onagawa-cho (Miyagi Prefecture), Okuma-machi, Naraha-machi and Hirono-machi (Fukushima), where nuclear power plants and large-scale thermal power plants are located, Shinchi-machi and Tomioka-machi (Fukushima), with their power stations and related corporations, and some municipalities of Sendai City, the business center of the Tohoku region where numerous plants and offices are located. They have little independent financial resources and are dependent largely on national taxes allocated to local governments. On the other hand, the financial index for Kobe City immediately before the Great Hanshin-Awaji Earthquake was 0.83. There are also many municipalities of which the actual debt expenditure ratio, which indicates the degree of financial burden caused by the actual national debt service expenditure (redemption money for principal and interest of local bonds), exceeded the national average (11.2 percent).

Next, with respect to the financial index in FY 2009 of the three prefectures, Iwate, Miyagi and Fukushima, although Miyagi (0.54) was a little higher than the national average (0.52), Iwate (0.31) and Fukushima (0.46) were both lower. Given such circumstances of being fundamentally poor in their independent financial resources, it is inferred to be difficult for the three prefectures to support their municipalities by carrying a large part of the burden of financial resources for reconstruction. Meanwhile, the financial index for Hyogo Prefecture immediately before the Great Hanshin-Awaji Earthquake was 0.70.

4.2 Recovery plan formulation process and structure by affected municipalities

4.2.1 Recovery plan formulation process

Contrary to the national government, which has been criticized for its slow response concerning reconstruction, the governments of the municipalities of Iwate Prefectures as well as those of Miyagi Prefectures have made efforts to formulate their reconstruction plans. Iwate Prefecture decided the Basic Guidelines for Reconstruction in response to the Great East Japan Earthquake and Tsunami in April 2011, and based on this, formulated the Iwate Prefecture Reconstruction Plan for the Great East Japan Earthquake and Tsunami on August 11, 2011 following approval by the regular prefectural assembly. Setting the plan period as eight years, it was divided into the first phase of infrastructure restoration (three years), the second phase of full-scale reconstruction (three years) and the third phase of consolidation for further development (two years). In Iwate Prefecture, the recovery plans were formulated by each of its 12 municipalities by the end of 2011, with Otsuchi-cho being the last.

Miyagi Prefecture announced the Basic Guidelines for Reconstruction in response to the Great East Japan Earthquake (draft) in April 2011, and then formulated the Miyagi Earthquake Reconstruction Plan on August 22 during the Miyagi Earthquake Reconstruction Meeting, which was approved by the regular prefectural assembly in September 2011. Setting the planning period as ten years, it was divided into the restoration phase (three years), the regeneration phase (four years) and the development phase (three years). In Miyagi Prefecture, Iwanuma City published the Reconstruction Plan Grand Design in early August 2011, followed by 18 municipalities, including Sendai City, Natori City, Watari-cho and Yamamoto-cho, by the end of the year.

Fukushima Prefecture, which suffered from nuclear disaster, formulated the Vision for Revitalization in Fukushima Prefecture on August 11, 2011, stipulating the basic concepts including "building a safe, secure and sustainable society free from nuclear power" and other major measures. Based on this vision, it also formulated the Plan for Revitalization in Fukushima Prefecture (First Version) in December 2011, describing concrete efforts and principal projects for the coming decade. The municipalities which had fallen far behind in formulation of reconstruction plans due to the nuclear power plant accident also completed such formulation by June 2013. However, the plans of those which have no prospect as to when their citizens can return home delineate nothing but an abstract future vision.

4.2.2 Structure of the recovery plan

The outline of overall recovery plans differs from those of the Great Hanshin-Awaji Earthquake. According to the publications (2003 and 2012) by Professor Haruo Hayashi, in the case of the Great Hanshin-Awaji Earthquake, the plan proceeded first from "infrastructure reconstruction" as the foundation of the reconstruction project, then to "rebuilding town and restoring economy" upon completion of the restoration, to "life recovery" on the premises of the former. While, in the case of the Great East Japan Earthquake, in the tsunami-devastated areas, one cannot simply carry out the "infrastructure reconstruction" as in the above first phase of the recovery plan, instead one is obliged to undertake the "well-planned rearrangement of infrastructure" in consideration of the risks of future tsunami.

This well-planned rearrangement of infrastructure can be summarized in the following five types primarily focusing on places of residence: (1) relocation to higher ground in the ria coastal areas, (2) relocation inland on the plains, (3) reconstruction of the original site, (4) restoration of infrastructure such as levees and development of tsunami countermeasure facilities such as disaster-prevention parks, and (5) restoration of developed/reclaimed land which suffered severe damage such as landslides and liquefaction (Figure 12.7).

4.3 Status of the implementation of reconstruction measures

In accordance with the aforementioned basic structure of the recovery plan, this section examines the status of the implementation of reconstruction measures.

4.3.1 Efforts regarding well-planned rearrangement of infrastructure

Based on the literature published by the Reconstruction Agency, the well-planned rearrangement of social infrastructure has been progressing at a

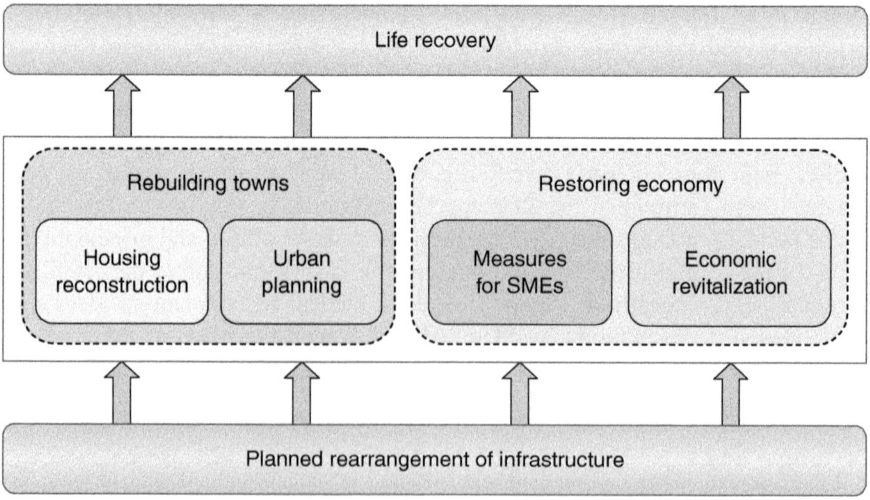

Figure 12.7 Basic structure of the recovery plan (source: Central Disaster Prevention Council Countermeasure promotion Council, material prepared by Haruo Hayashi).

considerably slow pace. As of the end of November 2013, with respect to the land readjustment project, the number of districts which had decided on implementation accounted for 94 percent of those surveyed for the reconstruction grants, the number of districts which had commenced land development was 65 percent, while the number of districts which had completed the land development amounted to nil. As of the same period, with respect to the Promoting Group Relocation for Disaster Mitigation project, the number of districts which had obtained approval from the Minister of Land, Infrastructure, Transport and Tourism concerning their project plans accounts for 100 percent, the number of districts which had commenced land development was 64 percent and the number of districts which had completed the land development accounted for 5 percent. Besides, there are differences in the extent of progress between municipalities.

The reasons for such delay in the progress of the well-planned rearrangement of social infrastructure are the scale of the project, consensus-building among parties concerned and shortage of professional staff. According to the results of a questionnaire conducted in Iwate, Miyagi and Fukushima Prefectures by the Ministry of Land, Infrastructure, Transport and Tourism, the total area combining three prefectures subject to the land readjustment project amounts to approximately 2,800 hectares, as of March 1, 2012, representing ten times that of the Great Hanshin-Awaji Earthquake. With respect to the disaster prevention group relocation promotion project, the total number of housing units in the three prefectures is approximately 23,300, representing more than 12 times the cumulative total of projects since 1972.

The reasons for the delay in consensus coordination among local residents are the fact that the expenses for the purchase of new land and building cost for dwellings have to be borne by residents, a long time is required to purchase the real estate with a mortgage and there is a sense of unfairness concerning the different amounts of compensation between residents whose houses were swept away and those whose houses remained. Professor Yuka Kaneko (2012) states that it was also because the governments made decisions concerning the safety measures of reconstruction plans without obtaining sufficient agreement from the community. She points out that, in many affected municipalities, the reconstruction plans were formulated under the initiative of governments and consultants with no substantial information made available to citizens during their formulation process. As a result, some affected residents now have doubts concerning effectiveness of the levees designed to withstand Level 1 tsunami, and designation of a disaster risk zone based on the two-meter inundation height standard, thereby hindering the obtainment of a consensus among residents.

The shortage of professional staff results from the following. First of all, the budget for the restoration and reconstruction is far greater than the level of each municipality's budget before the earthquake, while on the other hand many affected municipalities are relatively small in size with a small number of personnel to start with. Some of them also lost a large proportion of their personnel by the earthquake. Thus it is inevitable that the affected municipalities do not have a sufficient number of personnel required for the smooth and prompt implementation of massive-scale restoration and reconstruction projects. For example, Otsuchi-cho in Iwate Prefecture, which lost its mayor and a quarter of its personnel, is obliged to enforce a ten-times larger budget with personnel of only 1.5 to 2 times that before the earthquake.

The affected municipalities have taken various measures to overcome the shortage of manpower for reconstruction. They can be broadly categorized into the following two measures: (1) to obtain additional staff, by employing full-time, fixed-term, reappointed, temporary/part-time personnel or retired officials of other local governments; (2) to request other local governments to send their personnel for support. In this method, some affected municipalities themselves carry out the request and resources coordination, or the Ministry of Internal Affairs and Communications, Reconstruction Agency or other private sectors take charge of the reception, coordination and dispatch of personnel. Although such measures to counter the manpower shortage have been disseminating, the dispatching scheme operated by the Ministry of Internal Affairs and Communications shows that the number of personnel requested by the affected municipalities rose to 1,447 as of August 1, 2013, which is still short by 252.

4.3.2 Efforts for the reconstruction of housing

Referring to the estimation by Professor Yoshiteru Murosaki (2012), as there are no accurate statistics with respect to the number of required housing reconstructions, it is estimated that, one and a half years after the earthquake, 40,000 households have been rebuilt while 100,000 still require the recovery of housing. One of the measures for the reconstruction of housing is to take occupancy of public housing. According to the literature of the Reconstruction Agency, the required number of disaster public housings published by all prefectures except Fukushima was 21,811. In response, the number of disaster public housings which had started construction was 13,231 as of the end of November, 2013, showing a progress rate of only 61 percent.

The number of housings which had been completed was 509, representing only 2 percent of the total number required. Besides, Professor Murosaki (2012) pointed out that there was no guarantee that these housings can be completed as scheduled due to the fact that there had been delays in the securing of building sites for public housing and a shortage of manpower to carry out construction. He further stated that the reconstruction of housing had no prospect in sight when it was linked with group relocation and land adjustment.

4.3.3 Efforts for small and medium-sized enterprise measures

With respect to the reconstruction of small and medium-sized enterprises (SMEs), the SME Recovery and Reconstruction Support (Grouping) Subsidy Program was established for the first time. The purpose of this subsidy is to directly support the reconstruction of SMEs, and is granted by the national and prefectural governments in collaboration, with each bearing 50 percent and 25 percent respectively, when SMEs and other groups undergo restoration in accordance with the reconstruction project plan approved by the prefecture. As of August 9, 2013, a total subsidy of 414.4 billion yen (including national funds of 276.2 billion yen) for 537 groups had been decided. Professor Mitsuhiro Seki (2012) commended this group subsidy, stating, "Except for immobilized cases like Fukushima, motivated SMEs engaged in manufacturing have been recovering with the aid of the group subsidy program." However, Professor Kaneko (2012) raised the question as to whether such subsidy was allocated thoroughly among the enterprises which truly need subsidizing: "The group subsidy is allocated to enterprises based on their contribution to the regional economy, and to those which are likely to achieve early reconstruction, having a high capital investment and employment effect." The reasons for this are that the total amount of the subsidy is too little, while the certification criterion of the Small and Medium Enterprise Agency is too high to meet the actual situation.

The 32.4 billion yen project by the Organization for Small and Medium Enterprises and Regional Innovation, Japan (SME Support, Japan), through which it loans and transfers temporary plants and stores on a gratuitous basis to local authorities, has been implemented to 538 plants and stores, contributing to the swift recommencement of industry and commerce.

On the other hand, their support for small and medium-sized enterprises in terms of the double-loan issue has not been working efficiently. The Industrial Recovery Consultation Centers/Industry Reconstruction Corporation was founded in four disaster-affected prefectures with 200 billion yen, the reserve of SME Support, Japan. As of December 20, 2013, purchases had been decided for 213 companies only, and were limited to good-standing enterprises with the possibility of recovery. The question has been raised as to whether it is no longer functioning. To counter this, the Organization for Supporting the Turnaround of Businesses Damaged by the Great East Japan Earthquake was founded by a lawmaker-initiated bill, aimed at making purchases of up to 500 billion yen. It is intended to cover primarily small businesses, enterprises engaged in agriculture, and forestry, fisheries or medical/welfare services, which are difficult to support by the Industry Reconstruction Corporation. However, the number of supports decided as of December 20, 2013 was only 342. Despite these two organizations having been found to be redundant, the double-loan issue of the disaster-affected enterprises remains unsolved.

5 Conclusion

By taking a broad overview of the implementation status of reconstruction measures from the Great East Japan Earthquake, delays in reconstruction projects and disparities in the degree of recovery between affected municipalities were revealed. Some of the causes for the delay in reconstruction projects involved tasks concerning consensus-building among citizens prior to the implementation of projects, and a shortage of personnel in the municipalities. In terms of the difference in the progress of projects, delay was more prominent in the hard-hit areas and industrial field.

During the recovery process from large-scale disasters, qualitative changes to challenges awaiting solution emerge as time advances. The author learned through involvement in the process of reconstruction from the Great Hanshin-Awaji Earthquake how important it is to calmly watch over the problems which vary from hour to hour and to deal with them in a flexible manner.

As a method, the concept of the PDCA cycle introduced in line with the implementation of the Kobe City Recovery Plan was effective. In the reconstruction process from the Great East Japan Earthquake also, it has become difficult to see the picture of the actual situation of affected areas as they became differentiated and diversified over time. In order to proceed with reconstruction under such circumstances, one should flexibly meet the needs as required without being bound by the initial plans, based on the significance of the advancement and management of the recovery plan by the PDCA cycle; one of the lessons learned from the Great Hanshin-Awaji Earthquake.

Furthermore, another of its noteworthy lessons, "collaborative and participatory community development" as the essential key to the recovery of Kobe, together with its driving force, "fostering of social capital," are crucial to swiftly and effectively developing future reconstruction. The government alone cannot promote reconstruction; life and living can be restored only when people collaborate and participate in it.

Bibliography

Hayashi, H. (2003), *Inochi o Mamoru Jishin Bosai Gaku* [*Life Saving Seismology/ Disaster Prevention*]. Tokyo: Iwanami Shoten.

Hayashi, H. (2012), *The 3rd Committee for Policy Planning on Disaster Management under the Central Disaster Management Council*, data submitted by Hayashi, H., a Committee Member.

Honjo, Y. (2011), "Implementation of the Kobe City Recovery Plan," *Japan Social Innovation Journal*, Vol. 1.

Kaneko, Y. (2012), "Sangyo Keizai Fukko to Nariwai Sien [Reconstruction of Industry/ Economy and Support for Livelihood]", *Fukko*, Issue 5, Vol. 4, No. 1.

Kobe City (1995), *Kobe City Recovery Plan.* Kobe: Kobe City Government.

Kobe City (2010), *Comprehensive Strategy for Recovery from the Great Hanshin-Awaji Earthquake*. Kobe: Kobe City Government.

Kobe City Recovery and Rejuvenation Promotion Council (2003), *Kobe City's Comprehensive Assessment for Recovery.* Kobe: Kobe City Government.

Kobe City Research Committee on Disaster Recovery (2000), *Kobe City's Review for Life Recovery.* Kobe: Kobe City Government.

Murosaki, Y. (2012), "Fukko Machizukuri no Genjo to Kadai [Status and Issues Concerning Community Reconstruction]", *Fukko*, Issue 5, Vol. 4, No. 1.

Seki, M. (2012), *Higashi-Nihon Dai-Shinsai to Chiiki Sangyo Fukko II* [*Restoration from the Great East Japan Earthquake and of Regional Industry II*]. Tokyo: Shinhyo-sha.

13 Promptness and sustainability in town reconstruction following the 2011 Great East Japan Earthquake

Katsumi Matsuoka

1 Introduction

The coastal area of the Tohoku region in Japan was widely devastated by the Great East Japan Earthquake and Tsunami (GEJE) in March 2011. As a result, many towns required comprehensive spatial planning for reconstruction. To put this planning into practice, a new legislative regime was specifically established in combination with various other schemes and conventional disaster laws, so that town planning projects based on Disaster Risk Reduction (DRR) are now under way. The law has given impetus to reconstruction and rehabilitation, with legal enactments providing local governments with the authority and subsidies required for reconstruction from the disaster.

Nevertheless, many refugees from the disaster have had to live in temporary housing while awaiting permanent homes. The delay in residential reconstruction is conspicuous. One of the main factors in the delay is that a considerable number of the land acquisition contracts required to commence development have not been finalized in due course, as many pieces of the land in question are subject to rights held by many different people that have to be located and negotiated with. Lingering delays in public works arising from this land expropriation may prompt depopulation and protract community rebuilding.

Iwate Prefecture has proactively responded to this problem with a sense of urgency, ardently lobbying for more legislative reforms oriented towards prompt recovery. On the basis of these local needs, the national government has gradually implemented some legal measures; however, it cannot be said to be acting proactively as it is concerned that the prompt implementation of such laws may impinge upon the protection of private rights and due process of law under the Japanese Constitution.

The legal regime applicable in normal times may hinder the progress of reconstruction, whereas legal reform seems to need refined requirements. But then there is a further question which needs to be asked. Does the necessity of promptness outweigh the other elements of disaster recovery applicable within the legal regime?

The goal of this chapter is to present the relationship between the legal regime and prompt housing reconstruction in connection with sustainable recovery. The chapter first describes briefly the devastation in Iwate Prefecture caused by the tsunami following the GEJE and spatial planning in the legal regime for reconstruction. The focus then shifts to the reconstruction of housing from temporary dwellings to permanent homes, identifying factors causing its delay, the suspension of projects due to matters related to contracts and some legal responses in order to speed up housing reconstruction. On these observations, attention turns to the discussion about the legal regime under the due process of law. Finally, the article tries to evaluate "promptness", as a function in "sustainable recovery".

2 Topography of tsunami-affected Iwate

Iwate Prefecture is located in the Tohoku region of northeast Japan, facing the Pacific Coast along the Sanriku Kaigan, a coastal area that stretches from Iwate to Miyagi Prefecture.

The Sanriku coastline is one of the most disaster-prone areas in Japan and has historically suffered occasional damage due to tsunamis and earthquakes originating in the vicinity of the Japan Trench.

Notwithstanding this topography, town planning has been accustomed to developing the small indented portions of the Sanriku coast's jagged seashores and sandy estuaries built upon layers of silt. Once a tsunami wave arrives, it could dart upstream or sprawl out along the coast, destroying everything in its path. What was once beyond anticipation became a reality when many medium-sized cities with populations over 20,000 – Miyako, Kamaishi, Ofunato and Rikuzentakata – were heavily devastated by the GEJE tsunami. Of the 16,000 deaths caused by the earthquake, over 6,000 were in this area. The city of Rikuzentakata was the most badly damaged in the prefecture. The city is located along the saw-tooth shaped coast, centered upon the estuary of the Kesen River that flows into Hirota Bay. Famous as a beach resort, its beautiful pine forest scenery was totally lost to the monstrous tsunami, leaving a solitary pine tree (the "Miraculous Loan Pine Tree") standing from the 70,000 pine trees there previously. If you were to visit the city now for the first time, you may think it is a place at the frontier of development from the wilderness. But before March 11, 2011, there were streets, shops, houses and a railway station. The central part of the city has lost 50 percent of its population.

In the Great Hanshin Awaji Earthquake of 1995, the area that was struck by the disaster was limited compared with this time. The tsunami caused by the GEJE has totally changed the geological landscape and altered the national legal regime.

3 Spatial planning under the new legal regime after the tsunami

The Iwate Prefectural Government drew a roadmap for reconstruction (2011–2018) as "a blueprint for the future of the area" with a vision for "a renewed Iwate and Sanriku community where people's lives are protected in harmonious coexistence with the ocean and the land" (Iwate Prefecture 2014a); they divided the reconstruction period into three phases: fundamental reconstruction (2011–2013), full-fledged reconstruction (2014–2016) and progress leading to further development (see Figure 13.1).

Since the Great Hanshin Awaji Earthquake, it has been stressed that DRR is a national and local priority with a strong institutional basis and that within the planning of land use, the revision of existing or development of new building codes, standards, rehabilitation and reconstruction practices is one of the key activities (UN/ISDR 2007a, p. 6, 12; UN/ISDR 2007b, p. 7). Iwate Prefecture made proposals and initiatives related to DRR in its 2015 proposal document; for example, Proposal 1 denotes the "establishment of an institutional framework of disaster response support activities based on 'horizontal supplements' from cooperation of local governments" and Initiative 1, "establishment of widespread disaster risk reduction facilities effective in supporting damaged areas during large-scale disasters" (Iwate Prefecture 2015, p. 54).

"Building-Back-Better" (BBB) has attracted global attention since the reconstruction of Aceh, Indonesia from the Indian Ocean earthquake and tsunami in December 2004. BBB is not only about the reconstruction of safer housing and improved infrastructure but conceived of the empowerment of local community (Fan 2013, p. 9; UN/ISDR 2014). Iwate Prefecture set a goal "to create a new sustainable Sanriku for the future" in Phase 3 of the roadmap (see Figure 13.1): "to build something better – a community that is safer and more sustainable" (Farber *et al.* 2010, p. 348).

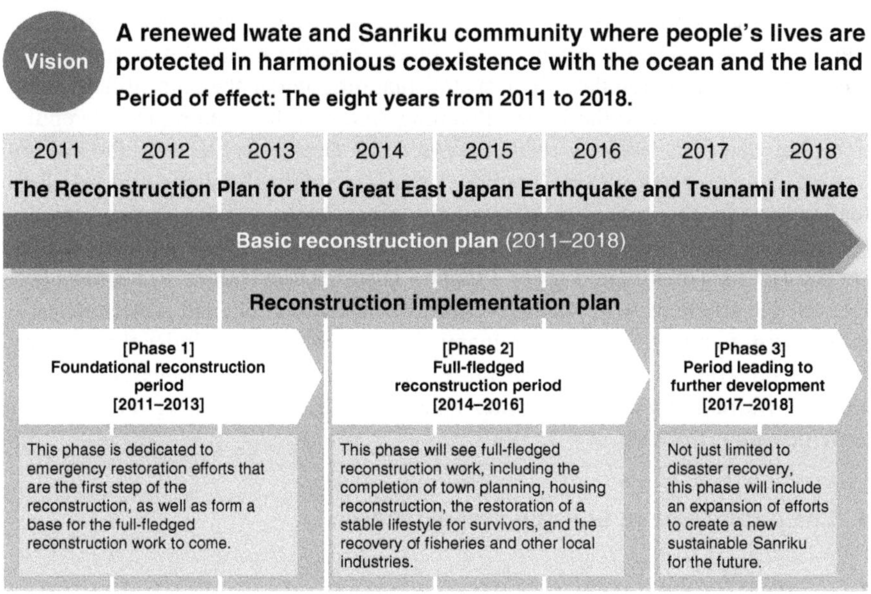

Figure 13.1 Reconstruction plan drawn up on August 11, 2011 (Iwate prefecture 2014a, p. 3).

Local governments in Iwate Prefecture also drew respective plans for reconstruction to rebuild their cities, financially backed up by the prefectural and national governments coupled with special laws and measures. They are planning central city areas under the principles of DRR as well as BBB.

There are too many laws pertaining to disaster prevention and reconstruction to refer to in full here. Therefore, this chapter focuses only on some of the new enactments after the GEJE. But attention has to be paid to their approaches to reconstruction when it comes to the question of whether they sufficiently concord with DRR and BBB (Ikuta 2013; Kaneko 2014).

The Basic Act on Reconstruction in Response to the GEJE 2011 (hereinafter the Basic Act 2011) prescribes that, considering the unprecedented national crisis caused by the GEJE, the act has the purpose of promoting the smooth and prompt reconstruction and revitalization of a vibrant Japan, securing financial resources, identifying afflicted areas as Special Zones for Reconstruction with institutional and tax measures and establishing a Reconstruction Agency to undertake tasks regarding integrated national measures (Art. 1).

The Basic Act 2011 then prescribes its basic philosophy, adopting the idea of the building back better concept, promoting dramatic measures for revitalization that are not limited to physical recovery of afflicted facilities, but also reconstruction measures to assist individuals to overcome the disaster and lead prosperous lives while honoring local culture and enhancing people's ties with the community (Art. 2).

The Act for Special Zones for Reconstruction 2011 was enacted as separate legislation from the Basic Act 2011 to implement the reconstruction measures. Under this legislation, afflicted local governments designated as special areas can acquire significantly larger budget funds from the national government for recovery and can deregulate their spatial planning under the Agricultural Land Act, the Forest Act and the Urban Planning Act. Via this funding and deregulation, they can plan recovery-related projects for disaster prevention: the promotion of collective relocation, functional reinforcement of fishery villages, land reallocation for the revival of affected city areas, basic construction to lead city centers towards recovery from the tsunami and disaster-resistant public housing.

The Act on Town Planning for Tsunami Disaster Prevention 2011 allows prefectural governments to set tsunami hazard zones and municipal governments to make integrated town plans for tsunami disaster prevention. Under the act, prefectural governments can set the presumed tsunami hazard zones and special tsunami warning zones. In the latter zone, normal town planning and building activities are restricted.

4 The public role in housing reconstruction

4.1 Options for permanent housing

The actual recovery process varies from the emergency response, restoration and reconstruction to BBB, in both time and space. In addition, the recovery process to be implemented through reconstruction planning is multidimensional: individual lives, local businesses, infrastructure and communities are involved. Notwithstanding the state's responsibility for disaster prevention under the Basic Act in Disaster Response 1961 (last revised in 2014), the nature of the responsibility is generally considered not as a legal liability burdened by the nation but as a sort of mission: there is implied a basic idea that in the case of natural disaster, it is the victim that is responsible for the emergency response and restoration (Ikuta 2010). Thus, responsibilities under the Act mainly encompass prevention and emergency response, but less so restoration and little regarding reconstruction. Since the Great Hanshin Awaji Earthquake, some legal scholars' interests have converged upon reconstruction from disasters and discussed it from various angles: the roles of the public and the state, public participation and civil rights (e.g. Abe 1995; Yasumoto 1995; Kaneko 2014). A further important point is a lack of laws about the restoration and reconstruction of individual lives and increasing available housing, in contrast to the numerous laws about the restoration of public infrastructure (Ikuta 2010). The disaster law system as a whole is weak in terms of recovery for disaster victims.

It is true that a cluster of laws related to supporting the lives of afflicted individuals in the aftermath of natural disasters has developed historically in the event of disasters. However, to what extent the state should support disaster victims still remains ambiguous as a result of the patchwork-style law making that lacks any coherent principle of disaster response (Kaneko 2014; Ikuta 2013, 2010). Put differently, the question is, regarding the support of disaster victims' lives and businesses, in what areas are public, self- and mutual support needed? It should be noted that this question becomes more serious when the present legal remedies result in disproportionate recovery between affected people who are affluent or resilient, and those who are socially vulnerable, as has happened in the United States (Beck 1992; Farber 2007; Verchick 2012).

Let us now focus on the housing recovery. Under the Disaster Relief Act 1946 (last revised in 2013), the temporary housing can be supplied for emergency relief in times of disaster. The period of the supply is normally two years (under the Building Standards Act) and, though intended for emergency use, supply can be extended year after year, but perhaps not for more than ten years as the prefabricated housing normally used is itself unsuitable for longer use. Then, in order to settle into permanent housing, there are generally three options for those who are currently living in temporary housing:

- Buy or rebuild houses either in their original location (if construction is legally allowed) or at a new location in an inland area. The Act on Support of Disaster Victims for Livelihood Reconstruction 1988 (last revised in 2007) was enacted to nationally subsidize disaster victims who rebuild houses with a maximum of 3,000,000 yen. Additionally, municipal governments have prepared other schemes to subsidize individual houses within their jurisdictions. A loan reduction program for those already burdened by housing loans has also been arranged in cooperation with banks. These subsidies and the program are also applicable to the latter two options. However, in this option, the person must find by themselves a new property via the real estate market. Consequently, this option is available only to those who are in a position to access funds and take out new loans.

- Collective relocation to higher ground planned and conducted by municipal government as disaster risk reduction-related public works. There are two types of relocation for permanent housing: land reallocation projects, where affected residents exchange their own old lands for newly plotted ones, and group relocation, where residents of a previous neighborhood establish a housing complex in a higher location, keeping original community ties. In both types, the municipal governments develop appropriated lands where prospective residents can build their own houses. This option is more readily available than the former self-help type recovery because people can obtain land via exchange, with adjustments made for the present value of the purchased land (the price of most allocated land is decreased for the purpose of this development) after the sale of their original land at the relatively reduced price set by the government. Although in each case the resident needs extra funds, the amount is lower than in the self-help option; to build a permanent house on the land requires at least 90,000 dollars.
- Apply for council housing (called 'public disaster housing') provided by local governments for moderate rent fees. There are plans to construct over 6,000 public apartments and flats (as of November 2013). Public housing is also available for those who had owned a house built on land subject to leasehold, as these people are unable to participate in the land reallocation or group relocation projects for landowners.

4.2 Delay of housing reconstruction

Whichever option above is selected, how far has housing reconstruction been progressed? In Iwate Prefecture, three years after the tsunami, 35,000 people still live in temporary housing out of an estimated 252,000 throughout Japan, including those residing in private apartments provided free as temporary housing (as of January 2014). Can this status be considered acceptable and normal in the course of reconstruction?

According to recent statistics published by the prefecture (as of January 2014), over 65 percent of the citizens in afflicted areas feel that the recovery as a whole is delayed or a little delayed. Among all aspects of the recovery, "support for disaster victims with regard to living and housing" and "city planning for disaster resilience: escape routes, roads, schools, and hospitals" are counted as priorities. Notably, they remarked there that "housing and residential development" is of highest need in the advancement of recovery; of the various priorities it is the slowest to progress in the phase of reconstruction. So it can be observed that, in terms of housing reconstruction, there is a big gap between the expectations of the people and the actual progress: it may be presumed that the housing reconstruction process is delayed, which is worthy of examination.

Generally speaking, delay in recovery may cause the loss of original community ties that give meaning to live in a location, leading residents to leave without returning, and progressing depopulation of the area.

What causes the recovery to be delayed? There are many factors for the delay; though mutually related, some are becoming conspicuous as the recovery process continues. Let us discuss some of those factors from the perspective of the spatial planning inclusive of housing (NRA 2015).

1 Limited land resources: The preferable option for housing recovery would be for people to relocate to safer areas. However, land resources for housing in the coastal areas of Iwate Prefecture are very limited. To resettle on higher ground, the reclamation of mountains is required. The limited land resources have influenced the local conditions, making low-income families struggle. Even when limited land is secured, the affected people have to move to narrower plot sizes than they had before the disaster; they are therefore becoming increasingly dissatisfied with the relocation planning.
2 Shortage of building materials: Post-disaster prices of construction materials have escalated in the market and become short in supply as a result of the urgent needs. The increase in market prices leads to delay in public procurement, thereby postponing the original reconstruction schedule.
3 Shortages in the workforce: Both professional personnel and general labor have been short in supply. Certainly, the region needs more experts for technical assistance in spatial planning. Ironically, in order to deploy and distribute experts in land acquisition, for example, to each district, even more, personnel are needed to administrate the expert personnel.
4 Failure of public tenders: Engineering companies have reduced their business capacity in recent decades due to the continuing recession. Thirty percent of tenders for public utility works have failed to find a successful bidder. Perhaps it is not viable for them to perform the works even at the cheapest successful price under the prevailing conditions of shortages in the workforce and materials.
5 Poor collaboration between governments: Among the factors giving impetus to recovery are "organizational, legal and policy frameworks" (UN/ISDR 2007a, p. 2) as well as disaster prevention and preparedness. Reinforcing national and local government capacities is also central to the concept of recovery.

The National Reconstruction Agency (NRA) was established under the terms of the Basic Act 2011, the main role of which is to speed up reconstruction operations, act as the contact point for reconstruction-related requests from local governments in disaster-affected areas and promote initiatives between various branches of government at the national level: in a sense, it is the "Control Tower" providing a thorough view over the disaster-afflicted areas.

Some local governments, however, have not only criticized the national government for being non-responsive to their requests but also expressed their dissatisfaction with the performance of the NRA as the Control Tower (*Iwate Nippo*, March 2, 2014; *Asahi Shimbun*, March 8, 2014). It is suggested that this problem is caused by the structure of the NRA's personnel, who have been scraped together via secondments from their original positions within the national government, so they are likely to be subjective to the wishes of their national government ministries rather than the urgent needs of local governments (*Asahi Shimbun*, March 8, 2014).

The NRA is authorized by law to make recommendations to other ministries to promote integrated reconstruction policies. However, this power has not been exercised so far. Under the powerful, complex and non-integrated Japanese ministry system, the NRA does not seem to take the initiative as the "Control Tower" and exert considerable influence over the other ministries (Johnson and Olshansky 2013).

6 Too many contracts: for public works to be set in motion, prefectural and municipal governments have to make private contracts independently with all parties who hold rights in the lands earmarked for reconstruction sites. However, before the contracts can be concluded, there are many parcels of land where finalization of ownership is required for the works to be registered, but the land is co-owned, inherited, used as collateral for loans or the whereabouts of the owners are unknown; municipalities must decide whether they await negotiation or compulsorily acquire the land.

4.3 Suspending matters of contract

Focusing on the last factor detailed above, the municipalities in Iwate Prefecture are required to conclude 20,000 private contracts to take control of lands required for town planning. Not all of them are supposed to be resolved via voluntary transactions. Sometimes they propose to use the power of eminent domain to acquire the remainder of land from unwilling owners and provide minimal compensation. However, whether lands should be voluntary purchased, exchanged or compulsory seized is a difficult question to answer because sometimes many pieces of land are subject to complex co-ownership arrangements as they were registered over 100 years ago. In those cases, a great number of the initial owners' successors must be identified in order to negotiate with them. Some lands have also been used as collateral for loans. Many refugees from the disaster cannot afford to take out a second loan to buy a new house. Moreover, even when the owners are identified, some of them are missing. In those cases, legal procedures for abandoned property must be followed, which takes at least seven months.

Table 13.1 shows reported findings of rights holders. Out of 4,759 contracts only addressing prefectural reconstruction projects, 1,501 cases involve rights holders that are difficult to identify and negotiate with for various reasons such as co-ownership, inheritance, absenteeism and unknown ownership.

For example, in a model case under a prompt recovery scheme conducted by the city of Kamaishi, the local office was confronted with a situation where a

Table 13.1 Reported findings of rights holders (as of November 2013)

Suspending matters of contracts	*Number (a)*[1]	*Ratio(a/4,759) %*	*Remarks*
Co-ownership/inheritance (number of rights holders)	850	17.9	75% inheritance not yet succeeded
Collateral	673	14.1	
Absentee	28	0.6	
Unknown	29	0.6	
Duplication deduction	(79)	(1.6)	
Total	1,501	31.6	

Source: provided by Iwate Prefecture and translated by the author.

Note

1 The numbers listed refer to the number of contracts (not land lots) in 146 districts where the investigation into rights holders has been completed, out of 162 districts that require land acquisition.

parcel of land was registered by 41 holders over 100 years ago but not subject to any subsequent succession procedures; the presumptive heirs of each of the 41 original owners needed to be identified for the purpose of contract negotiation, which consequently equated to a total of 601 heirs (Iwate Prefecture 2014b).

It seems that some of the lands that were registered in the Meiji period (1868–1912) as co-owned under the names of local representatives are often considered to be land held for the common good of local people as used since old times. It is said that following Japan's societal modernization, common property used under the feudal system was converted into western style co-ownership, with provisional registration that did not coincide with the actual circumstances of traditional land use.

Based on those findings of Table 13.1, it is estimated that 4,000 contracts are pending out of the total of 20,000 over the whole of Iwate Prefecture, including municipal-level reconstruction.

Notwithstanding some measures furthering the reconstruction process, municipal governments are still annoyed with time constraints.

Even if they deal with some land under compulsory purchase measures, some other projects, such as group relocation and fishing village projects for housing, are not within the scope of expropriation law, so the reservation of the lands are subject to the owners' willingness to sell or exchange the lands. For these projects to be launched, they have to find the vast number of stakeholders, induce them to participate in succession procedures and identify the contracting parties. As these processes are private matters dealing on a voluntary basis with individual properties owned by affected people, it undoubtedly takes a long time to negotiate with them.

5 Procedural barriers on expropriation of land

In response to these delay factors, in the middle of 2013 the NRA introduced measures to speed up housing reconstruction, such as improved administration of absentees' property and inheritance, and shortening periods within the eminent domain process, thereby bringing the schedule ahead by a few months. But Iwate Prefecture advocated that the system of eminent domain itself should be more drastically reformed for prompt recovery because the present system still necessitates enormous business formalities and long processing times.

This issue relates to the present legal procedure of land expropriation. Some parts of the public reconstruction works by the prefecture, such as public disaster housing, can be performed under the Land Expropriation Act. This enables governments to compulsorily purchase private lands, seeking a balance between the promotion of public interests and protection of private rights.

The process of expropriation is as follows and normally takes over two years, even without the factors mentioned above which have been causing delay.

1 Following public hearings, the ministry acknowledges the public benefit of the proposed work.
2 The local government (entrepreneur) identifies the relationship of the rights over the land and prepares registration documents for the lands registry.
3 The expropriation committee assesses the amount of compensation to be paid to each holder of a right coinciding with the changing of the real estate registration.

Local lawyers and prefectural officials responding to the prefecture's advocacy for legal reforms have recently proposed a new scheme: to empower the Council for Reconstruction (at the local government level) to acknowledge the public interest at step 1 and set up an independent agency that coordinates an integrated approach to steps 2 and 3 in the process. In response to this proposal, the Recovery Agency, being concerned that such shortcuts might conflict with the rule of law, has set a different solution to deal with the problem under a revision to the Act for Special Zones for Reconstruction 2011 (April, 2014).

Pursuant to the new system, local government can set forth simultaneously steps 2 and 3 in the process without an inventory and apply the provisions of the Land Expropriation Act in the case of collective relocation of more than 50 houses. Iwate Prefecture estimates that, even with this system, the process will speed up at most by one year and finds its effect as still unforeseeable. Still, this system indeed might endanger the due process of law because it does not seem to adequately secure public participation and protect private rights, while the original proposal by local groups could secure the input of affected peoples' opinions and fair compensation for expropriation by an independent board (Yoshie 2014, p. 26).

6 Promptness reconsidered with other elements

As mentioned before, delays in housing recovery may cause serious problems. While promptness is certainly one of the main targets of reconstruction, how to achieve it and its quality are different matters to be considered.

While progress has been seen to some extent by the legal measures and the special law, reconstruction processes have been chronically hampered by delaying factors. The reaction from the present legal regime seems to be based in improvements to existing laws on an ad hoc basis through broader application and relaxation. This technique seems to apply band-aid solutions. The legal regime for the reconstruction should be based on "disaster risk reduction" with a strong institutional framework (UN/ISDR 2007a, 2007b).

More or less, the present legal regime, as seen in the assembling of lands and expropriation, is presumed to operate in normal times under the due process of law. The regime of disaster law for reconstruction, by contrast, is expected to work in the context of incident management.

The Japanese Constitution guarantees the protection of property rights as prescribed by Article 29(1) and private property may be taken for *public use upon just compensation therefor.* Furthermore, Article 31 stipulates that due process under the law is applicable to administrative procedures, such as compensation for public use.

The approach by the national government and NRA is seemingly in accordance with the present hierarchy of norms, involving required procedures that comply with the Constitution and land expropriation laws. However, an ad hoc approach could backfire. Local governments are still required to exercise the power of expropriation cautiously, as myopic legal revisions may undermine the important step of public hearings in the name of "promptness". In this regard, the due process of law can take a role in favor of citizens, not only in solving conflicts between governments and citizens. Acceleration of reconstruction should also be an outcome involving fairness and community participation via due process. It is asserted that the increase of information flow, including providing information to citizens and facilitating communication among recovery participants, is a key element of disaster recovery and the most fundamental way to address the challenge of the tension between speed and deliberation in the recovery process (Johnson and Olshansky 2013, pp. 18–22). It follows that the quality of promptness is the key point. Human-centered promptness guaranteed by the due process can be authentic promptness.

In addition, promptness itself is not always welcomed in the process of disaster recovery. The author finds that, as time goes by, some projects in the afflicted areas are viewed as undesirable by local residents who are seeking their revision. For example, even though some public disaster housing has been completed three years after the GEJE, vacancy rates are over 10 percent because they have been built in areas inconvenient for permanent relocation; suffering from a lack of access to shopping, schools, hospitals and so on (*Iwate Nippo*, January 14, 2014; *Mainichi Shimbun*, March 2, 2014). From the author's interviews with the residents of temporary housing, some of them cannot afford to relocate to disaster public housing and are forced to stay in temporary housing on a permanent basis. If relocation is not conducted in accordance with their wishes, it may lead to "considerable social and psychological disruption, adding to the stress experienced by disaster victims" (Phillips 2009, p. 212). Even if the recovery is protracted, residents could be patient where they are well informed, persuaded, and finally satisfied with the result (Johnson and Olshansky 2013, p. 20; Sandel 2013, pp. 210–218).

7 Concluding remarks

Housing reconstruction mainly refers to the physical act of rebuilding houses. In contrast, housing recovery means "a process that involves communities and officials in a series of steps and stages through which households and businesses move at varying rates toward reestablishing normal routines" (Phillips 2009, p. 503); it is an ongoing process rather than an end point (Howitt 2013). In terms of long-term recovery, housing recovery requires more elements than promptness alone. As well as promptness, recovery should include human-centered recovery, deliberation, local needs, reconstruction of infrastructure, DRR, BBB, equity and recovery justice, and effective support for the vulnerable; however, these elements are competing and often difficult to reconcile (Howitt 2013). By contrast, if a suitably long time is taken, as if the town as it existed before the GEJE was being rebuilt over a period of decades, these elements could be synthesized. It would be naturally difficult to synchronize them in a short period.

Adherence to the established legal regime may hinder the progress of reconstruction. In this regard, the legal regime is required to be permissive of acceleration, while wary of jeopardizing the due process of law that ensures citizens' rights to the community. Then the quality of promptness will be more cardinal, compared with promptness driven only by the government side and physical reconstruction.

What is realistically needed at the local level is the community-based sustainable recovery in which those discrete goals described above compete and appropriately incorporate local needs; a process with speed, quality and timely assistance. In this sense, the legal regime should be more resourceful to find possibilities and feasibilities for a disaster-recovery continuum.

References

Abe, Yasutaka (1995) *Law and Policy in Big Earthquakes* (in Japanese), Tokyo: Nihon-hyouronsha.

Beck, Ulrich (1992) *Risk Society: Towards a New Modernity*, London: SAGE Publications.

Fan, Lilianne (2013) *Disaster as Opportunity? Building Back Better in Aceh, Myanmar and Haiti*, HPG Working Paper, London: Overseas Development Institute.

Farber, Daniel A. (2007) "Disaster Law and Inequality", *Law & Inequality*, Vol. 25, pp. 297–321.

Farber, Daniel A., Chen, Jim., Verchick, Robert R.M. and Grow Sun, Lisa (2010) *Disaster Law and Policy, 2nd ed.*, New York: Aspen Publishers.

Howitt, Arnold M. (2013) "Perspectives on Disaster Recovery", *The Canon Institute for Global Studies*. www.canon-igs.org/event/report/20130322_1750.html (accessed June 10, 2015).

Ikuta, Osato (2010) *Law and Machinery of Disaster* (in Japanese), Tokyo: Toshindo.

Ikuta, Osato (2013) *Disaster Law* (in Japanese), Tokyo: Shinzansha.

Iwate Prefecture (2014a) *Iwate Moving toward Reconstruction.* www.pref.iwate.jp/fukkounougoki/joukyou/033256.html (accessed June 10, 2015).

Iwate Prefecture (2014b) "Acceleration Measures of Site Acquisition pertaining to Reconstruction Projects from Great East Japan Earthquake" (in Japanese), *Youchi Journal*, Vol. 4, pp. 21–28.

Iwate Prefecture (2015) *Proposal from Iwate Prefecture about Disaster Risk Reduction and Reconstruction.* www.pref.iwate.jp/seisaku/bousaikaigi/033444.html (accessed June 10, 2015).

Johnson, Laurie A. and Olshansky, Robert B. (2013) "The Road to Recovery: Governing Post Disaster Reconstruction", *Lincoln Institute of Land Policy Land Lines*, July, pp. 14–21.

Kaneko, Yuka (2014) "State Involvement and Fate of Civil Rights in Post-Disaster Recovery: An Asian Comparative Approach to the Great East Japan Earthquake" (in Japanese), in Koyanagi, Shunichiro, ed. *Disaster and Law*, Tokyo: Kokusaishyoin.

National Reconstruction Agency (NRA) (2015) "Current Status of Reconstruction and Challenges", Tokyo: NRA.

Phillips, Brenda D. (2009) *Disaster Recovery*, Boca Raton, FL: CRC Press.

Sandel, Michael J. (2013) *Let's Talk about Justice in the World and a Special Lecture in the Tohoku University* (in Japanese), Tokyo: Hayakawa Publishing.

UN/ISDR (2007a) *Hyogo Framework for Action 2005–2015: Building the Resilience of Nations and Communities to Disasters* (A/CONF206/6), Geneva: United Nations Office for Disaster Risk Reduction.

UN/ISDR (2007b) *Words into Action: A Guide for Implementing the Hyogo Framework*, Geneva: United Nations Office for Disaster Risk Reduction.

UN/ISDR (2014) *Progress and Challenges in Disaster Risk Reduction*, Geneva: United Nations Office for Disaster Risk Reduction.

Verchick, Robert R.M. (2012) "Disaster Justice: The Geography of Human Capability", *Duke Environmental Law & Policy Forum*, Vol. 23, pp. 23–71.

Yasumoto, Norio (1995) "Disaster Recovery and Public Participation" (in Japanese), *Jurist*, Vol. 1070, pp. 87–92.

Yoshie, Nobuhiro (2014) "Some Problems on the Special Act in Acquisition of Lands for Reconstruction" (in Japanese), *Shintaku Forum*, 2014(2), pp. 21–27.

14 The complexities of land acquisition and zoning after the Canterbury, New Zealand earthquakes

Elizabeth Toomey

1 Introduction

The first of the serious earthquakes that occurred in the Canterbury region of New Zealand happened on September 2010. Immediately after that, Parliament passed the Canterbury Earthquake Response and Recovery Act 2010, which came into force on 15 September 2010. A second major earthquake occurred in the region on 22 February 2011. It was a devastating event that struck in the heart of the province's main city, Christchurch, and resulted in substantial loss of life and property destruction. On 28 March 2011 the Canterbury Earthquake Recovery Authority (CERA) was established.[1] The Bill that became the Canterbury Earthquake Recovery Act 2011 (CER Act 2011) was introduced to Parliament and passed through all parliamentary stages on 12 April 2011. It received Royal Assent on 18 April 2011 and came into force on 19 April 2011.

This chapter looks at Canterbury's progress as the province enters its fourth year of recovery. It focuses specifically on land recovery, namely the Crown's powers both to zone and to acquire land. It also looks briefly at the impetus of the overarching first insurer, the Earthquake Commission (EQC), and provides a snapshot of Canterbury's general recovery amid residents' continuing frustrations over rebuilding and building repair.

2 Insurance and the Earthquake Commission

The adequacy of a first loss insurance scheme for natural disasters is dealt with comprehensively in Chapter 9.[2] This chapter makes only brief mention of this extremely contentious aspect of Canterbury's earthquake recovery. The divide between the insured, and the uninsured or uninsurable, was a fundamental aspect of the Quake Outcasts' litigation detailed comprehensively in this chapter.

For any New Zealander who insures his or her buildings, insurance premiums include a low-level premium for earthquake damage. The earthquake premium is collected by the Earthquake Commission (EQC), a government-owned entity that was originally established in 1945 to provide earthquake and war damage cover for purchasers of fire insurance. Subsequently cover for natural disasters was included and, later still, cover for war damage ceased. This Natural Disaster Fund, called upon for isolated small disasters, faced its first major challenge when the Canterbury earthquakes hit. EQC's responsibility involves the building's replacement value to the amount as specified in the insurance policy, or $100,000, whichever is the lesser.[3] Any balance is the responsibility of the homeowner's private insurer. A whole region of dwelling owners lodged claims against it. In an attempt to limit its exposure, EQC adopted the stance that it was only responsible for one single big event, not a series of earthquakes. This was challenged successfully by the insurance industry in extensive litigation proceedings: *Re Earthquake Commission.*[4] The essential issue addressed by the High Court of New Zealand was how EQC cover responds to homeowners who made more than one claim for damage suffered in more than one earthquake where the damage exceeded, in aggregate, $100,000. Was EQC liable to pay up to the amount of $100,000 in respect of each occurrence of natural disaster damage to the residential building or was EQC liable for no more than $100,000 in total for the aggregate of all natural disaster damage caused by multiple events? The Court, after a careful analysis of the relevant legislation,[5] concluded that EQC was responsible for every significant earthquake or aftershock. This has led to significant delays in property settlements. Even four years after the February 2011 earthquake, there are still many disaffected homeowners awaiting repairs to their damaged homes.

3 The government's decision to zone Christchurch properties

Very soon after the 22 February 2011 earthquake, officials from Treasury, EQC and CERA began considering the impact of land and property damage in the Christchurch areas and the identification of the worst affected areas. Cabinet delegated power to act to eight Cabinet Ministers (the Cabinet Committee), of whom one was the Minister for Earthquake Recovery (the Minister), to make Cabinet decisions on matters relating to Canterbury earthquake land damage and remediation issues. Spurred on by a further serious earthquake on 13 June 2011, that group reached agreement on a detailed strategy for identifying "zones" of Christchurch land and for the Crown to offer to purchase properties in the worst affected areas. These worst affected areas were zoned red. Throughout this chapter, these properties are referred to as "red-zoned" properties.[6]

4 The empowering provisions to acquire land

The CER Act 2011 empowers the government to acquire property. The three pivotal statutory provisions for this chapter comprise ss 53, 54 and 55.[7]

4.1 Acquiring or disposing of property: s 53

The chief executive of CERA may, in the name of the Crown, "purchase or otherwise acquire, hold, sell, exchange, mortgage, lease, and dispose of land…"[8] If any such land is no longer required and is available for disposal, nothing in ss 40–42 of the Public Works Act 1981 (PWA 1981) (the offer-back provisions)[9] applies, whether by sale, exchange or otherwise, except as provided for in s 58.[10] If, however, the Minister, by notice in the *Gazette*, declares land held under the CER Act 2011 to be held for a public work in terms of the PWA 1981, offer-back requirements under that Act continue to apply.[11]

4.2 Notice of intention to take land: s 54

Proclamation: s 55

PROCLAMATION MUST BE REGISTERED AGAINST THE COMPUTER REGISTER TO THE LAND: S 56

The Minister may acquire land compulsorily by causing a notice of intention to take land in the name of the Crown to be published in the Gazette and twice publicly notified.[12]

The Minister must lodge a copy of the *Gazette* notice with the Registrar-General of Land, who must register it without fee against the computer register affected.[13]

There is no right of objection to a notice of intention to take land.[14]

If the relevant notice of intention to take in the *Gazette* has been registered in accordance with s 54, the Minister may recommend that the Governor-General issue a proclamation taking the land,[15] and the Governor-General may so declare.[16] The proclamation must then be published in the Gazette and publicly notified but is not invalidated by any error, defect or delay in any such publication or notification.[17] Unless otherwise provided in the proclamation, the CER Act 2011 or any other Act, the land specified in the proclamation under s 55 becomes absolutely vested in fee simple in the Crown and freed and discharged from all mortgages, charges, claims, estates or interests on the fourteenth day after the day the proclamation is published in the Gazette.[18]

If the land is compulsorily acquired under s 55, the Crown succeeds to all rights, entitlements and benefits that the owner has or may have against either the insurer of the land or the insurer of any building or other property on the land.[19]

The Minister must lodge every proclamation with the Register-General of Land, who must register it without fee against the computer register to the land.[20] Any error in any proclamation does not of itself prevent registration in respect of titles to land validly affected.[21] To avoid doubt, registration does not result in the cancellation of the title.[22]

5 The residential red-zoning decision

On 22 June 2011, the Cabinet Committee made the decision to create the four zones and also decided on the policy for the making of offers to purchase insured residential properties in the red zone. In its report dated 24 June 2011, the offer to purchase was in the following terms:[23]

53. I propose that the following offers be extended to landowners in the Red Zones.

Insured residential properties

54. Insured residential property owners will have the choice of two offer packages:

Option A

55. The Crown will offer to purchase the entire property at the 2007 capital value rating valuation (less any land and dwelling insurance payments already made). The Crown will also take an assignment of all earthquake related insurance claims. There will be a process through which any property owners who consider that there is a material discrepancy between the 2007 rating valuation and the market value of their property (e.g. because of subsequent improvements) can raise their concerns.

OR

Option B

56. The Crown will offer to purchase the land only at the greater of the following (less any EQC land payments already made):

    (a) 2007 land value rating valuation; or
    (b) EQC valuation for the minimum lot size applicable.

    The Crown will also take an assignment of the EQC land claim, and landowners will be free to pursue their private insurance company for any other insurance claims they have.

Subsequently, in August 2011, the chief executive exercised his power under s 53 of the CER Act 2011 to make offers to insured residents. The process involved seeking the consent of the insured owners to receive an offer and then making an offer to them. The fact sheet accompanying the offer made to each resident included the following statement:

> *What will happen to my property if I decide that I do not want to accept the Crown offer?*
> If you decide that you do not want to accept the Crown offer you should be aware that:
> The Council will not be installing new services in the residential red zone.
> If only a few people remain in a street and/or area, the Council and other utility providers may reach the view that it is no longer feasible or practical to continue to maintain services to the remaining properties.
> Insurers may cancel or refuse to renew insurance policies for properties in the residential red zone.

> While no decisions have been made on the ultimate future of the land in the residential red zones, CERA does have powers under the Canterbury Earthquake Recovery Act 2011 to require you to sell your property to CERA for its market value at that time. If a decision is made in the future to use these powers to acquire your property, the market value could be substantially lower than the amount that you would receive under the Crown's offer.

6 The results

A recovery milestone was reached on 31 January 2014 when the final flat land red zone settlements were completed. In total, 7,349 properties were zoned red and since the first red zone announcements were made in 2011, thousands of property owners have accepted the Crown offer and moved on from the worst affected areas. The cost to the Crown has been approximately $1.5 billion.

The then chief executive of CERA, Mr Sutton, made the following comment:[24]

> What we now know for certain, is that the majority of residential Red Zone property owners were able to stay close to their neighbourhoods. Based on Census 2013 information, over half of all movements by people in areas with high earthquake damage were within just four kilometres. This is particularly important for maintaining that sense of community belonging and pride that we as Cantabrians are known for.

6.1 Abdication to the free market

Despite the above public comment, there was no effort, by either local or central government, to facilitate movement of local communities, or parts of them, as communities. Landowners who took the Crown payout were left to fight in the free market, where housing demand quickly outstripped supply. Anecdotally, rapidly rising price rises left some residents unable to purchase a replacement property or, in some cases, purchasing a property far below the standard of housing to which they were accustomed. Individuals have, largely, made their own choices as to relocation[25] within the constraints of a free-market economy which has left the less wealthy only very restricted options.[26] Whether this has actually led to fractured communities and what long-term effects of dislocation may have arisen will be investigated in a major research project being conducted out of the University of Canterbury.

7 The Christchurch Central Business District

The Minister established a special unit within CERA, the Christchurch Central Development Unit (CCDU), which was tasked with developing a 100-day blueprint for the central city that would provide for the rebuild and create certainty designed to encourage and support investors.

The blueprint was released on 31 July 2012. It identified areas of land in the Central Business District (CBD) to be used for the development of anchor projects and precincts. The projects include a convention centre, Cathedral Square, a justice and emergency services precinct, a metro sports hub, a multi-purpose sports stadium and a performing arts and music precinct. The CBD area will be surrounded by green-space frames.[27]

Approximately 761 private ownership lots were affected and any land or building that does not fit within the scheme has been, or will be, acquired either by CERA or by the Minister. Pursuant to s 53 of the CER Act 2011, CERA has negotiated with affected landowners. The process is different from that of the residential red-zone. The negotations are simply the price for which the Crown will take the land, buildings included. In the event of those negotiations failing, the properties are subject to the compulsory acquisition powers under ss 54–56 of the CER Act 2011.

While the Christchurch community adjusts to the concept of a large-scale government land acquisition, progress on this front is proceeding pursuant to the Act's mandate for "focused, timely, and expedited recovery".[28]

8 The results

It is clear from the CCDU website[29] that a significant number of the property lots have been acquired by settlement negotiations under s 53 of the Act. Nonetheless, the string of notices of intention to take land compulsorily under s 54 of the Act signals that compulsory acquisition is the end point of any breakdown in settlement negotiations.

As at May 2015, several of the precincts are under construction and one has been completed. A press release on 27 November 2014[30] noted that the $300 million state-of-the-art Justice and Emergency Services Precinct had reached a key milestone with the final concrete pour and the installation of the first cranes. The precinct will be home to the Ministry of Justice, New Zealand Police, Department of Corrections, New Zealand Fire Service, St John, local and regional civil defence and emergency management teams, and the judiciary. It will comprise three buildings, each with five levels and 19 court rooms, and will accommodate 1,100 staff and 900 daily visitors. It is due for completion in early 2017.

Other key projects well under way include the Avon River Precinct, the Retail Precinct and the Health Precinct. The Bus Interchange was completed in May 2015.

The mandate of a high-profile transport project team, working very closely with Stronger Christchurch Infrastructure Rebuild Team (SCIRT), is to ensure that all the Anchor Projects link up and support each other, as envisaged by the CCDU Blueprint. This transport component – a plan called An Accessible City – will:[31]

> make real the vision of a green, vibrant, accessible and prosperous city: not just making roads for cars, but making them human scale and welcoming for people to walk, cycle, drive and gather within. These are the sort of things that make a city great.

9 The government's musings over vacant or uninsured red-zoned land

When the government released its residential red-zoning decision on 22 June 2011, it postponed any decision on other red-zoned land. This chapter concentrates on the class where properties had no insurance – either vacant land (it is impossible to insure vacant land in New Zealand) or uninsured residential properties. The decision for these red-zoned owners was released 15 months later, on 13 September 2012.

9.1 The background behind this September 2012 decision

A Cabinet decision was made on 3 September 2012.[32] A supporting paper, signed by the Minister on 31 August 2012, stated that, in relation to properties with no insurance, there were three broad options. They comprised:

a no offer;
b an offer at a reduced rate in valuation; or
c an offer on the same terms as for insured residential properties (that is, the same as the 100 per cent offer).

The first option was not recommended. The Committee considered there were "good reasons to support exit from the red zones".

The third option was also not recommended. The Cabinet paper stated:

> There are strong arguments for not extending an offer to these property categories on the same terms as for insured properties. It would compensate for uninsured damage, be unfair to other red zone property owners who have been paying insurance premiums, and it creates a moral hazard in that incentives to insure in the future where insurance is available are potentially eroded.

The second option was supported as the Committee considered it recognised that red zone properties were worth a lot less than they had been before the earthquakes, that the property damage they had suffered was not insured and that there was some residual property value.

The paper recorded 65 vacant sections, with market values of potentially only 10 per cent of pre-earthquake values. The Minister recommended 50 per cent of the rateable value on the basis that this would:

> ensure that the offer is not below the post-earthquake value (given individual properties' values may vary from the 10% estimate), and help support the signal that the Government wants to encourage property owners to move out of the red zone.

The paper recorded 50 uninsured improved properties in the red zones.[33] It also noted that some of these owners had consciously chosen not to insure, whereas others had been insured previously but did not meet the insurance continuity requirements for the 100 per cent offer. A 50 per cent offer of rateable land offer was suggested, with property owners retaining salvage rights to uninsured buildings. The objective for the 50 per cent offers was given as follows: "This offer supports the signalling objective for the red zone while providing some support for recovering elsewhere and acknowledging that the owners were not fully insured throughout the whole process." Following the Committee's decisions, the Minister publicly announced the 50 per cent offers on 13 September 2012 and material sent out with the offers included the same statement about the possible detrimental outcome for those who chose not to accept the offer as had been sent to the 100 per cent offerees.

10 The result – extensive litigation ensues

In *Fowler Developments Ltd v Chief Executive for the Canterbury Earthquake*,[34] an unincorporated group of land and property owners (the Quake Outcasts) together with a property developer (all owners of red-zoned land that was either vacant land or uninsured residential properties) applied for judicial review, the genesis of which was the decision-making behind the actual zoning of land after the earthquakes and subsequently the making of the 50 per cent offers to purchase these types of properties. In particular they considered that their treatment was unequal by comparison to that afforded to insured residential property owners who received a 100 per cent buy-out offer.

This chapter addresses the three Court decisions, all of which provide a rare glimpse of the intersection of public law and real property law as it is assessed under the overriding umbrella of New Zealand's emergency legislation, the CER Act 2011.[35]

It is concerned primarily with the fates of owners of uninsured (and uninsurable) vacant land but the litigation spreads across both these owners and those who could insure their residential property and didn't.

In the High Court, Panckhurst J determined that the original red zone decision (June 2011) had to be made pursuant to the powers contained in the CER Act 2011. The defendant contended that that decision could be, and was, made under the residual freedom of the government to do anything that is not in conflict with any obligation under common law or statute (commonly known as the "third source" of authority). It was common ground that the residual freedom did not provide authority to take action impacting on the rights of those affected by the action.

Panckhurst J described the combination of zoning decisions, purchase offers, announcements and a "clearance strategy" as:[36]

> essentially destructive of the residential zoning designations of the red zone land. In reality the decisions meant that over time the red zone would cease to be residential, and would become open space. In the meantime, the residential zones under the district plan subsisted, but in reality were no longer operative.

As a result, he concluded that the decision affected the rights of the owners to the enjoyment of their homes. Confirming the principle in *Attorney-General v De Keyser's Royal Hotel*,[37] he concluded that the zoning and purchase decisions were made under the CER Act 2011 rather than by prerogative power or the third source of power. That conclusion then led to an investigation as to whether the decision had been made correctly under the Act and Panckhurst J concluded that it had not. He held that there had been no deliberative process as required by the purposes of the Act as stipulated in s 3.[38]

The decision was appealed: *Minister for Earthquake Recovery v Fowler Developments Ltd*.[39] A fundamental issue in the appeal was whether the executive could exercise its residual freedom. The Court of Appeal held that it could. It considered that the June 2011 decision did not interfere with the rights of the respondents. It approved the finding of Asher J in *O'Loughlin v Tower Insurance*[40] that the red zone did not create the earthquake damage. It observed:[41]

> Even if the combined effect of the red zone and the 100 per cent offer is considered, we do not see these as having any legal effect on the rights or liberties of the affected residents. That is not to say they have not had a significant practical impact on land owners. But … it must be remembered that the creation of the red zone was a recognition of the severe damage caused by the earthquakes. It did not create the damage. The fact that land in the red zone is not, and will not for some time, be suitable for houses is a state of affairs caused by the earthquakes not by the decision to create the red zone. The respondents do not challenge the correctness of the assessment that land in the red zone is not suitable for houses. While the impact of the earthquakes has been devastating for the respondents and the red zone property owners in general, we do not consider that the June 2011 decision has interfered with their legal rights and liberties.

As a result, it concluded that the decision to declare the red zone was simply a dissemination of information made under the residual freedom banner. Nor (disagreeing with the lower Court) did it consider that the June 2011 decision should have been made under the CER Act 2011 (as a statute that "occupied the field" – an exception to the third source of power). Thus, the June 2011 decision to red zone was held to be lawfully made.

However, the Court of Appeal (agreeing with the lower Court on this point) concluded that the 50 per cent offer decision in September 2012 was not made in accordance with the recovery purposes of the CER Act 2011. It observed that the decision by the chief executive to make the 50 per cent offers was authorised by Cabinet and it was clear the Cabinet deliberations did not take into account the purposes of the CER Act (s 3). This contrasted starkly with the Cabinet deliberations in relation to the June 2011 decision where that did happen.

The Cabinet minutes of 3 September 2012 gave three "good reasons" for not extending the 100 per cent offer to properties without insurance:

a it would compensate for uninsured damage;
b it would be unfair to those who had paid for insurance; and
c it would create a moral hazard.

Recovery was not mentioned.

The Court made a declaration that the September 2012 decision by the chief executive to offer to purchase the properties of owners of vacant land and owners of uninsured improved properties in the red zone was not lawfully made.

The Quake Outcasts appealed to the Supreme Court, New Zealand's highest Court.[42]

In a majority decision, *Quake Outcasts v Minister for Earthquake Recovery*,[43] the Court ruled that the Cabinet Committee's zoning decision was illegal.

It did not accept the Crown's argument that, in making that zoning decision, the government was merely providing information to the public. After noting that the Cabinet committee made a number of decisions on important matter, Glazebrook J, delivering the majority decision, observed:[44]

> We are not suggesting that the decisions that were taken by the Cabinet committee and announced publicly on 23 July 2011 were not sensible decisions. They may indeed, given the situation facing Christchurch, have been seen by the Committee as the only sensible decisions that could be made. This, however, does not rob them of their character as decisions.
>
> ...
>
> The fact that decisions are based on information and that some or all of the information on which the decisions are based is communicated to the public at the same time as the decisions does not mean that the decisions are subsumed in the information upon which they are based. Nor does it mean that communication of the decisions is merely communication of information.

The Court considered that the CER Act 2011 "covered the field" and therefore the procedures under that Act should have been used for any earthquake recovery measures, including land zoning decisions. On that premise, the Court held that zoning decisions should have been made pursuant to the Recovery Strategy under the Act[45] but conceded that, because of the necessity to act quickly to restore confidence in the Christchurch community, a Recovery Plan[46] could, and indeed should, have been used instead:[47]

> This intention to facilitate and encourage voluntary withdrawal reinforces the link between the red zone decisions, the purchase offers and recovery from the earthquake and also reinforces the significant character of the decisions. It also highlights the need for such measures to have been the subject of a Recovery Plan. This would have required at least the minimum consultation provided by s 20 of the Act. Indeed, given the significance of the decisions made for all of Christchurch and in particular for those in the red zones, it may be that further consultation, albeit expedited, would have been required.

It was held that the decisions could not be characterised as funding decisions (and therefore not reviewable). The decisions were made outside the Act and that "undermined the safeguards, community participation and reviews mandated by … [it]".[48] Given the close relationship between the zoning decisions and the purchase offers and an area-wide approach, the Court concluded that at least the broad outlines of the purchase decisions should have been dealt with under the Recovery Plan processes. No s 53 offer could lawfully be made absent a Recovery Plan dealing with the red zoning decisions.

The Court also concluded that, while the insurance status of the properties (insured, uninsured or uninsurable) was not irrelevant, a number of relevant factors (including the wide applicability of the "moral hazard" argument; the fact that offers to the insured, not-for-profit organisations and owners of buildings under construction allowed for payment above that which was insured or uninsurable; and the concept that the harm suffered by the property owners related, at least to a degree, to government policy rather than insurance status) did not appear to have been taken into account in deciding whether or not there should have been differential treatment for the uninsured and uninsurable and, if so, the nature and extent of any differential.

Moreover, in making the decision as to any differential treatment of the uninsured or uninsurable, the recovery purpose of the Act had not been properly considered:[49]

> The area-wide nature of the decisions on the red zone suggests an area-wide community approach to recovery where practical.

The Court made a declaration that the decisions relating to the uninsured and uninsurable in September 2012 were not lawfully made. The Minister and the chief executive were directed to reconsider the decisions in light of the Court's judgment.

While the Court concluded that the June 2011 red zone measures should have been introduced under a Recovery Plan, in practical terms it was too late to implement this and "a declaration as to the unlawfulness of the June 2011 decisions would not serve any useful purpose and none is made".[50]

10.1 Observations

This chapter makes two brief but important observations[51] as to this ruling which was challenged stridently by one of the two dissenting judges.

First, the majority noted that participation from the affected communities, to the extent compatible with expedited recovery, was a key value to the Act. It also noted that, while the prescribed legislative mechanisms "may not be entirely suitable, convenient or perfectly 'aligned' with what the Executive desires to achieve"[52] this does not mean that statutory procedures should be bypassed. Therefore, the majority held that the community had to be consulted on zoning issues before decisions could be made. This was despite a Cabinet paper dated two days after the June 2011 decision that recorded the need for a "circuit breaker … to arrest the current decline in confidence and to form a solid basis for recovery".[53] There is a plethora of academic commentary as to what constitutes effective public consultation. One facet is particularly relevant. There are two types of public participation: "token" and "substantial". The former occurs when decisions are made at speed with little time for the public to engage; the latter when the result of the community's participation is influential on the final decision. In practical terms, it is difficult to imagine that, at that time, substantial participation would have occurred in zoning decisions made under a Recovery Plan.

Second, the majority refused to make an actual ruling on this point because it considered it was too late to reconsider the decision under a Recovery Plan. While this was made in the context of the residential red-zone decisions (by this stage, most had been purchased by the Crown) the June 2011 decision related to all zoning – green (land deemed suitable for repairs and rebuilding), red and the in-betweens (orange and white). The green zone was further divided into three categories: TC1, TC2 and TC3. TC3 land was deemed to be likely to suffer moderate to significant land damage in future earthquakes and any rebuilding is not allowed to commence before site-specific investigations are carried out. Four years on, rebuilding on TC3 land is extremely expensive. The author notes that that zoning mandate originates from an illegal decision.

11 Conclusion

In Christchurch and the surrounding environs, there is a cocktail of emotions. Many homeowners still await repairs to their homes and the four-year wait has sorely tried their patience. In the meantime, rebuilding in the Christchurch Business District has gained significant momentum in the past year and with designated completion dates for key projects, the city's inhabitants can finally see the green beginnings of a new city. There is no doubt that the city is recovering and there are tangible signs that life is slowly returning to normal. In the meantime, some of the Crown's processes throughout this recovery have been questioned. As this chapter describes, there has been significant high-level litigation that tests the Crown's ability to zone land and its rights and obligations under the CER Act 2011. The precedential value of this litigation will be a valuable resource worldwide for any future natural disasters.

Notes

1 It was established by an Order in Council made under the State Sector Act 1998.
2 See M. White, "Lessons From the Canterbury Earthquakes: Adequacy of a First Loss Insurance Scheme for Natural Disasters", at Chapter 9.
3 EQC's liability for household contents is $20,000.00. The High Court applied the same criteria for this liability as it did for EQC's building liability.
4 *Re Earthquake Commission* [2011] 3 NZLR 695.

5 Earthquake Commission Act 1993, s 18 ("Residential Buildings"); s 20 ("Personal Property"); Schedule 3, cl 6. ("Reinstatement of insurance on payment of claim"); and reg 5 of the Earthquake Commission Regulations 1993 ("Reinstatement of insurance on payment of claim").

6 The "red" zones were identified as areas where rebuilding might not occur in the short-to-medium term because the land was damaged beyond practical and timely repair, most buildings would generally be rebuilds, the areas were at high risk of further damage to land and buildings from low levels of shaking, floods or spring tides, and the infrastructure would need to be rebuilt. The "red" zone was one of four zones identified in the group's report to Cabinet on 24 June 2011. The other three comprised "green" (no significant issues, although subsequently this category was further divided), "orange" (further work required to identify extent of damage) and "white" (generally the Port Hills where the 13 June 2011 earthquake caused further extensive damage that required mapping and assessment).

7 For a detailed analysis of the effects of these provisions and accompanying appeal and compensation rights, see E. Toomey, "This Land is My Land, That Land is Your Land. A Challenge to Private Ownership: the Canterbury Earthquake Recovery Act 2011" (2012) *Property Law Review* (Syd) 2(2): 117–165.

8 Canterbury Earthquake Recovery Act 2011, s 53(1).

9 Sections 40–42 of the Public Works Act 1981. For detailed commentary on these statutory provisions, see E. Toomey, "The Offer-Back Provisions in the Public Works Act 1981 – A Fair Deal for the Parties" (1996) 6 *Canterbury Law Review* 272; E. Toomey, "The Offer Back Provisions of the Public Works Act 1981: A Minefield for the Crown or Local Authorities" (2001) 19(3) *New Zealand Universities Law Review* 310; and E. Toomey, "The Offer Back Provisions in the Public Works Act 1981: Former Owners Chase Potential Spoils" [2007] *New Zealand Law Review* 659.

10 Canterbury Earthquake Recovery Act 2011, s 58 ("Certain Land Must be Offered Back").

11 Canterbury Earthquake Recovery Act 2011, ss 53 (5) and (6).

12 Canterbury Earthquake Recovery Act 2011, s 54(1).

13 At s 54(3).

14 At s 54(5).

15 At s 55(3).

16 At s 55(4).

17 At s 55(5).

18 At s 55(6).

19 At s 55(7).

20 At s 56(1).

21 At s 56(3).

22 At s 56(5).

23 The author borrows this summary from the following two decisions: *Fowler Developments Ltd v Chief Executive of the Canterbury Earthquake Recovery Authority* [2014] 2 NZLR 54; *Minister for Canterbury Earthquake Recovery v Fowler Developments Ltd* [2014] 2 NZLR 587. See also E. Toomey, "The Canterbury Earthquake Recovery Act 2011: Land and Resource Management Issues" in J. Finn, E. Toomey (eds) *Legal Response to Natural Disasters* (Thomson Reuters, Wellington) (2015) at ch 11.

24 https://ccdu.govt.nz (accessed 17 November 2014).

25 For an interesting study of how individual reactions to disaster recovery are affected by expectations of government intentions and capabilities, see Emily Chamlee-Wright and Virgil Henry Storr, "Expectations of government's response to disaster", *Public Choice* (2010) 144: 253–274.

26 On the long-term effects of disaster recovery and social inequity, see Jeremy F. Pais and James R. Elliott, "Places as Recovery Machines: Vulnerability and Neighborhood Change after Major Hurricanes", *Social Forces* (2008) 86(4): 1415–1453.

27 For a map of the CBD blueprint, see https://ccdu.govt.nz (accessed 17 November 2014).
28 Canterbury Earthquake Recovery Act 2011, s 3(d).
29 See generally https://ccdu.govt.nz/projects-and-places (accessed 1 February 2016).
30 https://ccdu.govt.nz/our-progress/announcements/state-of-the-art-justice-precinct-reaches-key-milestone-27-november-2014 (accessed 1 December 2014).
31 Above.
32 Again, the author borrows this summary from the following two decisions: *Fowler Developments Ltd v Chief Executive of the Canterbury Earthquake Recovery Authority* [2014] 2 NZLR 54; *Minister for Canterbury Earthquake Recovery v Fowler Developments Ltd* [2014] 2 NZLR 587. See also E. Toomey, "The Canterbury Earthquake Recovery Act 2011: Land and Resource Management Issues" in J. Finn, E. Toomey (eds) *Legal Response to Natural Disasters* (Thomson Reuters, Wellington) (2015) at ch 11.
33 In relation to commercial properties that were insured but did not have EQC cover a variant on the offer was proposed, reflecting the absence of EQC cover. The options involved the most recent rating value as before the improvements and 50 per cent of the most recent valuation for the land, or 50 per cent of the most recent valuation of the land with the owner retaining the insurance claims in relation to the improvements.
34 *Fowler Developments Ltd v Chief Executive of the Canterbury Earthquake Recovery Authority* [2013] NZHC 2173 (HC), [2014] 2 NZLR 54; on appeal, *Minister for Canterbury Earthquake Recovery v Fowler Developments Ltd* [2013] NZCA 588, [2014] 2 NZLR 587.
35 This is very much a summary of the complex issues. For a full discussion, see E. Toomey, "The Canterbury Earthquake Recovery Act 2011: Land and Resource Management Issues" in J. Finn, E. Toomey (eds) *Legal Response to Natural Disasters* (Thomson Reuters, Wellington) (2015) at ch 11.
36 *Fowler Developments Ltd v Chief Executive of the Canterbury Earthquake Recovery Authority* [2013] NZHC 2173 (HC), [2014] 2 NZLR 54, at [62].
37 *Attorney-General v De Keyser's Royal Hotel* [1920] AC 508.
38 Canterbury Earthquake Recovery Act 2011, s 3 states: 3. *Purposes.*
The purposes of this Act are –

(a) to provide appropriate measures to ensure that greater Christchurch and the councils and their communities respond to, and recover from, the impacts of the Canterbury earthquakes;
(b) to enable community participation in the planning of the recovery of affected communities without impeding a focused, timely and expedited recovery;
(c) to provide for the Minister and CERA to ensure that recovery;
(d) to enable a focused, timely, and expedited recovery;
(e) to enable information to be gathered about any land, structure, or infrastructure affected by the Canterbury earthquakes;
(f) to facilitate, coordinate and direct the planning, rebuilding and recovery of affected communities, including the repair and rebuilding of land, infrastructure and other property;
(g) to restore the social, economic, cultural and environmental well-being of greater Christchurch communities;
(h) to provide adequate statutory power for the purposes stated in paragraphs (a) to (g);
(i) to repeal and replace the Canterbury Earthquake Response and Recovery Act 2010.

39 *Minister for Earthquake Recovery v Fowler Developments Ltd* [2014] 2 NZLR 587.

40 *O'Loughlin v Tower Insurance* [2013] 3 NZLR 275 at [27], 28]. The plaintiffs sought a payment from the insurer of $416,113.50, which, together with the EQC payment, totalled $620,000 for house damage, although the cost of a rebuild on a sound site was assessed at $540,000.
41 *Minister for Earthquake Recovery v Fowler Developments Ltd* [2014] 2 NZLR 587 at [108].
42 *Quake Outcasts v Minister for Earthquake Recovery* [2014] NZSC 51.
43 *Quake Outcasts v Minister for Earthquake Recovery* [2015] NZSC 27.
44 Above at [107], [108].
45 Canterbury Earthquake Recovery Act 2011, ss 11–15.
46 Canterbury Earthquake Recovery Act 2011, ss 16–26.
47 *Quake Outcasts v Minister for Earthquake Recovery* [2015] NZSC 27 at [137].
48 Above at [146].
49 Above at [197].
50 Above at [205].
51 These ideas are outlined by the author in a co-authored conference paper: E. Toomey, J. Finn, H. Holderness, "Paying out the Victims after a Natural Disaster: The Earthquake Commission, Private Insurance and Red-Zone Payouts after the Canterbury (New Zealand) Earthquakes)", Paper in Conference Proceedings, Australia and New Zealand Disaster and Emergency Management Conference, Surfers Paradise, Gold Coast, Australia, 3–5 May 2015.
52 *Quake Outcasts v Minister for Earthquake Recovery* [2015] NZSC 27 at [131].
53 Memorandum for Cabinet, "Land Damage for the Canterbury Earthquakes" (24 June 2011 at [19].

15 A comparative approach to the post-2001 Gujarat Earthquake recovery in India

Akihiko Hokugo

The Gujarat Earthquake occurred at 8.50 am on 26 January 2001, near Bhuj, a central city in Kutch District, Gujarat state. A wide area was damaged by the earthquake in and around the Kutch District, including 760 farm villages and local cities such as Bhuj, Bhachau, Rapar and Anjer.

According to the documents issued one year after the earthquake by the state government (Gujarat State Disaster Management Authority 2001), the damage was huge, with about 13,800 people dead, 167,000 people injured, 230,000 houses destroyed and one million houses in need of repair.

In rural areas, detailed support programs were proposed by the government and there was active cooperation with NGOs (Aota and Murosak 2001); restoration of livelihoods and housing reconstruction were almost complete within two years after the earthquake. On the other hand, city restoration and housing reconstruction in urban areas did not show much progress, even though the government prepared support programs for four cities – Bhuj, Bhachau, Rapar and Anjer – that incurred extensive damage.

In the central part of the urban area, within the walled city of Bhuj, reconstruction began about three years after the earthquake, having taken about eight months to draw up the urban reconstruction plans for all of Bhuj, about 14 months to create the town planning schemes for the inner-urban area and three years to start the reconstruction work in the walled city.

Field studies were conducted in December 2003 and in January 2005 to clarify the reason for the delay in the urban reconstruction process in Bhuj. In Gujarat state, India, the author visited the following organizations to carry out hearings and to collect documents: Gujarat State Disaster Management Authority (GSDMA) in Gandhinagar, the urban planning consultant Environmental Planning Collaborative (EPC) in Ahmedabad, the on-site office of the GSDMA in Bhuj, the Bhuj Area Development Authority, and Abhiyan (Kutch Nav Nirman Abhiyan), which is a collective of NGOs undertaking disaster-relief activities in Kutch. The author also visited the inner-urban district, temporary settlements and relocation sites in the quake-hit city of Bhuj.

The field study revealed the following points: reconstruction work has been proceeding with the establishment of the GSDMA and the time-limited Area Development Authority to enhance administrative capabilities in order to ensure human resources and quality for safety against earthquakes. It has taken an extended period of time to draw up the plans (a total of about two and a half years, including three months for the concept, eight months for the overall plan and 14 months for detailed schemes). A unique feature of housing reconstruction in Gujarat is that it has been owner-driven and has been carried out in partnership with the public sector and individuals; safety measures against earthquakes have been well considered during these processes. Interim inspection in the process of reconstruction is one of these safety measures. At the time of inspections, about four years after the earthquake, reconstruction work was in progress and housing construction was finally starting in the central urban area. For housing reconstruction, interim inspections are conducted in the course of building work to ensure quake resistance and to check the flow of funds. Consideration is also given to prevent the situation becoming even more dangerous in the case of a house collapsing. During reconstruction in the inner town, construction of roads for emergency access and partial relocation were planned, along with safer blocks being created by land readjustment, in order to solve the problem of congested and dangerous conditions. Consideration is given to minimizing the impact on post-reconstruction communities under a policy in which people who used to live in the same neighborhood should be able to live in the same place, by taking enough time for residents to take part in the planning, as well as attention being paid to ensuring the residents' safety against future earthquakes.

1 Extent of damage in Bhuj, a local city

Bhuj, a local city with a population of 150,000, is the seat of the provincial office of Kutch District (population 1.58 million). There are no major industries in Bhuj and about a quarter of the households depend on remittances from someone working away from home – either abroad or in a big city within India (Nagamatsu 2003).

In the walled city (about 1.3 square kilometers) of the inner town, which is located in the center of Bhuj, there were many decrepit, masonry buildings of more than 100 years old and other illegally expanded buildings. More than 50 percent of about 12,000 buildings collapsed in the 2001 earthquake. The percentage of collapsed buildings was around 15 percent in other areas of the city. The number of deaths in the entire city of Bhuj exceeded 7,000, with most of those occurring in houses which collapsed into narrow alleys (most of them with a width of around 2.5 meters) inside the walled city.

2 Situation of urban restoration and housing reconstruction in Bhuj

2.1 Administrative body in charge of restoration

As the administrative ability of Bhuj city hall was largely reduced by the disaster, the reconstruction of Bhuj was undertaken by the state government through the Kutch provincial office. The state government also established the GSDMA immediately after the earthquake and its on-site office served as the main body for technical support in Bhuj as well. The Bhuj Area Development Authority (BHADA), an independent administrative organization, was established in May 2001 with the intention of playing a pivotal role in the construction of urban infrastructure and support for rebuilding of housing (including building quality inspection).

2.2 Concepts of urban reconstruction, planning processes and state of implementation

Based on the urban reconstruction concept, a development plan (urban reconstruction plan) was drawn up as a master plan, targeting the entire city of Bhuj. Furthermore, town planning schemes were drawn up and carried out for the walled city as a means of implementing the development plan.

Town planning schemes in Gujarat state are generally created and implemented using a land readjustment method based on the Gujarat Town Planning and Urban Development Act, established in 1976, as the implementation method for the master plan. When an initial draft scheme for the town planning is completed, a meeting with the landowners is held for the draft to be modified. The modified draft scheme for town planning is made public in the government gazette, and opposing comments and arguments for the amendments are collected for one month so as to be reflected in the final draft scheme for urban planning. After that, town planning officers make preliminary schemes based on the draft. In this stage, various documents relating to the draft are consulted, and discussions with each landowner and office concerned are held. Then, with the approval of the state government, the scheme is put into practice. In this final stage, arguments from the people who will come under the influence of the scheme are received, and the final scheme with which the economic aspects are closely examined is developed. It is made public in the government gazette, then approved by the state government. The transparency of the planning is thus ensured and the communities which are to be influenced are encouraged to participate in the planning (Gurumukhi 2003).

During this planning process, from the draft scheme stage to the town planning scheme stage, and to the actual practice stage, people were continually encouraged to take part through NGO participation, discussions with specialist groups, hearing investigations of individuals and public meetings.

- January–February 2001: Emergency measures were central issues during this period. A comprehensive relocation of the inner-town district was also proposed. Building restrictions were in place until February 2003 in the inner town (walled city). About 600 buildings were constructed in violation of the building restrictions, but they were removed after the restrictions were lifted.

- March–April 2001: The fundamental concept for the city reconstruction was under consideration and the Earthquake 2001 Rehabilitation Package No. 5 for Earthquake-Affected Areas was approved by the state government. It was decided that the inner town was basically to be reconstructed in the same location, with congestion being reduced to improve safety and access. There were also plans to construct relocation sites, where building owners in the inner town who wished to move there could do so. Each of the considerations at each stage, as stated below, were all based on this Package No. 5.
- May–December 2001: An urban planning project for the entire area of Bhuj city (56 square kilometers) was decided upon. This planning process was handled by the EPC, an urban planning consultant company that had been engaged in the planning of the master plan for Bhuj since before the quake. The EPC set up the job in May 2001, prepared an original plan within five months, by September, and completed the urban planning procedures for it to be a master plan in December.

  A development plan covering the entire area was then decided upon as part of the urban reconstruction planning project, which included redevelopment of urban infrastructure, such as roads with a total length of 152 km, water supplies, sewage, commercial facilities, theaters and other public buildings.

  Four relocation sites with a total area of 160 hectares and 3,500 housing plots were planned for safe reconstruction in solving the problem of the congested inner town. One of the four sites, called the GIDC district, was initially prepared as a temporary settlement, but was later converted into the fourth relocation site.
- January 2002–February 2003: Eight town-planning schemes for the walled city (a total of 131 hectares, with 12,000 buildings and 50,000 residents) were decided upon. Housing construction in the relocation sites began in June 2002. The Gujarat Urban Development Company (GUDC) started working on improvements in the urban infrastructure in the inner town in July 2002. Draft schemes for town planning had been drawn up by September 2002, followed by the successive holding of public meetings and decisions being made on the housing plots for the post-redevelopment (land readjustment) period.
- May 2003: Housing construction in the inner town started.
- October 2003: Building permits for 1,900 buildings at relocation sites and 3,263 buildings within the development-planned districts were issued. Construction work on 1,500 residential buildings, including 1,053 in the relocation sites, was underway. Land acquisition for construction of roads of 90 km total in length, which was planned for the first stage of the project, had almost been achieved. Public works on main roads in the inner town were started.
- December 2003: Although urban infrastructure works were scheduled to be completed, road construction works in the inner town were still in progress at this time.

- January 2005: Urban infrastructure works were still in progress, but the authorities had finished with the construction work of the main roads and had started construction of slightly narrower roads. In the four relocation sites, the main roads had been constructed, housing construction was going on and many houses were already occupied. In the inner town, housing construction was also in progress and there were many observed signs of recovery, such as the reopening of a vegetable market that had been reconstructed.

2.3 Situation of housing reconstruction at relocation sites

The situation of housing reconstruction at the three sites initially planned is shown in Table 15.1. The sites have been supported for housing construction in consideration of the following factors:

- Community meetings held regularly to promote reconstruction;
- Building materials provided at on-site material banks;
- Offices established for on-site technical advice;
- Free water supplied for construction work;
- Efforts made to link people in need of support to an NGO.

In the first field research, residential areas of single-family housing and that of terraced housing built in cooperation with NGOs (hereinafter referred to as NGO housing) were seen within the same district. The three relocation sites, as it turns out, are located within a 3 km diameter of the city center.

When the author visited the sites for the second time, the provision of building materials had ended because the materials had already become available in the market, and NGOs were moving forward with housing construction for people in need of support.

The GIDC district (within a diameter of 5 km from the city center, 22 hectares) was planned as a temporary settlement – mainly for dwellers in rental housing – and was turned into a relocation site afterward. Permanent housing construction has already been started there by Abhiyan, an NGO network. In this

Table 15.1 Situation of housing reconstruction in the relocation sites (three sites planned in the early stage) as of October 2003

District	*Number of plots*	*Number of plots already allocated*	*Number of housing units being constructed*
Rawalwadi	1,431	685	369
Mundra	1,097	845	357
RTO	702	676	327
Total	3,230	2,206	1,053

Source: BHADA (2003).

district, the construction of permanent housing for dwellers in rental housing and squatters is planned, which will be the first such experience in the state of Gujarat. The housing being constructed by Abhiyan will be provided for those who lived in rental housing before the earthquake in the inner town. There was still much temporary housing remaining at the time of the author's second visit, but it was scheduled to be replaced by a series of reconstructed permanent housing projects. There are 28 communities in this district and the people of each community live closely together.

The permanent reconstruction of 160 housing units has been done by Abhiyan on a government-owned wasteland site. Residents are supposed to buy it for a very low price from the government after moving in. Abhiyan built the housing at a low cost so as to be able to provide it for free. The funds are obtained from the World Bank. Single mothers, widows and the disabled are given priority for the housing. A cluster consists of five housing units and four clusters are put together, making up a group of 20 units. People from the same community are to move into the same cluster. Regarding the other blocks, NGOs are being sought to work in cooperation with authorities. Two or three housing cooperation unions have also been established for future construction works. The unions will be owners of the constructed housing. The establishment of a housing cooperation union is planned for each community to facilitate community-based life in each block.

Abhiyan worked mainly in the farm villages for the first two years after the disaster. Then, a certain level of reconstruction having been done, it started to work in the urban areas, particularly in the temporary settlements where many people still face difficulties.

2.4 Redevelopment and housing reconstruction in the walled city

Before the 2001 earthquake, there were only narrow streets and buildings with poor quality of construction in the walled city. Town planning schemes were drawn up and carried out for this walled city as a means of implementing the development plan. The draft schemes for town planning for the walled city, which was divided into eight districts, were later dramatically changed, based on overtures made by residents and through the various meetings, including public meetings, held after the announcement of the schemes. The length of roads to be constructed was reduced and the access to be improved was minimized by utilizing the existing roads. During this period, the EPC held about 150 meetings with people from different ranks, including above-mentioned public meetings, in efforts to incorporate their opinions.

According to the EPC, the draft schemes for urban planning were created with the top priority put on people who used to live in the same neighborhood to enable them to live in the same place once again. It was also decided early on that religious institutions, large trees and non-collapsed buildings should be kept as they were as much as possible. It was also decided to expand some roads and to construct a set of new wide loop roads utilizing patches of open land created by collapsed buildings because rescue teams could not get into the area, due to the roads being narrow and blocked with collapsed buildings (Balachandran 2003).

Community-based shopping arcades were kept in situ in the end, with the widening of the roads, though there was some consideration of relocating the arcades in the draft schemes. The fact that the shopping streets were kept in the same place and buildings that did not collapse were not relocated – along with the policy of "people who had lived in the neighborhood should be able to live in the same place" – indicates that consideration is given to minimize the impact on communities when reconstruction is achieved.

The principle behind relocation in Bhuj is that the owners of collapsed houses in the inner town should have an option for relocation. Remaining houses which may obstruct adequate town planning will be removed. Also, because the inner town had been congested, residents were asked to move into the relocation sites if they so wished. As a result, about 40 percent of the residents decided to move. It is compulsory for them to surrender their original plots and, in return, they are given some land at the relocation site. When the price of the original land is higher than that of the newly given land, the difference will be paid to the beneficiary on surrender of the land. In some cases, people keep their shops only in the walled city, as it is not possible to start a business in the new residence.

In cases where a house exists at a site of newly built roads or roads planned for widening, the house is usually purchased.

In cases of vacant land where a house had collapsed, according to the land readjustment method, a certain proportion of the contributions from each plot was required for the infrastructure. The proportion is decided so as to make the burden lighter for those with smaller plots. The actual proportion is: 0 percent for a plot of less than 30 square meters, 10 percent for a plot of 30–100 square meters, 20 percent for 100–200 square meters, 30 percent for 200–500 square meters and 35 percent for 500 square meters or more, based on the Gujarat Town Planning and Urban Development Act 1976.

Table 15.2 indicates the process of housing reconstruction in Bhuj up to now. In the relocation sites, as of 2006, housing construction for most of the scheduled plots had been successfully completed or was underway. In the development-planned districts in the inner town, on the other hand, the number of issued building permits was only 2,066, and it can be deduced that housing construction had not started at all on about half of the plots.

2.5 Reconstruction of private housing in urban areas and support for individuals

A unique feature of housing reconstruction in the State of Gujarat, India is that it has been right-owner-driven and is being carried out in partnership with the public sector and individuals. Although it is the right owners who lead the reconstruction, there is sufficient technological and financial aid offered by the government.

Table 15.2 Process and situation of housing reconstruction in Bhuj city

District	*Number of plots*	*Number of completed houses*			*Under construction, 2006*	*With permits, construction not started*
		2003	*2004*	*2006*		
Within the development-planned area[1]	6,000[2]	0	150	831	913	322
Outside the development-planned area	–	581	660	1,753	1,440	1,089
Three relocation sites	3,230	283	1,760	2,238	854	18
NGO housing	–	–	–	3,188[3]	–	–
Total[4]	–	–	–	8,010	3,207	1,429

Source: compiled by GSDMA (Oct. 2001, Dec. 2004, March 2006), BHADA (2007).

Notes

1 "Development-planned area" refers to the area in which a town planning scheme was decided.

2 Estimated by calculation: 12,000 (the number of plots in the development-planned area) multiplied by the collapse rate of 0.5. This number is, however, expected to decrease because some residents will move out due to road construction projects, etc.

3 NGO housing units (1,191 units in three relocation sites, 280 units in the GIDC, 1,717 units outside the development-planned area) (– indicates not known).

4 The number of building permits is the total of the numbers of completed houses by 2006, houses under construction in 2006 and building permits issued, though construction has not yet started.

For the post-quake housing reconstruction, building restrictions were in place because of the fact that Kutch district is in a Level 5 earthquake zone. In order to prevent collapsed houses from blocking roads, a building should be two stories or lower regardless of its structure, in the inner town the second story should be set back to a distance of five meters from the median of the road and in relocation sites a house should be built a distance of two meters from the boundary line with the street.

The owner of a collapsed house is provided with a total of 150,000 rupees for house reconstruction by the government in three installments. The amount is regarded to be almost equal to, if slightly smaller than, the reconstruction cost of a 50-square-meter house. At first, 60,000 rupees is to be given when the building permit is issued. Then, when the building is approved by building inspection after completion of the foundation and walls, an additional 50,000 rupees is to be given. This interim inspection is designed to secure the safety of the building, as well as to make sure that the assistance has been used for the building construction. The last installment of 40,000 rupees is to be given after the second interim building inspection.

A tenant is provided with a quarter of the above-mentioned amount when a house is reconstructed in situ. Usually the tenant pays the amount to the landlord.

3 Reasons why urban reconstruction planning has required more time

It took about eight months to draw up the urban reconstruction planning for all of Bhuj, about 14 months to create the town planning schemes in the inner town and three years to start the reconstruction work in the walled city. This was due to careful attention being paid to democratic procedures, which required time. There are, however, some other reasons, as noted below:

1. Land prices in the inner town were high and landowners and/or building owners were financially well off. Also, some landowners live in another city. Thus, there is no need for them to hurry with reconstruction.
2. A law established about 20 years ago greatly protected dwellers in rental housing units. They had been living on low rents but since their homes collapsed in the earthquake, they have no place to go back to unless the housing is reconstructed. Most of them have by now moved to the above-mentioned temporary settlements. Owners of rental housing have only a minimal desire to reconstruct housing because, when housing is reconstructed, the rights of the tenants are treated accordingly.
3. Owners of single-family housing with land (especially people in the commercial field) were willing to reconstruct their buildings in situ. The pressure on them to reconstruct, however, has been decreasing as land use in the surrounding area has changed, resulting in complementing the urban functions in the inner town.

While housing reconstruction has been showing progress (though it is taking time), the support for securing a "job," which should be the means of regaining financial strength for individuals, has been insufficient. It should not be overlooked that the NGO Abhiyan pointed out that the reconstruction policy and support of putting too much importance on "housing" and/or "urban development" has weakened the strength of individuals, especially the owners of small businesses, as the reconstruction is being extended.

4 Conclusions

Characteristic aspects of the Gujarat Earthquake reconstruction developments can be concluded as follows:

1. Reconstruction work has been proceeding with the establishment of the GSDMA and the time-limited Area Development Authority to enhance administrative capabilities in order to ensure human resources and quality for safety against earthquakes.
2. At the time of inspections, three years and four years after the earthquake, reconstruction work was in progress and housing construction was finally starting in the central urban area. It has taken an extended period of time to

draw up the plans (a total of about two and a half years, including three months for the concept, eight months for the overall plan and 14 months for detailed schemes).

3 For housing reconstruction, interim inspections are conducted in the course of building work to ensure quake resistance and to check the flow of funds. Consideration is also given to prevent the situation becoming even more dangerous in case of a house collapsing.
4 On the occasion of reconstruction in the inner town, construction of roads for emergency access and partial relocation were planned along with safer blocks being created by land readjustment in order to solve the problem of congested and dangerous conditions.
5 Consideration is given in order to minimize the impact on post-reconstruction communities under a policy in which people who used to live in the same neighborhood should be able to live in the same place.

In the case of the Great Hanshin Earthquake, large-scale redevelopment planning was decided for the central urban areas, where the development had been delayed and the damage was huge. It took only two months to complete the planning without encouraging much participation of the local residents. The slogan for the planning was "Disaster Prevention and Safety," and it was expected that land use would be enhanced and new people should come to live in those areas. There was some lack of consideration concerning the original residents being able to live in their original living places. In contrast, in the case of Bhuj, consideration was given to disaster-affected people being able to live in their original living places by taking enough time for residents to take part in the planning, as well as attention being paid to ensure the residents' safety against potential earthquakes – in other words, safety for the future – which should be regarded as a good example. There remain, however, some questions about care for the livelihood of quake-stricken people who have to survive through an extended reconstruction period.

References

Aota, R., and Y. Murosaki (2001). Support for Community and Reconstruction of Lives with NGO Activities after the Earthquake in Gujarat, India, *Journal of Institute of Social Safety Science*, 3, 163–172. (in Japanese).

Balachandran, B.R. (2003). The Reconstruction of Bhuj, Case Study: Integration of Disaster Mitigation into Planning and Financing Urban Infrastructure after an Earthquake, *Course on Role of Local Governments in Reducing the Risk of Disasters*, pp. 95–124, 28 April–2 May 2003, Istanbul.

Bhuj Area Development Authority (BHADA) (2003). *BHUJ: Urban Rehabilitation*, PowerPoint file offered by the Bhuj site office of GSDMA.

Bhuj Area Development Authority (BHADA) (2007). www.bhujada.com, 2 February.

Gujarat State Disaster Management Authority (GSDMA) (2001). *Gujarat Earthquake Reconstruction and Rehabilitation Policy*. Gandhinagar: Gujarat State Disaster Management Authority.

Gujarat State Disaster Management Authority (GSDMA) (Oct. 2001, Dec. 2004, March 2006). *Gujarat Emergency Earthquake Reconstruction Project*, Quarterly progress report. Gandhinagar: Gujarat State Disaster Management Authority.

Gurumukhi, K.T. (2003). Land Pooling Technique: A Tool for Plan Implementation – An Indian Experience, *Map India Conference 2003*, GISdevelopment.net.

Nagamatsu, S. (2003). Impact on the Local Economy by the 2001 Gujarat Earthquake and Characteristics of the Reconstruction Policy, *Research of International Public Policy*, 6(2), 193–208 (in Japanese).

16 Post-disaster reconstruction in Taiwan

Yung-Fang Chen

1 Introduction

Taiwan is an island surrounded by the Pacific Ocean to the east, and the Taiwan Strait to the west, in which lie the Pescadores islands, the East China Sea lies to the north, the Bashi Channel to the south and the South China Sea to the south-west. It comprises the island of Taiwan and some smaller islands, including Kinmen, Matsu and Penghu. The main island is 394 km long and 144 km at its widest point; it has a total area of 35,873 square kilometres with a population of 23.39 million people (CIA 2015).

Two-thirds of Taiwan is mountainous, the highest point being 3,950 m; the flat to rolling coastal plain in the western part of the island accommodates the bulk of the population and the national commerce, industry and agriculture. The climate is tropical marine with persistent cloudy conditions. The monsoon rains fall between May and June, whilst July, August and September is the typhoon season (Central Weather Bureau 2015). Heavy storms transform the short and precipitous rivers and streams into torrents of water, sweeping down the mountains carrying a large amount of mud and silt.

Taiwan is one of the most vulnerable places on the planet to natural hazards due to its East Asian location on both the Tropic of Cancer and the junction of the Manila and Ryukyu Trenches. A global risk analysis summarised that 92.5 per cent of the total land and 95.5 per cent of its population are situated in areas subject to high mortality risk from multiple hazards, including typhoons, floods, mass movement (landslides) and earthquakes (Dilley *et al.* 2005: 8).

Over the years these hazards have brought about many fatalities and loss of properties, which have, as a consequence, resulted in the need to resettle large numbers of affected populations. According to statistical data collected by EM-DAT (2015), from 1900 to 2015, the total number of the affected population was almost 4 million, resulting in claims for more than 213 billion US dollars. In particular, climate-related disasters (storm, flood and landslides) have impacted on 87 per cent of the population and 30 per cent of total damage reported (EM-DAT 2015).

Post-disaster recovery and reconstruction has become a big challenge to the government and communities, in particular in terms of shelter and resettlement.

Emergency management related laws were only enacted in 2000 after the deadly earthquake in Jiji (1999) and have been through a further revision after Typhoon Morakot (2009).

The aim of this chapter is to evaluate the post-disaster recovery strategies. The objectives include: (1) to investigate the development of disaster management systems in Taiwan; (2) to provide an extensive understanding of post-disaster reconstruction arrangements in Taiwan by using the case of post-Morakot reconstruction programmes; and (3) to provide recommendations to policies and theories which might benefit similar countries or areas.

2 Historical development

The development of disaster management practices in Taiwan can be divided into four periods: (1) post Japanese colonial period, 1945–1965, (2) post 1965, (3) during the 1990s, and (4) post Ji-Ji Earthquake, 1999. The section attempts to explain the development of these four phases with a focus on the recovery and reconstruction phases.

2.1 Post Japanese colonial period, 1945–1965

The first disaster management system in Taiwan was very heavily influenced by Japan during its colonial period. The Japanese government introduced the first government-led emergency procedures between 1894 and 1945. The Japanese army and the police were used to lead Taiwanese civil groups when operating the emergency services (Wu 1998).

After the Chinese Nationalist Party, or so-called Kuomintang (KMT), moved from mainland China after the 1940s, the existing emergency service system was adopted, but it played more of a reactive role. Normally it was the responsibility of the police and the military to initiate action after a hazard or an emergency took place. These organisations were therefore under pressure of setting up their own strategies to cope with disasters. Consequently, they quickly constructed networks with other agencies involved as a result of responding to disasters. During this period the focus of disaster management was principally based on post-disaster compensation measures.

2.2 Post 1965

The first specifically disaster-related law was enacted in 1965, *The Measure of Natural Hazards Mitigation and Recovery in Taiwan Province*. It divided the disaster management structure into three levels: the province (and the metropolis), the counties and the township levels. Although the head of the administration took the political responsibility, the police was the key organisation when facing disaster response. It is noted that during this period, the government utilised a more decentralised approach to carry out response tasks.

This arrangement of the law in the prevention and response to disasters was very similar to the systems set up by the Japanese during the colonial period. Since the reactive framework to disasters prevented the effectiveness of disaster response and recovery, there was a demand for specifying a permanent operational organisation for the implementation of approved practices when responding to disasters (Sa 2002).

2.3 The 1990s

A more modernised and detailed plan – the *Disaster Preparedness and Response Plan* (1994) – was only revised after a series of catastrophic events took place globally, for example, the Northridge Earthquake (1994) and China Airline plane crash in Nagoya, Japan (1994). Learning from these events, the plan started to include the covering of the management of man-made disasters as distinct from purely nature disasters.

To make sure of the effective coordination of personnel and resources during a disaster, the National Fire Agency under the Ministry of Interior was established to carry out operations when responding to disasters. This meant that the disaster management structure had one extra layer at national level. At the same time, a new framework for the emergency services was formulated: the fire service was separated from the police, and the collaborative framework between the fire and ambulance services was determined. The restructure revealed the serious shortage of fire fighters and an insufficient budget for the improvement of search and rescue equipment. The lack of coordination between the police and the fire services had also prevented effective response (Li 2000).

Due to a lack of consensus on what constituted or what a holistic disaster management framework should be like and what the best distribution of relevant tasks was, it was difficult to formulate an effective plan. In addition, the government at the same time was undergoing a restructuring process – the abandonment of the provincial level. Consequently, the legislative progress of the emergency management was postponed for six years.

2.4 Post Ji-Ji Earthquake, 1999

The *Disaster Prevention and Protection Act* was finally agreed and enacted in 2000, under the public demand after the catastrophic Ji-Ji Earthquake in 1999. Although the Act has undergone several revisions, it is still under enforcement. The *Disaster Prevention and Protection Act* includes 8 chapters, with 52 articles, covering the whole range of disaster management cycle, including general introduction, organisations for disaster prevention and rescue, disaster plans, disaster prevention, disaster response, reconstruction, penalties and an appendix.

As a result of the downsizing of government levels, the emergency system has returned to a three-level arrangement: nation, county/metropolis and township/district. The new Act utilises a centralised approach to implementing disaster management. A national level institute – the National Disaster Prevention and Protection Commission (NDPPC) – has been created to implement overall policy responsibility for major disasters and to ensure the effectiveness of coordination and communication among agencies involved. The purposes of this committee are to:

- upgrade operation performance and efficiency of the Central Disaster Response Centre
- handle disaster prevention and protection drills
- establish mutual-aid agreements on disaster rescue
- promote civilian education and advocacy on disaster prevention.

(National Fire Agency 2014)

It is noted that NDPPC only took a small part of the decision-making role at the national level. At the national level, the Administration Yuan, the top administration institute of the political system, takes the political responsibility. The assigned lead department has operational responsibility for different hazards. For example, the Ministry of Interior is responsible for typhoons, the Ministry of Economics for flooding and the Council for Agriculture for landslides. The relevant leading department is responsible for calling meetings at the Emergency Operation Centre (EOC) if it foresees any emergencies. At the same time, the National Fire Agency (NFA) leads the process of search and rescue.

It seems to be reasonable to have a lead department to coordinate a potential disaster; however, the complexity of the environment in Taiwan means that, if there is a typhoon, flooding and landslides will ensue. Quite often this results in undefined 'ownership' of the disaster and the arrangement becomes inefficient when dealing with complexities (Professional Advisory Committee of Disaster Reduction 2010).

The complexity of the organisational management structure at the national level proved to paralyse the decision-making and command and control mechanism during a disaster event (Tsai and Chi 2010: 7). Lessons have been identified in several big disasters, such as Kaohsiung gas explosions (2014), dust explosion at the Formosa Fun Coast Water Park (2015), and oil spill disaster of the T. S. Line container ship (2016). An all-hazard approach for disaster management structure has been called (Tsai and Shi 2010).

Learning from the experience of responding to and recovering from the Ji-Ji Earthquake, the *Disaster Prevention and Protection Act* ensures that post-disaster recovery and reconstruction phases are included in Articles 36 and 37. In particular, Article 36 requires the government to implement post-disaster reconstruction programmes that include the social, economic, resettlement, infrastructure and other development dimensions. For the contents of Article 36, see Box 16.1. These requirements correspond to the international guidelines for reconstruction (Oxfam 1995; Collins 2009). However, there is still a criticism that these two articles are not sufficient to provide adequate guidance on the implementation of the necessary work when responding to a catastrophic event (Lu *et al.* 2011).

Box 16.1 Article 36: Implementation of recovery and reconstruction after disaster

1 Investigate, study, evaluate and analyse disaster situations and needs of victims.
2 Authorize and implement program and proposals for recovery and reconstruction after a disaster.
3 Record and allot volunteers.
4 Distribute and handle donated resources and money and allocate relief.
5 Attend to casualties, settle people and order maintenance in disaster areas.
6 Medical care, epidemic prevention and psychological counselling.
7 Rebuild school dormitories and its supplementary public facilities.
8 Schooling and boarding of affected students.
9 Approve or assist the drafting of urgent repair and recovery of heritage, historical sites and buildings.
10 Emergency responses, including investigation of damage of heritage, historical sites and buildings, urgency repair and reinforcement.
11 Safety evaluation and handling of damaged structures.
12 Recovery of houses, public buildings, urban renewal and handling of land ownership.
13 Repair utilities, including water conservancy, soil and water conservation, environmental protection, tele-communications, electricity, water, oil and gas, and regulate resource supplies.
14 Repair tracks, roads, bridges, mass transportation, airports, ports and agriculture and fisheries.
15 Environment disinfection and reject processing.
16 Employment services for people and reconstruction of industry.
17 Other issues related to recovery and reconstruction.

Various tiers of governments shall depending on its functional authorities include the mitigation affairs under the preceding paragraph to each prevention and protection plan.

Public enterprises shall depending on its functional authorities depend on its disaster prevention and protection operation plan to implement mitigation affairs.
Source: Disaster Prevention and Protection Act 2012

3 Post-disaster arrangements after Typhoon Morakot

The effectiveness of the *Disaster Prevention and Protection Act* was challenged by the impact and consequences of the Typhoon Morakot disaster in 2009. Typhoon Morakot triggered many floods, landslides and debris flows in the mountainous areas of Taiwan. It resulted in 699 deaths and nearly 40 per cent of the homes of the population affected were either destroyed or damaged. The estimated financial loss from the typhoon was nearly US$61.17 billion (Morakot Post-Disaster Reconstruction Council 2014). The scale and magnitude of the disaster challenged the capability and ability of the Taiwanese emergency response systems to cope with needs of the post-disaster recovery and reconstruction.

According to the *Disaster Preparedness and Response Act* (2000), the government has the responsibility to organise the rebuilding or reconstruct housing for the affected populations. However, due to the catastrophic impact of the disaster, the government had to pass a *Special Law of Reconstruction After Morakot Typhoon Disaster* (2009) as guidance for reconstruction.

Learning from the Ji-Ji Earthquake, the government very quickly proposed a strategy for short, medium and long-term recovery measures (see Figure 16.1). After the emergency shelter phase, the affected populations could choose to use the emergency fund or to arrange a loan to purchase a new home or attempt reconstruction of the damaged property. They could also choose to stay in temporary pre-fabricated houses, government settlements or private rental houses. Following the medium-term settlement, the affected population could then apply for permanent housing.

After the post-disaster environment impact assessment, it was realised that many communities had now been newly classified as high-risk areas because the landslides or floods had weakened the land and these areas had become unstable. The government had to make the decision that the populations could not be allowed to live in these areas for safety reasons. This decision caused many disputes as to whether or not the population could return to their own homes and to which degree they would be able to use their homes (Chen 2016).

To compare the settlement plans between post Ji-Ji Earthquake and Morakot, one notable difference was that the government made it compulsory after Morakot to ask the population living in the high-risk areas to choose the resettlement plan. Although it sounds to be right to relocate these people due to safety considerations, many did not agree with the policy. Shieh *et al.* (2013) criticised the government for utilising the policy to maintain its own economic interests rather than assisting the affected populations. Valuable resources are stored in

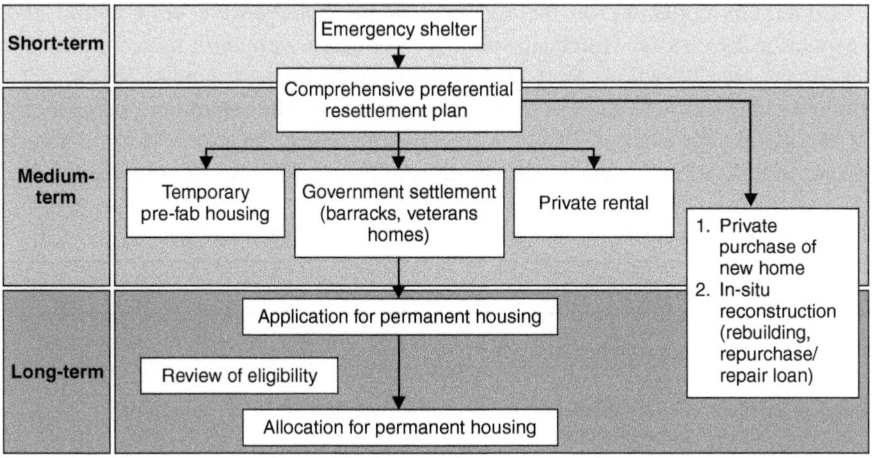

Figure 16.1 Resettlement strategy and implementation (source: Morakot Post-Disaster Reconstruction Council 2014: 28).

the mountains; the government has for a long time been working with big commercial enterprises to gain control of these resources (Xiao 2012).

Facing the challenges of scarce available land, the government decided to use the 'one stop housing policy', which was to abandon the pre-fabricated housing phase and move to a permanent housing phase directly. This resulted in more pressure on the government to find alternative land for the re-settlement programme. This forced 88.7 per cent of the applicants into permanent housing, and as a result to be relocated to another location distant from their original homes. Since most of them were aboriginals, this caused additional problems.

It should also be noted that the decision had left half of the temporary pre-fabricated houses built by the government and NGOs empty (Morakot Post-Disaster Reconstruction Council 2012a). Many affected populations were encouraged to stay in the military barracks and then move to the permanent housing, which further increased the problem of empty pre-fabricated houses.

It was the first time that the Taiwanese Government had liaised with local authorities and NGOs, such as the Tzu-Chi Foundation, Taiwan World Vision, Taiwan Red Cross, Dharma Drum Mountain and others, in its efforts to implement the necessary construction work. The government met with these NGOs to determine methodologies on how to build these new communities, including the size of the houses, the inclusion of responsible organisations and also the establishment of preferred sites, as examples (Morakot Post-Disaster Reconstruction Council 2012b). It was decided that NGOs were responsible for building the houses while the central government was responsible for the establishment of key infrastructure to support these newly built communities (Table 16.1). Local government played a supportive role to make sure the quality control and administration procedures were done effectively. Although the collaboration between the government and NGOs received high appraisal, the centralised system limited the possibilities of the local involvement to participate fully (Shen 2011).

Under this collaboration model, most of the houses were built within two years after the disaster struck. In total, 3,045 houses were built to accommodate 8,873 people (Morakot Post-Disaster Reconstruction Council 2012a: 62). However, the ultimate success of the model relied on the capability and capacity of the NGOs. For example, Tzu-Chi received the most donations and had a very strong mobilisation system to distribute resources and tasks to volunteers; they

Table 16.1 The responsibility/deliverables for the respected lead agencies

Lead agency	*Responsibilities*
Central government	Policy, law, budget, land offer, cut short procedures matching resources, major infrastructure construction
Local government	Qualification review, building administration, community management
NGOs	Fund raising, buildings and local infrastructure construction

Source: Chern and Hung (2012).

successfully completed the construction of 628 households within 88 days: for the Da-Ai Community.

Although Tzu-Chi also provided these new residents with furniture and daily necessities, most of the residents were not happy with the arrangements due to religious reasons. Tzu-Chi is a Buddhist organisation while most of the aboriginals are Christians. The new residents felt the overall plan of the community and the interior design of the houses was too religious (Knight *et al.* 2013) – for example, the entrance gate of a community was built with a very clear Buddhist symbol. In addition, some residents felt the design of the house looked like a temple (Quan 2010).

It was found that the experience and network between the NGO and the communities played a crucial role for the satisfaction of the residents. For example, World Vision Taiwan had been working in the aboriginal tribes for more than four decades so they had gained social trust within these communities. It is argued that World Vision Taiwan understood the aboriginals' culture so they could understand the need and demand from the affected populations better than other organisations (Knight *et al.* 2013).

Most of the applicants for the permanent houses were aboriginals; historically they live in the high mountains and have their own language, culture and way of life. They also have their own economic livelihood in the mountains. The government had to take these factors into consideration during the reconstruction phase. Several strategies had been made to accommodate their lifestyle and culture. For example, the government provided funding for these households to decorate their gardens in their traditional style. Each household was also provided with some farm land inside the newly built community. However, due to a lack of effective risk communication, many disputes took place in many communities as the aboriginals did not feel that their needs had been heard during the public consulting process. This resulted in several protests and made it more difficult to achieve an agreement between the government and the affected population (Quan 2010).

In general, the reconstruction programme received very positive appraisal as most of the projects were completed between six months and two years. Research shows that Taiwan is one of those countries which recover faster from disasters than many others due to its economic advantages (Aldrich 2012).

3.1 The Rainbow Community

Complying with the *Post-Morakot Reconstruction Special Act* and *Post-Morakot Life Reconstruction Service Centre Implementation Measures*, the Taiwanese Government had to facilitate the use of an all-inclusive approach for community development to ensure the sustainability of the livelihood of the relocated populations. Once the new communities were built, the government continued to work with NGOs to establish 'Life Reconstruction Service Centres' to help the affected populations re-build their ways of living as well as their livelihoods. The involvement of these Centres in the communities has already become well established. The services provided by these Centres include: mental health, education, employment, welfare, community development and citizen advice facilities (Table 16.2).

The government also set up priorities of the work required: starting with the needs assessment of each individual household, and then to facilitate the development of each individuals' priorities and requirements, and finally to promote the development of the whole community. Training and development plans were provided for these communities.

The government claimed success in the implementation of these projects (Morakot Post-Disaster Reconstruction Council 2012b) – for example, the satisfaction survey conducted by the Ministry of Interior in 2010 showed 89 per cent of the residents were satisfied with the permanent housing and 85 per cent were happy with the overall quality of life. Nevertheless, there was a continually declining trend of satisfaction. The results from Knight *et al.* (2013) showed only 76 per cent of the population were satisfied with the condition of their houses and 30 per cent of the residents were not happy with the way the government had worked with the NGOs in the promotion of the reconstruction and development programmes.

Many of these newly built houses have become 'emergency shelters' for aboriginal residents. From a positive point of view, 'permanent houses have encouraged residents to be evacuated from the mountainous areas because they now have houses in the urban area so they have accepted evacuation before a further typhoon impacts' (Quan 2010). These development programmes have lasted five years and most are now complete, although not all communities are back to 'where they were', and indeed, some are worse off.

4 The revisions of the Disaster Preparedness and Response Act (2000) post Morakot

The catastrophic disaster challenged the capabilities and ability of the emergency response systems and the post-disaster recovery and reconstruction. The

Table 16.2 Six dimensions of service provided by the Life Reconstruction Service Centre

Mental health	Mental consultant and medical transfer assistance
Education	Student schooling and counselling assistance
Employment	Assisting the jobless to apply for unemployment payment, attend professional training and apply for jobs
Welfare	Sustaining needs of elders, youngsters, single-parented or low-income families
Community development	Helping create local job opportunities and enhance development of local industries
Citizen advice facilities	Transferring legal, community industry reconstruction, cultural display news

Source: Chiayi County Government (2015).

government carried out a post-disaster inquiry to identify lessons learnt and organised a series of conferences to receive recommendations from academics. Key recommendations regarding post-disaster response and reconstruction are summarised below.

4.1 To clarify the role and responsibilities of government at each level

It was indicated in the previous section that the arrangement of the disaster management structure in Taiwan was quite complex, in particular at the national level. To meet relevant organisations on an ad hoc basis and call for committee meetings just before or immediately after a disaster takes place is not effective; it is suggested that it would be better to establish a permanent institute to monitor, mitigate and manage all types of disaster (Shen 2011), such as the civil protection mechanism utilised in Italy. The permanent institute could also formulate appropriate warning systems and informing strategies in order to communicate risks to relevant stakeholders and the general public. Appropriate progressive training and exercises could be planned and delivered to enhance the knowledge and skills of relevant personnel and to encourage team working practices.

After Typhoon Morakot in 2009, the district office has been empowered as an extra level of authority to implement strategies to intervene and respond to disasters. It is argued that the roles and responsibilities between governments at each level should be clarified and determined. At the same time, local governments should be empowered for decision-making and should be fully equipped with sufficient personnel, resources and budget. By doing this, it would be possible to achieve the effective and rapid operational responsibilities and reactions to emergencies.

4.2 Worst-case scenario should be included in the emergency planning

Although many reports identifying lessons learnt have been published after the Morakot disaster, the main recommendations remain focused on the pre-disaster mitigation and preparedness and the revision of the disaster management framework; little has been input into the improvement of the reconstruction strategies. The worst-case scenario should at all times be taken into consideration to ensure a holistic plan can be formed. A clear guidance on the responsibilities of departments involved, potential models for compensation and also alternatives should be included. Although it could be argued that each disaster is different, it is recommended that the recovery and reconstruction measures should be included during the immediate disaster response phase (Cabinet Office 2013: 93).

4.3 Encourage effective public engagement and participation

Many criticisms have been raised by the affected aboriginal population. Their argument was that they had different cultures, beliefs and lifestyles, so decision-makers should work with their needs and demands in mind when informing them of any new policies. From this point of view, the main issue was the consultation procedure during the construction phase. The government should provide channels for discussion at a very early stage, thus allowing time for in-depth and considered discussion. At the same time, a programme of educating the public on the concept of 'public participation' should be implemented.

One of the reasons why the public disliked the resettlement plan was that they were not aware of any new potential risks after Morakot struck. The foundation of risk communication lies in whether information delivered has been received and been acted upon. The communication flow should not only descend from top to bottom but also rise from the bottom up. Risk communication and reliable information between the government and the public during normal times is essential to build the required level of trust and confidence between government and public.

5 Conclusion

The chapter illustrates the development of the disaster management framework in Taiwan. It has used post-Morakot reconstruction programmes as a case study to further explain and evaluate the current arrangements of post-disaster reconstruction measures in Taiwan. Recommendations have been made to improve the disaster management framework, including simplified and unified disaster management systems, embedded in the discussion of recovery and reconstruction strategies as early as possible, and promoting a culture of public engagement.

The best practices that can be shared include the following points:

1 The effective coordination and collaboration between the government and the NGOs: A clearer definition of the role and responsibilities between the government and NGOs enables more effective collaboration between these two sectors. A transparent recording of the income and expense and regular and routine audits enhances public trust on the reconstruction programmes and facilitates more and continuous donations.
2 The utilisation by the government of a holistic way for reconstruction: The Taiwanese Government proactively included reconstruction in the *Post-Morakot Reconstruction Special Act* and stressed that it is necessary to take a holistic approach for further development, including the growth of infrastructure, community resilience and individual skills and knowledge.

References

Aldrich, D.P. (2012) *Building Resilience: Social capital in post-disaster recovery*. Chicago and London: The University of Chicago Press.

Cabinet Office (2013) *Emergency Response and Recovery: Non statutory guidance accompanying the Civil Contingencies Act 2004*. London: Cabinet Office. Available online: www.gov.uk/government/uploads/system/uploads/attachment_data/file/253488/Emergency_Response_and_Recovery_5th_edition_October_2013.pdf.

Central Weather Bureau (2015) *Weather Phenomena*. Available online: www.cwb.gov.tw/V7/knowledge/encyclopedia/me034.htm.

Chen, Y.F. (2016) Post-disaster reconstruction strategies: A case study in Taiwan. In T. Sternberg (Ed.) *Climate Hazard Dilemmas: Risk, Environment and Security in Asia*. London: Ashgate. Revision in progress.

Chern, J.C. and Hung, S.Y. (2012) The strategy of community reconstruction after a mega disaster: The case of post Typhoon Morakot reconstruction in Taiwan. *Journal of Management* 1(1): 63–79.

Chiayi County Government (2015) *Disaster Prevention and Rescue Management & Post-Morakot Reconstruction*. Presentation.

CIA (2015) *The World Factbook: Taiwan*. Available online: www.cia.gov/library/publications/the-world-factbook/geos/tw.html.

Collins, A.E. (2009) *Disaster and Development*. Oxon: Routledge.

Dilley, M., Chen, R.S., Deichmann, U., Lerner-Lam, A.L., Arnold, M., Aqwe, J., Buys, P., Kjevstad, O., Lyon, B. and Yetman, G. (2005) *Natural Disaster Hotspots: A Global Risk Analysis*. Disaster Risk Management Series No 5. Washington DC: World Bank.

EM-DAT (2015) *The International Disaster Data Base – Country Profile: Taiwan*. Available online: www.emdat.be/database.

Knight, C.L., Burgin, G. and Chen, Y.F. (2013) *Living with Typhoons: Disaster management in rural Taiwan*. Final report to the Royal Geographical Society (with IBG).

Li, Z.X. (2000) 我國緊急救災體系整建及運作功能之探討–以九二一地震為研究對象。公共行政學報，第四期，323–362 [A study on the construction and operational function of emergency rescue systems – the analysis of Taiwan's 921 Earthquake. *Public Administration* 4: 323–362].

Lu, J.C., Chen, S.Y., Zhang, Z.R., Li, Y.N. and Zhuang, M.R. (2011) *Analyses of Recovery Issues and Policies after Typhoon Morakot*. NCDR 99-T36. New Taipei City: National Science and Technology Centre for Disaster Reduction.

Morakot Post-Disaster Reconstruction Council (2012a) 莫拉克颱風災後救助與安置。行政院莫拉克颱風災後重建推動委員會 [*Post Morakot Disaster Relief and Settlement*. Kaohsiung: Morakot Post-Disaster Reconstruction Council].

Morakot Post-Disaster Reconstruction Council (2012b) 創新、效率的家園重建新思維：高雄山林大愛園區。行政院莫拉克颱風災後重建推動委員會 [*Innovative, Effective Reconstruction: A case study in Da-Ai Community in Kaohsiung*. Kaohsiung: Morakot Post-Disaster Reconstruction Council].

Morakot Post-Disaster Reconstruction Council (2014) *Rebuilding a Sustainable Homeland with Innovation and United Efforts*, 2nd edition. Kaohsiung City: Morakot Post-Disaster Reconstruction Council.

National Fire Agency (2014) *Services*. Available online: www.nfa.gov.tw/main/Content.aspx?ID=2&MenuID=665.

Oxfam (1995) *The Oxfam Handbook of Development and Relief*. Oxford: Oxfam.

Professional Advisory Committee of Disaster Reduction, Executive Yuan (2010) 莫拉克颱風災害課題分析與政策建議。行政院災害防救專家諮詢委員會 [*Analysis and Policy Recommendation for Lessons Identified from the Morakot Disaster*. New Taipei City: Professional Advisory Committee of Disaster Reduction].

Quan, K.C. (2010) 以原住民的重建需求為觀點–探討家園重建政策與原鄉期待的落差與衝突 社區發展季刊，第131期，213–232頁 [An investigation of the differences and conflict of reconstruction strategies between the government and aboriginals: From the view point of aboriginals. *Community Development Quarterly* 131: 213–232].

Sa, Z.P. (2002) 我國防救災體系介紹。[*The Introduction of the Disaster Management in Taiwan*. In 921 Earthquake Reconstruction Site, Emergency Operation Centre, Administration Yuan Disaster Education Training Programme, National Cheng Kung University Disaster Prevention Research Center]. Available online: http://210.59.250.229/TNDS/Data/School/School_06.pdf.

Shen, Z.Z. (2011) 未來十年我國災害管理發展趨勢 研究報告 內政部消防署 [*The Development Trend of the Disaster Management System in Taiwan in the Next Ten Years*. Research Report. Funded by National Fire Agency].

Shieh, J.C., Chen, J.S. and Lin, W.I. (2013) Skip to permanence without transition? Policy-making in post-Morakot reconstruction. *Taiwan: A Radical Quarterly in Social Studies* 93: 46–89.

Tsai, J.S. and Chi, C.S.F. (2010) Dysfunction of governmental emergency systems for natural disaster management: A Taiwanese case study. *Working Paper Proceedings: Engineering Project Organisations Conference*. South Lake Tahoe, CA. Available online: http://academiceventplanner.com/EPOC2010/Papers/EPOC_2010_TsaiChi.pdf.

Wu, K.S. (1998) 我國災害防救體系之研究 – 以社子島防颱執行過程為例。國立中興大學公共政策研究所，碩士論文 [*The System of Disaster Management in Serzi Island*. MA Dissertation. Taipei: Department of Public Policy, National Chung Hsing University].

Xiao, H.Z. (2012) 新自由主義下原住民族土地的發展地景：一個新夥伴關係的初探。文化研究雙月刊，第132期，44–68頁 [The development of aboriginals' land under New Liberalism: An investigation of the new partnership relation. *Cultural Studies Bimonthly* 132: 44–68].

17 The framework of international cooperation for disaster management and Japan's contribution

Toshihisa Toyoda

1 Introduction

The international community – inclusive of countries, international organizations, NGOs, and private sector organizations – has increasingly provided active support to countries affected by large-scale natural disasters. Obviously, support activities and agendas vary depending on how much time has elapsed since the natural disaster in question. The response stage, the period immediately after a disaster, is the most urgent and important because disaster victims may be at high risk for disease and injury and may have lost their homes and other assets. Thus, at this stage in particular, the international community provides support based on the principles of humanitarianism.

In the recovery stage, affected countries require financial, physical, and human resources for restoration and recovery. Procurement of these resources can be difficult even for advanced countries. However, developing countries require assistance from advanced countries, international financial institutions such as the World Bank and regional banks, and NGOs. Many developing countries in Asia and Africa are increasingly vulnerable to hazards; some of these hazards have been exacerbated by global warming and social factors such as rapid increases in population and urbanization.

Since the 1990s, the international community, led by the United Nations (UN), has paid greater attention to prevention, risk reduction, and preparedness rather than emergency response and recovery. In discussions of the social (including legal) aspects of natural disasters, the concept of "disaster risk reduction" (DRR) has become the most important of all.

In this chapter, I discuss recent trends in international cooperation for disaster management and Japan's contribution to this issue with special reference to disaster laws, regulations, and rules. First, I review trends in international cooperation related to supporting countries affected by natural disasters. I show that the UN played an important role in establishing objectives and general rules for international cooperation in this field since no clear international laws on this matter had existed previously. While relief activities were originally a major concern, gradually the international community's focus has shifted to activities related to DRR. I also show that the concept of DRR is reasonable and, with recent emphasis, has become widely accepted; however, caution is necessary when applying the concept to the least developed countries.

Second, I review the characteristics of Japan's disaster management system with special reference to its legislative and financial system. It is pointed out that, although Japan's disaster laws have historically embodied the DRR principle, less importance has been attached to assisting disaster victims with livelihood recovery. Japan, together with relevant members of the international community, is at the fore of mainstreaming DRR into development. However, it is desirable for Japan's domestic experiences and lessons related to DRR to be disseminated. Although many good practices have emerged in Japan due to the emphasis on the DRR principle, some victims of large-scale disasters have experienced delays in the provision of assistance for livelihood recovery.

2 Humanitarian approach to international cooperation

2.1 Cooperation in the global community led by the United Nations

Typically, when major disasters occur, the international community provides support by dispatching relief teams to the affected country on humanitarian grounds immediately afterwards. UN General Assembly (1991) Resolution 46/182, "Strengthening of Coordination of Humanitarian Emergency Assistance of the United Nations," provides a conceptual definition for humanitarian assistance.[1] It states that "humanitarian assistance must be provided with the principles of humanity, neutrality and impartiality" and that "assistance must be provided with the consent of the affected country and in principle on the basis of an appeal by the affected country." The international community has accepted these points as the basic principles undergirding assistance activities for disaster relief and recovery.[2]

The UN Office for the Coordination of Humanitarian Affairs (OCHA), which was established in 1997, is the organization tasked with coordinating urgent humanitarian support activities. The UN Disaster Assessment and Coordination Team (UNDAC) has more recently been established under OCHA; UNDAC's disaster emergency experts undertake initial coordination, quick disaster assessment, and information dissemination activities. When disasters occur, various UN organizations undertake relief activities in their fields of specialization under the coordination of OCHA.

2.2 International Federation of the Red Cross and Red Crescent Societies

The Red Cross and Red Crescent Society, which operate in 152 countries and 33 countries, respectively, have a long history of humanitarian support activities in the form of national organizations in various countries. They undertake their own relief activities, but their most important functional and operational role lies in processing financial support and donations from inside and outside affected countries.

2.3 NGOs

Some established international NGOs work on a global scale to support the victims of various disasters. Medicins Sans Frontiers is one renowned NGO that specializes in providing medical relief. Certain global NGOs, such as Oxfam, Save the Children, and World Vision, engage in non-disaster-related activities at normal times and provide relief when large-scale disasters occur.

In Japan, attention has only recently turned to how NGOs can provide disaster relief; few organizations at present specialize in overseas disaster relief and recovery cooperation. The largest Japanese NGO is Japan Platform; it was established by several NGOs and corporations with the support of the government to provide relief to disaster victims and refugees. It is active in 40 countries.

Regulations pertaining to disaster relief activities undertaken by foreign NGOs vary by country. For example, in Japan, such activities are unrestricted unless illegal. Subsequent to witnessing the substantial participation of foreign NGOs in relief and recovery, the Indonesian government clarified its position concerning foreign NGOs in a regulation (No. 23/2008). The regulation states that while the government guarantees that foreign NGOs can undertake activities, such activities must be based on the principles of the Disaster Management Law (No. 24/2007) and are subject to various other conditions. In short, foreign NGOs are protected but must work together with the government under the Disaster Management Law.

3 Era of disaster risk reduction

3.1 Disaster management cycle and paradigm shift

The disaster management cycle – the sequence of disaster management activities – has typically been considered as follows: disaster occurrence → response → restoration → reconstruction → preparedness. There have been debates over what "recovery" and "reconstruction" entail and various definitions have been proposed. Here, I use the term "recovery" to encompass both "restoration" and "reconstruction." Reconstruction is a lengthy process by which affected areas are restored at least to as they were before. Regarding recovery, I follow the UN definition:[3] "recovery is the restoration and improvement, where appropriate, of facilities, livelihoods and living conditions of disaster-affected communities, including efforts to reduce disaster risk factors." This conceptualization of recovery is well aligned with the concepts of Build Back Better (BBB) and DRR, both of which have recently become popular. BBB entails not only restoring areas to their original state but also making communities more resilient by improving physical, social, environmental, and economic conditions. DRR is based on the fact that hazards are not in human control but DRR is; it has become mainstream in the international community in the last two decades. Rather than focus exclusively on response and relief activities, the international community has begun to direct attention to DRR.

In the following, I examine the past three meetings of the World Conference on DRR to sketch recent trends. Subsequently, I highlight a few problematic issues.

3.2 From the Hyogo Framework for Action to the Sendai Declaration

The First World Conference on DRR was held in Yokohama, Japan in May 1994. The Japanese government called the meeting as a mid-term evaluation of the International Decade for Natural Disaster Reduction (IDNDR), 1990–1999, which had been proclaimed by the UN General Assembly in 1989. At base, IDNDR was motivated by the belief that natural disasters could be ameliorated by utilizing disaster prevention and early-warning technology.

The Great Hanshin-Awaji Earthquake occurred and struck Kobe about half a year after the Yokohama meeting. The earthquake mercilessly caused structures that had been built with the most advanced technology in the world, including expressways, railroads, and high-rise buildings, to collapse. The earthquake was a lesson not only for Japan but also for the international community that there are limits to the artificial prediction and amelioration of natural disasters. After the Great Hanshin-Awaji Earthquake, a paradigm shift in the field of disaster reduction occurred: in academia and government, there was a shift from "disaster prevention" to "disaster risk reduction." Accordingly, the UN International Strategy for Disaster Reduction (ISDR) was instated, superseding the IDNR. The ISDR's main headquarter was established in Geneva and ten other active headquarters were established worldwide, including in Kobe, Japan.

The Second World Conference on Disaster Risk Reduction was held in Kobe in January 2005. It has been said that the most important result of the Kobe Conference was the declaration of the Hyogo Framework for Action 2005–2015: Building the Resilience of Nations and Communities to Disasters (HFA).[4] The HFA was the first plan to describe the work required from all sectors and actors to reduce disaster losses.

The HFA was expected to result in "the substantial reduction of disaster losses, in lives and in the social, economic and environmental assets of communities and countries." Based on these three strategic goals, the framework established five practical priorities for action. The first priority was to ensure that DRR became a national and a local priority with a strong institutional basis for implementation. The second priority was to assess DRR and enhance early-warning systems. The third priority was to use knowledge, innovation, and education to build a culture of safety and resilience at all levels. The fourth priority was to reduce underlying risk factors. The fifth priority was to strengthen preparedness for effective response at all levels.[5]

While the priorities pertain to both structural (hard) and non-structural (soft) measures for DRR, most concern soft measures. Of the soft measures called for, the most important is the call to make DRR a national and a local priority with a strong institutional basis for implementation. To that end, it was proposed, among other things, that legislation to promote DRR be enhanced; that responsibilities and resources be decentralized; that community participation, as well as training and study pertaining to DRR, be facilitated; and that emergency funds be provided.

In the last decade, numerous countries in the international community, primarily thanks to the leadership of the UN, have engaged in various efforts for DRR. Many documents report that, overall, HFA has been an important instrument for raising public and institutional awareness and eliciting action from a wide range of stakeholders at all levels (e.g. UNISDR, 2015a, p. 3). According to an evaluation report by the UNISDR on the HFA, the HFA has not significantly reduced global disaster risks. While improvements in risk management have resulted in reductions in mortality, the economic losses from disasters have increased, particularly in certain developing countries. More critically, in developing countries, mortality and economic losses associated with extensive risks are trending up (UNISDR, 2015b, p. 14).

The Third World Conference on Disaster Risk Reduction was held in Sendai, Japan in March 2015. In the conference, the Sendai Framework for Disaster Risk Reduction 2015–2030 was declared. The framework was subsequently approved by the UN General Assembly in Resolution 69/67. The framework aims to substantially reduce disaster risks and losses in terms of lives, livelihoods, and health and in economic, physical, social, cultural, and environmental assets held by people, businesses, communities, and countries (UNISDR, 2015a, p. 3). The framework states a need for focused action in the following four priority areas (UNISDR, 2015a, pp. 9–15):

- a Understanding disaster risks;
- b Strengthening disaster risk governance to manage disaster risks;
- c Investing in disaster risk reduction for resilience;
- d Enhancing disaster preparedness for effective response and to Build Back Better in recovery, rehabilitation, and reconstruction.

Based on these four priorities, the framework describes both necessary domestic (national and local) and international (global and regional) measures in detail. In my view, the Sendai Framework is an advancement compared to the HFA that preceded it in at least the following two points. First, it clearly states the roles each stakeholder must fulfill – in particular, it identifies the measures that national and local stakeholders must undertake. In addition, it recommends that the international community (advanced countries, international organizations, the private sector, etc.) recognize that disaster risks are increasing in developing countries (including the least developed, small-island, landlocked, and African countries) as well as in middle-income countries; as these countries face specific risks, it is recommended that the international community support them through bilateral and multilateral commitments to facilitate capacity-building and technology transfer and to provide financial and technical assistance. Second, certain economic considerations that had been basically neglected in the preceding HFA are explicitly described in this new framework. In both developed and developing countries, policy must consider that the implementation of disaster risk management (DRM) at every stage requires the more efficient and effective use of limited financial resources. Furthermore, countries must establish recovery funds and/or risk-sharing financial mechanisms at the pre-disaster stage as this is an important aspect of preparedness.

4 Mainstreaming disaster risk reduction and Japan's contribution

Vulnerable to sporadic large-scale natural disasters due to geographical, meteorological, and geological factors, Japan is experienced with various difficult recovery stages. In Japan, countermeasures to prepare for possible future events have developed in an evolutionary way. Naturally, sharing with other countries Japan's experiences and records related to disasters, pertaining to both structural and non-structural factors, could be useful. This may be why the Japanese government has been so keen to host UN World Conferences on DRR, as observed in the last section, and has conducted many training programs on disaster reduction management in Japan to which it has invited relevant central and local government administrators as well as professionals and scholars from developing countries.

In the following section, I inquire into certain characteristics of Japan's domestic DRR practices; I point out some peculiar aspects that, in my view, should be modified or improved.

4.1 Legal system

Japan's disaster management system has been fine-tuned on a step-by-step basis in reaction to a succession of devastating disasters. The central disaster law is the Disaster Management Basic Law, which was enacted in 1961 to systematize disaster prevention and response. The law specifies relevant agencies' scope of authority and duties, as well as some financial and monetary measures (basically for the recovery of public facilities) and prevention measures. The basic law also incorporates provisions from the Disaster Relief Act (1947), which was enacted to serve as the basis for public aid at the response stage and remains in force. The basic law states that local governments (municipalities) are, in principle, responsible for disaster management, including in regard to financing. However, it also states that the central government supports municipalities based on separate laws and rules. These separate laws include, in addition to the Disaster Relief Act, the Public Facility Recovery Expenses Treasury Burden Act (1951), which enables the central government to subsidize up to 80 percent of the cost of recovering public civil engineering facilities depending on financial status of the affected municipality. The Law Concerning Special Fiscal Aid for Coping with Devastating Disasters (1962) authorizes the central government to increase subsidies to municipalities when disasters are classified as "devastating." There are also several other laws that pertain to particular types of disaster, such as, the Flood Control Act (1949), the Act on Special Measures for Volcanoes (1978), and the Act on Special Measures for Nuclear Disasters (1999). In addition to these laws, several acts on special measures for various aims were enacted, for example, after the large-scale disasters of the 1995 Hanshin-Awaji Earthquake and 2011 East Japan Earthquake. Therefore, Japan's DRM system is quite complicated. It is not rare even for staff members in the response/recovery sections of municipal offices to be unclear regarding the system of disaster laws and to need to research various laws before they can take firm action. Only a limited number of specialists in the government and academia understand the disaster law system in detail. The laws exist for the general public and general officials in charge of DRM at municipalities. Thus, the whole system should be reorganized, integrated, and simplified. Furthermore, unless this is done, Japan's DRM system will not be comprehensible to the international community, limiting Japan's international contribution in the area of disaster legislation.

The table in the Appendix (Table A17.1), adopted from a recent publication by IFRC and UNDP (2014), compares disaster laws in the Asia-Pacific region in their special aspects. It compares how countries prioritize DRR. It shows how each country's DRM system incorporates DRR as an objective (even when the phrase "DRR" is not used), how financial provisions are legalized for DRR, and how community participation and education are legislated. Certain countries, including the Philippines, Indonesia, and Mexico, have recently enacted or amended their basic disaster laws in accordance with HFA principles to systematically and explicitly prioritize DRR.

Although Japan's basic DRM law (1961) is quite old and the system has become quite complex, as noted before, it prioritizes DRR and emergency response. The DRM budget is allocated through the national budgetary process; from 1999–2015, the DRM budget amounted to approximately 5 percent of general accounts. Measures for disaster prevention, preparedness, and national land conservation accounted for 55.4 percent of the DRM budget from 2006–2015. This means that DRR investment accounts for around 2.7 percent of Japan's national budget. However, since 2011, a large portion of the regular DRM budget has been specially transferred to fund various measures for recovery from the 2011 East Japan Earthquake. Considering the decade before 2011 (i.e. 2001–2010), DRR investment can be considered to have accounted for 3.9 percent of the national budget, a significantly higher value.[6]

In Japan, although pre- and post-disaster budgets allocated for DRR measures have been substantial, the budget allocated for assisting victims with livelihood recovery has traditionally been small. At the response stage, the Disaster Relief Act (1947) and other relevant laws guarantee support for severely affected victims through the construction of shelters and temporary housing, and later, through providing assistance in renting permanent housing. However, there is a customary principle peculiar to Japan of not carrying out individual compensation. Therefore, the government, in principle, has assisted victims by the provision of goods such as food and water and by building public housing facilities.

In principle, no cash payments are made to victims except for small sums of condolence money. The government has stubbornly clung to this practice for years.[7]

A strong outcry among citizens (specifically, those affected by the 1995 Hanshin-Awaji Earthquake) and the obvious plight of victims who lost their houses persuaded Diet politicians to unanimously vote for the Act on Support for Livelihood Recovery of Disaster Victims in 1998, which was amended in 2007. In Japanese disaster law, this is a rare case in which citizens initiated the legislative process. The amended law allowed for cash assistance of up to ¥3 million for reconstructing severely collapsed residences. The amendment also enabled the law to be applied to all large-scale disasters occurring after 1999. Although there remain some limitations to the applicability of the law, this amendment represented a symbolic shift toward a greater emphasis on assisting victims with livelihood recovery in Japan's DRM mentality and practice. After the 2011 East Japan Earthquake, many local municipal governments provided some additional cash benefits to severely affected victims in addition to the amounts designated by the amended law (2007).

4.2 Mainstreaming DRR

Since the late 1990s, there has been increasing recognition of the importance of mainstreaming DRR into development. Facilitating such recognition is explicitly the first of the three principal strategic goals of the HFA 2005–2015: the framework calls for "more effective integration of disaster risk considerations into sustainable development policies, planning and programming at all levels, with a special emphasis on disaster prevention, mitigation, preparedness and vulnerability reduction" (UN, 2005). This integrated approach is considered essential in view of the fact that development initiatives do not necessarily reduce vulnerability to natural disasters but, instead, may create new forms of vulnerability (i.e. as "reduced disasters"). Disasters may cause failed development, but failed development may also result in disasters.

As Benson and Twigg write:

> "Win-win" solutions for securing sustainable development, reducing poverty and strengthening hazard resilience therefore need to be explicitly and actively sought … Such solutions are best derived by integrating disaster risk reduction strategies and measures within the overall development framework, viewing disaster risk reduction as an integral component of the development process rather than as an end in its own right.
>
> (Benson and Twigg, 2007, p. 6)

Mainstreaming DRR in development requires an integrated approach inclusive of both hard and soft measures. Caution is necessary when applying the concept to the post-disaster recovery stage. Too much attention to physical structural aspects as compared to non-structural aspects in the post-disaster recovery stage sometimes causes delay and/or failure of victims' livelihood recovery.

Three examples are illustrated as follows:

a I observed certain scenes of failed development (or recovery) in Aceh, Indonesia, which was devastated by the 2004 Indian Ocean Tsunami. Using foreign funds and based on the DRR concept, many houses for victims were constructed in the highlands. However, most of the victims were fishermen and had difficulties pursuing their livelihoods as they were relocated far from the ocean; thus, later many left the highlands to which they had been relocated. This case indicates that policy measures that solely target DRR cannot contribute to livelihood recovery or poverty reduction.

b After the 1995 Hanshin-Awaji Earthquake, the central government spent approximately ¥6 trillion mainly on the recovery of physical facilities and infrastructure; the government stubbornly kept to the principle of not carrying out individual compensation. The local governments spent about twice this amount, of which approximately two-thirds was directed to the recovery of physical facilities and infrastructure and the remaining one-third to various projects for public housing, welfare, culture, supporting small and medium-sized enterprises through low-interest loans, and supporting severely affected victims through compensating them for only the interest portion of their housing loans. Most victims built or repaired their houses by themselves, which resulted in macroeconomic decline and the prolonged stagnation of the regional economy: many households were forced to spend their income on housing and furniture, and subsequently, as unemployment increased, there were decreases in disposable income, consumption, and final demand. Facing worsening fiscal conditions, local governments cut expenditures, accelerating declines in final demand, particularly following the five-year concentrated recovery period. This case indicates that concentrating the allocation of financial resources on DRR measures to the detriment of livelihood recovery measures does not lead to sustainable development but rather leads to delays in the recovery of victims' livelihoods and the regional economy.[8]

c The central government spent about ¥30 trillion on the restoration and recovery of areas affected by the 2011 East Japan Earthquake, five-fold what had been spent on restoration and recovery after the 1995 Hanshin-Awaji Earthquake. Although a greater portion of the total budget was allocated for assisting victims with livelihood recovery, approximately three-quarters of the total budget was spent on restoration, reconstruction, and purchasing pertaining to physical structures related to various infrastructure works, public facilities, and land for permanent housing projects. Most civil engineering recovery projects were based on the principles of DRR and BBB. In one typical but controversial example, huge, tsunami-resistant seawalls are being built to reduce future risk of tsunamis. Currently, with the support of the central government, prefectural governments are constructing 370 km of seawalls approximately 10 m high along nearly all the beaches and ports on the seashore of eastern Japan. The central government is covering the approximately ¥1.0 billion cost.

In some coastal communities, the residents are strongly opposed to the construction of such huge seawalls, and are requesting some more reasonable measures aiming at risk reduction from both tsunamis and losing their work places. If some portion of the budget for constructing the huge seawalls was reallocated to supporting the victims (e.g. those who still live in temporary houses or some other places), the recovery of their livelihoods would be more advanced.[9]

4.3 Challenges for the Japanese system

Japan has experienced major disasters since ancient times. Consequently, the concept of DRR is built into the Basic Act on Disaster Management (1961). Although many humanitarian measures have also been taken based on the Disaster Relief Act (1947), after every disaster, huge problems emerge at the recovery stage – problems related to delays in the recovery of victims' livelihoods. This peculiar aspect may be ascribed to the persistence of the customary principle of not carrying out individual compensation, as was previously mentioned. Although Japan's disaster management system is improving, delays in the recovery of victims' livelihoods remain a problem for which solutions are elusive. This problem is not only legal but also financial. For example, allocating half of the seawall construction budget, say ¥500 billion, to victims who remain in severe need in temporary housing would enable them to recover their livelihoods faster. However, whereas my proposal is based on humanitarian reasons, it is clear that the mainstream DRR approach is more or less based on economic rationality and efficiency.

It seems that a gap exists between domestic DRR management and the internationally advocated DRR approach. As mentioned previously, Benson and Twigg (2007) wrote that the DRR approach is legitimate if we "view disaster risk reduction as an integral component of the development process rather than as an end in its own right."[10] In Japan, this integrated approach has not been well implemented.

The Japan International Cooperation Agency (JICA) is the main player in the implementation of Japan's overseas development assistance projects; it is at the fore in implementing DRR principles in developing countries.[11] According to JICA (2015), its approach is strongly based on economic rationality and efficiency. My hope is that Japan can contribute to enhancing DRR to support developing countries, the least developed countries in particular, not based on the principles of economic rationality and efficiency, but based on the integral approach, which implies a humanitarian approach.[12]

5 Conclusion

In this chapter, I have discussed recent trends in international cooperation for disaster management and Japan's contribution to this issue with special reference to disaster laws, regulations, and rules. First, I briefly reviewed trends in international cooperation pertaining to supporting countries affected by natural disasters. I show that the UN played an important role in establishing objectives and general rules for international cooperation in this field as no clear international laws on this matter had existed. For the international community, relief activities were originally the major concern; however, in a gradual shift, activities related to DRR have begun to attract the most attention. Thus, the main idea and objective undergirding the international cooperation framework has gradually shifted from humanitarianism to economic rationality. The recent emphasis on DRR is reasonable and DRR has become widely accepted; however, caution must be taken when applying the principles of DRR to the least developed countries.

Second, I reviewed the characteristics of Japan's disaster management system with special reference to its legislative and financial system. Although Japan's disaster laws have historically embodied the principle of DRR, less importance has been attached to assisting victims with livelihood recovery. Japan, together with relevant members of the international community, is at the fore of mainstreaming DRR into development. It is desirable for Japan to disseminate domestic experiences and lessons related to DRR. Although Japan employs many good practices based on the DRR principle, among other problems, there have been delays in assisting the victims of large-scale disasters with livelihood recovery.

Appendix

Table A17.1 DRR in DRM legal frameworks in Asia-Pacific countries

Country	*DRR priority in objectives and mandates*		*Local DRR mandates*	*Financing for DRM (budget line)*	*Financing for DRM (special fund)*	*Civil society and community participation*	*DRR education*
	Law	*Policy*	*Law*			*Law*	*Law*
Australia	Medium	Yes	Yes	n. a.	n.a.	n.a.	No
China	Medium	Yes	Yes	Yes	Yes	Yes	No
India	Medium	Yes	Yes	n.a.	Yes	n.a.	Yes
Indonesia	Medium	Yes	Yes	Yes	Yes	Yes	Yes
Japan	High	Yes	Yes	Yes	Yes	Yes	Yes
Mexico	High	Yes	Yes	Yes	Yes	Yes	Yes
Nepal	Low	Yes	n.a.	Yes	Yes	Yes	No
New Zealand	High	Yes	Yes	Yes	n.a.	Yes	Yes
Philippines	High	Yes	Yes	Yes	Yes	Yes	Yes
United States	Medium	Yes	Yes	Yes	Yes	Yes	Yes
Vietnam	High	Yes	Yes	Yes	Yes	Yes	No

Notes

Compiled from Table 2 in IFRC and UNDP (2014), p.40. The author added the data pertaining to Indonesia and amended one entry for Japan – specifically, in the "'Financing for DRM (special fund)" column, the entry was amended because the government has funds for covering earthquake insurance and also for supporting victims' livelihood recovery in cooperation with prefectural governments. In the US, the legal system differs by state; the states of Illinois and Louisiana, in addition to the federal system as a whole, are taken into consideration here.

Notes

1 See UN (1991).
2 Study Group on Great Disasters and International Cooperation (2013), pp. 84–88.
3 UNISDR (2009).
4 UN (2005).
5 Ibid.
6 The author calculated these values based on the official data for annual DRM budgets from the Cabinet Office, Government of Japan, *White Paper on Disaster Management 2015*, Appendix, pp. 52–53.
7 It is likely that central government bureaucrats insist on retaining this principle because they fear that, should cash benefits be awarded to victims of major disasters, the government's coffers would be emptied by the next disaster to hit, for example, metropolitan Tokyo.
8 See Toyoda (2008).
9 As of June 30, 2015, the number of total refugees is 207,000.
10 Benson and Twigg (2007), p. 6.
11 JICA (2015).
12 For more detail, see Toyoda (2013).

References

Benson, C. and Twigg, J. (2007) *Tools for Mainstreaming Disaster Risk Reduction: Guidance Notes for Development Organizations.* Geneva: IFRC and RCS/ProVention Consortium.

IFRC and UNDP (2014) *Effective Law and Regulation for Disaster Risk Reduction: A Multi-country Report*. New York: IFRC, UNDP.

Indonesia. National Agency for Disaster Management (BNPB) (2008) *Disaster Management Law and Its Ancillary Regulations*. Jakarta: BNPB.

Japan International Cooperation Agency (2015) *Toward Mainstreaming Disaster Risk Reduction*. Tokyo: JICA.

Study Group on Great Disasters and International Cooperation (2013) *Japan and the World Coping with Great Disasters: Disasters and International Cooperation.* Tokyo: Saeki Printing (in Japanese).

Toyoda, T. (2008) Economic Impacts of Kobe Earthquake: Quantitative Evaluation after 13 Years. *Proceedings of the 5th International ISCRAM Conference*, pp. 606–617. Available from: www.iscramlive.org/dmdocuments/ISCRAM2008/papers/ISCRAM2008_Toyoda.pdf.

Toyoda, T. (2013) International Cooperation for Disaster Relief and Recovery: Is Japan's Experience Incorporated? *Disaster Recovery and Revitalization Review*, 8, pp. 11–18 (in Japanese).

UN (1991) *General Assembly, 46/182, Strengthening of the Coordination of Humanitarian Emergency Assistance of the United Nations*. New York: United Nations.

UN (2005) *General Assembly, General Assembly, 60/195, Hyogo Framework for Action 2005–2015: Building the Resilience of Nations and Communities*. New York: United Nations.

UNISDR (2009) *Terminology on Disaster Risk Reduction*. New York: UNISDR. Available from: www.unisdr.org/files/7817_UNISDRTerminologyEnglish.pdf.

UNISDR (2015a) *Sendai Framework for Disaster Risk Reduction: 2015–2030*; Also, UN, General Assembly, 69/67, *Sendai Framework for Disaster Risk Reduction 2015–2030*. New York: UNISDR.

UNISDR (2015b) *Global Assessment Report on Disaster Risk Reduction 2015*. New York: UNISDR.

Index

Page numbers in *italics* denote tables.

For Product Safety Concerns and Information please contact our EU
representative GPSR@taylorandfrancis.com
Taylor & Francis Verlag GmbH, Kaufingerstraße 24, 80331 München, Germany

www.ingramcontent.com/pod-product-compliance
Ingram Content Group UK Ltd.
Pitfield, Milton Keynes, MK11 3LW, UK
UKHW020020200926
475702UK00014B/1984

* 9 7 8 0 8 1 5 3 6 1 4 8 0 *